Islamic Sufism Unbound

SCHOOL OF ORIENTAL AND AFRICAN STUDIES
University of London

Islamic Sufism Unbound

Politics and Piety in Twenty-First Century Pakistan

Robert Rozehnal

ISLAMIC SUFISM UNBOUND
Copyright © Robert Rozehnal, 2007.

First published in hardcover in 2007 by
PALGRAVE MACMILLAN®
in the United States - a division of St. Martin's Press LLC,
175 Fifth Avenue, New York, NY 10010.

Where this book is distributed in the UK, Europe and the rest of the world,
this is by Palgrave Macmillan, a division of Macmillan Publishers Limited,
registered in England, company number 785998, of Houndmills,
Basingstoke, Hampshire RG21 6XS.

Palgrave Macmillan is the global academic imprint of the above companies
and has companies and representatives throughout the world.

Palgrave® and Macmillan® are registered trademarks in the United States,
the United Kingdom, Europe and other countries.

ISBN-13: 978–0–230–61896–1 paperback

Library of Congress Cataloging-in-Publication Data is available from the
Library of Congress.

A catalogue record for this book is available from the British Library.

Design by Newgen Imaging Systems (P) Ltd., Chennai, India

First PALGRAVE MACMILLAN paperback edition: August 2009

10 9 8 7 6 5 4 3 2 1

Printed in the United States of America.

Transferred to Digital Printing in 2009

CONTENTS

List of Illustrations   vii

Acknowledgments   ix

Introduction: Mapping the Chishti Sabiri Sufi Order   1

1   Sufism and the Politics of Islamic Identity   19

2   Muslim, Mystic, and Modern: Three Twentieth-Century
    Sufi Masters   39

3   Imagining Sufism: The Publication of Chishti Sabiri Identity   89

4   Teaching Sufism: Networks of Community and Discipleship   129

5   Experiencing Sufism: The Discipline of Ritual Practice   173

Conclusions   227

Notes   231

Bibliography   257

Index   269

List of Illustrations

Figures

I.1   Women Dancing in Ecstasy at the Shrine of 'Ala ad-Din
      'Ali Ahmad Sabir (d. 1291), Kalyar Sharif, India   2
1.1   The Shrine of Baba Farid ad-Din Mas'ud Ganj-i Shakkar
      (d. 1265), Pakpattan, Pakistan   25
2.1   The Shrine of Shaykh Shahidullah Faridi (d. 1978),
      Karachi, Pakistan   61
2.2   The Shrine of Shaykh Wahid Bakhsh Sial Rabbani (d. 1995),
      Allahabad, Pakistan   75
5.1   The Shrine of Shaykh Isma'il 'Abd al-Qadir Thani,
      Pulau Besar, Malaysia   201
5.2   Qawwali Singers at the 2001 'urs Festival of Wahid
      Bakhsh Sial Rabbani, Allahabad, Pakistan   213

Map

1.1   Map of Pakistan   20

ACKNOWLEDGMENTS

The field research for this study was supported by a fellowship from the International Dissertation Field Research Fellowship Program of the Social Science Research Council, with funds provided by the Andrew W. Mellon Foundation. Additional funding was provided by fellowships from the American Institute of Pakistan Studies, and Duke University's Graduate School and Center for International Studies. The writing stage was funded by a Charlotte W. Newcombe Doctoral Dissertation Fellowship, and Franz and Class of 1968 Fellowships from Lehigh University. I am extremely grateful to all these institutions for their generous support.

This project would not have been possible without the kindness, cooperation, and hospitality of many Chishti Sabiri disciples in both Pakistan and Malaysia. I thank them all and sincerely hope this book honors their tradition. I owe a special debt of gratitude to a host of friends in Pakistan: Dr. Mansoor Hashmi and family, Tahir Maqsood and family, Lubna Shah Anwar and family, Moinuddin Hashmi, Jawwad and Bina Khwaja and family, Suroosh Irfani, Rashida Hamid, Aamir Ali, Yawer Ansari, Shaffaq and family, Muhammad Razzaq, Mushtaq Muhammad, Shahnaz Hassan and family, Riaz Ibrahim and family, Irfan Khan, Madni and family, Tariq Nazir, Altaf Siddiqui and family, Bilal, Muhammad Haroon Riedinger, Masood Hasan, Abdul Razzaq, Muhammad Saalim Shaheedi, Fayyaz Hussain Gilani and family, Tehzeeb un-Nissa Aziz, Saleem and Humaira Aziz and family, Gulfizah Afzal Khan, Ayesha Salam, Salma Khan, and Asadullah Sumbal.

In the end, I am solely responsible for the views, as well as the mistakes, expressed in this work. Even so, I want to acknowledge the influence of many wonderful colleagues and friends whose insights and encouragement helped bring it to life. In its earliest stages this project was shaped by my doctoral dissertation committee at Duke University—a unique group of scholars representing three institutions and three academic disciplines: Professors Carl Ernst (University of North Carolina-Chapel Hill), Katherine Ewing (Duke University), David Gilmartin (North Carolina State), Bruce Lawrence (Duke University), and Ebrahim Moosa (Duke University). I thank them all for their enthusiasm, patience, and unfailingly constructive criticism. I am especially indebted to Carl Ernst for opening the door to this research and to Bruce Lawrence for skillfully guiding it to completion. Among the many others whose wisdom and insight contributed to this work I would especially like to thank Vincent Cornell, Omid Safi, Scott Kugle, Kecia Ali, Rick Colby,

Jamillah Karim, Zia Inayat Khan, Naveeda Khan, Asad Ahmed, and Najeeb Jan. I am particularly grateful to Anna Bigelow for her careful and critical reading of the text at a crucial stage in its evolution. The encouragement and collegiality of my colleagues in the Department of Religion Studies at Lehigh University over the past several years has been equally invaluable. Lastly, I thank my wife, Kelly Choi—for her boundless patience, humor, and perspective. I owe the ultimate debt to my parents, Ellen and Richard Rozehnal, for their unwavering support and for first introducing me to the world of books and travel.

Introduction

Mapping the Chishti Sabiri
Sufi Order

This book is a study of a living Sufi tradition. Drawing on both textual and ethnographic materials, I trace the identity politics and ritual practices of a contemporary South Asian Sufi order (*silsila*) through the contexts of late colonial India and postcolonial Pakistan. My analysis focuses on the use of sacred space, ritual, and mass media among the followers of a particular sub-branch of a prominent Sufi lineage: the Chishti Sabiri *silsila*. These modern Sufi adepts preserve a distinctive Muslim identity that is legitimized through spiritual genealogy, inscribed in texts, communicated in the intimate exchange between master and disciple and, above all, experienced through ritual performance. Though connected to a sacred past, they are also fully enmeshed in the living present. In response to shifts in the social, cultural, ideological, and technological landscape of South Asia, Chishti Sabiris have embraced a series of practical strategies designed to adapt Sufism to the contingencies and complexities of twenty-first-century life.

As the inner or "mystical" dimension of Islam, Sufism (*tasawwuf*) stands as an alternative nexus of Islamic authority, piety, and practice.[1] Neither a sect nor a cult, it is best understood as a spiritual quest, experienced and expressed via an interpersonal teaching network centered on the fundamental master-disciple relationship. Pushing the boundaries of normative Islam, Sufis strive for a direct, intimate, and unmediated experience of the Divine. Sufi adepts tend to emphasize the inward over the outward, intuition over intellect, spiritual contemplation over scholarly debate, and ecstatic poetry over legalistic prose. Since the twelfth century, Sufi institutional orders—discrete spiritual "paths" (*tariqas*)—proliferated throughout the Muslim world. Though they vary in their teachings and techniques, most Sufis strictly follow the dictates of the Qur'an and the *shari'a* (Divine law), and model their behavior on the example of the Prophet Muhammad (*sunna*).

Despite its deep roots in Islamic history, Sufism remains a controversial and contested tradition. With their bold claims to experiential knowledge and authority, Sufis have often been misunderstood. Much of this dissonance stems from the fact that such a broad range of practices are subsumed under the rubric of "Sufism." At the level of everyday social practice, Sufism is often equated with "popular" worship at shrines. In South Asia, the tombs of Sufi saints provide an alternative outlet for piety and pilgrimage, especially for women who are often marginalized from the public, gendered space of the mosque (figure I.1).

This photograph captures a typical scene at Kalyar Sharif—a rural shrine complex north of Delhi and the final resting place of the eponymous founder of the Chishti Sabiri order: 'Ala ad-Din 'Ali Ahmad Sabir (d. 1291). Here women dance in a state of ecstasy in front of the saint's tomb while a group of musicians (*qawwals*) perform to a crowd of pilgrims. In many ways, this image encapsulates popular Sufism in the Subcontinent. However, these same practices are flashpoints in public debates over Islamic authority and authenticity. For conservative Islamist critics who reject any intermediaries between human beings and God, the cult of Sufi saints is blasphemous idolatry and the worship at shrines corrupt superstition. Yet the story of Sufism in South Asia does not end with saints and shrines. Throughout the Subcontinent, Sufism has inspired myriad forms of artistic and aesthetic expression—from vernacular poetry, to painting and architecture, to music and

Figure I.1 Women Dancing in Ecstasy at the Shrine of 'Ala ad-Din 'Ali Ahmad Sabir (d. 1291), Kalyar Sharif, India

Source: Photograph by Robert Rozehnal

dance traditions. Above all, Sufism in twenty-first-century South Asia remains a spiritual teaching tradition—mediated in the intimate exchange between master and disciple and experienced through ritual performance.

Who are the Chishti Sabiri Sufis? In South Asia—the vast geographic and cultural zone encompassing modern-day India, Pakistan, and Bangladesh—the Chishtiyya has been the most prominent Sufi brotherhood since the twelfth century.[2] With its doctrine of social equality, tolerance, and spiritual discipline, the order spread rapidly eastward from its roots in the remote town of Chisht in central Afghanistan. Under the guidance of charismatic spiritual leaders (*shaykhs* or *pirs*) who embodied Islamic doctrine through their piety, Sufism helped translate Islam for the indigenous population. Versed in local customs and proficient in vernacular languages, Chishti *shaykhs* established centers of learning and hospices (*khanaqahs*) that offered food and shelter for the wayfarers and mendicants who survived on their charity, solace for the pilgrims who visited them for spiritual blessings (*baraka*), and intensive spiritual training for their select disciples.[3] The posthumous reputation of many Chishti *shaykhs* often led to the development of elaborate shrine complexes (*dargahs*) where devotees continued to flock in search of spiritual power to alleviate their worldly troubles. As loci of sacred geography and fonts for public social welfare, these regional shrines continue to thrive as pilgrimage sites and symbols of local Muslim culture and identity.

In South Asia the Chishti Sufi order developed two primary genealogical branches: the Nizamiyya and Sabiriyya. Breaking from the lineage of the dominant Nizami branch in the thirteenth century, the eponymous founder of the Chishti Sabiri subbranch, 'Ala ad-Din 'Ali Ahmad Sabir, initiated an alternative model of spiritual asceticism. From the beginning, Chishti Sabiri spiritual masters were much less visible than their Nizami counterparts, withdrawing from public, urban life, and the allure of the royal courts. Renowned for their intense, awe-inspiring (*jalali*) personalities, Sabiri *shaykhs* stuck to more rural locales, made fewer public appearances, trained fewer devotees, wrote fewer books, and generally avoided the construction of large shrine complexes (*dargahs*). As a result, much of the *silsila's* early history is elusive and opaque, shrouded in legend.

All this changed during the era of British colonialism, however. In the face of rising communal polemics and competition, select Chishti Sabiri leaders came to view silence and withdrawal as untenable. In the late nineteenth century, prominent *shaykhs* linked themselves to social reform movements, founding educational institutions and publishing a broad range of texts. For example, both Hajji Imdad Allah al-Muhajir Makki (1817–1899) and Rashid Ahmad Gangohi (1829–1905)—the spiritual founders of the famous Deoband *madrasa*—were Chishti Sabiri masters.[4] The activism of these nineteenth-century *shaykhs* mirrored the efforts of numerous Sufi leaders from diverse institutional orders across the Muslim world who resisted European colonialism and vigorously defended Sufi doctrine and practices.[5] For the Chishti Sabiri order, however, this model of socially engaged Sufism represented a radical break with historical precedent.

Today's Chishti Sabiri disciples (*murids*) embrace the reformist spirit of their nineteenth-century predecessors, even as they perpetuate the core ritual practices that are the enduring bedrock of their Sufi identity. Contemporary *murids* remain deeply attuned to historical memory. The order's family tree (*shajara*) charts a spiritual heritage that links the current generation of disciples directly to the authority and legacy of the Prophet Muhammad. To a large extent, ancestry defines identity for Chishti Sabiri devotees who recite the following genealogy in a ritual liturgy:

1. The Prophet Muhammad (d. 632)
2. 'Ali ibn Abi Talib (d. 661)
3. Hasan al-Basri (d. 728)
4. 'Abd al-Wahid ibn Zaid (d. 792)
5. Jamal ad-Din Fuzayl ibn 'Iyaz (d. 803)
6. Ibrahim ibn Adham al-Balkhi (d. 779)
7. Huzayfa al-Mar'ashi (d. 823)
8. Abu Hubayra Amin ad-Din al-Basri (d. 895)
9. 'Alu Dinawari (d. 911)
10. Abu Ishaq Chishti (d. 941)
11. Abu Ahmad 'Abd al-Chishti (d. 966)
12. Abu Muhammad Chishti (d. 1020)
13. Abu Yusuf Chishti (d. 1067)
14. Mawdud Chishti (d. 1133)
15. Sharif Zandani (d. 1215)
16. 'Usman Harwani (d. 1220)
17. Mu'in ad-Din Hasan Sanjari (d. 1236)
18. Qutb ad-Din Bakhtiyar Kaki (d. 1237)
19. Farid ad-Din Mas'ud Ganj-i Shakkar (d. 1265)
20. 'Ala ad-Din 'Ali Ahmad Sabir (d. 1291), eponymous founder of the Chishti Sabiri order
21. Shams ad-Din Turk Panipati (d. 1316)
22. Jalal ad-Din Kabir al-Awliya' Panipati (d. 1364)
23. 'Abd al-Haqq Rudawlwi (d. 1434)
24. Ahmed 'Arif Rudawlwi (d. 1477)
25. Muhammad 'Arif Rudawlwi (d. 1492)
26. 'Abd al-Quddus Gangohi (d. 1537)
27. Jalal ad-Din Thanesari (d. 1582)
28. Nizam ad-Din Balkhi (d. 1626)
29. Abu Sa'id Gangohi (d. 1630)
30. Muhibb Allah Allahabadi (d. 1640)
31. Muhammad Fayyaz (d. 1696)
32. Muhammad Makki (d. 11 Rajab, no date)
33. 'Azd ad-Din 'Aziz Amrohi (d. 1759)
34. 'Abd al-Hadi Amrohi (d. 1776)
35. 'Abd al-Bari Amrohi (d. 1811)
36. 'Abd al-Rahim Shahid (d. 1831)

37. Nur Muhammad Jhanjanawi (d. 1843)
38. Hajji Imdad Allah al-Faruqi al-Muhajir Makki (d. 1899)
39. Rashid Ahmad Gangohi (d. 1905)
40. Shah Sayyid Waris Hasan (d. 1936)
41. Muhammad Zauqi Shah (d. 1951)
42. Shahidullah Faridi (d. 1978)—Wahid Bakhsh Sial Rabbani (d. 1995)
43. Siraj 'Ali Muhammad

This study focuses on the final links in this chain of spiritual authority. In particular, I explore the lives and enduring legacies of Muhammad Zauqi Shah and his two principal successors, Shahidullah Faridi and Wahid Bakhsh Sial Rabbani. This trio was profoundly shaped by the spatial and cultural context of twentieth-century South Asia. They were each acquainted by education and experience with the institutions and ideology of the colonial state. As writers and ideologues, these *shaykhs* resolutely defended the orthodoxy of Sufism on the contested public stage of postcolonial Pakistan. As spiritual guides, they understood Sufism as a personal struggle for self-mastery, experienced and expressed within a moral community. The *shaykhs* communicated the disciplinary techniques of embodied and enacted ritual performance (*suluk*) to their loyal followers. Their teachings aimed to cultivate a modern, virtuous self through interpersonal networks of knowledge and practice. Today this legacy is perpetuated by a new generation of Chishti Sabiri disciples in Pakistan. Recently the order has stretched its reach across the Indian Ocean to include a growing contingent of followers in Malaysia. From Karachi to Kuala Lumpur, these twenty-first-century Sufi adepts perpetuate a tradition that remains grounded in Indo-Muslim history, even as it continues to expand into new and uncharted territory.

FRAMING "TRADITION" AND "MODERNITY"

This book traces Chishti Sabiri politics and piety within the context of twentieth- and twenty-first-century South Asia. Throughout this survey, I frequently employ two key terms: "tradition" and "modernity." Though often invoked in academic scholarship and public policy debates, these ambiguous concepts are rarely explained. They are typically paired in opposition—with "modernity" encompassing everything that is "nontraditional," and vice versa. Invariably, one is valorized and the other discredited. The ubiquity of these kinds of reductive, dichotomous definitions only serves to reify both "tradition" and "modernity" as static categories, however. In this study, by contrast, I approach them as malleable and contingent constructs, subject to continuous reformulation and reinvention. Since both terms surface in my analysis of the public and private dimensions of contemporary Chishti Sabiri practice, they each merit some initial consideration here.

"Tradition" is an ambivalent and ambiguous concept. Much of this fuzziness results from the term's elasticity. In contemporary Islamic religious discourse, tradition often constitutes an idealized, sacralized, timeless order—the antithesis of the profane, lived-in world of temporal change and historical context. When defined in relation to a lost Golden Age, tradition sets a standard against which the present is measured (and invariably found lacking). While articulations of sacred history and genealogy differ across the Islamic world, in all contexts they provide Muslims with a powerful sense of orientation, meaning, and purpose. Especially in the midst of unsettling times, appeals to a direct and unbroken link with the past provide a vital sense of continuity and community. Recent scholarship challenges the very notion of a pristine, primordial, and unchanging tradition, however. As historian Muhammad Qasim Zaman notes, dichotomous constructions of "tradition" and "modernity" are increasingly challenged by scholars who argue that "appeals to tradition are not necessarily a way of opposing change but can equally facilitate change; that what passes for tradition is, not infrequently, of quite recent vintage; and that definitions of what constitutes tradition are often a product of bitter and continuing conflicts within a culture."[6]

All Muslims everywhere look to the Qur'an, the dictates of Divine law (*shari'a*), and the model of the Prophet Muhammad (*sunna*) for guidance and inspiration in their spiritual lives. Yet despite frequent claims to a timeless, immutable universality, the interpretation and implementation of Islamic tradition remains remarkably fluid and dynamic. In today's postcolonial Muslim world, the authority of the '*ulama*—religious scholars, literally "those who know"—as arbiters of tradition is increasingly challenged. Shifting geopolitical and socioeconomic boundaries, competing nationalist identities, and the cumulative effects of mass education and mass communication have all contributed to an increasing "objectification of Muslim consciousness."[7] As a result, Muslim identity politics across the globe now more than ever constitutes a dynamic struggle over multivalent religious symbols.In this exchange, a diverse range of social actors—the state, '*ulama*, Islamists, secular intellectuals, and even Sufis—wrestle over the mantle of Islamic authority and authenticity in a complex and fluid process of bargaining and protest, accommodation and conflict. Within the charged ideological landscape of the post-9/11 Muslim world, this internal wrangling has intensified exponentially. Tradition, in short, is up for grabs.

"Modernity" is an equally problematic construct, a malleable and contested term that is "easy to inhabit but difficult to define."[8] This is not to say that scholars have shied away from the subject. Indeed, there is a voluminous scholarship that attempts to delineate and deconstruct modernity by exploring its genesis and genealogy, its causes and effects, from multiple theoretical and disciplinary perspectives.[9] Despite its volume, this scholarly debate has often produced more heat than light. While a consensus on terminology and definitions has proved elusive, modernity is typically associated with a particular worldview and a discrete set of practices, ideas, and institutions. These include such concepts as "citizenship, the state, civil society, public sphere, human rights, equality before the law, the individual, distinctions between public and private, the idea of the subject, democracy, popular sovereignty, social justice, scientific rationality," and secularism.[10] For many scholars such as the Indian historian Dipesh Chakrabarty, the one common denominator underlying any genealogy of "modernity" is the looming presence of the Europe. Other scholarship, however, tracks divergent trajectories of modernity—from its roots in European colonialism to its appropriation and reconstitution among non-European peoples in the postcolonial world. While scholars disagree on its utility as a universal, cross-cultural category, however, one thing does seem clear: in the twenty-first century, the discourses and practices associated with modernity have gone global. As anthropologist Talal Asad illustrates, despite its inherent ambiguity modernity is now a universal political-economic "project":

> It is right to say that "modernity" is neither a totally coherent object nor a clearly bounded one, and that many of its elements originate in relations with the histories of peoples outside Europe. Modernity is a *project*—or rather, a series of interlinked projects—that certain people in power seek to achieve. The project aims at institutionalizing a number of (sometimes conflicting, often evolving) principles: constitutionalism, moral autonomy, democracy, human rights, civil equality, industry, consumerism, freedom of the market—and secularism.[11]

This book aims to decenter modernity. In my view, modernity is neither monolithic nor hegemonic—it has no metanarrative, no universal form, no singular function. As both a discourse and a practice, modernity is encountered, experienced, and shaped by individual social agents (real people) in specific historical moments (discrete places and times). In tracing the multiple vectors of Chishti Sabiri identity, I make no attempt to theorize, delineate, or deconstruct "modernity" as an abstract, disembodied, decontextualized signifier. Instead, following the lead of historian Timothy Mitchell, I chart "the local articulation and dissemination of modernity" by "paying less attention to the grand designs of the colonizing or modernizing state and more attention to the myriad local sites where the modern is realized and continually translated, in its articulation with and production of the non-modern."[12] In short, this book is less concerned with defining what modernity *is* than in exploring *how* it is experienced and explained. To be specific, I am interested in how Chishti Sabiris have endeavored to rethink, reform, and represent their own Sufi identity and practices within the social and historical context of late twentieth-century India and early twenty-first-century Pakistan and Malaysia.

Beyond its usage as a generic marker of temporality—a synonym for "now"—modernity often creates more confusion than clarity as an analytical framework. Nevertheless, I employ the term because the Chishti Sabiris I study do. For them, modernity is not a theoretical abstraction. Nor is it a totalizing system, a zero sum game that must either be appropriated or rejected as a prepackaged whole. Instead, disciples use the term as shorthand for the specific social, political, cultural, and religious ideas and institutions they encounter in the lived-in, real-world landscape of their daily lives. When they describe themselves as "modern" Muslims, Chishti Sabiri disciples do not bother to articulate a detailed definition of the concept. They most certainly do not quote from Western theorists. In practice, the *silsila*'s appropriation of the panoply of modernity—its language, its logic, and its institutions—is a selective and utilitarian bricolage.

So what do contemporary Chishti Sabiris make of modernity? Though far from a homogenous group, disciples could be generally described as global cosmopolitans. The inner circle of *murids* is comprised largely of urban, middle-class professionals who are fully integrated into the global, capitalist economy. Many of them are active participants in public life and civil society. On both sides of the Indian Ocean, Chishti Sabiris also champion their national identities as patriotic citizens of Pakistan and Malaysia. They embrace science, rationalism, and technology, all of which they see as entirely compatible with Islamic piety and Sufi practice. A significant number of disciples have lived or traveled abroad for education and work, and others have extended networks of family and friends overseas. Thus, in both their personal and professional lives, *murids* move fluidly through the diverse modalities and multiple locations of twenty-first-century life.

Yet even as they accept implicitly many of the benefits of modernity, Chishti Sabiris explicitly reject many of the ideologies and institutions associated with it. In public writings and private conversations, for example, *shaykhs* and disciples decry the political and economic hegemony of the West. They are equally critical of many of the excesses of global consumer culture—its shallow materialism, exploitation, and blatant disregard for religious sensitivities. Most significantly, Chishti Sabiris utterly reject any attempt to defend or promote secularism. This distinguishes them (and Pakistanis generally) from their Muslim counterparts in India who—amid a vast Hindu majority—equate secular politics with the defense of religious pluralism and the protection of religious minorities. As citizens of the Islamic Republic of Pakistan, by contrast, Chishti Sabiris define secularism as the removal of religion from the public sphere and insist that God cannot and must not be marginalized from human affairs. Though they embrace many of the instruments of modernity, Chishti Sabiris are critical of modernism as a holistic ideological framework. In this sense, they "are moderns, but not modernists."[13]

When asked to articulate their identity as twenty-first-century Muslims and Sufis, disciples often employ another vocabulary altogether. In their assessment, the central issue they face is how to accommodate a life of spiritual discipline and religious piety to the myriad demands of their daily experiences. Chishti Sabiris do not view this conundrum as something unique to "modernity," however. Instead, adopting a well-known adage, they assert that the real struggle—the true *jihad*—is the age-old dilemma of balancing religion (*din*) with worldly life (*dunya*). Invoking the paradigmatic example (*sunna*) of the Prophet Muhammad, disciples insist that Islam mandates a symbiotic relationship between *din* and *dunya*. The mundane world of everyday life, they argue, is itself the ultimate testing ground for a Muslim's faith. In this, the Chishti Sabiri order bears a striking resemblance to the transnational Daudi Bohra community studied by anthropologist Jonah Blank.

As Blank notes,

> The Bohras have been able to integrate and utilize modernity because they regard it as a friend rather than a foe. When modernity is cast as the obstacle to be overcome, the battle is already more than halfway lost. By reorienting the mindset of the community, [the Bohras] have succeeded in reorienting modernity to serve as a bolster for the group's fundamental traditions. The Bohras regard the *deen* and *dunya* (spiritual and temporal concerns) as two halves of an integrated whole: it's not an either-or proposition, but a way of looking at both religious and everyday concerns in a holistic manner.[14]

Much like their South Asian Shi'a counterparts, contemporary Chishti Sabiris have essentially formulated their own version of postcolonial modernity. Today's disciples—young and old, male and female—appear perfectly comfortable with studying at a secular university, working at an international bank, surfing the Internet, speaking both Urdu and English, arguing about domestic and global politics, voting in national elections, and traveling abroad. At all times and in every location, however, they preserve a religious identity, a discursive tradition, and a ritual discipline that links them to a deeper, sacred Sufi history. Unbound from its premodern geographical and cultural locus in South Asia, the twenty-first-century Chishti Sabiri *silsila* has transformed itself. At the level of everyday practice, disciples in both Pakistan and Malaysia have adopted a range of practical strategies to integrate Sufism into the complex matrix of twenty-first-century life. Yet even as they experience their faith in new forms and spaces, Chishti Sabiris emphasize the underlying *continuity* of the doctrinal teachings and ritual practices of their Sufi tradition.

I view the Chishti Sabiri project of reimagining postcolonial Sufism as further evidence of the malleability and fluidity of modernity. The meanings and applications of modernity are constituted in localized, particularized settings—often outside the geography and categories of the West and beyond the gaze of the colonial and postcolonial state. As anthropologist Katherine Ewing illustrates, "In order to avoid exaggerating its power, it is important to recognize that modernity itself is not a single force but rather the temporary conjunction of practices and ideologies that have diverse sources and divergent trajectories. Current technologies are, of course, taken up into Sufi practice, but they are transformed and encompassed in local circles of meaning. Sufism, itself a diverse phenomenon, thus has a historical trajectory that has been affected but not determined by the composite of forces that we call modernity."[15] Over the past sixty years, the Chishti Sabiri order has marshaled a critical and creative response to the shifting landscape postcolonial South Asia. By selectively appropriating and then reshaping the constitutive discourses and practices of modernity, Chishti Sabiri *shaykhs* and disciples have adapted Sufi tradition to changing contexts. As the following chapters of this book will illustrate, Chishti Sabiris have thus shaped their own *alternative modernity*—an identity that is simultaneously Muslim, mystic, and modern.

Inside or Out?: Negotiating Boundaries

In a strange and wonderful way, my own introduction to the world of living Sufism was facilitated by a photograph. I spent the academic year of 1995–1996 as a graduate student studying Urdu in Lahore, Pakistan. During the course of my studies, I also had the opportunity to meet and interact with a number of Chishti Sabiri disciples. In April 1996, I accompanied a group of *murids* on a pilgrimage to the rural village of Allahabad—sixty miles southwest of the city of Bahawalpur—in southern Punjab to commemorate the first death anniversary (*'urs*) of Shaykh Wahid Bakhsh Sial Rabbani. I remained there for a full week, living among disciples, sharing their meals and company, listening to their stories, and observing their ritual devotions. It was my first real taste of the intensity and transformative power of Sufi piety in practice. And to say the least, it left an impression.

After the week's festivities concluded, a senior disciple invited me to accompany him to the nearby town of Uch Sharif. Together we spent a day wandering through the magnificent blue and white tiled mosques and desolate tombs of this ancient center of learning, trade, and pilgrimage built on a hill overlooking the confluence of the Sutlej and Chenab rivers. That afternoon, near the crumbling tomb of Bibi Jawindi—the wife of the renowned fourteenth-century Suhrawardi *shaykh*, Sayyid Jalal ad-Din Bukhari (1303–1383)—we were approached by an elderly gentleman. I remember being both surprised and impressed by his sudden appearance. The man was tall, thin, and dark-skinned, with long, flowing white hair and a beard. He was dressed in a plain, white *shalwar kamiz*, with simple leather sandals on his feet, a thick white blanket draped over his shoulders, and a white cap covering his head. He also wore a pair of thick, black glasses. In one hand he carried a string of prayer wooden beads, and in the other a long wooden staff. I distinctly remember shaking the old man's hand. We exchanged a few pleasantries and then I wandered off by myself to take more photographs. When I returned a short time later, I found my friend seated on the ground, still engaged in conversation with the stranger. With their approval, I snapped a picture of the two of them. Soon after, we bid our farewells and went our separate ways. When I returned to the United States that summer, I sent this photograph—along with a series of others from the Allahabad *'urs*—to several friends in Lahore as a small gesture of gratitude for their hospitality and kindness.

In August 2000 I returned to Pakistan for my dissertation fieldwork research. While I hoped to pursue an ethnographic study of the contemporary Chishti Sabiri *silsila*, I was unsure how my intentions would be received. It had been four years since that April day in Uch Sharif, but not long after my arrival I discovered that in the interim my photograph had assumed a life of its own. Piecing together the story, I learned that the picture had caused an immediate sensation when the elderly stranger in the picture was identified as the deceased spiritual master Shaykh Wahid Bakhsh Sial Rabbani. This was, to put it mildly, perplexing since the *shaykh* had been deceased for more than a year when the photograph was taken. I was also told that the photograph had been shown to Wahid Bakhsh's wife shortly before her death. She declared it authentic, noting that the glasses, staff, and shoes were those of her late husband. To my further surprise, this photograph had also been copied and widely distributed among Shaykh Wahid Bakhsh's disciples—along with the story of my role as the photographer. As a result, *murids* I had never met would inevitably ask, "Are you the one who took the picture of my *shaykh*?" In their eyes, this photograph legitimized my presence and my work. And during the ensuing fifteen months of research, it facilitated an access and accessibility to the *silsila* that I could never have otherwise anticipated.

With this remarkable introduction, I was drawn deeper into the world of Chishti Sabiri Sufism. From the start, my research raised a host of issues that anyone who undertakes ethnographic fieldwork must be prepared to deal with—complicated questions about the boundaries between participation and observation, scholarly objectivity and self-positioning. Many scholars have written about the ethics of ethnography and the complex power dynamics in the act of re-presenting others.[16] Is there such a thing as objectivity in the study of religion? Should there be? Who is more qualified to interpret religious practice—religious actors themselves (the *emic* voice), or outside academic observers (the *etic* voice)? How should the scholar mark her/his presence in the text? Is authorial voice best left at the margins, or should the interpreter reflexively insert herself/himself into the narrative?

These are important and vexing ethical questions with profound implications because when scholars speak for others, "power, not just meaning, is at stake when we do our work."[17] In any ethnography, the playing field is not level—and these sorts of ambivalences only threaten to complicate matters further. Reflecting on her own work with a *guru* in India, anthropologist Kirin Narayan notes that there is "a raw nerve for every fieldworker: the ethical dilemma involved in appropriating fragments from others' lives. While this appropriation serves the ends of academic careers, the uncomfortable question remains as to how the people concerned, who provided hospitality, time, and insights, might gain."[18]

I wrestled with these very same questions during my fieldwork, and yet again while writing this book. In translating the visceral, three-dimensional experiences of fieldwork to the flat, black-and-white space of the written page, I have been constantly aware of a slippage, a loss, an underlying tension, and ambiguity that is never fully resolved. In narrating the Chishti Sabiri story, I begin with the assumption that all interpretations emerge from a particular site. I acknowledge my own positioning as a white, middle-class, American male of Christian background. Further, I am aware that my training in Islamic Studies and the History of Religions profoundly impacted the questions I asked of Chishti Sabiri disciples in Pakistan. Without a doubt, my own biography and biases have colored the writing of this book as well. I mark this as a process of both translation and transition, a movement *across* the boundaries of physical, temporal, and epistemological space. To quote from religious historian Thomas Tweed,

> Where do scholars of religion stand? We are neither here nor there and do not remain on the boundary for very long. Rather, interpreters are constantly moving back and forth—across the terrain between inside and outside, fact and value, the past and the future . . . But the interpreter can never be fully or permanently inside. We move across—but only partially and temporarily. The act—or, more precisely, the process—of interpretation inevitably distances. It pushes us away. But, at its best, interpretation closes that distance and comes back across.[19]

This book explores both the public and private dimensions of contemporary Chishti Sabiri practice. I quote at length from the *silsila's* texts as well as from a host of recorded interviews to allow—to the greatest extent possible—Chishti Sabiri *shaykhs* and disciples to speak for themselves. At the same time, I recognize that my questions, the way I organize the material, and the theoretical and interpretive tools I bring to the analysis inevitably inserts my own voice into the narrative. In the end, this is not the book Chishti Sabiri disciples would write. Many *murids* will see their own words reproduced on these pages. No doubt, some will wonder why certain things were said and others omitted. Still other readers will, I imagine, lament the frequent emphasis on politics and ideology and see my analysis as too laden with theory and academic abstractions. This is all to be expected, especially given the *silsila's* emphasis on the importance of firsthand experience. Chishti Sabiri disciples view books, at best, as invitations to practice.

And this is the ultimate, insurmountable barrier. As an academic outsider, I claim no direct knowledge of the inner states and experiences that are the essence and goal—the raison d'etre—of Sufi practice. While there is much I did not experience and still do not fully understand, I acknowledge that I have been profoundly impacted by my interactions with the Chishti Sabiri community. To paraphrase a Sufi metaphor, I have seen the fire and sensed its heat. I have watched others burn and have encountered people who were clearly well cooked. But ultimately I make no claims to having burnt myself; in fact, I would say that I remain quite raw. At most I have taken a small sip from a vast ocean. There are certainly other stories to tell here, and I leave them for future interlocutions and other narrators. As for this telling, while it is not a hagiography, it is narrated with humility, gratitude, and profound respect.

METHODS, SOURCES, AND STRUCTURE

The title of this work, *Islamic Sufism Unbound*, demands some explanation. For some "Islamic Sufism" may sound redundant; others may find it novel, even counterintuitive. For twenty-first-century Chishti Sabiri adepts, however, it is an absolutely essential pairing. Chishti Sabiris view Sufism as the essence of Islamic orthodoxy, an authentic discourse and practice firmly grounded in the dictates of normative law (*shari'a*) and prophetic precedent (*sunna*). At the same time, they champion Pakistan as the teleological culmination of Islamic history. In this sense, the order's historical narrative is *unbound* from the prevailing story of the nation and its religious roots. As its transnational reach continues to expand, the order is increasingly *unbound* from its historical moorings in South Asia as well. Furthermore, by adapting its teaching networks and ritual performances to changing contexts, contemporary Chishti Sabiris have effectively *unbound* the trajectory of their own tradition. To keep pace with these momentous shifts, I believe scholars need to do some *unbinding* of their own. Sufism's complexity and dynamism have consistently evaded the gaze of the postcolonial state, the critique of Islamist detractors, and the purview of academic scholarship as well. To capture Sufism's inherent complexity, the scholar's methodology must be equally malleable and responsive.

With certain notable exceptions, however, academic studies of Sufism have generated more heat than light. As Carl Ernst has illustrated, the term "Sufism" is itself an invention of late eighteenth-century European Orientalist scholarship. In current academic language it serves as a generic, catch-all sociological term "for anyone connected to the texts, saints, shrines, orders, and practices broadly associated with Islamic spirituality."[20] Most Western scholars of Islam interpret Sufi thought and practice through an essentializing and reductive lens. Typically, Sufism is characterized as one of three things: an abstract mystical philosophy inscribed in "classical" texts; a thinly veiled political ideology; or an ossified relic, a once dynamic tradition now devolved into popular tomb cults.[21] The result is an entrenched view of contemporary Sufism as a monolithic, superstitious, syncretistic cult mired in profiteering and political wrangling. Ironically, this simplistic model parallels the attacks leveled against Sufism by its Islamist detractors. As Ernst notes, Euro-American scholars and Muslim fundamentalists "share (for somewhat different reasons) a 'Golden Age' view of history, which lauds safely dead 'classical' Sufis while scorning more recent examples of the tradition."[22]

Both Islamicists and social scientists favor one-dimensional models of Sufism.[23] Echoing early Orientalist scholarship, specialists in Islamic Studies tend to focus on the literary texts of select premodern Sufi masters. Abstracting Sufi doctrine from its broader social milieu, their work emphasizes hagiology, detailed descriptions of saintly piety, and the saint's inner metaphysical journey to God. For their peers in the social sciences, however, such God talk is anathema. With rare exception, anthropologists dismiss mystical experience as elusive and ultimately ineffable. Downplaying the doctrinal dimensions of Muslim sainthood, they focus instead on the public negotiation of Sufi power and authority. Not surprisingly, most anthropological studies of South Asian Sufism concentrate on "objectively" visible phenomena such as saintly charisma and the popular ritual practices at Sufi shrines.[24] In my view, each of these approaches precludes an understanding of the full complexity and multivalence of Islamic sainthood. What is needed therefore is a more nuanced, multidimensional, interdisciplinary reading of

Sufism's multiple dimensions—its public and private manifestations, its doctrines and practices, its piety, and its politics.

This book argues that Sufism (like the broader category of "Islam") is best understood as a verb rather than a noun. Sufism is not a static, homogenous "thing" that can be studied in isolation. Rather, it is a discursive tradition and an embodied practice that is experienced in discrete temporal and cultural locations.[25] Furthermore, there is no Sufism without Sufis. Even when they share a common corporate identity connected to specific genealogies of teachers, Sufi adepts are each unique individuals. Any study of Sufi piety and practice, therefore, needs to account for time, place, and agency. With this in mind, I view Sufi identity as textual and contextual. It is envisioned and articulated in *texts*. At the same time, it is experienced and expressed in ritual *contexts*. Moreover, texts and contexts intertwine. As Catherine Bell reminds us, "The dynamic interaction of texts and rites, reading and chanting, the word fixed and the word preached are practices, not social developments of a fixed nature and significance. As practices, they continually play off each other to renegotiate tradition, authority, and the hegemonic order. As practices, they invite and expect the strategic counterplay."[26] With attention to both continuity and change, this study engages both written texts and ethnographic contexts to chart Chishti Sabiri Sufism as a multidimensional, dynamic and adaptive Islamic tradition.

Combining manuscript research and fieldwork my methodology aims to bridge a disciplinary divide. I seek a middle space between the philological approach of Islamicists who often overlook the dynamics and diversity of localized, ground-level contexts, and the overdetermined theorizing of social scientists who frequently gloss the impact of historical change and import of textual traditions. In this I follow the lead of several recent publications that aim to rethink and retool the standard approaches to the study of South Asian Sufism.[27] Katherine Ewing, for example, provides unique psychological insights into contemporary Pakistani Sufism in her book, *Arguing Sainthood*, though her ethnography gives less attention to Sufi ritual practices. In similar fashion, Pnina Werbner's recent study explores a Pakistani Naqshbandi order with a growing transnational reach in England. Werbner examines a range of public rituals, but glosses over the essential core of Sufi practice: the master-disciple teaching relationship.[28] And Arthur Buehler's detailed study offers new perspectives on the history and practices of the Naqshbandi Sufi order in South Asia, though it focuses largely on premodern texts and lacks a nuanced theoretical framework.[29] For my purposes, however, the most relevant contribution is Carl W. Ernst and Bruce B. Lawrence's monograph, *Sufi Martyrs of Love: The Chishti Order in South Asia and Beyond*. This comprehensive overview provides an unparalleled account of the Chishti order, both past and present. Even so, it focuses predominantly on premodern *shaykhs* within the Chishti Nizami lineage, with less attention to the Sabiri subbranch.[30] Though indebted to all these works, this book aims to fill in some of the remaining gaps. In tracking contemporary Chishti Sabiri Sufism, I employ a wide array of interdisciplinary lenses—an approach that should resonate with readers interested in the theory and practice of modernity, postcoloniality, religious nationalism, transnational identity, mass media technology, and ritual.

This project draws on fifteen months of fieldwork research in Pakistan (August 2000–September 2001) and Malaysia (October 2001–November 2001). In Pakistan, I was based in the cultural capital of Lahore. I also traveled frequently to Islamabad, Bahawalpur, Allahabad (southern Punjab), and Karachi to interact with the Chishti Sabiri disciples. In the aftermath of September 11, 2001, I transitioned to Kuala Lumpur, Malaysia to further explore the order's growing transnational dimension. In both countries I recorded extensive personal interviews and oral histories. These interviews were conducted in Urdu, English, or a combination of both. During my fieldwork, I observed the *silsila's* myriad ritual activities as well. This included communal prayers, Qur'an recitations, meditative chanting (*zikr*), contemplation (*muraqaba*), musical assemblies (*sama'*), and pilgrimages (*ziyarat*) to Sufi tomb complexes. Wherever I traveled, I collected an array of texts that encompass several distinct genres, from the discourses of Sufi masters (*malfuzat*), to private letters, diaries, and photographs.

Throughout the book, I draw liberally on textual translations and quotations from personal interviews. Unless otherwise noted, all translations of the original Urdu sources are my own. In the interest of accessibility for a general readership, I avoid the use of diacritics; only '*ayn* (as in *shari'a*) and *hamza* (as in Qur'an) are marked. In similar fashion, the plural forms of words are indicated by adding an "s" to the singular, as in *shaykhs* (rather than *masha'ikh*). When quoting directly from Chishti Sabiri informants, I note the date and location of the interview. At the request of senior figures in the *silsila*, however, I have withheld the names of individual respondents in the interest of privacy and anonymity.

This book is not a comprehensive history of postcolonial Pakistan. Nor is it an exhaustive account of either Indo-Muslim culture or Sufi tradition. By narrowing my focus, I aim instead for a multilayered, nuanced, "thick description" of a living Sufi order—on the ground, in context, and through the words of its contemporary adepts. The following chapters explore Chishti Sabiri Sufi identity from a variety of perspectives:

Chapter 1, "Sufism and the Politics of Islamic Identity," contextualizes the twenty-first-century order in Pakistan's religious and political landscape through a story of personal tragedy and national trauma. In April 2001 over a hundred devotees were crushed to death in a mob stampede during the annual pilgrimage at the shrine of Pakistan's most famous Sufi saint, Baba Farid ad-Din Ganj-i Shakkar (d. 1265). This chapter provides a firsthand account of this accident and its aftermath. My analysis examines the diverse responses of the state authorities, the shrine custodians, and the Chishti Sabiri disciples to this incident. In doing so, I illustrate how Sufi piety and practice act as a lightening rod in the public debates over Islamic authority and authenticity in today's Pakistan.

Chapter 2, "Muslim, Mystic, and Modern: Three Twentieth-Century Sufi Masters," charts the construction of contemporary Chishti Sabiri sainthood in sacred biographies. Drawing on Urdu manuscripts and personal oral histories, I trace how the lives and legacies of three modern Chishti Sabiri masters are remembered in both texts and story-telling networks. I argue that the hagiographical accounts of Muhammad Zauqi Shah, Shahidullah Faridi, and Wahid Bakhsh Sial Rabbani offer unique insights into the historical context of twentieth-century South Asia. At the same time, they each conform to the traditional model of Indo-Muslim sainthood established in premodern Sufi biographical literature.

Chapter 3, "Imagining Sufism: The Publication of Chishti Sabiri Identity," surveys how Chishti Sabiri Sufi identity is imagined, articulated, and disseminated in texts. Focusing on the *shaykhs* as writers and public ideologues, I explore how their literary legacy positions Sufism as the essence of Islamic orthodoxy and the foundation of Pakistani national identity. I focus in particular on two works by Wahid Bakhsh Sial Rabbani that together encapsulate the key themes and rhetorical strategies of the contemporary Chishti Sabiri writing project. The chapter concludes with an analysis of the *silsila's* ongoing publication campaign in Pakistan and Malaysia, highlighting its adroit use of mass media technology to reach a broad, international audience.

Chapter 4, "Teaching Sufism: Networks of Community and Discipleship," traces how Chishti Sabiri knowledge is transmitted via interpersonal teaching networks. My analysis explores the contemporary Chishti Sabiri order as a moral community mediated by strict rules of etiquette and decorum (*adab*). Drawing on extensive interviews, I survey the background and demographics of Chishti Sabiri disciples in Pakistan and Malaysia. Through personal oral histories, *murids* narrate their own experiences of initiation (*bay'at*) and interaction with a spiritual guide. These accounts reveal both the transformative power and underlying tensions of the fundamental master-disciple relationship. This ethnography also demonstrates how disciples draw upon texts as well as the collective wisdom of their peers to make sense of their own doubts, ambiguities, and experiences. I argue that these supplemental sources of knowledge complement and clarify the hierarchical relationship with the teaching *shaykh*.

Chapter 5, "Experiencing Sufism: The Discipline of Ritual Practice," explores how Chishti Sabiri identity is embodied and expressed in ritual performance. My analysis combines theories of the body with a detailed ethnography to illustrate how the rigorous discipline of the Sufi path (*suluk*) transforms the acculturated, social self into a sacralized, moral self. The chapter details three separate ritual complexes: dreams and dream interpretation; rituals of remembrance (prayer, *zikr*, and *muraqaba*); and the annual pilgrimage networks and musical assemblies at Sufi shrines ('*urs* and *sama*'). I argue that the continuity of these technologies of the self cements contemporary Chishti Sabiri identity. These rituals connect the current generation to its premodern antecedents. At the same time, Chishti Sabiri spiritual practices have been reformulated to accommodate the changing ground-level realities of everyday life in twenty-first-century Pakistan and Malaysia.

Engaging both texts (the written word) and ethnographic contexts (the lived reality), each chapter in this book explores a different perspective on Chishti Sabiri identity. Throughout, I emphasize the power of agency by highlighting the distinct characters and personal histories of individual Chishti Sabiri spiritual masters and their disciples. The resulting portrait marks the contemporary Chishti Sabiri *silsila* as a complex, multidimensional entity that is simultaneously

- a central marker in an imagined Pakistani (and now Malaysian) national identity;
- a discursive tradition, inscribed in texts and debated in the public sphere;
- an expression of Muslim subjectivity that constructs a modern, moral self;
- and above all a spiritual discipline, communicated in a dynamic teaching network and embodied in ritual performances.

In charting these interdependent trajectories, this book demonstrates how, at the dawn of the twenty-first century, Chishti Sabiri Sufism remains a dynamic, adaptive, living spiritual path—firmly rooted in tradition, yet responsive to change.

CHAPTER 1

SUFISM AND THE POLITICS
OF ISLAMIC IDENTITY

On the night of April 1, 2001 more than one hundred Pakistani men lost their lives, crushed to death in a mob stampede at the tomb of one of South Asia's most renowned Sufi saints: Baba Farid ad-Din Mas'ud Ganj-i Shakkar (d. 1265). Drawing on ethnographic fieldwork and a range of personal interviews, this chapter offers a firsthand account of this tragedy and its aftermath. My analysis surveys the divergent interpretations of the state authorities, the shrine's hereditary custodians, and a group of Chishti Sabiri Sufi disciples to the causes and meanings of the disaster. I do so to explore a broader issue: how Sufism functions as a lightening rod in the public debates over Islamic identity and authority in today's Pakistan. In a competition over the mantle of Islamic authenticity, competing groups—state officials, Islamists, secular nationalists, *'ulama*, and Sufis themselves—frequently invoke Sufi doctrine, history, and piety, alternatively defending and decrying the tradition's Islamic credentials. Most Pakistanis view Sufi saints such as Baba Farid as the embodiment of Islamic virtue—true *faqirs* ("impoverished ones"), who are committed to a life of piety, self-sacrifice, and public service. Yet the tradition's detractors dismiss them as charlatans and fakers. *Faqir* or faker? The disparate answers to this deceptively simple question reveal a great deal about the way in which Sufism is framed in contemporary Pakistan and throughout the modern Muslim world. As a case study of the politics of Islamic identity, this chapter highlights how Chishti Sabiris transformed the Pakpattan tragedy from story of personal loss and national trauma into a narrative of sacrifice and sacralization, with Sufism repositioned as the center of Islamic orthodoxy.[1]

FAQIR OR FAKER? THE PUBLIC BATTLE OVER SUFISM

The 2001 Pakpattan tragedy and its consequences are an outgrowth of Pakistan's current ideological landscape (map 1.1). After all, Sufism does not exist in a vacuum. Though rooted in personal spiritual piety, Sufism is always mediated in public spaces. Like any religious discourse and practice, it is impacted by (and responsive to) broader social, cultural, and political forces. This has always been true, but global religious traditions have increasingly assumed public, political roles since the 1980s. As sociologist Jose Casanova illustrates, "Religions throughout the world are entering the public sphere and the arena of political contestation not only to defend their traditional turf, as they have done in the past, but also to participate in the very struggles to define and set the modern boundaries between the private and public spheres, between system and life-world, between legality and morality, between individual and society, between family, civil society and state, between nations, states, civilizations, and the world system."[2] Undermining

Map 1.1   Map of Pakistan
Source: The World Factbook

entrenched theories of modernization and secularization, the progressive deprivatization of religion is a growing phenomenon in the twenty-first century. The implications of this trend for social theorists are profound, mandating a wholesale rethinking of the parameters of modernity.

While the public emergence of religious symbols and actors may be a growing trend in the predominantly Christian West, this is nothing new in the Muslim world. In fact, traditional networks of Islamic patronage, religious leadership, and political organization blurred the boundaries between the public and private spheres.[3] This is certainly the norm in Pakistan where sixty years after the nation's traumatic birth religion and politics remain inextricably linked. In a nation deeply divided along ethnic, linguistic, economic, and sectarian fault lines, both state policy and public discourse focus on the relationship between religious and national identity. In the face of the growing threats of regional instability and internal implosion, politicians, the military hierarchy, religious leaders, and average Pakistanis alike grapple over the roots of Islamic authority and authenticity and, by extension, religion's relationship to the ideology of the state. What is Islam and who speaks for the tradition? What precisely is the role of religion in framing the nation's educational, legal, economic, social, and administrative policies? Beyond the geopolitical realities of passports and maps, what exactly does it mean to be Pakistani, and who represents the nation? Where is the center of political authority and religious authenticity? Is it located in the political machinery of the state within the nation's capital, Islamabad (the "abode of Islam"), the religious schools (*madrasas*) of the traditional religious scholars (*'ulama*), the public mosques, or the ubiquitous shrines of Sufi saints? Who knows and who decides?

These questions have dominated public discourse since the end of British colonialism and independence in 1947. From the beginning there has always been an unresolved tension in the constructions of a Pakistani national identity, despite frequent appeals to a reified, universal Islam. As anthropologist Katherine Ewing notes, "The idea of a distinctive 'Pakistani Islam,' the principle of difference that is the rationale for the founding of a nation-state separate from other nation-states, was inconsistent with the universality of Islam at the ideological level and with reality of diversity amongst the practitioners of Islam who were to be subsumed under the signifier 'Pakistani.'"[4] Neither Islam nor Pakistan are inherently united. Yet in a time of immense ambiguity and acute anxiety, the contestation over Pakistan's Islamic identity has assumed an unprecedented urgency with profound implications for Muslims throughout South Asia, and beyond.

Living in an embattled region of fluid borders and contested identities, twenty-first-century Pakistanis are confronted daily with the legacy of Partition: the political entrenchment of the Pakistani military, the instability of regional politics, burgeoning economic debt and endemic unemployment, waves of Afghan refugees, the explosion of drug and smuggling operations, the proliferation of a culture of guns and violence, and the spread of militant Islam and sectarianism. In the aftermath of September 11, 2001, and the fall of the short-lived Taliban regime in Afghanistan, these trends have only been amplified and exacerbated.[5] As the struggle between the military state, independent political parties, and a wide array of religious groups continues to intensify, the country now finds itself at yet another crossroads.

The national elections of October 2002 appear to signal a further shift in the local political landscape. Though never successful at the ballot box before, a coalition of religious political parties, the Muttahida Majlis-i Amal (MMA), made unprecedented gains, capturing 19 percent of the seats in the National Assembly, a controlling majority of the Provincial Assembly of the Northwest Frontier Province, and an upper hand as the largest party in Baluchistan. Pro-Taliban, anti-American, predominantly ethnic Pashtun, and fervently opposed to the government's attempts to reform *madrasa* education and reign in the Kashmir insurgency, the MMA now presents a direct challenge to the government of General/President Pervez Musharraf and its pledge to turn the country back toward democracy.[6]

These electoral results were not entirely unexpected, however. The integration of religious parties within the institutions of the national government can be seen as the culmination of a gradual process of Islamization that has dominated Pakistani politics for the past quarter of a century. Islamic symbols and rhetoric have been increasingly visible in the Pakistani public sphere since the late 1970s. As a new, multiethnic postcolonial state with weak notions of national identity, the Pakistani state opportunistically embedded Islam in politics in order to legitimize its hegemony and expand its powers. As Seyyed Vali Reza Nasr illustrates, "[S]tate-led Islamization is in essence the indigenization of the postcolonial state—embedding it in the local value systems. The dialectic of state expansion and social resistance to it has forced at least some postcolonial states to realize that it is more efficient to be Islamic than not."[7] Although Islamist values and rhetoric now frame public debate in Pakistan as never before, the discourse over Islam is neither static nor monolithic. In fact, it never has been. Yet today the expanding numbers of new religious intellectuals and social actors who openly contest the mantle of Islamic authority and authenticity in the Pakistani public sphere have only raised the stakes even higher.

The increased fragmentation of religious authority is a common trend not just in Pakistan but throughout the contemporary Muslim world. Within this ongoing debate over the parameters of Islamic orthodoxy, Sufism remains an emotive, multivalent, and highly contested signifier in postcolonial Pakistan. With their bold claims to experiential knowledge, authority, and authenticity, individual Sufis have found themselves embroiled in controversy throughout Muslim history. The polemics against the tradition were further intensified and amplified under colonial regimes and the subsequent proliferation of independent, neocolonial Muslim states.[8] The increasing attacks on and widespread marginalization of Sufism by both secular nationalists and Islamists are a distinctly modern phenomenon, however. In fact, the attack on Sufism runs counter to Islamic intellectual history and pervasive cultural norms. As Carl Ernst notes,

> Ironically, as a result of strategic successes by fundamentalist movements in certain key regions like Arabia, and the massive oil wealth that fell into the lap of the Saudi regime, many contemporary Muslims have been taught a story of the Islamic religious tradition from which Sufism has been rigorously excluded. It is ironic because as recently as the late eighteenth century, and for much of the previous millennium, most of the outstanding religious scholars of Mecca, Medina, and the great cities of the Muslim world were intimately engaged with what we today call Sufism. It is doubly ironic because the fundamentalist story is belied by the religious practices of more than half of today's Muslim population.[9]

In South Asia, the British Raj attempted to appropriate and manipulate Sufi tradition—its sacred sites and heroes—for political gain. Recognizing the importance of Sufi shrines as loci of regional identity and the power of hereditary Sufi leaders as moral exemplars and mediators, the British colonial administration actively incorporated Sufism into its system of local politics and patronage. As Ewing argues, "The hereditary saints [*sajjada nishin*] were seen primarily in terms of their economic power. British policy, especially in the Punjab and Sind, was to treat them in essentially the same way that landlords and tribal leaders were treated . . . They tried to maintain the traditional social structure intact, securing the loyalty of the *pirs*, landlords, and chiefs by reinforcing their economic positions and educating them in the British tradition."[10] At times, the British interfered directly in the administration of local shrines such as Pakattan, going so far as to mediate succession disputes in colonial courts. As historian David Gilmartin demonstrates, under colonial rule the Sufi shrine's traditional position "as a hinge between the culture of the locality and the larger Muslim community" remained intact while the role of the saint's living heirs was increasingly politicized.[11]

The politics of Sufism were only amplified in the wake of Partition. In an effort to embed Islamic symbols in a political ideology, the architects of the fledgling Pakistani state continued the British policy of direct control over Sufi shrines and Sufi leaders. Beginning with the secular government of the military leader Ayub Khan (1958–1969), successive Pakistani regimes attempted to link themselves with Sufi religious authority. "The Sufi was the symbol these secularists chose to represent their position and to legitimate their position as leaders of a Muslim democracy," argues Ewing. "They strove to enhance the shrines and the Sufi origins of these shrines for the glorification of Islam and Pakistan. At the same time they sought to strip the hereditary *pirs* of their traditional functions."[12] The state's hegemony over religious spaces and local religious leaders was formally institutionalized with the passage of the West Pakistan Waqf Properties Ordinance of 1959. This act provided legal precedent for the state to appropriate control over religious endowments and to manage shrines, mosques, and other properties dedicated to religious purposes. The result was a further dissolution of the independence and political power of both the hereditary Sufi families and the local *'ulama*.

The Pakistani state used this newfound platform to aggressively forward its own economic and social policies. As Nasr notes, "By taking over the management of the shrines, state leaders were able to use them to propagate a new interpretation of Sufism and rural Islam as compatible with development. Sufi doctrines were depicted as enjoining a positive work ethic, and rural religious festivals were used as venues for agricultural and industrial fairs. By becoming the keeper of shrines, the state was able to find a presence in rural areas, which was otherwise closed to it by the landed elite."[13] This official policy of co-optation and control expanded under the successive regime of Zulfikar 'Ali Bhutto (1971–1979) and during the Islamization campaign of General Zia al-Haq (1979–1989). In Pakistan, Sufi history, sacred spaces, and spiritual luminaries now form an important component of the administrative machinery and political theater of the state. In official government literature and the public posturing of politicians, Sufi shrines are marked and celebrated as sacred national spaces, while premodern Muslim saints are publicly embraced as poets, social reformers, and protonationalists.

Despite these determined efforts to appropriate the tradition's symbolic capital, however, the state's relationship with Sufism has always been plagued by an underlying ambiguity. The colonial and postcolonial state's policies, in fact, never fully erased a deep-seated ambivalence toward contemporary Sufi masters and the continuity of Sufi ritual practices. Never fully integrated into the state's ideology and institutions, the living Sufi master always remained an ambiguous, liminal figure. In Ewing's assessment,

> Within the framework of a colonial ideology, the Sufi *faqir* (mendicant) represented the epitome of indifference, a refusal to be captured by the "naturalness" of the colonial order. The more threatening the presence of the *faqir*, the more demeaning were the images used to "capture" him, images that continue to circulate in postcolonial discourse as versions of modernity, Islam, and secularism vie for dominance in the political arena. The Sufi saint occupies a contested position in these contemporary debates, which have inevitably been molded by the colonial experience out of which Pakistan emerged as a nation.[14]

In spite of its best efforts, Sufi doctrine and ritual practice have never been fully preempted and controlled by the state. Communicated orally via the intimate master-disciple (*pir-murid*) relationship and experienced primarily in private ritual arenas, Sufi knowledge and technologies of selfhood survived and thrived beyond the purview of the state. In Ewing's apt summation, "[U]ltimately, there is an excess of meaning embodied in Sufi practice and expressed in Sufi identities. It is an excess that escaped colonial gaze(s) and is not fully captured by modernity as a discourse or a practice."[15] In my view, it is precisely this "excess of meaning" that is the key to understanding the Chishti Sabiri response to the tragedy in Pakpattan.

THE 2001 PAKPATTAN TRAGEDY

The regional shrine complex in the small pilgrimage town of Pakpattan—120 miles southwest of Lahore—has for centuries served as a central marker in the regional history of Punjab (figure 1.1). Since the thirteenth century, the tomb of the saint, Baba Farid, has linked the local population to a wider universe of Islamic piety and Chishti Sufi spiritual hierarchy. As historian Richard Eaton notes,

> The shrine of Baba Farid in Pakpattan provides a striking example of how Islam, the religion par excellence "of the Book," has been in one instance mediated among common villagers most of whom were illiterate. For them it was the shrine, and less so the Book, which manifested the juncture "where the contrasted poles of Heaven and Earth met." Through its elaborate rituals, grand processions and colorful pageantry, the shrine displayed a sense of divine magnificence and divine mercy. It displayed, in short, the Court of God. Not that Baba Farid himself was confused with God. This could of course have been blasphemous idolatry . . . Rather, though the Court of God as a cosmological construct seemed to lie beyond the devotee's immediate grasp, he did have a "friend in court," as it were, who represented his interests there. This "friend in court," this special pleader, was Baba Farid.[16]

The legacy of Partition has arguably elevated the shrine's symbolic position even higher. In the absence of other religious communities—the Hindu, Jain,

Figure 1.1   The Shrine of Baba Farid ad-Din Mas'ud Ganj-i Shakkar (d. 1265), Pakpattan, Pakistan

Source: Photograph by Robert Rozehnal

or Sikh "Other"—Pakpattan is no longer a site of intercommunal conflict or cooperation. Instead, the shrine is now marked as exclusively Muslim space—a controversial signifier where the parameters and practices of Islam itself are defined, delineated, and contested. In similar fashion, shifting geopolitical boundaries effectively disrupted Sufi sacred geography (*wilayat*). The realities of new passports and the redrawing of local maps made pilgrimage to the major Chishti shrines in India—including Ajmer Sharif, Kalyar Sharif, and Nizam ad-Din in Delhi—prohibitively difficult for Pakistani Muslims. As a result, Pakpattan now stands as the unrivaled center of a distinctly Pakistani Sufism.

Late in the night of April 1, 2001—the fifth day of Muharram, the first month of the Muslim lunar calendar—an atmosphere of intense piety pervaded the shrine complex. It was the eve of Baba Farid's death anniversary (*'urs*) and, as they have for centuries, tens of thousands of devotees inundated the provincial town of Pakpattan to pay their respects to the preeminent saint of Pakistan's Punjab.[17] In keeping with tradition, the faithful waited for hours in the long lines weaving through the town, hoping to eventually pass directly through the narrow Gate of Heaven (*bihishti darwaza*) and into the holy man's presence. This famous southern door of the saint's tomb remains closed throughout the year until the evening of the anniversary when it is opened by the Diwan, a direct lineal descendant of the saint and the shrine's official representative (*sajjada nishin*). To pass through this threshold is the ultimate goal of every pious pilgrim—a direct, salvational encounter with Baba Farid's living grace (*baraka*), a ritual reenactment of the saint's eternal union (*'urs*, or "marriage") with God. A description of this ceremony recorded by a European visitor in 1833 conveys something of the intensity—and continuity—of this transformative experience:

> Numbers of pilgrims, both Hindus and Mussalmans, come to visit the shrine, and all who pass through this doorway are considered saved from the fires of perdition. The doorway is about two feet wide, and cannot be passed without stopping, and the apartment itself is not capable of containing thirty people crowded together . . . A superlative heaven is allotted to those who are first to enter the tomb on the day mentioned. The rush for precedence may, therefore, be better imagined than described. The crowd of pilgrims is said to be immense, and as they egress from the sacred doorway, after having rubbed their foreheads on the foot of the saint's grave, the air resounds with their shouts of "Farid! Farid!"[18]

The night of April 1, 2001 was a night unlike any other, however. As the pious pilgrims flocked to the shrine, jostling toward Baba Farid's tomb in eager anticipation, a tragedy was unfolding that would transform the occasion from a raucous public celebration into a somber mass funeral, a tableau of confusion, chaos, and grief.

The majority of the victims had been among the first to offer their devotions at the saint's tomb. Exiting the crowded central courtyard, they ascended the narrow stairwell at the extreme north end of the shrine, a passageway typically reserved for the Diwan and his personal guests. At the same moment, an impatient crowd of several thousand onlookers broke through a weak police cordon and descended upon them from above. In the melee that followed, the pilgrims were knocked backward and pinned against the staircase's thick stone walls. Panicked by the violent onslaught, a police contingent posted at the entrance point made the fateful decision to close and lock the doors, sealing off the only means of escape. In an instant, a private exit became a public entrance—with disastrous consequences. By the time it became clear what had happened and the heavy wooden doors were thrown open it was too late. Pilgrims had become martyrs, crushed to death. Reporter Tahir Jehangir recounted the disturbing scene for the Lahore-based English language weekly, *The Friday Times*. His sense of helplessness and outrage are palpable:

> Soon the commotion was replaced by a deathly silence. When the gate was opened again the sight was ghastly. I am told that many men had been crushed against the walls . . . it was like a wall of dead bodies. They started pulling people out. Some were still alive but most were dead. All night the dead were being carried out. How many died? The newspapers reported over forty, but I can vouch for the fact that there were many more. The poor families just took their dead away, leaving officialdom to do its count, carry out the enquiries, pass the blame to somebody else, and rule on.[19]

I too was there that night, accompanying a select group of Chishti Sabiri Sufi disciples (*murids*). The group included more than a hundred and fifty men and women, most of them Pakistanis but including a large contingent from Malaysia as well. They had traveled to Pakpattan along with their spiritual guide, Shaykh Siraj 'Ali, for a week of intensive spiritual immersion. At the personal invitation of Diwan Maudud Mas'ud Chishti, the disciples entered the shrine complex early in the evening, long before the doors were opened to the public. Dressed in white *shalwar kamiz* and following the strict rules of etiquette and decorum (*adab*), the male disciples formed a series of straight rows parallel to the main door of the saint's tomb. Surrounding Shaykh Siraj, they sat or stood in quiet contemplation (*muraqaba*) as the female disciples looked down from the rooftop balcony above. This meditative calm was gradually eclipsed by a growing tumult as the crowds began to pour into the compound to participate in the public ritual ceremonies. Following evening prayers, the Chishti Sabiri disciples dispersed into smaller groups, merging into the waves of humanity awaiting the highlight of the evening: the opening of the *bihishti darwaza*.

After a prolonged delay, the Diwan arrived along with his entourage. A small group, among them Shaykh Siraj 'Ali and a number of senior Chishti Sabiri disciples, accompanied the procession into the shrine's inner sanctum for ritual prayers. At the end of this private ceremony, the door was opened and the surging crowds began filing into the cramped space of the saint's grave to the clamorous shouts of "Ya Farid, Haq Farid!" As the Diwan mounted a large stage in the center of the courtyard to distribute saffron-soaked strips of cloth known as *pechas* to the assembled masses, the Chishti Sabiri group exited the compound through the northern gate, as was the custom. This time, however, they were trapped in the stampede. When the barricaded doors were finally opened, Shaykh Siraj and a dozen of his disciples were found among the wounded, stunned, and battered but alive. A fourteen-year-old boy from the group was not so fortunate, however, perishing amid the melee. And this was no ordinary boy. He was the son of a prominent devotee and, significantly, the great-grandson of the prominent Chishti Sabiri master, Shaykh Muhammad Zauqi Shah (1877–1951).

I reached the northern gate a half hour after the incident, having made my way along with the enraptured throng through the *bihishti darwaza* and into the cramped quarters of the saint's tomb. It was a harrowing and moving experience. I emerged from the inner sanctum both exhausted and exhilarated. The reverie, however, did not last long. In the hope of locating my hosts whom I had lost in the crowd, I made my way toward the shrine's northern exit through a narrow passageway that suddenly opened onto a surreal scene—the aftermath of the stampede. In a great tumult of commotion, people were frantically struggling to assist groups of injured men while others carried off the broken bodies of their fallen relatives and friends. Stretched out in the middle of the white marble courtyard were lines of twisted, contorted corpses, strangely silent amid the unfolding chaos.

While searching for my hosts, I met two Malaysian *murids*, both of them medical doctors. They recounted the horrific events and their own efforts to help revive and resuscitate the victims, including the group of Chishti Sabiri *pir-bhais* (fellow disciples) injured in the crush. Overwhelmed by this sobering news and the devastation around me, I returned to the Chishti Sabiri compound via the narrow, twisting alleyways that flank the shrine's northern border. There I found groups of disciples huddled together in stunned, muted grief. They were deeply concerned about the condition of Shaykh Siraj and a number of other senior disciples, but they were devastated by the loss of the young boy.

As the scale of the horror became evident, the Chishti Sabiri disciples tried to make sense of what had happened. They struggled to find a deeper meaning for this unprecedented tragedy at the sacred site of one of the spiritual luminaries of their own tradition.[20] What had gone wrong? Why had so many died at Pakpattan of all places, and on this of all nights? Who was to blame? What did this tragedy signal for the shrine of Baba Farid, for the life of the Chishti Sabiri order, and for the future of Sufi pilgrimage and ritual practices? In the days and weeks that followed, the Pakistani press investigated these same questions, spurring a lively public debate.

The Pakpattan tragedy immediately brought the latent tensions and ambiguities in the state's relationship with institutional Sufism into full view. In response to the public outcry over the loss of life and widespread accusations of corruption and incompetence in the local and national press, the government conducted a hasty inquiry. The local police and district administration were quick to blame the incident directly on the actions of the shrine's chief custodian, Diwan Maudud Mas'ud Chishti. According to the authorities, the Diwan had delayed the public ceremonies and the opening of the *bihishti dar-waza* by four hours while bickering over the annual payment allotted to him from the Awqaf Department. The day after the incident, the lead article in the national Urdu newspaper *Jang* quoted the district commissioner who insisted that this financial quarrel precipitated the crisis, forcing the long delays that prompted the impatient crowds to overrun the helpless police forces.[21]

As part of an investigation ordered by the governor of Punjab in Lahore, I was subsequently invited to accompany three senior Chishti Sabiri disciples to the home of a prominent minister assigned to assist the local authorities in their investigation. After listening to the testimonies, the minister promptly summarized his own findings in the case. Predictably, his opinions echoed the modernist and rationalist rhetoric that characterized the official government response. While acknowledging that Baba Farid had been a great saint and poet, the minister dismissed the shrine custodians as profiteers, mired in nepotism, intransigence, and greed. The events of the *'urs*, he insisted, had little to do with "real Islam," and the mob stampede was only to be expected from the illiterate, ignorant masses drawn to the shrine's carnival-like atmosphere. The police and district administration, the minister maintained, were simply overwhelmed by an unruly mob—and understandably so since their resources were already stretched thin by the state's concerted efforts to prevent sectarian violence throughout the district during the month of Muharram. While acknowledging that further precautions and logistical changes would be needed to avoid a repeat of this incident in the future, he concluded that the Diwan was ultimately responsible for the tragedy (April 11, 2001, Lahore).

In response to the public declarations of the state authorities, the shrine's hereditary custodians spoke out publicly against the heavy-handed tactics and culpability of the local police and district administration. In an article in the English daily newspaper *The Nation*, Badr Moeenuddin, the Diwan's maternal uncle, denounced the government's accusations while defending his family's honor. With photographs and a schematic drawing of the shrine complex as evidence, his article offers a detailed summary of the mechanics of this unprecedented logistical breakdown. Describing how the newly appointed district administration altered long-standing policies, Badr Moeenuddin blames poor crowd control and security arrangements as the underlying cause of the stampede. Attacking the state's version of the incident, he notes that the tragedy took place some two hours after the Diwan's arrival for the door-opening ceremony—a fact, he asserts, that proves that the delay had absolutely nothing to do with chaos that followed. In a final rhetorical move, Badr Moeenuddin defends the sanctity of the *'urs* itself, condemning unwarranted police violence as the real cause for the crowd's unruliness: "They [pilgrims] are full of reverence with a burning desire to pass through the door, but are frightened of the police *lathi*-charge so at the slightest chance they tend to make a dash to the entrance. Invariably they are beaten back, but they keep waiting for the rare opening. This was the cause of the tragedy."[22]

These widely divergent renditions of events typify the public discourse (and dissonance) over Sufism in contemporary Pakistan. Though the state authorities and shrine custodians held each other ultimately responsible, both camps viewed the tragedy as the result of administrative mismanagement—a breakdown in logistics, communication, and the allocation of resources. What is missing from both accounts are the experiences and views of actual participants, the voices of everyday people who made the pilgrimage to the shrine that night and suffered the consequences. Among Chishti Sabiri Sufi adepts, the suffering and loss at Pakpattan was interpreted in a remarkably different fashion. While defending the Diwan, they turned to more spiritual explanations, sacralizing the loss of life in terms of ritual sacrifice and martyrdom (*shahadat*). An outgrowth of a fundamentally different epistemology and worldview, this alternative interpretation stands in marked contrast to the logic of the modernist, rationalist state. In my view, it can also be read as a statement of resistance, a counternarrative to the hegemony of the state. As Pnina Werbner and Helene Basu suggest, "For the citizens of postcolonial societies, it is often the *opposition* between a morally grounded charisma and the rationalized authority of the state which more accurately reflects the experiential reality of modernity. What needs thus to be theorized is the nature of charismatic (saintly) *dissent and opposition* to the bureaucratic domination of the state."[23] With this in mind, I examine the Chishti Sabiri interpretation of the Pakpattan tragedy as a salient example of the order's overarching project to reclaim Sufism as Islamic orthodoxy.

CHISHTI SABIRI SUFISM AS ISLAMIC ORTHODOXY

Among Chishti Sabiri disciples, the death of the great-grandson of Shaykh Muhammad Zauqi Shah, along with the injuries to Shaykh Siraj 'Ali and a number of prominent *murids*, elicited a great deal of personal and collective introspection. When asked about their experiences and reflections, disciples uniformly expressed profound sorrow at the appalling loss of life. At the same time, they voiced anger and disgust at what they perceived as a gross distortion of the facts—and a woeful ignorance of Sufi traditions—in the newspaper coverage and the public statements of local authorities. According to disciples, both the state and certain religious leaders used the incident for political leverage. Both glossed over the spiritual dimensions of the 'urs in an attempt to assign blame elsewhere. Condemning the pilgrimage rites as little more than the superstitious customs of the uneducated rural masses, these critics of Sufism dismissed the tragedy as the regrettable—but altogether predictable—outcome of a frenzied mob. In response to such critiques, a senior *murid* argued,

There have since been rather strange suggestions from some of the local 'ulama who say that they should just keep the door (*bihishti darwaza*) open all year long. They do not realize that people would still just come on those nights [of the 'urs celebration]. Reading the newspaper report it is clear these people just do not understand the rituals at all. They assume that these are all just simple, ignorant, rural folks who have these beliefs. These reporters are as ignorant as foreign outsiders. People have become so distant from Sufism . . . There is a Wahhabi in my office and he told me, "This is what happens at these shrines!" I asked him to explain the stampedes at Hajj. He had no response. (April 8, 2001, Lahore)

By drawing a direct parallel between the loss of life in Pakpattan and the frequent incidents that occur during the paradigmatic annual pilgrimage to Mecca, this devotee implies that both rites exhibit an orthodoxy incumbent on all Muslims.

Other disciples were even more pointed in their critique, defending the shrine custodians while attacking the hypocrisy of the state. A German convert and prominent disciple who has lived in Pakistan for almost thirty years wrote a response to the tragedy, which he subsequently shared with me. Surveying the recent history of Sufism's relations with the state, he laments that the shrine custodians were "coerced into surrendering the management of the shrine" to the Awqaf Department. This co-optation, he asserts, constituted a radical break with a six-hundred-and-fifty-year-old tradition that "not only violated the natural propriety rights of the Diwan's family but dragged an institution of an essentially spiritual nature for reasons of revenue collection onto the mundane plane of government administration, and this in itself constitutes a very serious breach of etiquette. Things like this never go unpunished, even though the reprisal might not strike right away."[24]

Turning his attention to the root causes of the tragedy, the author points to the opportunistic posturing of local authorities at the 'urs ceremonies. He laments the officials' utter disregard for the sanctity of the space and the proper decorum (adab) mandated by the occasion. From this perspective, the crass violation of the sacred realm of religion (din) by the profane politics of the mundane world (dunya) is the real cause of the unprecedented disaster at Pakpattan. This written account echoes what I heard from numerous murids in person. It constitutes, in effect, a counterpolemic to the state's official interpretations of the causes of the tragedy.

Disaffected by the response of the state, Chishti Sabiri disciples turned to more spiritual explanations for the traumatic events that impacted them so profoundly. With a firm belief that nothing accidental happens in proximity to a saint's tomb, murids reasoned that the loss of life must be sacralized and understood in terms of martyrdom (shahadat). The German disciple makes this logic explicit: "Against whom was this outburst of divine vengeance directed? Certainly not the more than one hundred people who breathed their last there. They, or at least a good number of them, embraced shahadat (martyrdom) . . . It is part of our faith to believe that every man's time of death is predestined, and the fact that those people died there in these circumstances instead of at home in their beds, or anywhere else, I would see rather as a reward than a punishment."[25]

In the Chishti Sabiri alternate narrative, the death of the young boy is rationalized as a ritual sacrifice. As a member of a *sayyid* family (i.e., a lineal descendant of the Prophet Muhammad) and the great-grandson of a renowned Sufi *shaykh*, his martyrdom becomes an act of Divine will—an atonement for the lack of piety and propriety shown by others at Baba Farid's *'urs*. In the words of a prominent female disciple, "I believe it was ordained to happen. Sometimes the saints, they do interfere in things, in worldly matters. Maybe now some changes will take place. Our Holy Prophet—God bless him and grant him salvation—his family is always there to give sacrifices. Right from the day of Karbala, the Prophet's family has offered themselves for sacrifices like these . . . He [the young boy] was a lovely child, a perfect human being. I really believe he had completed *suluk* [the Sufi path]" (June 17, 2001, Lahore).

This revealing account memorializes the deceased child as the very embodiment of Sufi virtue. For an audience steeped in Sufi tradition, his preternatural knowledge of spiritual matters, mastery of ritual practices, and careful attention to the rules of decorum affirm his lofty spiritual status as a successor to the legacy of his great-grandfather and, by extension, the Prophet himself. The memory of the young boy's precocity also marks a sharp contrast to the clumsy and disrespectful actions of the representatives of the state who, by implication, are ultimately held responsible for his untimely death. The invocation of Karbala in this context is a particularly resonant and evocative rhetorical device. It links the Pakpattan tragedy to sacred history by suggesting that, once again, the Prophet's heirs have suffered at the hands of corrupt political rulers obsessed only with worldly power.

While sacralizing the tragedy in terms of martyrdom, Chishti Sabiris also drew broad moral lessons from the painful events in Pakpattan. As *murids* recounted their experiences in private and public contexts, the tragedy came to serve as an important heuristic device. Another senior female disciple, for example, recounted how the women disciples had responded to the news of the tragedy with pious resignation and patient forbearance, even in the midst of overwhelming pain and grief. In her words,

> Whatever God wants, it has to happen. People who had to learn something, and they will learn from this incident. It could have happened anywhere, but the best thing is that it happened there, right in front of Hazrat Baba Sahab. He [the young boy] was only fourteen years old. It was terribly sad, but it gave us patience. I was amazed, among the women, even the boy's mother did not cry out. There was no wailing and no one had to carry her. We all just sat and prayed. Everyone knew that this was the will of God. When every leaf moves only with the will of God, how can you start wailing and crying over this? (June 17, 2001, Lahore)

According to disciples, this ability to maintain comportment in the face of trauma is itself a sign of advanced spiritual development—the realization of the key Sufi virtues of patience (*sabr*) and selfless surrender to the Divine will (*tawwakul*).

This emphasis on the power of redemptive suffering was further high-lighted in descriptions of Shaykh Siraj 'Ali's endurance and unwavering calm in the face of the chaos. In the weeks and months following the incident, anecdotes about the *shaykh's* conduct and composure circulated widely. These accounts provided Chishti Sabiri disciples with instructive examples of the transformative power of faith. The intensity and importance of the experience is clearly conveyed in the words of a female Malaysian *murid*, a medical doctor who helped treat Shaykh Siraj's injuries:

> I touched his wounds and the *faizan* [spiritual grace] was very strong. That is when I understood the meaning of the majesty of a saint. You read about it, but you do not understand it until you see it. He was in pain, he was in trouble, yet there was this calm. His face was so serene, so beautiful. In my whole life I will never forget that night! Somehow along with the majesty of Hazrat Siraj Sahab, I could feel the majesty of Allah. I felt His presence. Being in the *shaykh's* presence is Allah's presence. I felt it so strongly that night, even amid all the tears, all the sadness. I just remember all the *faizan*. There was electricity in the air. (October 6, 2001, Kuala Lumpur, Malaysia)

Faizan—literally meaning "overflowing" or "abundance"—is a common term used to describe the Divine blessing and power that radiate from sacred places and holy persons.[26] Similar to the Arabic term *baraka*, it is understood as a marker of sacrality, here described in visceral, material terms as an electric charge or a surge of energy.

The palpable sense of intensity and awe conveyed in this anecdote is echoed the recollections of numerous Chishti Sabiri disciples present in Pakpattan that April night. In interviews, many disciples recalled strange circumstances and portents of impending disaster—signs they had failed to understand fully and interpret at the time but which later appeared highly significant. A number of disciples narrated dreams that they experienced in the days leading up to the *'urs*: visions of Chishti Sabiri *shaykhs*, the death of family members and, in the case of one female *murid*, an attack by a black goat. Several disciples recalled being plagued with feelings of unease and anx-iety on the day of the tragedy, while others noted sudden shifts in the weather as the ceremonies began that evening. Significantly, recollections of the limi-nality of that particular night were not limited to those present in Pakpattan. A group of Malaysian disciples who were unable to make the trip to Pakistan gathered together at a private home in Kuala Lumpur on the evening of the *'urs*. Listening to recordings of *sama'* on a small cassette player, they com-memorated the death of anniversary of Baba Farid on the opposite side of the Indian Ocean. As a female Malaysian disciple attests, these women experi-enced something of the intensity of the experience as well:

> We celebrated the Muharram *'urs* here [in Kuala Lumpur], a small gathering in our house. It was mostly women. The *faizan* that night was fantastic. We thought we were going into *hal* [a state of ecstasy], all of us. We were so scared that we immediately stopped. It was fantastic though. You feel it yourself. The

rhythm of the *qawwali* [music], you want to go along with it. Your body wants to get up and dance along with the rhythm. That was the first time I experienced this—and not just me, all of us who were there that night. It was that same night, around the time of the mob stampede in Pakpattan Sharif. (October 3, 2001, Kuala Lumpur, Malaysia)

Narrated and circulated among Chishti Sabiri disciples, these stories and retroactive interpretations now form part of the order's collective memory. For Sufi disciples who live in a sacralized universe, these oral accounts imbue the trauma suffered at the saint's *'urs* with a deeper sense of meaning and purpose. In sharing their personal experiences with their peers, *murids* have effectively discovered a "mode of narrating, imagining, re-presenting those events that, at least to some extent, does their extremity justice."[27] In effect, the Chishti Sabiris' alternative response to the Pakpattan tragedy shifts the discursive frame from the level of personal tragedy into a story of national trauma. It transforms the loss of individual lives at the shrine into a symptom of the internal moral decay of the nation. According to this reading, Pakistan's fundamental loss of values and betrayal of tradition had to be accounted for and rectified—and here death is transformed into a ritual sacrifice that allows for healing, renewal, and redemption. Through a logic and worldview directly opposed to the rationalist discourse of the state, these oral testimonies do more besides providing suture to the pain and trauma of suffering: by sacralizing the suffering at Pakpattan, this counternarrative also marks the shrine—and the legacy of its patron saint, Baba Farid—as the rightful inheritance of the contemporary Chishti Sabiri order.

The Chishti Sabiri response to the Pakpattan tragedy exemplifies the order's overarching project to put Islam back into Islamic Sufism. In response to their detractors who denigrate Sufism as a perversion of Islam's normative traditions, Chishti Sabiri practitioners are quick to defend the orthodoxy of Sufi piety. They reclaim the Prophetic model (*sunna*) and the normative boundaries of Islamic law (*shari'a*) as the foundations of their own faith and practice. In the words of one *murid*, a conservative, middle-aged woman who lived for twenty years in both Saudi Arabia and Turkey and who now runs an informal religious school (*madrasa*) for women in Lahore,

Our Prophet, God bless him and grant him salvation, was the greatest Sufi. Self-negation in everything, that was his way. Yet, at the same time, he was so disciplined. Each moment of his life was within the *shari'a*. What is Sufism [*tasawwuf*]? It is self-negation, controlling your self [*nafs*]. And what is *shari'a*? *Shari'a* is there to guide you, to keep you within bounds. If you do not have boundaries, you just do whatever you want to do . . . *Tasawwuf* keeps the Prophet's life, his role model alive. For the *'ulama*, for the people who are just practicing the *shari'a* without the spirit of it, it is dry. The spirit of *shari'a* is *tasawwuf*. (March 9, 2001, Lahore)

This is a typical refrain. Far from being a peripheral practice, or the outgrowth of external cultural accretions, Sufism is repositioned in Chishti Sabiri narratives—both oral and written—at the very heart of Muslim history, belief, and practice.

This is further exemplified in a private letter written by Shaykh Wahid Bakhsh Sial Rabbani to a female disciple in Malaysia. In a didactic voice, the *shaykh* explains that Sufism is sanctioned by both the Qur'an and the Prophet Muhammad. Critiquing Islamist—in this case, Wahhabi—ideology, he valorizes Sufism as the very essence of Islam:

> Sufism is not against the Qur'an or Hadith, even by a fraction of an inch. In fact, no one in the world has obeyed the Qur'an and Hadith as much as the Sufis have. They are the most ardent lovers of Allah Most High, and sacrifice everything for him. The Holy Prophet preached this sort of life, and turned his Companions into the greatest *awliya' Allah* ["Friends of God" or saints, nearest the Almighty. The Wahabbis do not believe in the *awliya' Allah*. They simply ignore the verse in the Qur'an which says, "The *awliya' Allah*, neither do they fear nor despair" [Qur'an 10:63].[28]

What is at stake here is the definition of Islamic orthodoxy. All sides claim authority and authenticity, arguing about who knows and who has a right to speak for Islam. Of course, this is nothing new and certainly not unique to the Chishti Sabiris. In fact, the public wrangling over the roots of orthodoxy has continued unabated throughout Islamic history. As historian Daniel Brown notes, this underlying ambiguity has never been resolved: "It is a tension between principles of stability and of flexibility, between the authority of the past and the exigencies of the present, and between scripture and tradition. Most fundamentally, however, it reflects a struggle over the question of who has the authority to represent the Prophet. What individuals, groups, or institutions are the true mediators of the Prophetic legacy, standing in his place and speaking with his voice?"[29] Like many premodern and revivalist Sufi masters before them, contemporary Chishti Sabiris see themselves as the rightful heirs to the legacy of the Prophet. The order is distinguished, however, by its unique response to the challenges and changes spurred by Partition and its particular vision of a *sunna*-centric and *shari'a*-minded Sufism couched in a distinctively Pakistani idiom. Subsequent chapters explore this complex dynamic in detail. Here, however, it is important to highlight how contemporary Chishti Sabiris claim the mantle of Islamic orthodoxy in order to defend their tradition against its critics and detractors in the highly contested public sphere of today's Pakistan.

In interviews, disciples frequently expressed anxiety over what they saw as the increasing politicization of Islam in contemporary Pakistan. They bemoaned the growing hegemony of Islamist readings of Islamic history, social relations, and ritual practice. After the tragedy at Pakpattan and, in particular, in the wake of the attacks of September 11, *murids* became increasingly vocal about their frustration over exclusivist and extremist versions of Islam. When asked to articulate their criticism of Islamist ideology, for example, disciples generally focused on their coreligionists' singular obsession with outward displays of piety. The simplistic equations of "true Islam" with a person's style of dress, the veiling of women, and rigid, inflexible attention to the mechanics—instead of the intention—of ritual practices, *murids* asserted, only conceal a woeful ignorance of Islam's deeper meanings. The increasing "Talibanization" of Pakistani society outrages a senior disciple, even as his discourse synthesizes the Chishti Sabiri counterpolemic:

> The Taliban see themselves as reformers, a movement to restore past glory. Their logic is that we must become exactly like the *Sahaba* [the early community surrounding the Prophet Muhammad]. No one can be like that. The Prophet and the *Sahaba* are not coming back. This is just imitation [*taqlid*], nothing else—imitating them without their purification and perfection. A focus on outward display is an easy way out for something that is simply not so easy. The *sunna* of the Prophet is beyond the capacity of any Muslim. I think it is incumbent on all Muslims to try to follow the *sunna* of the Prophet in all areas. But there is a difference between imitation and *sunna*. The outward becomes mere imitation. (October 1, 2001, Lahore)

I heard Chishti Sabiri disciples level a similar critique—often couched in stories of direct personal confrontation—against a number of Pakistani religious parties and revivalist movements. This included the Ahl-i Hadith, Wahhabis, Jama'at-i Islami, Tablighi Jama'at, and a variety of pro-Taliban religious parties—the very groups who dismiss Sufism as an un-Islamic cultural accretion in public discourse.[30] Predictably, some of the most pointed criticism fell on the contemporary Deoband—a religious educational institution with roots in nineteenth-century India that is most often associated with the radical and extremist doctrines of the Taliban. Not surprisingly, the legacy of the Deoband *madrasa* is hotly contested by contemporary Chishti Sabiris who view the contemporary movement as a complete betrayal of the teachings of its founders, men such as Hajji Imdad Allah al-Faruqi al-Muhajir Makki (1817–1899) and Rashid Ahmad Gangohi (1829–1905), who were themselves Chishti Sabiri masters.[31] Disciples argue that the logic and intention of Deoband's initial conservatism was subsequently distorted and perverted, leaving behind a hollow shell devoid of all Sufi spirituality. In the words of one senior male *murid*, "Throughout the British period, this was the institution [the Deoband *madrasa*] that preserved religion [*din*] in its purest form. Now, however, there is a great misunderstanding. The Deobandis have strayed from the path of their elders" (February 21, 2001, Lahore).

Significantly, Chishti Sabiris also avoid association with the pro-Sufi Barelwi movement. In the words of another senior disciple, the contemporary order effectively steers a course between the doctrinal conservatism of the contemporary Deoband movement and the populism of the Barelwis: "Our *shaykhs* have come from Deoband. Today we go to the Sufi shrines [*mazars*] like the Barelwis, but we are neither Deobandis nor Barelwis. We simply are following the way of our spiritual masters" (May 21, 2001, Karachi).[32] In articulating their own distinct identity, Chishti Sabiris remain wary of all political labels and actively avoid direct involvement in any political party or movement.

Who then speaks for Islam? For Chishti Sabiri practitioners, the answer is unambiguous: only the *awliya' Allah* (the "Friends of God," the Sufi saints) and their living heirs (the Sufi *shaykhs*) carry the mantle of the Prophet. In the words of another senior male disciple,

> We reject all elements of compulsion or force—if they are there, the sincerity [*khalus*] is not there. There is a saying of Hazrat Shahidullah Faridi that a person cannot proselytize *da'wa* without permission. Until you are explicitly given permission, you are just a student, and you have no business proselytizing. So many preachers [*maulvis*] give passionate speeches. People leave in tears, but people do not change. This is because these *maulvis* do not have permission to speak. The Sufi *shaykhs* do not say a word, but people's lives are profoundly changed. Only they have the express permission for *da'wa*. (April 24, 2001, Lahore)

As this quote suggests, Chishti Sabiris reject all simplistic attempts to reify, synthesize, codify, and systematize Islamic piety and practice. Unlike the representatives of the state, the religious scholars (*'ulama*), the preachers attached to local mosques (*maulvis*), or the genealogical heirs to the Sufi saints (*sajjada nishin*), they mark the Sufi master's authority as an unrivaled status that must be *earned* through self-discipline and experiential knowledge. Proper spiritual guidance, therefore, is ultimately available only under the watchful tutelage of an accomplished *shaykh*. To use Sufi vocabulary, Chishti Sabiris assert that the moral reform of individuals as well as society must be cultivated through the discipline of *'ibadat* (normative ritual practice), channeled through a strict adherence to *shari'a* (the dictates of Divine law), and perfected through the rigors of *tariqa* (the Sufi path).

CONCLUSION

Sufism remains a malleable and controversial signifier within the combative discursive landscape of twenty-first-century Pakistan. In an attempt to appropriate the tradition's symbolic capital, Sufi leaders are co-opted into the ideology and institutions of the state as political agents and power brokers, mediators in regionalized networks of local identity and power. At the same time, Sufism remains deeply rooted in everyday practice. The lives of Sufi saints are woven into local poetry and legends, and Sufi shrines such as Pakpattan serve as vital centers of popular piety—nodal points of local identity and culture. Even so, many of the activities associated with popular Sufism are viewed with intense ambiguity and suspicion, particularly by Islamist groups who dismiss them as impure, un-Islamic accretions. As a result, questioning Pakistanis about their views on Sufism may elicit any number of responses—from reverent, extemporaneous recitations of the poetry of a local saint to harsh invectives against the moral depravity of the uneducated masses who flock to shrines. In today's Pakistan, Islam itself is argued and debated. And when it comes to Sufism, lines are drawn and sides are chosen.

The events of the night of April 1, 2001 framed these issues in the starkest of terms. In the wake of the disaster, the tragedy at Pakpattan was read in diverse ways by multiple audiences. Local politicians and police attributed the chaos, confusion, and deaths to the greed of the local shrine authorities and the lawlessness of an unruly, uneducated mob. The heirs of Pakpattan's holy man, by contrast, condemned these same administrators for overturning established crowd control policies and shirking responsibility. For the Chishti Sabiri Sufis who traveled to the rural tomb complex in Pakpattan that night and suffered grave losses, however, this was no mere accident. Living in a sacralized universe, these pious Sufi devotees found a deeper meaning and, ultimately, a transformative sense of redemption amid their grief. As heirs to the spiritual legacy of the shrine's holy man, they interpreted the loss of one of their most promising young disciples—and the injuries to their own living master and several prominent devotees—as a ritual sacrifice demanded by the saint. In this alternative Sufi narrative, pain and suffering are transformed into acts of atonement in which death is understood as a sign of Divine favor and surrender to the inscrutable will of God, a marker of spiritual strength.

The 2001 Pakpattan tragedy locates the Chishti Sabiri order within Pakistan's contested political landscape. A deeper and more nuanced appreciation of the *silsila's* makeup and modus operandi requires a shift in focus, however. Why? Because ultimately today's Chishti Sabiris do not look to politicians, civil society, or public institutions for answers to their religious questions. Instead, they seek knowledge, inspiration, and guidance from the internal resources of their own Sufi community and the collective wisdom of its spiritual heritage. Through their piety and practices, Chishti Sabiris seek to articulate and preserve an alternative religious identity that repositions Sufism as the essence of Islamic orthodoxy.

The remaining chapters of the book each focus on a particular dimension of contemporary Chishti Sabiri identity. Chapter 2 maps the construction of Sufi sacred history and modern sainthood through an exploration of Chishti Sabiri hagiographical texts. My analysis traces the lives of three twentieth-century spiritual masters whose legacies serve as the touchstone for twenty-first-century Chishti Sabiri identity: Shaykh Muhammad Zauqi Shah (1877–1951), Shaykh Shahidullah Faridi (1915–1978), and Shaykh Wahid Bakhsh Sial Rabbani (1910–1995).

CHAPTER 2

MUSLIM, MYSTIC, AND MODERN: THREE TWENTIETH-CENTURY SUFI MASTERS

In this book, the discourses (*malfuzat*) and selected incidents from the life of the Sun of Sainthood, Candle of Righteousness, Lamp of the Sufi Travelers, King of the Gnostics, our master and teacher, Hazrat Sayyid Muhammad Zauqi of the Chishti, Sabiri, Qadiri, Naqshbandi, and Suhrawardi orders have been collected for the guidance of the searchers for truth.

In the present time, new inventions and theories such as communism, socialism, capitalism, materialism, democracy and fascism have deeply afflicted the world. At every step, it has steadily become more complicated and contorted. Hazrat's blessed life offers a complete lesson on how to live for every rank of person, whether a seeker of the world or a Westernized person who has strayed far from the path of religion. This is because as a graduate of Aligarh College he was well acquainted with both traditional and modern learning. He was aware of the dangers of modern culture and well versed in national and international affairs. With his capacity as a Perfect Man (*insan-i kamil*), a Friend of God (*wali Allah*) and a Divine gnostic, he knew the true nature of reality—the secrets and signs of the universe.

Solutions to all problems, complications, and difficulties in human life are found in his collective discourses, especially those problems in which there is endless disagreement between the purveyors of the new sciences and the religious scholars (*'ulama*). With reference to religious principles, he perceptively and openly discussed the veiling of women, music, photography, cinema, religion and science, religion and communism, religion and democracy, materialism and capitalism. He has made luminous insights into the real Islamic system, the office of the ruler, the duties of the religious scholars, and the domestic and foreign policies of the state, all of which light the path for the government and common people alike.

In addition to this, the book contains a complete course in the eradication of base qualities; the cultivation of laudable attributes; developing spiritual power; obtaining the abilities of visions (*kashf*) and saintly miracles (*karamat*); and knowledge of the doctrines and paths through which a person, having annihilated himself in the Prophet (*fana' fi al-rasul*) and in God (*fana' fi Allah*), becomes absorbed in Divine attributes and achieves worthiness as His vicegerent (*khilafat*). Not only novices and commoners can receive guidance from this book. It contains rare, sublime, and novel insights relating to esoteric Divine knowledge (*ma'rifat-i ilahi*) for the adepts and spiritually elect as well.[1]

This glowing panegyric comes from the introduction to *Tarbiyat al-'ushshaq* ["The Training of the Lovers"]. First published in 1958, this voluminous Urdu text is a compilation of the spiritual discourses (*malfuzat*) of a major twentieth-century Chishti Sabiri master, Shaykh Muhammad Zauqi Shah. This hagiographic account begins by duly noting the *shaykh's* identity as a Chishti Sabiri master with additional initiations in multiple Sufi orders. Invoking this genealogy affirms Zauqi Shah's authority and authenticity within established lineages of piety, learning, and practice. But beyond his impeccable spiritual credentials, the cumulative record of the *shaykh's* teachings is said to illuminate multiple dimensions of human existence. His life provides guidance on all matters, we are told, from the sublime to the mundane. With knowledge of science and politics to match his spiritual acumen, the *shaykh* emerges as an inquisitive and eclectic scholar who immersed himself in the Sufi path. At the same time, he remained fully engaged with the modern world. In essence, this revealing passage eulogizes Zauqi Shah as a model of Islamic piety for an age corrupted by ideology, whether capitalist or communist. Muslim, mystic, and modern, the *shaykh* is championed as an exemplary model for religious scholars, politicians, Sufi adepts, and spiritual aspirants alike.

This paradigmatic portrait of a modern Sufi master provides a useful backdrop for an analysis of the construction of Islamic sainthood in contemporary Pakistan. For today's Chishti Sabiri disciples, three spiritual masters set the standard for Sufi piety and practice. They are Muhammad Zauqi Shah (1877–1951) and his two principal successors (*khalifas*): Shahidullah Faridi (1915–1978) and Wahid Bakhsh Sial Rabbani (1910–1995).[2] These twentieth-century Sufi leaders embodied the complexity and contradictions of their times, and their lives paralleled the birth and development of Pakistan itself. Zauqi Shah was an early graduate of Aligarh Muslim University. He went on to pursue a career in journalism and politics before emigrating to Pakistan and devoting himself exclusively to his spiritual duties as a Chishti Sabiri teaching *shaykh*. His designated successor Shahidullah Faridi was an Englishman from an exceedingly wealthy industrialist family in London. He converted to Islam along with his elder brother in 1937. Together they traveled widely throughout the Muslim world in search of spiritual knowledge. Moving to Pakistan with his spiritual mentor following Partition, Shahidullah spent the last thirty years of his life in Karachi immersed in Sufi practice, guiding his own devoted corps of disciples. Wahid Bakhsh Sial Rabbani served in the British Indian Army in Malaysia during the Second World War. He returned to Pakistan to work as a civil servant before committing himself to a life of scholarship and piety as a Chishti Sabiri teaching *shaykh*.

The lives and enduring legacy of this trio of twentieth-century Chishti Sabiri *shaykhs* offer a unique perspective on postcolonial subjectivity and its relation to religious identity and expression. This chapter draws on both hagiographical texts and ethnographic interviews to assess how these modern Sufi exemplars are now remembered and memorialized by contemporary disciples. My analysis is informed by three fundamental assertions:

1. *Sainthood blurs the boundaries between history and myth.* For devotees who live within a sacralized universe, sainthood signals a manifestation of the sacred, affirming the living connection between humanity and divinity. For a pious reader, the narrative structure of hagiography—or to borrow Thomas J. Heffernan's apt phrase, "sacred biography"—is simultaneously historical (a story of individual sanctity) and metahistorical (an affirmation of cosmic order).[3] Since the primary goal is to edify and inspire, a hagiographer is more interested in articulating a vision of sanctity than in documenting historical events. As a result, the scholarly interpretation of sacred biography demands a creative and empathetic approach that transcends the limits of positivist history or empirical biography.

2. *Sainthood is simultaneously paradigmatic and protean.* Hagiography is fundamentally a didactic genre. Prophets and holy men/women establish a blueprint for virtue against which all subsequent exemplars are measured. The inscription of a saintly life, therefore, establishes an enduring *model of* and *model for* moral and ethical behavior—a paradigm I refer to as the *hagiographical habitus.*[4] At the same time, no saintly paradigm can remain static, rigid, or unyielding. While certain hagiographical motifs persist across time, constructions of sainthood must also adapt to changing cultural settings and localized discourses.

3. *Sainthood is socially constructed.* The recollection and recording of a saintly life is more than the cumulative sum of names, dates, and events that mark a holy person's passage from cradle to grave. As a public marker of personal piety, sainthood is an ascribed status. It is negotiated in public discourse *before* it is inscribed in sacred biographies, assimilated within institutional structures, and narrated in story-telling networks. To a large extent, a spiritual leader's reputation depends on the response of her/his followers. If disciples fail to recognize and publicize their master's piety, the aspiring saint is doomed to historical anonymity. Although the negotiation of sainthood often begins during the holy person's lifetime, the most important phase in establishing a saint's reputation depends on the posthumous compilation of a sacred biography. A written record survives. It can be memorized, reproduced, and disseminated to new audiences—an ever-expanding readership that, in turn, brings its own distinct interpretations to the hagiographical

text. In the end, any claim to spiritual authority and authenticity is ultimately socially mediated in a dynamic process of negotiation, competition, and compromise. It is impossible to abstract a holy person's life and legacy from the concrete, lived in world of the everyday. Saints, after all, are human beings, albeit extraordinary ones. Though sainthood deals with transcendent matters, it remains firmly rooted in the mundane world of public discourse and social practice.

ISLAMIC SAINTHOOD: THE SUFI "FRIENDS OF GOD"

Islamic sainthood engages both the inner/private (*batini*) and outer/public (*zahiri*) dimensions of faith and practice. From its earliest stages, Sufism developed a distinct vocabulary to distinguish between these realms of experience. In most scholarship, the Arabic terms *walaya* and *wilaya* are each translated as "sainthood." Yet this semantic conflation veils a subtle but significant difference. In Arabic, *walaya* conveys a sense of "closeness." The saint, or *wali Allah*, is therefore a "friend of God" by virtue of this intimate association. Conversely, *wilaya*—alternatively translated as "manager," "guardian," "protector," or "intercessor"—carries a connotation of power, patronage, and authority.[5] In short, *wilaya* describes a function, and *walaya* a state of being. Early Sufi masters recognized this distinction, even if they sometimes disagreed on the terminology. According to Shaykh Nizam ad-Din Awliya' of Delhi (d. 1325), one of the spiritual luminaries of the Chishti order,

> The saint possesses both *walayat* and *wilayat* at the same time. *Walayat* is that which masters impart to disciples about God, just as they teach them about the etiquette of the Way. Everything such as this which takes place between the Shaykh and other people is called *walayat*. But that which takes place between the Shaykh and God is called *wilayat*. That is a special kind of love, and when the Shaykh leaves the world, he takes his *wilayat* with him. His *walayat*, on the other hand, he can confer on someone else, whomever he wishes, and if he does not confer it, then it is suitable for God Almighty to confer that *walayat* on someone. But the *wilayat* is the Shaykh's constant companion; he bears it with him (wherever he goes).[6]

Here Nizam ad-Din reverses the definitions, equating *wilaya* with closeness and love, and *walaya* with power and authority.

Western scholars of Sufism debate this taxonomy as well. Some such as Michel Chodkiewicz argue that *walaya* most accurately conveys what we in the West think of as sainthood.[7] Yet as Vincent Cornell demonstrates, "Only when *wali Allah* is used in the plural, as in the verse: 'Verily for the *awliya' Allah* there is no fear, nor shall they grieve' (Qur'an 10:62), does the idea of closeness to God come to the fore. Thus, according to Qur'anic usage, the term *wali Allah* has a social as well as a metaphysical signification: the Muslim saint protects or intercedes for others as Allah's deputy or vicegerent."[8] For premodern Sufi masters and contemporary academics alike, there is no consensus on the interpretation of *walaya* or *wilaya*. In the end, they are best understood as symbiotic concepts, "semantic fraternal twins that coexist interdependently, like yin and yang. Each relies on the other for its meaning."[9]

Leaving this etymological debate to the grammarians, one thing is amply clear: both in terms of language and social practice, Sufism emphasizes the dual nature of sainthood. The *wali Allah* combines piety and sanctity with power and authority. Though he lives, works, and worships in the world, the Sufi saint is unbound from the laws of nature by virtue of his intimacy with God. In Cornell's words, the *wali Allah* is "above all else an empowered person—empowered to perform miracles, empowered to communicate with God, empowered to help the weak and oppressed, empowered to act on behalf of others, empowered to mediate the course of destiny, and empowered to affect the behavior of other holders of power."[10] This power continues even after the saint's physical death. For the faithful who flock to Sufi shrines on pilgrimage, the *wali Allah* represents a tangible and renewable source of blessing.

Sacred biography plays an essential role in cementing a Sufi master's posthumous reputation as a "Friend of God." Sufi hagiographers employ a distinct stockpile of tropes and spiritual heroes. Drawing on eyewitness accounts, historical precedents, doctrinal evidence, and a rhetorical flair they construct a story of sanctity. As Bruce Lawrence argues, Sufi biographies "are not random life stories designed to impress or elicit awe. They are constructions of a tradition of piety, the evidence of believers transmitted by other believers for the purpose of gaining still further believers."[11] Sufi biographers are especially careful to integrate their subjects into a broader historical narrative that links each Sufi master with an established chain (*silsila*) of sacred authority that extends backward in time to the Prophet Muhammad himself. As the living embodiment of tradition, "each major saint becomes a crucial, indispensable link extending the spiritual charisma—and hence the institutional longevity—of his order (*tariqa*). Inevitably the shaykh as shaykh reshapes the way in which his followers think about all antecedent—and also all subsequent—saints."[12] A Sufi family tree is based not on blood but on an intimate—and intuitive—knowledge and experience of the Sufi path.

For all Muslims everywhere, the supreme prototype of human perfection is the Prophet Muhammad. He is revered as the final messenger of Divine revelation; his roles as legislator, political leader, husband and father, and spiritual guide mark the standard for a socially engaged spiritual life.[13] In both spiritual and worldly matters, the Prophet is the "beautiful model" (*uswa hasana*; Qur'an 33:21). His words, actions and exemplary conduct (*sunna*) are recorded in *hadith* (the reports or traditions about the Prophet, transmitted by his Companions), eulogized in poetry, folktales, legends and songs, and evoked in daily worship. For the global *umma*—diverse in culture and divided by language, custom, ethnicity, class, nationality, and geography—the Prophet serves as a potent and enduring symbol of unity.

Sufis view the Prophet Muhammad as the paradigmatic *shaykh*, the supreme spiritual master, and the first and essential link in any chain of spiritual authority. In an intriguing passage from his spiritual discourses, Shaykh Muhammad Zauqi Shah outlines the relationship between sainthood and prophecy:

> The rank of sainthood [*walayat*] is higher than prophecy [*nubuwwat*]. Sainthood is the name of a personal relationship with God, and prophecy is an office for the guidance of people. It is a mistake, however, to say that a saint [*wali*] is superior to a prophet [*nabi*]. Every prophet, in addition to holding the office of prophecy, is also a saint. For this reason, the prophet's rank is greater than that of the saint. It is like a king who has two friends. If one of them is appointed viceroy of an area then his status is higher than the one who is merely a friend. The viceroy is both a deputy and a friend.[14]

In the eyes of many Muslims, this is a controversial claim. Some would even find it blasphemous. Sufis, however, assert that the *wali Allah's* closeness to God is matched by an intimacy with the Prophet. The central importance of the Prophet in Sufi thought and practice is beyond question. To aid them in their spiritual quest, Sufi adepts draw particular inspiration from the story of the Prophet's Night Journey from Mecca to Jerusalem (*isra*) and his Ascension to heaven (*mi'raj*).[15] Dreams and visions of the Prophet serve as key markers of spiritual progress along the path. And most importantly, the Prophet's day-to-day activities define the benchmark of correct, moral behavior (*adab*), which every devotee seeks to emulate. For Sufis everywhere the Prophet is the indispensable tour guide on the spiritual journey to God. At the same time, however, models of Sufi sainthood are neither synchronically nor diachronically uniform. Emerging from local contexts, Sufi sacred biographies mirror the remarkable cultural variety of the global Muslim world.

THE CHISHTI SUFI MASTER: PAST AND PRESENT

> Having collected everything which I heard from that candle of the angelic assembly [the Chishti Shaykh Nizam ad-Din Awliya' of Delhi, d. 1233–1325], I have written down the distillation of his blessed discourse and what it means—at least to the extent that I understood it. Since the heart of the spiritually aroused will benefit from it, I have named this work *Morals for the Heart* (*Fawa'id al-Fu'ad*). God alone is our helper, on Him do we rely.[16]

With these words, Amir Hasan Sijzi—poet by day and spiritual seeker by night—established a new genre of Sufi sacred biography that profoundly reshaped the construction of Islamic sainthood in South Asia. In time, the Chishtiyya "produced a broader and more sustained literary tradition than any other Indian Sufi order."[17] And, in no small way, it was the singular impact of Hasan Sijzi's foundational *malfuzat* text that opened the floodgates. This unique work records the teachings of Shaykh Nizam ad-Din Awliya' on a wide range of topics over a fifteen-year period, from 1307 to

1322. With its eclectic and informal style, the text brought the saint's personality to vivid, three-dimensional life for an audience well beyond his inner circle of devotees. As historian K.A. Nizami notes, "With *Fawa'id al-Fu'ad*, Sufi literature entered a new phase and assumed a more lively, realistic, and concrete form related to actual circumstances. It made Sufi teachings accessible to a broad audience of Indian Muslims."[18] The continued popularity and influence of Sijzi's account through the centuries did much to secure Nizam ad-Din's enduring reputation as one of the spiritual giants of the Chishti order. On a broader level, it also enshrined a portrait of Islamic sainthood that remains the hagiographical habitus for the Chishti order up until the present day.

What exactly are the defining characteristics of the premodern Sufi saint that emerge from Indo-Muslim sacred biographies? In order to be acknowledged as a great *shaykh* during his lifetime and a *wali Allah* for posterity, a Chishti Sufi master had to possess several salient—and often paradoxical—qualities. In a survey of the scholarship of South Asian Sufism, Bruce Lawrence offers the following profile of the premodern Indo-Muslim Sufi *shaykh*:

1. Well born into an established Muslim family, the saint must yet be motivated to seek a Sufi master in order to improve the quality of his Islamic faith.
2. Well educated in Qur'an, *hadith*, theology, and also Sufi literature as well as Persian poetry, he must yet be able to intuit the deepest truths behind, and often beyond, the written word.
3. Initiated by a *shaykh* (usually after an epiphanic moment) and acknowledging his *shaykh* as the sole vehicle of Divine grace for him, he must yet strive to attain his own level of spiritual excellence, often through severe fasting and prolonged meditation.
4. Living in isolation from the company of others, he must yet constantly attend to the needs of his fellow Muslims, or at least to those needs evidenced by his disciples and visitors to his hospice [*khanaqah*]. (He is seldom expected to concern himself with non-Muslims).
5. Married and the father of sons, he must yet be celibate in temperament and disposition.
6. Capable of performing miracles [*karamat*, "saintly graces"], he must yet be careful to suppress them on most occasions.
7. Prone to ecstasy, whether in silent solitude or abetted by music and verse while in the company of other Sufis [*sama'*], he must yet be able to recall and to perform his obligatory duties as a Muslim.
8. Poor and unmindful of worldly possessions, he must yet be receptive to large donations of money and be able to dispense them quickly for the benefit of those in need.
9. Avoiding the company of worldly people, merchants, soldiers and government officials, including kings, he must yet live in proximity to them (i.e., near a city) and stay in touch with them through his lay disciples.[19]

In the following pages, I demonstrate how this typology of the premodern Indo-Muslim Sufi master continues to inform the contemporary construction of Chishti Sabiri sainthood. While tracing the continuity of tradition, I also mark how South Asian Sufism has accommodated to the momentous changes of the colonial and postcolonial eras. My survey is by no means an exhaustive, year-by-year recounting of the lives of Muhammad Zauqi Shah, Shahidullah Faridi, and Wahid Bakhsh Sial Rabbani.[20] Here I am less concerned with compiling historical "facts" than in measuring how the legacies of these modern Sufi exemplars are remembered and re-presented in hagiographical narratives. Communicated in texts and oral histories, the story of this trio of Chishti Sabiri masters is firmly grounded in the context of twentieth-century South Asian history. Yet what is immediately striking is how closely the sacred biographies of these modern masters adhere to the premodern model of Indo-Muslim sainthood. I argue that Sufi masters—both past and present—are revered as the physicians of human souls, the agents of the miraculous, and the heirs to Prophet Muhammad. As mortal men, however, they remain fully immersed in the social, cultural, and political life of their times. In the cultural contexts of South Asia, Sufi sainthood continues to engage both *din* (religion) and *dunya* (the world).

SHAYKH SAYYID MUHAMMAD ZAUQI SHAH (1877–1951)

The life of Shaykh Muhammad Zauqi Shah stretched from the twilight of British colonial rule to Pakistan's formative period in the wake of political independence. The *shaykh* passed away during the Hajj pilgrimage in September 1951 and lies buried in an unmarked grave on the plain of 'Arafat. Many of his disciples are also now deceased, and those still alive were quite young when he died. As a result, recollections of Zauqi Shah are based largely on a combination of inherited stories and, more importantly, references to the hagiographical accounts of his life and teachings. The contemporary *silsila's* collective memory, in other words, is maintained through an interdependent nexus of oral narratives and written texts.

The following survey is based primarily on the two principal sacred biographies that document Zauqi Shah's long life. Both were written in Urdu in the late 1950s and are now published in Pakistan by the contemporary Chishti Sabiri order. *Tarbiyat al-'ushshaq* ["The Training of the Lovers"], is the order's most important *malfuzat*. A weighty compilation of Zauqi Shah's spiritual teachings, it comprises four separate works:

1. *Muqaddama* ["Introduction"]: a lengthy and detailed introduction to Zauqi shah's legacy written by Wahid Bakhsh Rabbani.[21]
2. *Sirat-i Zauqi* ["The Path of Zauqi"]: a brief biography based largely on the *shaykh's* diaries composed by a disciple named Sayyid Sharif al-Hasan.[22]

3. *Malfuzat* ["Spiritual Discourses"]: compiled by Shahidullah Faridi and detailing a series of Zauqi Shah's lectures delivered to disciples between 1942 and 1950.[23]

4. *Malfuzat* ["Spiritual Discourses"]: compiled by Wahid Bakhsh Rabbani and covering the period from 1940 to 1951.[24]

A separate account, *Hajj-i Zauqi* ["Zauqi's Hajj Pilgrimage"] also written by Wahid Bakhsh, complements and completes this quartet with a detailed account of Zauqi Shah's final Hajj pilgrimage to Mecca in 1951.[25] Together, these sacred biographies constitute a distinctively twentieth-century portrait of Indo-Muslim sainthood while still preserving the essential markings of the premodern paradigm.

Zauqi Shah is an intriguing and complicated figure. In many ways, he stands at a historical crossroads. Though steeped in Sufi tradition and deeply indebted to his Chishti Sabiri predecessors, his personal experiences and worldview were profoundly colored by twentieth-century, postcolonial South Asian history. Zauqi Shah's spiritual teachings and political activism reflect an attempt to bridge these two worlds. He was acutely aware of the challenges posed by science, nationalism, secularization, and Western cultural and political hegemony. For him, the fundamental question was how to make Sufism relevant for a new age. Zauqi Shah's biographers detail the experiences of this complex spiritual master for a contemporary Pakistani (and international) audience. For the current generation of Chishti Sabiri disciples, distanced from Zauqi Shah's life but keenly aware of his enduring legacy, these hagiographical texts remain a vital source of information and guidance.

Family Background and Spiritual Initiation

Zauqi Shah was a descendent of a prominent *sayyid* family. *Sirat-i Zauqi* traces his family genealogy back thirty-six generations directly to the Prophet Muhammad. The family's patriarch, Sayyid Jalal Gul Surkh, emigrated to India from Bukhara, residing for some time in the hospice (*khanaqah*) of the well-known Suhrawardi saint of Uch Sharif, Baha ad-Din Zakaria. A close affiliation with the Suhrawardi order was a hallmark of the family through the generations. The most important link in this chain was Gul Surkh's grandson, the famous fourteenth-century Suhrawardi master of Multan, Sayyid Jalal ad-Din Bukhari Makhdum-i Jahaniyan. According to *Sirat-i Zauqi*, Jalal ad-Din "completed his training under Shaykh Rukn ad-Din Abul Fatah Suhrawardi and Nasir ad-Din Chirag-i Delhi. Thus both the Suhrawardi and Chishti systems were followed in the family."[26] In an intriguing lecture, Zauqi Shah reveals to his disciples that his family's lineage was confirmed for him in a vision of the Prophet himself.[27] Today's disciples highlight this genealogy as an auspicious marker of Zauqi Shah's own spiritual status and authority. Though he would eventually make a name for himself as a Chishti Sabiri master, Zauqi Shah's family tree further cements his posthumous status and reputation.

Zauqi Shah's father, Sayyid Abu Muhammad Jamal ad-Din (d. 1914), was born in 1850 in Farrukhabad. He is remembered as a strict follower of *shari'a* and a member of the revivalist movement, Ahl-i Hadith. He studied traditional medicine (*tibb*) and was appointed as a physician in the colonial administration, receiving a pension when he retired from service in 1898. He was transferred to various places, including the town of Khori (Sagar District) where Zauqi Shah—born Sayyid Muhammad Ibrahim—was born on September 15, 1877.[28]

While his hagiographers reveal very little about Zauqi Shah's early childhood, they do record a transformative experience from his youth. In April 1888 at the age of ten, he accompanied his family on his first Hajj. In the holy city of Mecca he had the opportunity to meet the famous Sufi master Hajji Imdad Allah al-Faruqi al-Muhajir Makki (1817–1899) who "placed his hand on his head and prayed for him."[29] The *shaykh's* biographers highlight this as highly significant and propitious encounter. Hajji Imdad Allah was a prominent nineteenth-century Chishti Sabiri master. A reformist, social critic, and political activist, the *shaykh* supported the 1857 uprising against the British and subsequently fled to Mecca. Living in exile, he became the spiritual mentor for a dynamic group of young Muslim scholars who went on to establish the Deoband *madrasa* after the British sacked Delhi in 1857. Hajji Imdad Allah is a prominent figure throughout Zauqi Shah's discourses. He is characterized as an advanced spiritual master and political leader known for his activist social ethics and close relationship with the Prophet. Zauqi Shah clearly maintained a deep affinity for Hajji Imdad Allah throughout his long life. His hagiographers stress that he remained in direct spiritual contact with the saint throughout his life via dreams and visions. In short, Zauqi Shah is positioned as the twentieth-century equivalent of his nineteenth-century predecessor. Yet despite these deep personal links, Zauqi Shah came to reject the scripturalist reformism of the later Deoband movement. In its critique of Sufi piety and practices, he argued, the Deobandis had betrayed Hajji Imdad Allah's true legacy.

In the hagiographical account of Zauqi Shah's life, this early meeting with Hajji Imdad Allah clearly signals an initiation on the Sufi path. It also foreshadows his future as a Chishti Sabiri spiritual master. Zauqi Shah's full immersion in Sufi practice, however, was delayed until much later in life after an active career in journalism, business, and politics. According to his biographers, his life took a dramatic turn in 1913 when he traveled to the shrine of Mu'in ad-Din Chishti in Ajmer in search of spiritual guidance. There he prayed for guidance and was rewarded with a vivid dream of a mysterious Sufi master. Inspired by this vision, Zauqi Shah resolved to leave his worldly life behind and traveled to various places in search of this unknown spiritual guide—a common trope in Sufi hagiographical literature. Eventually he made his way to Lucknow where he was introduced by his brother-in-law to the Chishti Sabiri *shaykh* Shah Sayyid Waris Hasan. Zauqi Shah immediately recognized him as the Sufi master from his dream.

He immediately took *bay'at* (the ceremony of formal initiation) in Lucknow on February 14, 1914 at the relatively advanced age of thirty-six.[30] It was Shaykh Waris Hasan who guided Zauqi Shah along the Sufi path. In true Chishti fashion, Zauqi Shah fastidiously recorded his master's discourses. This Urdu compilation is now published by the Chishti Sabiri *silsila* in Pakistan under the title *Shamamat al-'Ambar*. A partial English translation by Wahid Bakhsh Sial Rabbani entitled *A Guide for Spiritual Aspirants* has recently been published by Chishti Sabiri disciples in Kuala Lumpur, Malaysia as well.

Education

Zauqi Shah's early education was thoroughly traditional. As a young boy he attended a local school in Khori while studying the Qur'an and Arabic at home with his father. His education took a marked turn, however, during adolescence. From 1893 to 1896, Zauqi Shah enrolled at the bastion of nineteenth-century Indo-Muslim modernism: Muhammadan Anglo-Oriental College at Aligarh (subsequently renamed Aligarh Muslim University). Graduating from the famous academy founded by Sir Sayyid Ahmad Khan (1817–1898) likely made Zauqi Shah the first Chishti master to be educated in a modern university.[31] This distinction marks a major deviation from the premodern paradigm of Indo-Muslim sainthood. It signals a clear break from established tradition and a major accommodation to the changing landscape of twentieth-century South Asia.

Unlike many of his Sufi predecessors and contemporary *'ulama* counterparts, Zauqi Shah received no formal *madrasa* training in Qur'an interpretation (*tafsir*), *hadith*, theology (*kalam*), or the intricacies of legal interpretation (*usul ul-fiqh*). His formal education did provide him access to alternative networks of social patronage and new mediums of knowledge, however. Zauqi Shah's proficiency in English, for instance, facilitated a career as a journalist and political activist. As a Sufi master, it spurred his interest in and interaction with numerous foreign associates and disciples as well. Throughout his long life Zauqi Shah displayed an abiding interest in Western thought and, in particular, science. His discourses abound with references to the wonders—and limits—of scientific knowledge and technological discovery. In numerous passages, he praises Einstein's Theory of Relativity, which, he asserts, parallels but does not equal the essential teachings of Sufism regarding space and time.[32] To say the least, Zauqi Shah's intellectual interests were broad and deep.

A love for learning and an enduring obsession with writing are among the hallmarks of Zauqi Shah's legacy. He was a voracious reader of newspapers, books, and periodicals and clearly benefited from the rapid spread of print technology. Zauqi Shah is said to have been especially fond of poetry. In fact, he used many of his favorite Persian verses to adorn his own mystical Urdu novel *Bada u saghir* ["The Wine and the Cup"]. In the introduction to

Tarbiyat al-'ushshaq, Wahid Bakhsh Rabbani comments on his mentor's bib-
liophilism and active literary life:

> There were all kinds of books in his personal library, including various books
> concerned with scientific knowledge. All of them were well maintained. Each
> book was wrapped with a paper cover, on which the title had been written with
> great care. It was his habit that if a particular book did not have an index, he
> would prepare one himself . . . He preserved copies of all the letters he wrote to
> Qaid-i Azam [Muhammad Ali Jinnah], Pickthall [English convert and famous
> Qur'an translator], Habib Allah Lovegrove [an English convert], and other
> important personages. He always used to write in a diary in which he recorded
> the important events of the day . . . From all this it is apparent how regulated
> and disciplined Hazrat's daily life was. He used to say, "If a person's world is
> not in order, how can his religion be sound?"[33]

As a professional journalist, and later as a Chishti Sabiri teaching *shaykh*,
Zauqi Shah's own literary production was voluminous. Besides his spiritual
novel, he also wrote and published an encyclopedic lexicon of Sufi terminology entitled *Sirr-i dilbaran*, as well as numerous articles, essays, and pamphlets in both Urdu and English.[34] With his eclectic background, Zauqi Shah
was convinced that Sufism had to be personally experienced and publicly
articulated. The sheer scope and scale of his literary corpus is testament to the
range of his energy and interests. Zauqi Shah's love of books is evidenced in
his expansive personal library preserved in a house near the shrine of
Shahidullah Faridi in Karachi. The library contains a large collection of
Arabic, Urdu, and Persian texts on *tafsir* (Qur'an interpretation) and *fiqh*
(Islamic law), along with a broad selection of Sufi poetry and biographical
works. Catalogued and well maintained, the *shaykh's* personal collection is
accessible to Chishti Sabiri disciples.

Spiritual Training

Zauqi Shah's own spiritual training at the hands of his Sufi teacher, Shah
Sayyid Waris Hasan, was firmly in keeping with the long-standing practices of
the Chishti order. This included a strict adherence to the dictates of the
shari'a, supplemented by a demanding daily regimen of extra spiritual exercises (*mujahada*), including supererogatory prayers, meditative *zikr* (the
"remembrance" of God), contemplation (*muraqaba*), and fasting. *Tarbiyat
al-'ushshaq* records a revealing memory of his early spiritual training:

> Sometimes my Maulana Sahab [Shaykh Waris Hasan], may God have mercy on
> him, prescribed a spiritual exercise [*mujahada*] that initially seemed very diffi-
> cult. But actually it was quite simple. For example, once during Ramadan I was
> extremely thirsty in the evening . . . That day I had undertaken a special exer-
> cise that had caused my body to heat up. Maulana Sahab then told me, "Zauqi,
> keep the fast today." I was suffering greatly, but it is imperative to carry out the
> *shaykh's* wishes. I firmly resolved that I would force myself not to break my fast.

When it was time to break the fast, Maulana Sahab said, "Come, Zauqi. Take some breakfast." In this way I received mental exercises which appeared very difficult. Yet I only had to battle with my lower self [*nafs*] for a short while and in the end I enjoyed a great reward.[35]

Even after completing his formal Sufi training under the tutelage of Shah Sayyid Waris Hasan, Zauqi Shah is said to have maintained a regimented spiritual discipline. He constantly pushed his physical and mental boundaries in the pursuit of further spiritual growth. His biographers recollect Zauqi Shah praying alone under the blazing heat of the summer sun or, amusingly, with a radio on full volume as a test of his powers of concentration. This emphasis on the *shaykh's* asceticism and unrelenting self-discipline is echoed in the account of his final days during Hajj in 1951. While others retired to their beds, exhausted by the heat and the day's trials, Zauqi Shah continued his spiritual rigors: "Hazrat's [Zauqi Shah's]—may God have mercy upon him— courage and persistence was miraculous. He had endured rigorous spiritual exercises without interruption from the time of afternoon prayer ['*asr*], and even after we went to sleep, he remained sitting in the chair. The next morning when we awoke for the morning prayers, Hazrat, may God have mercy upon him, was still seated in the chair, deep in meditation [*muraqaba*]."[36]

Zauqi Shah's training in the Sufi path tested the limits of his mental and physical endurance. His sacred biographies emphasize that the *shaykh's* spiritual knowledge and insight were acquired through immense sacrifice and unwavering discipline. According to *Sirat-i Zauqi,* "Hazrat Shah Sahab, may God have mercy on him, was a dervish in the truest sense. He had neither inherited it as a *sajjada nishin,* nor was it founded on an empty display of spirituality. He personally endured all the hardships that are part of being a dervish. In the beginning he did exceedingly difficult spiritual exercises. For almost five full years, he lived in jungles, enduring hunger and thirst while engaging in constant worship."[37] The denigration of hereditary Sufi leaders (*sajjada nishin*) in this passage is particularly telling. It suggests that they may not have any particular spiritual accomplishments to match their auspicious family lineage. By contrast, the hagiographer asserts that Zauqi Shah earned his lofty spiritual status through personal effort and raw determination. Each of the *shaykh's* discourses, in fact, recount a range of experiences meant to demonstrate his advanced level of intuitive, experiential, esoteric knowledge (*ma'rifa*).

Of particular interest are the accounts of Zauqi Shah's frequent visionary experiences and Uwaysi-style mystical connections. For example, his discourses record an early encounter with the immortal prophet Khizr along with frequent visions of the Prophet Muhammad.[38] There are also numerous descriptions of spiritual encounters with a host of premodern Chishti luminaries. For example, Zauqi Shah narrates a lengthy and detailed dream in which he meets Khwaja Mu'in ad-Din Chishti who appears as a handsome and richly dressed youth of seventeen. Together they travel instantaneously from Ajmer to Multan where the Khwaja helps a sick friend of Zauqi Shah's who lacks the money to return to Delhi. According to Zauqi Shah, his friend subsequently verified that he had been miraculously cured and woke to find a stash of money under his pillow.[39] A parallel narrative records that Zauqi Shah also received news of his status as the successor (*khalifa*) to Waris Hasan Shah directly from Khwaja Mu'in ad-Din Chishti in a dream during pilgrimage to the saint's shrine in Ajmer in 1914.[40] In yet another anecdote Zauqi Shah accompanies his own *shaykh* on a visit to the *mazar* of Nizam ad-Din Awliya' in Delhi. There they encounter a Punjabi mendicant (*majhzub*) who asks Zauqi Shah for money. Later, Waris Hasan Shah tells him that the *majhzub* was none other than Nizam ad-Din himself in disguise.[41] And on a subsequent pilgrimage to the shrine at Kalyar Sharif, Zauqi Shah experiences a vision of 'Ala ad-Din 'Ali Ahmad Sabir—the eponymous founder of the Chishti Sabiri order—who gives him a lengthy discourse on the spiritual qualities and benefits of listening to music (*sama'*).[42] The sheer abundance of these encounters is clearly meant to signal Zauqi Shah's acceptance into the Chishti pantheon.

Hagiographic accounts of other transformative dreams highlight Zauqi Shah's connection to prominent nineteenth-century Chishti Sabiri masters as well. In a remarkable passage, the *shaykh* narrates a vivid dream he experienced on October 24, 1927 during a prolonged period of fasting. In the dream, he meets Hajji Imdad Allah—the famous Chishti Sabiri master and Deoband leader—who teaches him a mystical breathing exercise that allows him to merge into the Divine essence (*dhat*). Afterward, the two of them visit the shrine of the Prophet Yusuf (Joseph) where they are joined by Zauqi's Shah's master. According to the text, when Waris Hasan Shah visited Bombay several days later and was told about this vision, he immediately announced that it was an indication that Zauqi Shah had been granted *wilayat-i Yusufi* (the station of the "authority of the Prophet Joseph").[43] During an extended retreat at Ajmer Sharif where he was immersed in spiritual exercises (*mujahadat*), Zauqi Shah had another vivid, life-altering dream. In this vision, Rashid Ahmad Gangohi—the other major Deoband founder and nineteenth-century Chishti Sabiri *shaykh*—appears as a young man dressed in royal garb. The saint questions Zauqi Shah, and then announces that he is ready to teach disciples of his own. When Zauqi Shah recounts this dream to his own *shaykh*, he is immediately granted permission to initiate his own disciples in the name of Waris Hasan Shah (*wilayat-i niyabati*).[44] For an audience steeped in Sufi sacred biographies, these dreams serve as vital markers—direct and unambiguous signs of spiritual power and accomplishment. Zauqi Shah emerges from these accounts as a pious, disciplined, and highly accomplished Sufi spiritual master: the twentieth-century reflection of his nineteenth-century Chishti Sabiri predecessors.

Qualities as a Teaching *Shaykh*

Throughout his adult life, Zauqi Shah led a peripatetic life, traveling frequently between Agra, Jaipur, Bombay, Peshawar, Hyderabad, Ajmer, and, finally, Karachi. Somewhat paradoxically, he was also known to retreat from social life for prolonged periods of isolation, especially in the early years of his spiritual training. His *malfuzat* recounts two forty-day spiritual retreats (*chilla*) in particular, one in Delhi at the *mazar* of Nizam ad-Din Awliya' and another in Kalyar Sharif.[45] The vast majority of the *shaykh's* time and energy, however, was spent attending to the needs of his disciples. Time and again his biographers emphasize that Zauqi Shah was, first and foremost, a spiritual mentor. He is characterized as the embodiment of *shari'a* and the paragon of decorum (*adab*). Unlike his Chishti ancestors, Zauqi Shah never lived in a traditional *khanaqah*—the premodern Sufi hospice where disciples and visitors either lived or visited for spiritual guidance. Instead, he met privately with disciples in his modest home in Karachi or traveled to meet them in person. Under his leadership the *silsila's* collective gatherings were limited to weekly *zikr* sessions (also in the Zauqi Shah's home), along with the annual pilgrimages to local shrines for the death anniversaries (*'urs*) of prominent Sufi saints.

Zauqi Shah's attitude toward outsiders represents another important break from the traditional paradigm of Chishti leadership. In his sacred biographies, the *shaykh* appears remarkably open and accessible to *murids* and non-*murids*, Muslims and non-Muslims alike. According to *Sirat-i Zauqi*:

> Hazrat Shah Sahab's—may God have mercy upon him—circle of followers included people from every religion and social class. There were no restrictions against Muslims, Hindus, Parsis, or Christians. His discussions always struck the heart, and whoever heard him became persuaded. He never insisted that Muslims had to be strict in following *shari'a* in the beginning, nor did he demand that non-Muslims convert. He often said that his only function was to encourage people to remember God. He used to say, "Our work is to bring people to the remembrance of God. This remembrance will itself bring them to the straight path."[46]

This account portrays Zauqi Shah as a wise and generous teacher who convinces others through the force of his personality and the power of personal example. The frequency of such cross-creedal encounters in his hagiographies is best understood against the backdrop of the late colonial period. Faced with the confrontational politics of religious communalism, Zauqi Shah became a public apologist for Sufism.[47] Within the charged polemical atmosphere surrounding Partition, he actively defended Sufi piety and practice from its detractors, both Muslim and non-Muslim alike.

While he recognized the integrity of other monotheistic religions, Zauqi Shah aggressively championed the superiority of Islam as the final revelation and Sufism as the most highly developed spiritual path. This is illustrated in a number of edifying interactions with both Christians and Hindus. In certain lectures the *shaykh* describes non-Muslim spiritual luminaries—Krishna, Rama, Sita, Lachman, and Guru Nanak—as believers in the one true God and religious leaders with "Divine connection" (*nisbat*).[48] In practice, however, he openly encouraged the conversion of non-Muslims to Islam and frequently accepted foreigners as disciples. Among them were Dr. Abdul Aziz—a Hindu convert—as well as Habib Allah Lovegrove and Fazl al-Haq Berkley, both Christian converts from England.[49] Zauqi Shah communicated with foreigners outside the boundaries of the *silsila* as well. A particularly fascinating exchange is found in a lively correspondence with Mohammed Marmaduke Pickthall (1875–1936), the famous British convert and Qur'an translator. In a series of letters written in 1932, Zauqi Shah critiques Pickthall's ecumenicism, insisting that salvation demands belief in Islam and the Prophet Muhammad as the final messenger.[50] On the whole, Zauqi Shah emerges from these hagiographical accounts as a learned, tolerant, and tireless teacher. At the same time, he is portrayed as a firm advocate of Islamic orthodoxy and a staunch defender of Sufi doctrine and ritual practices.

Married Life

Although select Chishti luminaries such as Nizam ad-Din Awliya' and 'Ali Ahmad Sabir remained bachelors for life, Zauqi Shah followed the precedent of the Prophet Muhammad in the conduct of his own personal life. The *shaykh* first married in April 1896 at the age of nineteen and soon after became a father with the birth of his first daughter. Following the sudden death of his wife in 1911, Zauqi Shah was extremely reluctant to remarry, preferring instead to remain single and celibate to focus on his spiritual life. His *shaykh*, Waris Hasan, firmly rejected this idea, however, exclaiming, "We are following the way of Muhammad, and not of Isa (Jesus)."[51]

In deference to his master's wishes, Zauqi Shah married the widowed daughter of a local landowner (*jagirdar*) of Fatehgar in September 1918. Together they too had a daughter named Rashida Khatun. In a lecture to his own disciples many years later, Zauqi Shah echoed the words of his *shaykh*, drawing a line between the Christian and Muslim spiritual life to stress the importance of the institution of marriage. In his words,

> The path of Muhammad [*suluk-i Muhammad*], God bless him and grant him salvation, demands spiritual striving [*mujahada*] from everyone, and this is exceedingly difficult work. The path of Jesus [*suluk-i Isa*] is easy. Hazrat Isa, peace be upon him, had neither a house nor a wife and children. He would sit and lie down under any tree he came across. He owned nothing. He used to drink water from the palm of his hand. In his ragged garments [*khirqa*] he carried only a needle and some thread, and on reaching the Fourth Heaven he said that even those worldly things were useless. But our Holy Messenger, God bless him and grant him salvation, went up to the throne of God with his shoes on.[52]

Zauqi Shah's youngest daughter was eventually married to his principal *khalifa*, the Englishman Shahidullah Faridi. On that occasion, he again commented on the paradoxical nature of marriage, telling his disciples, "People call marriage happiness [*shadi*], but in my opinion it is really a misfortune [*musibat*]. With marriage, one's freedom comes to an end. This isn't happiness, it's an occasion for mourning."[53] Though hardly an encouraging endorsement for his son-in-law's marital future, Zauqi Shah clearly viewed marriage as a religious duty—a fitting test of character and faith for a Sufi spiritual seeker obliged to live in the world.

Miracles

Sufis distinguish between the confirmatory miracles of the Prophet Muhammad (*mu'jizat*), and the occasional, nonconfirmatory feats performed by saints (*karamat*).[54] In *Fawa'id al-Fu'ad*, Shaykh Nizam ad-Din Awliya' cautions against any public display of control over the forces of nature. In his view, miracles are merely a distraction on the spiritual path: "God Almighty has commanded His Saints to conceal their miracles (*karamat*), just as He has commanded His prophets to demonstrate theirs (*mu'jizat*). Since anyone who performs a miracle is disobeying God, what sort of work is this? There are one hundred stages on the spiritual path. The seventeenth stage provides divine inspiration to perform miraculous acts. Now, if the traveler stops at this stage, how will he reach the other eighty-three?"[55] Echoing his premodern Chishti ancestor, Zauqi Shah dismissed miracles as child's play. "The real purpose is to keep busy in God's work," the *shaykh* reminds his disciples in one recorded lecture. "Unveilings [*kashf*] and saintly miracles [*karamat*] are insignificant matters."[56] While acknowledging the reality of the miraculous, Zauqi Shah's biographers stress that the *shaykh* was extremely reluctant to demonstrate his own powers. This is evident, for instance, in an anecdote from his final Hajj journey. Amid the chaos and confusion of the pilgrimage, Zauqi Shah's followers come to him to express their concern over the delayed arrival of several prominent *murids*. In response, Zauqi Shah encourages patience, saying, "If I so desired, I could find out through inspiration, but it is against the etiquette [*adab*] of this place to display inspiration and saintly miracles. Whatever I learn from 'official channels' [in English], through outward means, will be sufficient."[57]

Despite this reticence, Zauqi Shah's sacred biographies do document numerous occasions when the *shaykh's* spiritual powers were unveiled. *Sirat-i Zauqi*, for example, records a brief but revealing encounter between Zauqi Shah and the Chief Minister of Hyderabad Maharaja Krishna Prashad. Meeting for the first time, the *shaykh* immediately asks the politician why he has abandoned a particular meditation exercise. Duly impressed, the prime minister promises to return to the practice.[58] Another intriguing story describes an occasion when Zauqi Shah traveled to the *ashram* of Mahatma Gandhi. Finding the Hindu leader absent, the *shaykh* takes the opportunity to assist a young Hindu woman who complains of difficulty concentrating during meditation. When Zauqi Shah's advice to her pays immediate dividends, the young woman tells him, "[Y]ou are a very spiritual man and I will certainly tell Mr. Gandhi about you."[59] For a Sufi audience, this anecdote obviously serves a dual purpose. It highlights Zauqi Shah's powers of observation and concentration while simultaneously implying that his spiritual powers eclipse those of his famous Hindu counterpart.

Other hagiographical stories document miracles of healing. In one incident, a young boy with a severe mental illness is brought before Zauqi Shah. Although all previous efforts to find a medical explanation have been fruitless, the *shaykh* immediately perceives the cause of his ailment and sets about curing him:

> As soon as he saw the boy he perceived that he had been so overwhelmed by excessive illuminations from continuous acts of worship that his heart was not able to withstand it. As a result, his mind had gone bad. He told the boy to return the next day before breakfast. That night, Hazrat Shah Sahab, may God have mercy upon him, ate a heavy meal and, after the morning prayers, gathered within his heart all kinds of base thoughts. When the boy arrived, he transferred the effects of the food and the filth of those base thoughts into the boy's heart through concentration. From that day onward the boy's mind and senses began to improve, and within a few days the condition of his mind was completely sound. Hazrat Shah Sahab mentioned this cure to his own *shaykh* who was quite pleased and said, "You have done the right thing. A dervish ought to exercise this kind of independent reasoning [*ijtihad*]!"[60]

In a personal interview, one of Zauqi Shah's oldest and most revered disciples related a similar incident. As a child, this man suffered from tuberculosis of the spine. When the treatments prescribed by his medical doctors failed, he was taken to Zauqi Shah who cured his condition by breathing into his open mouth (May 21, 2001, Karachi).

Hajj-i Zauqi records Zauqi Shah's final and most dramatic miraculous display, however. According to Wahid Bakhsh's emotional narrative, when Zauqi Shah unexpectedly expired during the waning days of the pilgrimage, he left his *murids* with a powerful sign: "The strangest thing of all was that his heart continued beating. In order to confirm this we called a Pakistani doctor. He too opened Hazrat's blessed eyes and examined them, felt his pulse and then exclaimed, 'There is no doubt that he has passed away [*wisal*], but amazingly his heart continues to beat as before!'"[61] For a Sufi audience, all of these extraordinary displays of knowledge, insight, and control over the forces of nature signify Zauqi Shah's lofty spiritual status as a *wali Allah*. On a more mundane level, the *shaykh's* basic empathy for the suffering of others—and his consummate skills as a spiritual physician—suggests that a Sufi saint's powers trump the wisdom and technological wonders of Western science and medicine. Taken together, such miraculous anecdotes mark Sufism as an alternative episteme—a parallel system of inner, esoteric knowledge with real power and efficacy in the mundane world.

Ecstasy and Sobriety

Throughout his sacred biographies, Zauqi Shah displays a highly developed aesthetic and spiritual sensibility. In one particular lesson, he compares life to a dance, and God to an enraptured dancer: "The entire universe is a dance. Dance is the beauty of movement, just as music is the beauty of sound and poetry the beauty of words. We think that we are the ones doing this and that. But everything is Him. What else is there? There is only Him. He appears in various forms. He moves around, dances, sees, and is in ecstasy."[62] In true Chishti fashion, Zauqi Shah was particularly fond of *qawwali* (poetry put to music) and Sufi musical assemblies (*sama'*). He was unwavering in his defense of the tradition and had little regard for anyone who questioned its Islamic credentials. When asked by a disciple to explain the controversy surrounding *sama'*, he replied, "[T]hose preachers [*maulvis*] whose hearts are not moved by music are worse than snakes!"[63]

Zauqi Shah viewed *sama'* as a powerful tool and a vital catalyst for spiritual development. In fact, his name—*zauqi*, meaning "tasting"—was given to him by Shah Sayyid Waris Hasan to reflect his thirst for the direct, unmediated experience of spiritual ecstasy.[64] Yet the *shaykh's* enthusiasm for music was tempered by a firm insistence on ritual decorum. According to *Sirat-i Zauqi*,

> Hazrat Shah Sahab, may God have mercy upon him, had a great fondness for *sama'*. He did not listen to it often, but on the occasion of the death anniversaries ['*urs*] of Sufi saints he always listened to it. He was never seen in ecstasy. He always continued to sit with complete composure until the end. He never used to wave his hands, nor did he cry out. Instead, he always remained seated in silence. While younger persons became tired and began to move about, he continued to sit in one place like a block of stone, his posture never changing. He had a very refined taste for both music and poetry, and for this reason his gatherings were of high standard. There were no outcries of ecstasy, and no unrefined poems [*ghazals*].[65]

Given this emphasis on sobriety and self-control, Zauqi Shah found the carnival-like atmosphere of many public *qawwali* sessions especially distasteful. As with miracles, he viewed any public displays of ecstasy as a sign of spiritual immaturity. *Malfuzat-i Zauqi* contains a revealing discourse in this regard:

> Hazrat, may God have mercy upon him, was reading a book when he remarked: "In *qawwali*, ecstatic trance [*wajd*] is a great feat for a beginner, but a weakness for one who is spiritually advanced. In the beginning, when the soul [*ruh*] is delighted by something new it goes into ecstasy. Later on, once that state has been experienced several times, the pleasure continues but ecstasy does not come. Similarly, when a person eats a delicious mango or sweet for the first time he shakes with rapture. But once he's eaten it several times, he still feels the pleasure but not with such ecstasy."[66]

For Zauqi Shah, *sama'* was appropriate only for the elite practitioners on the Sufi path.

Zauqi Shah's unwavering faith in the efficacy and legality of Sufi music are most clearly revealed in a remarkable incident recorded in *Hajj-i Zauqi*. During his final Hajj pilgrimage in 1951, the *shaykh* managed to arrange for a *qawwali* performance in a private home within the sacred precincts of

Mecca—a practice prohibited by anti-Sufi, Wahhabi doctrine. According to the text,

> In Saudi Arabia, *qawwali* is prohibited, but Allah Almighty arranged for *qawwali* inside the noble sanctuary [*haram sharif*] in Mecca. A *qawwali* master Rahmat Allah Shah Sahab was living there at that time. He was invited one evening and the *qawwali* was held in a house inside the noble sanctuary. It was an incredibly intoxicating *sama'*. Shah Sahab presented the finest poetic verses and created a wonderful mood. When he sang in praise of Khwaja Gharib Nawaz [Mu'in ad-Din Chishti (d. 1236)], may God have mercy upon him, it seemed as though the saint was actually present. Afterwards when I asked Hazrat—may God have mercy upon him—about this, he replied, "I offered *Fatiha* for him [i.e., reciting the opening chapter of the Qur'an], so from the very beginning he was attentive to us."[67]

This extraordinary story serves several hagiographical purposes. By emphasizing Zauqi Shah's role as a patron and apologist for *sama'*, the *shaykh's* biographers mark him as a quintessential Chishti master. Zauqi Shah's link to the Chishti legacy is made explicit through his direct connection with the paradigmatic Chishti saint: Mu'in ad-Din Chishti of Ajmer. By offering prayers in honor of his spiritual predecessor, Zauqi Shah marks the piety and power of his South Asian Sufi lineage in the precincts of Islam's most holy site—a gesture, we are told, that is reciprocated by the saint's blessing of this unique spiritual gathering.

Lifestyle

Zauqi Shah's biographers continuously emphasize his disregard for material possessions and worldly power. Numerous accounts highlight his willful acceptance of a life of poverty, simplicity, and asceticism. According to *Sirat-i Zauqi*, for example, "Even in the face of poverty he was satisfied and patient. In his early days as a dervish there were many times when he went without food, but the countenance of his face never showed his condition, even as he met with his friends and followers until late at night. He followed the path of Hajji Imdad Allah Muhajir Makki Sahab, may God have mercy upon him, insisting that *dervishes* should avoid directly asking for assistance."[68]

Zauqi Shah viewed physical suffering and deprivation as useful spiritual tools. A life of poverty, he believed, taught the Sufi to surrender to the Divine will (*tawwakul*) and helped to tame the lower self (*nafs*). "Allah brings misfortune to his servants in order to weaken the strength of their lower selves and draw them nearer to Him," he explains to his disciples. "In a life of pleasure and ease, egotism gains the upper hand, and a person is distanced from God."[69] Zauqi Shah's biographers also note, however, that the *shaykh* recognized the importance of accepting donations and handling money in the interest of social welfare. His hagiographies each portray the *shaykh* as willfully engaged in worldly matters but only to the extent that such activities would forward spiritual development or provided succor for others. In one particular lecture the *shaykh* remarks, "The status of those saints [*awliya' Allah*] who have worldly possessions and wealth is very high. Their powers are so strong that they can perform both their spiritual and worldly duties."[70]

Public and Political Life

Throughout his life, Zauqi Shah remained engaged with the world and active on the public stage. As a vocal advocate for an independent Muslim nation in South Asia, he participated directly in politics as a writer, an active member of the Muslim League, and a personal confidant of Muhammad Ali Jinnah. The level and duration of the *shaykh's* political commitments are indeed remarkable. They also deviate sharply from the traditional, premodern pattern of Chishti leadership that favored withdrawal from public, political life.

Zauqi Shah's biographers chart his political activities. At the same time, there is a marked attempt to downplay their importance for his legacy as a Chishti Sabiri spiritual master. *Sirat-i Zauqi*, for example, contains a revealing discourse in which the *shaykh* orders his *murids* to avoid all contact with government officials and wealthy people. According to the text, Zauqi Shah never initiated such contact himself: "Hazrat Shah Sahab, may God have mercy upon him, never flattered wealthy people or government officials, nor did he follow their orders. Some such people certainly did go to him, but they were his followers or friends from earlier days. If someone came to him and requested a favor from such people he used to say, 'My work is to break connections with these people and bind myself to God, but you drag me towards worldly people!'"[71] In another passage, Zauqi Shah stresses the importance of inner, spiritual development as a precursor to outer, societal reform. "The progress of the nation depends on its moral improvement [*akhlaqi islah*]," he tells his followers. "Instead of preaching to the whole nation, I have begun to reform just one person, and that person is myself. If each one of us were to act similarly, the whole nation would improve."[72] Clearly, Zauqi Shah found no contradiction in balancing his duties as a spiritual teacher with his strong political commitments. As we will see in chapter 3, among today's Chishti Sabiri disciples the *shaykh* is remembered as both an enlightened Sufi master and an ardent nationalist—the de facto spiritual founder of Pakistan.

SHAYKH SHAHIDULLAH FARIDI (1915–1978)

The life and legacy of Shaykh Shahidullah Faridi represent an anomaly in the history of the Chishti Sabiri order. The details of his personal history and spiritual quest diverge sharply from the traditional mold of Indo-Muslim sainthood. An Englishman born into a family of immense wealth and privilege, he converted to Islam as a young man. In the twilight of the British colonial era, he left his family and his inheritance behind to travel throughout much of the Muslim world in search of spiritual guidance. Shahidullah's journey eventually took him to South Asia—not, as for so many of his British contemporaries, in pursuit of a career as a colonial administrator but instead for a life of sacrifice, poverty, and piety as a Sufi adept. The shrine of Shaykh Shahidullah Faridi in Karachi, Pakistan, is shown in figure 2.1.

From his childhood in London to his final decades in Karachi as a Chishti Sabiri teaching *shaykh*, the trajectory of Shahidullah Faridi's life inverts the dynamics of the colonial encounter. For contemporary Chishti Sabiri disciples he remains a shining example of the universal truth of Sufism's power to transcend the mundane boundaries of class, ethnicity, and race. The words of a senior male *murid* encapsulate the pervasive sense of awe and respect that disciples invariably express when considering Shahidullah's legacy:

> Hazrat Shahidullah Faridi, may God have mercy on him, was one of the great friends of Allah, and thousands of people received spiritual knowledge [*ma'rifa*] and nearness to Allah from him. Even now he is training people! His life and his teachings are a great lesson for all the nations. The Creator of the Universe is kind to human beings without regard to race, religion, or any other distinction. He is kind to all, and all can achieve His nearness. If Hazrat Shahidullah Sahab has been given such a great status, everyone who comes in this path can receive it! (May 2, 2001, Bahawalpur)

Today Shahidullah Faridi's life is memorialized through both texts and oral narratives. The *shaykh's* own corpus of writings in Urdu and English are printed and distributed by the contemporary order. In addition, a record of his spiritual discourses—compiled by his designated successor, Shaykh Sira 'Ali Muhammad—was published by the *silsila* in 1996. This book titled *Malfuzat-i shaykh* comprises nineteen eclectic lectures dating from September 1970 to August 1977. It offers an intimate portrait of Shahidullah's personality, worldview, and teaching style.[73] Beyond this text, the *shaykh's* disciples continue the dynamic process of emplotting his sacred biography through a story-telling network. More than a quarter of a century after Shahidullah's death, this repository of personal memories remains the primary source of collective knowledge about his life and legacy.

Family Background and Spiritual Initiation

Shahidullah Faridi was born John Gilbert Lennard in London in 1915. His father, John William Lennard, came from a family of German descent and rose to wealth and social prominence during the nineteenth century as one of the largest paper manufacturers in all of Great Britain. Shahidullah was raised with three siblings: an elder sister and two brothers. The eldest son, christened John William after his father, was born in 1913 and also converted to Islam. Beyond these skeletal details, virtually nothing is recorded about Shahidullah's upbringing in the *silsila's* records. Contemporary disciples, however, do narrate a few select anecdotes from his childhood, events that are seen to prefigure his future conversion. For example, as boys both he and his brothers reportedly rebelled against attending Christian church services, and both had a lifelong aversion to eating pork. Such stories are clearly meant

Figure 2.1 The Shrine of Shaykh Shahidullah Faridi (d. 1978), Karachi, Pakistan

Source: Photograph by Robert Rozehnal

to bend the contours of biography to fit the hagiographic mold. Shahidullah encouraged this pervasive biographical erasure with his own silence regarding his personal background. As a senior male disciple told me, "Hazrat Sahab never liked to talk about his past, about his parents, about his family. I even went to England in 1958 when his father was still living in London. But Hazrat Sahab never gave me the address, he never encouraged me to go to him, and I didn't have the courage to ask about it" (September 2, 2002, Karachi). After leaving England in his early twenties, Shahidullah returned only once—to visit his dying mother who, according to the hagiographical record, converted to Islam on her deathbed.

Following Partition in 1947, Shahidullah surrendered his British passport and accepted Pakistani citizenship. While the *shaykh's* physical appearance always marked him as a foreigner in his adopted homeland, in speech, dress, and demeanor he conformed to local customs. As the following anecdote narrated by another senior male *murid* illustrates, Shahidullah clearly viewed his own past as irrelevant to his central identity as a Chishti Sabiri Sufi master within the tradition of the Prophet Muhammad:

> Once Captain Wahid Bakhsh Sahab and Hazrat Shahidullah Sahab went to visit the shrine of the saint Miyan Mir in Lahore. A Sufi mendicant [*majhzub*] stood in their way. The man was very dirty and unkempt, but Hazrat Sahab was very kind to him. Then the *majhzub* asked, "Where is your hometown?" Hazrat replied, "My hometown is London." Then he laughed and said, "No, no. Your hometown is Medina!" He repeated this many times. Hazrat Sahab enjoyed this immensely.
>
> Whenever someone would ask him about his past life in England or about his family or his brother, questions concerned with his previous life before coming to India, he became very angry. He would say, "I have come out of that gutter, why do you want to put me in that gutter again? Please don't ask such questions!" (May 2, 2001, Bahawalpur)

For the chroniclers of Shahidullah's life, his sacred biography effectively begins with a search for spiritual truth. Quitting his studies at Oxford University, he was overcome by an insatiable curiosity, wanderlust, and spiritual restlessness. Shahidullah's interest in Sufism was reportedly sparked by his discovery of Reynold A. Nicholson's (1868–1945) translation of *Kashf al-mahjub* [The Unveiling of the Secrets], the famous Persian treatise on Sufism written by the eleventh-century master 'Ali Hujwiri (d. 1072).[74] In 1936, both he and his elder brother, John William, converted to Islam in an East End mosque at the hands of a Bengali *imam* who gave them their Muslim names: Shahidullah ("Martyr of God") and Faruq Ahmad. Determined to find a Sufi master to guide them, the brothers then left England. They traveled throughout Europe and then onward to Morocco, Egypt, and Syria.

In 1937 their quest brought them to India. They initially stayed in Dera Nawab—a town in the southern Punjab, south of Multan—as the guests of the local Nawab of Bahawalpur. The Nawab had previously met the brothers in England shortly after their conversion to Islam while vacationing as the guest of their father, John William Lennard. Impressed with the young men, the Nawab had encouraged them to come to India in their search for a spiritual guide. His patronage proved invaluable to the young Englishmen.[75] Soon after their arrival the brothers were introduced to Maulana Asraf Ali Thanawi, one of the leaders of the Deoband *madrasa* and a prolific writer and activist (interviews: April 28, 2001, Bahawalpur and September 2, 2002, Karachi).[76] Though Thanawi agreed to accept the Englishmen as disciples, Shahidullah had a dream that indicated they should continue their search.

Subsequent travels, however, proved fruitless. Disheartened, the brothers made their way to Bombay where they planned to book a ticket on a steamship for a return trip to England. There by chance Faruq Ahmad met a man known as Khatib Sahab, the caretaker of a local Sufi shrine in Bombay and a disciple of the Chishti Sabiri master Shaykh Waris Hasan. Khatib Sahab advised Shahidullah and Furuq Ahmad to travel to Hyderabad, Deccan, where his teacher's successor, Muhammad Zauqi Shah, lived and guided a group of disciples. With this recommendation as an introduction, the brothers received permission to visit and departed for Hyderabad.

Their first encounter with Muhammad Zauqi Shah took place on September 18, 1938. Upon meeting the young Englishmen, the *shaykh* is reported to have commented, "If you have come to me to witness supernatural acts, this is the wrong place. However, if you have come to find God, you must be prepared for a long and arduous journey."[77] Convinced that he had finally discovered his designated spiritual guide, Shahidullah took formal discipleship (*bay'at*) on October 3. Since Faruq Ahmad had previously become a disciple of Frithjof Schuon in Paris, however, Zauqi Shah insisted that he must obtain permission from his *shaykh* before he could accept him as a *murid*. When Schuon's response arrived by letter, Faruq Ahmad joined his younger brother as a full-fledged initiate in the Chishti Sabiri order (interview: September 2, 2001, Karachi).[78]

Education

After converting to Islam and leaving behind his Oxford education, Shahidullah Faridi immersed himself in studies on Islamic history and faith. While he never received formal *madrasa* training, he eventually became well versed in the Qur'an, *hadith*, and Sufi literature.[79] In one of his published discourses, Shahidullah asserts that his own authority rests on direct, personal experience. Here he draws a sharp distinction between inner (*batin*) and outer (*zahir*) dimensions of knowledge and practice, saying, "Those noble Sufis who have gained acceptance in genuine *silsilas* are the true rulers. As Hajji Imdad Allah al-Muhajir Makki Sahab, may God have mercy upon him, has said, unless there is inner knowledge [*batini 'ilm*], outward knowledge [*zahiri 'ilm*] is worthless. This is the truth. In the absence of inner manifestation and vision a human being simply cannot have the correct perspective."[80]

As a Sufi master and a teaching *shaykh*, Shahidullah privileged the insights of inner, intuitive experience over the discursive knowledge found in books. Even so, he maintained an interest in worldly matters throughout his life. Much like his own mentor, the *shaykh* frequently punctuated his theological discussions with references to the lessons (and shortcomings) of science.[81] From the perspective of Shahidullah's disciples, however, the *shaykh's* unusual background and experiences only made his erudition and advanced spiritual status all the more remarkable and convincing. In the words of a senior male *murid*,

> Hazrat Zauqi Shah Sahab was a descendent of the Holy Prophet, God bless him and grant him salvation. Yet he granted succession [*khilafat*] to Hazrat Shahidullah, an English gentleman! He was a newcomer, a new convert. He was not a religious scholar, an expert in Qur'an interpretation, or a scholar of *hadith* who is born into the Muslim community and acquires a great status. He never had these qualifications. He never received any degrees of scholarship from any Muslim university or *madrasa*, only the training of his *shaykh*. Of course, his knowledge was vast. More than that of any scholar! So he became the principal successor [*khalifa-i azim*]. It was all the order of Allah, because of the fire of love, the sincerity, and the devotion in his heart. (April 30, 2001, Bahawalpur)

Spiritual Training

Shahidullah Faridi's religious education consisted of years of rigorous spiritual training (*suluk*). This was a hands-on, experiential introduction to the inner dimensions of Sufi doctrine and ritual practice. In September 1939, on the advice of Zauqi Shah, he and Faruq Ahmad moved from Hyderabad back to the state of Bahawalpur. There they enjoyed the patronage of the local Nawab who was so impressed with the young English converts' dedication that he secured a position for them as captains in the Bahawalpur State Army. This arrangement allowed the brothers to commit themselves to their spiritual disciplines while avoiding conscription in the British Army during the course of the Second World War.[82]

In between their military duties, Shahidullah and Faruq Ahmad maintained a strict regimen of ritual practices as prescribed by their *shaykh*. This involved an intense program of daily prayers, *zikr*, and *muraqaba*, augmented by prolonged periods of fasting and isolation. The brothers also traveled frequently to Sufi shrines for extended spiritual retreats and regularly attended the annual '*urs* celebrations of local saints. At Ajmer Sharif they often worked in the *langar*, serving food and water to impoverished pilgrims (interview: March 24, 2001, Islamabad). In *Tarbiyat al-'ushshaq*, Shahidullah recalls an extended pilgrimage to a number of Sufi shrines in the company of his *shaykh*:

> Once we went with Hazrat [Zauqi Shah], may God have mercy upon him, to Hyderabad, Deccan, and from there we also visited Daulatabad and Khuldabad

where there are countless shrines of the noble saints. It is reported that fourteen hundred saints went together from Delhi to Hyderabad and their tombs are in Daulatabad and Khuldabad. We presented ourselves at those shrines. But at the shrine of Hazrat Sayyid Yusuf Husseini, may God have mercy upon him—the father of Hazrat Sayyid Muhammad Gesu Daraz, may God have mercy upon him—I did not perceive any spiritual blessings in my heart.

I asked for Hazrat's guidance about this and he replied, "When a person becomes a disciple, his *shaykh* prepares a 'skeleton program' [*sic*, in English] for him. After this, all of his training proceeds according to this program. It is possible, however, that certain events and experiences are simply not included in that program, and for that reason the seeker is not affected by them . . . This illustrates the power of the *shaykh* in controlling the disciple's spiritual course [*suluk*]. Tomorrow after morning prayer go there again by yourself." Thanks to Hazrat's spiritual influence, during this second visit I began to feel the spiritual blessings and sensed a strong connection [*nisbat*] [with the saint].[83]

This anecdote gives some sense of the intimacy and intensity of the master-disciple relationship—the backbone of Sufi ritual practice that will be discussed in detail in chapter 4. Shahidullah and Faruq Ahmad's spiritual training was completed under the strict supervision of Zauqi Shah. Yet remarkably the brother actually spent relatively little time in the presence of their *shaykh*. In *Malfuzat-i shaykh*, Shahidullah notes that Zauqi Shah purposefully limited their interactions with him to no more than fifteen days at a time in order to encourage their independence and spur their self-discipline.[84]

Shahidullah's journey became significantly more difficult, however, when Faruq Ahmad died in Lahore on February 13, 1945 after a prolonged bout of pneumonia. The details of his tragic death and burial within the tomb complex of his patron saint 'Ali Hujwiri are outlined in *Tarbiyat al-'ushshaq*. In an emotional letter written to Zauqi Shah, Shahidullah recounts the scene of Faruq Ahmad's burial, along with a powerful vision of the Prophet Muhammad that confirms for him his brother's advanced spiritual status:

> When Faruq Ahmad was in the agonies of death, I saw the Master of the Two Worlds [the Prophet Muhammad], God bless him and grant him salvation, at his head with you [Zauqi Shah] standing by his side. The saints [*Awliya' Allah*] had formed a circle and were dancing . . . When Faruq Ahmad, may God have mercy upon him, was being lowered into the grave, once again I saw that the Pleasure of the Two Worlds [the Prophet], God bless him and grant him salvation, was standing at the side of the grave and you were there next to him. A host of saints came forward in turn and paid their respects. Everyone present there also saw that at the time of prayer a small cloud appeared directly over the site and stopped there. Throughout the time of the funeral, a light rain fell from that cloud of mercy only above that spot in Lahore.[85]

According to the text, there were insufficient funds to fulfill Faruq Ahmad's desire to be buried in the compound of Hujwiri's shrine, and an alternative location was hastily arranged. As the burial was about to commence, however, a stranger suddenly arrived and announced that he would provide a plot within the *mazar*. Faruq Ahmad's grave can still be found within a small, subterranean room under the large shrine complex. In interviews, I was told that when an underground parking garage was constructed at the shrine during the 1980s, many such tombs were exhumed and relocated. Workers reportedly attempted to move Faruq's tomb as well. Yet when they began to unearth his grave, they discovered that his body was still fresh and had not decomposed—one of the well-known tropes of sainthood. Though it is impossible to verify this remarkable story, Faruq Ahmad's tomb was indeed left undisturbed. Today it is maintained by an elderly devotee and frequently visited by Chishti Sabiri *murids*.

In the years following his brother's death, Shahidullah continued his ritual practices while simultaneously participating in business and family life. On the advice of Zauqi Shah, he moved from Bombay to Karachi in February 1947. On September 7, 1947 Zauqi Shah and his family joined him in Pakistan.[86] Along with several *murids*, their families shared a humble two-bedroom flat on the upper floors of a building near the main railway station. One small room was reserved for Zauqi Shah and his wife, while the other room was partitioned, half for women in the family and the other for the men (interview: September 2, 2001, Karachi). These cramped living quarters doubled as a space for spiritual practices, including the weekly performance of communal *zikr*. In the final years of Zauqi Shah's life, Shahidullah often led these *zikr* sessions as his *shaykh's* health progressively deteriorated. For disciples, this provided a clear indication of his advanced spiritual status and potential to inherit the *khilafat* as a Chishti Sabiri master.

Qualities as a Teaching *Shaykh*

Zauqi Shah died during Hajj on September 13, 1951. According to several senior disciples, before his death he appointed both Shahidullah and Wahid Bakhsh as his spiritual heirs, distinguishing Shahidullah as his principal successor (*khalifa-i azam*). At the time, however, none of this was made public, and for the next four years the *silsila* was effectively without a guiding *shaykh*. During this interim period, senior disciples implored Shahidullah to accept disciples of his own. He resisted, however, asserting that he had not yet received explicit permission to do so. This situation changed dramatically in 1955. After returning to Karachi from the '*urs* of Baba Farid ad-Din Ganj-i Shakkar in Pakpattan, Shahidullah had a vivid dream in which his status as *khalifa* was confirmed by the patron saint himself. This paradigmatic experience is not recorded in any text, but during my interviews I heard it narrated—with slight variations—on numerous occasions. The account of a highly respected male *murid*—a disciple of Zauqi Shah and close personal friend of Shahidullah—illustrates how even private dreams are progressively incorporated into the *silsila's* collective memory:

> On the ninth of Muharram, Hazrat Shahidullah had a dream. He saw a vision that he was standing in the shrine (*darbar*) of Hazrat Baba Sahab, may God

have mercy upon him. There was a large group of people gathered there and Baba Sahab himself was standing at the door of his *mazar*. The people were shouting at him, "Please, we want to become your disciples (*murids*). Make us your disciples!" Baba Sahab looked around the crowd, as though he was search- ing for somebody. And then he stared directly at Hazrat Sahab and called to him by name. He said, "You make these people *murids*!" Hazrat Sahab replied, "My *shaykh* has not allowed me." And then Hazrat Zauqi Shah Sahab, may God have mercy upon him, appeared and said, "Of course I've allowed you!" Then Baba Sahab said, "Make them disciples and inform the people of this." (May 21, 2001, Karachi)

When this revelatory dream was made public, Shahidullah entered an entirely new phase of his life. Soon after he officially dropped his surname, Lennard, and adopted the moniker "Faridi" to mark his special relationship with the saint in Pakpattan (interview: September 2, 2001, Karachi). For a number of years, Shahidullah accepted *murids* in the name of his teacher, Zauqi Shah (*khilafat-i niabati*), but eventually he accepted *bay'at* independ- ently. For the final twenty-three years of his life, Shahiduallah Faridi guided a large and diverse group of disciples as a full-fledged Pakistani Chishti Sabiri spiritual master. An English convert was transformed into a teaching *shaykh*.

Among his many disciples, Shahidullah Faridi is remembered as a man of immense sophistication, integrity, and piety. As a spiritual mentor, he was renowned for his openness and tolerance. In the words of a female disciple who took *bay'at* with Shahidullah as a young woman in Peshawar,

> Our Hazrat Sahab was never concerned about the outward appearance of a per- son. Back in the 1970s in Pakistan, it was the fashion for women to wear very short skirts and trousers. I remember a woman and a couple of her friends in Karachi who would come and meet Hazrat Sahab, dressed up as they wanted. One day, somebody raised an objection and said, "They should at least be dressed in a graceful and dignified manner." To that Hazrat Sahab replied, "No, we Sufis have nothing to do with a person's appearance. It is the inward that we deal with." In that manner, I think he was very broad-minded, relaxed, and not at all strict. (October 31, 2001, Lahore)

As this narrative illustrates, Shahidullah was fully accessible to women and treated them as the spiritual equals of his male *murids*. The *shaykh*, in fact, had a large number of female disciples, many of whom were particularly active in the order's daily life. In a last will and testament (*wasyat nama*) com- posed a year before his death in 1978, Shahidullah singles out several senior female disciples by name, praising them for their knowledge and lofty spiri- tual status. If the Chishti Sabiri tradition allowed, he asserts, he would have named them his successors.[87] Shahidullah's legacy continues to inform con- temporary Chishti Sabiri opinions and practices. To this day, many of the most respected disciples in the *silsila* are women. Their wisdom and advice is eagerly sought after by all *murids*, female and male, young and old alike.

While no official records were ever maintained, Shahidullah's formal disci- ples are said to have numbered in the thousands. His Pakistani *murids* were

scattered across the country and represented a broad spectrum of socioeconomic and ethnic backgrounds. Given his own personal background, it is not
surprising that Shahidullah attracted a large number of foreign converts and
Muslims from diverse nationalities as well. In the last decades of his life, he
met regularly with a group of foreign students at a large Islamic Center in
Karachi, giving lectures in both English and Urdu, some of which were
recorded on tape. Many of these foreign students eventually became disciples, and several of them remain in Pakistan to this day. Significantly, the
shaykh also had a number of followers from East Pakistan—today's
Bangladesh—and traveled himself on one occasion for an extended stay in
Rangpur to visit them. The story of this connection was narrated to me by a
senior disciple. During a stay in Ajmer Sharif in 1956, Shahidullah was
approached by a man named Yasin who was "clad in a *lungi* and *kurta*,
bearded, with a cap." Yasin told him that he often came to Ajmer Sharif and
had been searching for a *shaykh* for many years. This time, however, Khwaja
Sahab himself—the saint of Ajmer, Mu'in ad-Din Chishti—had specifically
directed him in a dream to seek out Hazrat Shahidullah. For contemporary
disciples this is a significant story. This mystical, Uwaysi connection also prefigures Wahid Bakhsh Rabbani's subsequent relationship with a large contingent of *murids* from Malaysia (interview: September 2, 2001, Karachi).

Shahidullah is remembered as a patient but firm teacher. He mentored disciples who were committed to the discipline of *suluk*, and his discourses are
full of practical advice on the details of ritual performance. The *shaykh* had little regard for those who came to him only with worldly problems, however,
and discouraged disciples from sending anyone to him merely for amulets
(*tawiz*).[88] Shahidullah maintained a busy schedule attending to his disciples.
Just as Zauqi Shah before him, he never lived in a *khanaqah*. Instead, he held
weekly *zikr* sessions and met individually with disciples at his home near the
central train station in Karachi. He also traveled frequently both to visit
murids and to participate in pilgrimages to Sufi shrines. Following a heart
attack in the late 1960s, Shahidullah moved his family to another house in
the north of the city where they lived until his death in 1978. He was buried
nearby in a large cemetery called Sakhi Hassan. According to a senior disciple, the complex arrangements necessary for the construction of a shrine
were made with remarkable speed and ease—a fact that *murids* see as nothing short of miraculous (interview: September 2, 2002, Karachi). Today
Shahidullah's marble tomb is housed in a whitewashed *mazar* adjoining a
spacious mosque. An adjacent graveyard contains plots for *silsila* members
who wish to be buried near their spiritual master. This simple, elegant shrine
complex is the final resting place of the first and only Chishti Sabiri *shaykh*
from outside South Asia.

Married Life

In keeping with prophetic tradition and the norms of the Chishti hagiographical habitus, Shahidullah Faridi viewed marriage as an essential component of

Sufi training. In one of his lectures, he quotes from a *hadith* to define marriage as an expression of faith, arguing that piety should always take precedence over wealth and beauty in choosing a mate.[89] The anchor of Shahidullah's own personal and spiritual life was his wife Rashida Khatun. On numerous occasions, *murids* recounted the story of his first encounter with his future wife, known affectionately among disciples as Ammi Jan. During his prolonged search for a spiritual guide in the 1940s, Shahidullah had a vivid dream of an unknown *shaykh*, holding the hand of a small girl. Years later, he was living with Zauqi Shah as a novice disciple when he met the young woman from his dream. A senior male *murid* narrates the story:

> Hazrat Sahab was living upstairs [in the home of Zauqi Shah]. Ammi Jan was coming down the stairs, and he was going up. On the way they crossed paths. Hazrat Sahab just stopped and looked at her, and this annoyed Ammi Jan a great deal. In Islam, it is not proper to stare at a woman who is not in your family. Later when they were married, Ammi Jan asked him, "Why did you look at me that way that day we met? It's against the *shari'a* and against the etiquette [*adab*] of sainthood." Hazrat explained, "When I saw a dream of Hazrat Zauqi Shah Sahab for the first time, the young girl with him resembled your face. When I looked at you I thought, 'It's the same girl who was with Hazrat Shah Sahab!' I was astonished by this. That's why I looked. Otherwise there was no intention." (April 28, 2001, Bahawalpur)

Several disciples recounted a similar story about the saint Baba Farid Ganj-i Shakkar who also met his future wife in a prescient dream. These hagiographic parallels of Shahidullah Faridi and his namesake are seen as another important marker of legitimacy, authority, and authenticity.

Shahidullah and Rashida Khatun were married in March 1946. Disciples who knew them best attest that their relationship was based on a deep mutual respect and admiration. "I have never seen any person with such respect for his wife," said one male *murid*. "He [Shahidullah Faridi] was her servant. One could say that she was the daughter of his *shaykh*, so that's why he respected her. But I know that even if she wasn't he would have respected her. It was part of his nature. This is an example for us all" (April 28, 2001, Bahawalpur). As a convert and a cultural outsider, Shahidullah's marriage into the *sayyid* family of his own mentor was seen as a vital public affirmation of his spiritual status. Zauqi Shah made this explicit, describing the marriage as a salient example of the primacy of meritocracy over blood genealogy in Sufism. *Tarbiyat al-'ushshaq* records the *shaykh's* views: "In Islam we are all brothers and there is no family superiority. In the Holy Qur'an there is only the command that virtuous men are for virtuous women and evil men are for evil women. This is the only statement to be found. Family and genealogy are not important. Look at what I have done, I have given my daughter to a Muslim convert! He left his own country and had not thought to take a wife. Yet his heart is filled with passion for the true Islam and for this reason there was no obstacle to the match."[90]

Chishti Sabiri hagiographies emphasize that Ammi Jan was herself deeply immersed in Sufi practices from childhood. As a young girl she received *bay'at* at the hands of her father's guide, Shah Sayyid Waris Hasan. And growing up in Zauqi's Shah's house she endured great privations but benefited from the atmosphere of intense religious devotion. Among Chishti Sabiri *murids*, Ammi Jan was revered for her piety and sanctity. In the words of a senior male disciple who knew her well,

> Ammi Jan was a unique person; she was not of this world. Her father used to nearly starve her and the family for weeks at a time. Right from the cradle she was used to spiritual striving [*mujahada*]. Shah Sahab, may God have mercy upon him, used to follow his own *mujahada* with the whole family, it was not done individually. And then she was married. She was the daughter of a *qutb* [axis or pole, the apex of the hierarchy of Sufi saints], and was married to a *qutb*! And she was the disciple of yet another *qutb*, Mawlana Waris Hasan Sahab, may God have mercy upon him. (September 1, 2001, Karachi)

These lofty claims place Ammi Jan at the very center of an elect circle of spiritual masters.

Like her husband, Ammi Jan is remembered for her unique connection to the saint, Baba Farid ad-Din Ganj-i Shakkar. With great emotion, another senior disciple elaborated on this lifelong link with the saint of Pakpattan:

> Ammi Jan was of very high status. She was a favorite of the saint. Whenever the door was closed to the room of Hazrat Zauqi Shah Sahab, it was a sign that some saint, or even the Holy Prophet, God bless him and grant him salvation, was present there. Once he was talking to a person and the door was closed. Ammi Jan was then a very small child. She opened the door and Hazrat Zauqi Shah Sahab just pointed [to the doorway], saying, "Go. Go away." But the saintly person with him was sitting there and said, "No, no. Let her come. She is my daughter." And then he put her on his lap. Afterward Hazrat Sahab told Ammi Jan that the man was Baba Sahab [the saint, Farid ad-Din].
>
> Whenever she would visit his *mazar* [Pakpattan Sharif], there was a wonderful scene. People would gather, and there were such blessings. She attracted a lot of women; no queen could receive such a reception. She had a very high status. Even after the passing away of Hazrat Shahidullah Sahab she had a very strong hold on the *silsila*. Everything was run under her guidance. (April 29, 2001, Bahawalpur)

While this intriguing hagiographic anecdote is not recorded in any text, it too is now integrated into the contemporary *silsila's* collective memory.

In his last will and testament written a year before his death in 1978, Shahidullah outlines a unique role for Ammi Jan in the *silsila*, asking his disciples to honor her and follow her advice. In the *shaykh's* words, "My first command concerns the daughter of my *shaykh* who has been my life companion for over thirty years and who is the priceless treasure entrusted to me. Once I am no more, no one must cause her hardship or grief . . . This counsel is for the entire *silsila*. She is the mother to all of you, and she should be given the treatment due to a mother and her counsel must be included in every matter."[91] Though they never had children, Ammi Jan and Shahidullah Faridi adopted Ammi Jan's nephew who was raised in their home and treated as their own son. For the last twelve years of her life, she lived with this young man and several close disciples in a house near Shahidullah's tomb in the Sakhi Hassan cemetery. And just as her husband envisioned, she proved to be a solidifying influence during this period. In effect, she served as a surrogate *shaykh*—her opinions and insights on both spiritual and worldly matters were regularly solicited by both male and female *murids*. Reflecting on this legacy, several *murids* highlighted the symbolic significance of twelve years, noting that the saints Baba Farid Ganj-i Shakkar and 'Ali Ahmad Sabir both underwent twelve years of spiritual training before completing *suluk* (interview: September 2, 2001, Karachi). Such parallels reveal the depth of reverence for Ammi Jan prevalent among Chishti Sabiris to this day. Ammi Jan died in February 1990 and is buried in a place of honor near her husband at the shrine.

Miracles

Shahidullah's discourses offer relatively few insights on his attitude toward miracles (*karamat*), but personal narratives suggest that here too he is remembered as the model of propriety. Numerous disciples, however, did recount examples of the *shaykh's* powers over the forces of nature. For example, his keen knowledge of numerous regional languages—Arabic, Persian, Sanskrit, Hindi, and even Saraiki—was considered miraculous. On a less mundane level, individual *murids* recalled demonstrations of Shahidullah's knowledge of future events and his powers as a healer and protector—all common hagiographic motifs in Sufi hagiography. A young male *murid* from a family with long Chishti Sabiri roots narrated an especially remarkable event:

> Hazrat Shahidullah Sahab, may God have mercy upon him, had a disciple in India. This man wished to go to Medina and remain there until he died. He was called to work there as a government servant and was given a stipend. When he was sent back to Pakistan, he was very upset. He went to Hazrat Sahab and said, "Huzur, I wanted to die there, but now I'm back. You have to pray for me. I want to go back." Hazrat Shahidullah Faridi said, "Yes, I'll pray." The man replied, "No! I want you to pray with me now." Hazrat Sahab took him into the next room. The man died suddenly a few days later and was buried somewhere near Maleer. That night his wife saw him in a dream and said to her, "When you come to my grave tomorrow, do not worry. I am here in Medina." The next morning they went to the grave site and found only an empty hole there. His body and even the soil was gone. This is a living miracle of Hazrat Sahab! (September 2, 2001, Karachi)

It is of course impossible to objectively verify such accounts—in this case, a secondhand retelling of an orally transmitted story of anonymous origin.

Nonetheless, their impact on the lives of contemporary disciples is beyond question. Such hagiographical stories serve as key tropes in the construction and narration of sacred biography. They mark moments of rupture in the natural order that, for Chishti Sabiri believers, confirms the tangible reality of Islamic sainthood.

Ecstasy and Sobriety

Despite his atypical background, Shahidullah's temperament, lifestyle, and teaching style conformed to the premodern paradigm of an Indo-Muslim Sufi *shaykh*. Though a great lover of poetry and, in particular, *sama'* (music), he is remembered for his constant sobriety and careful attention to the dictates of propriety and etiquette (*adab*). Significantly, when narrating his sacred biography Chishti Sabiri disciples often draw explicit parallels between his life and that of the Prophet Muhammad. A prominent female *murid* expresses a common sentiment about the *shaykh's* unique spiritual status:

> I feel that Hazrat Shahidullah Faridi was very close to the Prophet, in all his actions. This is my own interpretation. He lived to the age of sixty-three, like the Holy Prophet, God bless him and grant him salvation, and became *khalifa* at age forty . . . Hazrat Shahidullah's personal migration (*hijrat*) was even more difficult than our Prophet's, may God bless him and grant him salvation, because he left behind his religion, his language, his family. It was something that no human being can do, honestly. He was the chosen one. When people who do not believe in these things hear about him and read his books, they say the same thing—that he was the chosen one and nobody can be like him. I think he was the biggest saint of the century. (June 17, 2001, Lahore)

When he was nearing the age of sixty-three, Shahidullah's heart condition worsened. His personal physician told him that his heart had become enlarged and recommended that the *shaykh* travel abroad for medical treatment. "I will never go abroad for treatment," Shahidullah reportedly said, "My life is in accord with that of the Holy Prophet, and living on earth more than sixty-three years is itself against the *sunna*" (May 2, 2001, Bahawalpur). In life and even in death, Shahidullah is remembered as the very embodiment of both *shari'a* and *sunna*—a living reflection of the Prophetic model, *murids* insist, all the more impressive given his British upbringing.

Lifestyle

Though first and foremost a Chishti Sabiri teaching *shaykh*, Shahidullah was also a full participant in the daily affairs of family and business. For him, this too was a key component of Sufi practice and a vital element distinguishing Sufism from other spiritual traditions. *Malfuzat-i shaykh* documents Shahidullah's views on comparative mysticism:

> There is a striking difference between Islamic spirituality [*ruhaniyat*] and that of other religions. Our spiritual people continue to live in the world as normal

Muslims after completing their training. This is one of the distinctions. Their contemplation is not like that of the Christians. Most of the Christian mystics have been monks who have abandoned the world. It is the same with the Hindus . . . Those who say that the Sufis teach people to abandon the world and not to engage in worldly work are mistaken. It is absolute foolishness for a Sufi to think that he should have no connection with the world or that Sufism has nothing to do with worldly matters. This too is a mistake.[92]

Shahidullah owned and operated a small business importing high-quality paper and stationary when he first lived in Bombay. Originally called J.G Lennard and Company, he later transferred the company to Karachi following Partition (interview: September 1, 2001, Karachi). Disciples note that Shahidullah's experiences in worldly matters added another dimension to his role as a teaching *shaykh*. The *shaykh* encouraged his followers to discuss all kinds of matters with him as well, both spiritual and worldly. According to a senior disciple, a *murid* of Waris Hasan who first met Shahidullah Faridi as a young man in 1949,

> After my father's death and after the passing away of Shah Sahab [Muhammad Zauqi Shah], there was a big vacuum for me. So it was Hazrat Sahab, may God have mercy upon him, who became a father figure for me. I used to talk to him about very intimate matters which I would not tell anyone else. And he encouraged me to talk to him about anything. At times I used to hold myself back and not tell him things, but he used to ask me about them. He used to draw me into talking about them. I felt that talking about the everyday world [*dunya*] with him was too mundane, so I would avoid talking about it. Then he would ask me, "How is business? How is your factory? What are you doing?" All those things. (May 21, 2001, Karachi)

The *shaykh's* own lifestyle was marked by extreme frugality and simplicity—a stark contrast with the life of wealth and comfort he had known as a child. After leaving England, Shahidullah never accepted the offers of financial support from his concerned family. At one point, his father learned about his difficult living conditions in Karachi. Determined to help, he arranged to purchase a thousand Morris Minor taxis so that Shahidullah might start a new business and generate a large income. According to a *murid*, his father wrote to him and said, "For generations we have built a sound financial empire. Though you have converted to Islam, so what? You are my son. Come and take it." Hazrat Sahab responded, "I am a *faqir* of Allah. These things have no attraction for me" (March 24, 2001, Islamabad). Shahidullah then distributed the taxis to those in need around the city, keeping nothing for himself.

Another oft-repeated anecdote echoes this salient theme of indifference to worldly possessions. In the words of another male disciple,

> Hazrat Sahab was living almost at the level of starvation, but he did not accept a penny from his father. There is a very intimate story about this. His father told him, "You won't accept anything from me, but I have some of your mother's

jewelry. Since your elder brother is no longer alive, I'm sending it to you." Hazrat said, "No! I don't need anything. I have so much, I don't need it. You give it to my sister in Paris." When Ammi Jan heard about this, she said, "Why did you do that? You denied yourself all of the things your father offered you. Why did you deny me this?" The reply he gave her was fantastic. He said, "In comparison with the blessings your father has given us, you prefer these stones?" Ammi Jan related this story to my mother and told her, "After he said that, I felt so small. There was no question then of accepting it." (May 21, 2001, Karachi)

Such stories reinforce the Chishti hagiographical habitus. As a devoted Sufi teacher, Shahidullah engages the world in order to serve others. Leading by example, the *shaykh* willfully surrenders his material possessions in favor of the riches of spiritual wealth.

Public and Political Life

Like his predecessors, Shahidullah was politically savvy. Even so, a survey of his public writings reveals relatively little commentary on political matters. This pervasive silence is mirrored in Shahidullah's public persona. After immigrating to Pakistan, the *shaykh* never formally joined a political party, and he was never as politically outspoken as either his spiritual master, Zauqi Shah, or his friend and fellow disciple Wahid Bakhsh. Perhaps his status as an outsider—and an Englishman living in South Asia in the twilight of the British Raj, no less—prompted Shahidullah to be wary of voicing his personal political views in public. Regardless of the motivation, the consequences are predictable: among today's Chishti Sabiris, the *shaykh* is remembered more for his personal piety and spiritual teachings than for his political opinions. As a citizen of Pakistan, however, Shahidullah was clearly concerned with the country's well-being and development. While his collective discourses and writings overwhelmingly focus on the Sufi path, he does occasionally address an array of social issues, from political administration and sectarianism to the institutionalization of Islamic law. Not surprisingly, his opinions, when voiced, echo those of his mentor, Zauqi Shah.

There is one common theme in Shahidullah's teachings that sets him apart, however. Time and again he emphasizes that spiritual development is an essential prerequisite for anyone who hopes to engage in meaningful political activism or institutional reform. In a lecture recorded in *Malfuzat-i shaykh*, Shahiduallah exclaims, "If a person wants to examine the political facet of Islam, or its economic or judicial dimensions, he can look at all of them. But first of all his faith and connection with Allah, his inner spiritual state and his heart, should be correct. Only then can such work be done. In this way, he will acquire strength and good results will be achieved. If he is not spiritually strong, how can he hope to understand Islamic politics, Islamic economics or other branches of knowledge?"[93] The implications of this statement for political leadership and state building are clear. For Shahidullah Faridi, Pakistan could never hope to fulfill its promise as an

Islamic republic in the absence of widespread, fundamental moral reform. Avoiding the glare of the public spotlight, Shahidullah Faridi immersed himself in the Sufi path—guiding his loyal followers to a deeper awareness of the meaning of Islamic piety and virtue by his own personal example.

SHAYKH WAHID BAKHSH
SIAL RABBANI (1910–1995)

The sacred biography of Shaykh Wahid Bakhsh Sial Rabbani signals a reaffirmation of the traditional trajectory—the hagiographical habitus—of Chishti Indo-Muslim sainthood. At the same time, his personal biography and worldview were profoundly shaped by the politics of Partition. A *khalifa* of Muhammad Zauqi Shah and close friend of Shahidullah Faridi, Wahid Bakhsh continued the efforts of his predecessors to root the Chishti Sabiri tradition within the spatial and cultural landscape of postcolonial, independent Pakistan. The *shaykh*'s legacy is distinguished by his vast literary output. His voluminous corpus of books and articles includes translations of classical Persian *malfuzat* texts, original commentaries on Sufi practice, and polemical tracts on Pakistani identity and political life. The shrine of Shaykh Wahid Bakhsh Sial Rabbani in Allahabad, Pakistan is pictured below in figure 2.2.

Wahid Bakhsh is remembered for his alluring personality, his remarkable openness and accessibility, and his resolute defense of the Sufi tradition against its critics and detractors. A recent edition of the *silsila's* English

Figure 2.2 The Shrine of Shaykh Wahid Bakhsh Sial Rabbani (d. 1995), Allahabad, Pakistan

Source: Photograph by Robert Rozehnal

magazine *The Sufi Path* offers a portrait of the *shaykh* through a collection of short articles, poems, and letters composed by several of his disciples. In a eulogy to Wahid Bakhsh—the first trace of an incipient, proto-*malfuzat*—the magazine's editors write,

> The spiritual guide, renowned scholar, practicing Sufi, saint par excellence, and spiritual *khalifa* of Hazrat Zauqi Shah, may God have mercy upon him, departed from this world after a long illness on 20th Ziqad, 1417 Hijri (April 21, 1995) at the age of eighty-five, leaving behind hundreds of followers at home and abroad. All those who were blessed with his companionship (*suhbat*) during his lifetime mourn an irreplaceable loss. As one ardent lover of his remarked, "The world is poorer without him."
>
> Having authored a large number of books on various facets of Islamic spirituality, writing thousands of letters to his *murids*, besides spending endless hours meeting those visiting him, traveling frequently within the country and abroad, eating only to live, and spreading kindness, warmth and mercy to old and young, rich and poor, powerful and helpless, he embodied the highest traits of the best of Sufis to such a degree that one found full confirmation in the famous saying, "Sufis in their communities are like the Prophet, God bless him and grant him salvation, amongst his Companions."[94]

The exuberance of this prose encapsulates the reverence and enthusiasm of Wahid Bakhsh's disciples. It is also mirrors the premodern paradigm of Indo-Muslim sainthood—affirming the continuity of the Chishti Sabiri discursive tradition even in the face of widespread societal transformation. The *shaykh* passed away in 1995 after a prolonged battle with prostrate cancer. He is buried in a shrine complex in his birthplace, the village of Allahabad in the southern Punjab (sixty miles southwest of the city of Bahawalpur). His recent death, coupled with the fact that he did not name a direct successor, means that Wahid Bakhsh's legacy remains an open book. The details of his personal history have yet to be inscribed in a sacred biography. Instead, they are preserved in a nexus of oral narratives. In this complex story-telling network, the *shaykh's* words and deeds are remembered and retold among contemporary Chishti Sabiri disciples. It is safe to assume that in time Wahid Bakhsh's teachings and life experiences will also be permanently recorded for posterity in a formal hagiography. But for the moment he remains a saint under construction.

Family Background and Spiritual Initiation

Wahid Bakhsh was born in 1910 in the village of Allahabad into a family of modest means but deep piety. His parents both came from families with long-standing ties to the Qadiri Sufi order. They are remembered for their affinity for Persian poetry, profound love for the Prophet, and strict adherence to both *sunna* and *shari'a*.[95] Wahid Bakhsh was raised in a devout household along with four siblings: an elder brother and sister, and a younger brother and sister. At the age of fourteen, his father passed away, leaving the young boys to provide for the family. Recalling the family's intense spirituality, a senior male disciple narrated the following miraculous anecdote about the death of Wahid Bakhsh's father:

> When he [Wahid Bakhsh] was fourteen and his younger brother was just two and a half, his father died. His father was a great lover of the Holy Prophet. He would recite *Durud Sharif* [prayers for the Prophet Muhammad] five thousand times daily. There is a tradition in the villages that when a person dies his feet are bound together. His large toes are tied together so the position is maintained, and then butter is applied to the eyes so that they remain soft. His father had died, but he suddenly sat up and said, "Why have you tied my toes? What is this you have put over my head?" He stood up and in the prayer position started repeating, "Blessings and peace be upon you, of Prophet of God." He addressed everyone there, saying, "The Holy Prophet has come, all of you should stand up!" After repeating this several times, he laid down in the same position [and passed away]. This was his father, such a spiritual person. (April 29, 2001, Bahawalpur)

For an audience steeped in the hagiographical tropes of the Sufi tradition, this narrative strikes a powerful, responsive chord. It simultaneously affirms the intense piety of Wahid Bakhsh's family lineage and prefigures his own emergence as a Sufi master.

Education

Like his mentors, Wahid Bakhsh never received formal *madrasa* training. Instead, his exposure to and knowledge of the Qur'an, *hadith*, theology, Islamic law, and Sufi literature were forged through self-study and direct, personal experience as a Sufi adept. As a young boy, Wahid Bakhsh attended government school in Allahabad. He remained there until the tenth grade when he transferred to Bahawalpur for his secondary and university education. Under the patronage of the local Nawab, he was subsequently commissioned in the British Indian Army in 1933. He went on to qualify for studies at the prestigious British military academy in Dehra Dun, India. This school—located approximately one hundred and twenty miles northeast of Delhi—maintained an exclusive quota for the sons of nawabs. Many of its graduates went on to positions of high rank in the Indian and Pakistani armies following Partition (interview: April 28, 2001, Lahore). With the support of the Nawab of Bahawalpur, Wahid Bakhsh enrolled at the academy from 1935 to 1937. After graduation, he was then transferred back to the Punjab to serve as a captain in the Bahawalpur State Army.

At this time, Wahid Bakhsh was the epitome of the English gentleman in dress and behavior: "He represented a typical Indian Army officer, more proud of his recently acquired British manners and customs than of his own traditional Islamic heritage."[96] A female member of the *shaykh's* family describes her own memories of Wahid Bakhsh in those days:

> He was a real British officer then. My mother used to tell me that in her childhood she saw him as a very sophisticated man, with very proper manners. She even remembered that he had a box with a compartment in it just for his ties.

He was so prim and proper that they always had to be creased. The family was living in a village, and when he returned from wherever he was posted, he would come and teach them. They were young girls, my mother, and my aunt, and he would teach them everything, like table manners. But when he left the military, he gave away all his clothes, his suits, everything. When he left the army, he gave up that lifestyle. My mother has told me a lot about this. (June 17, 2001, Lahore)

At the outbreak of the Second World War, Wahid Bakhsh's entire regiment was transferred to Malaysia. His stay there, however, was short-lived. Charged with insubordination for refusing—on the advice of his *shaykh* Muhammad Zauqi Shah—to cut his beard or wear shorts, he was discharged from military service and returned to India. During wartime, this could have resulted in the death penalty. Instead—in keeping with the hagiographical model—it saved Wahid Bakhsh from disaster. According to a short biography published in *The Sufi Path*, the Japanese overran the garrison just days after his departure. The entire regiment was taken as prisoners of war.[97] For many disciples, Wahid Bakhsh's experiences in Malaysia during the Second World War foreshadow his future connection with a large following of Malaysian *murids*.

Returning to South Asia, Wahid Bakhsh retired from military service altogether in 1946. With the Nawab's continued support he joined the Civil Secretariat, serving as the personal assistant to the prime minister of the state of Bahawalpur. In 1955 he was transferred to the West Pakistan Secretariat in Lahore where he worked as a civil servant until his retirement in 1968.[98] Both personally and professionally, therefore, Wahid Bakhsh was fully acquainted with the ideology and institutions of the colonial and postcolonial state. His experiences as a military officer and a civil bureaucrat had a profound impact on his worldview and political perspective.

Spiritual Training

Wahid Bakhsh's introduction to Chishti Sabiri Sufism came from the most unlikely of sources. In 1937, during his stint in the Bahawalpur State Army, he was introduced to the young English brothers, Shahidullah and Faruq Ahmad, who were visiting as the royal guests of the Nawab in the midst of their travels. Before resuming their search for a *shaykh*, the brothers met a number of army officers who were duly impressed with their sincerity and determination. *The Sufi Path* records this pivotal event in Wahid Bakhsh's own spiritual life: "Since the search for a *shaykh* was the only concern for these men, they soon cast an awe inspiring influence on those around them who, suffering from the complex of being a subjected nation, felt pleasantly surprised and elated on seeing these two men emulating and rigorously practicing the Islamic prayers. Judging by their sincerity that their's was the true cause, Captain Wahid and a few other officers requested of them that once they found a true *shaykh* they would also benefit from their efforts and follow their path."[99]

When Shahidullah and Faruq Ahmad returned to Bahawalpur in 1939, Wahid Bakhsh learned of their experiences with Shaykh Muhammad Zauqi Shah. Convinced that he too should follow the Chishti Sabiri master, he traveled to Ajmer Sharif. At that time, Zauqi Shah had taken up residence in a house immediately facing the shrine of the preeminent saint of the Subcontinent: Khwaja Mu'in ad-Din Chishti. Significantly, this residence at Ajmer was subsequently named Zauqi Manzil. It remains a central fixture adjacent to the shrine complex and now serves as a hostel for pilgrims. In recent years, its caretakers have increasingly distanced themselves from the *silsila*, however, and its affiliations with the Chishti Sabiri order now appear somewhat ambivalent. Even so, the name remains unchanged, and individual Chishti Sabiri *murids* who visit the city on pilgrimage (*ziyarat*) occasionally stay there. I visited the house in 2001, though I was not able to stay there. This humble hospice was an important site during the early years of Wahid Bakhsh's Sufi apprenticeship.

Wahid Bakhsh received formal initiation on June 24, 1940. In the following years, he frequently spent time in the company of Zauqi Shah, taking leave from military duties to travel to Ajmer Sharif during Ramadan and to attend the annual *'urs* celebrations. In between these meetings, Wahid Bakhsh maintained a strict regimen of prayer, *zikr*, fasting, and meditation. This relationship continued after both Zauqi Shah and Shahidullah moved to Karachi in the wake of Partition. All told, Wahid Bakhsh's training in the discipline of *suluk* lasted eleven years. By all accounts the relationship between master and disciple was intimate and intense. Wahid Bakhsh accompanied Zauqi Shah on his final Hajj pilgrimage in 1951—a transformative experience he later recorded in detail in his book, *Hajj-i Zauqi*.

Wahid Bakhsh's emergence as a teaching *shaykh* in his own right came decades later. According to several senior disciples, he was granted *khilafat* during Zauqi Shah's life. He concealed this fact from the *silsila*, however, in deference to Shahidullah Faridi. "He had been granted *khilafat*," a senior disciple told me, "but due to etiquette [*adab*], he would say, 'I respect Hazrat Shahidullah Faridi, may God have mercy upon him, as my *shaykh*.'" These were his words. "I consider him my *shaykh* because he is the *khalifa-i azam* [principal successor] of my *shaykh*. So I will not make *murids*" (April 29, 2001, Bahawalpur). Instead, for twenty-eight years—from Zauqi Shah's death in 1951 to Shahidullah's in 1978—Wahid Bakhsh remained largely in the background. After his retirement from public office in 1968, he immersed himself in spiritual devotions. During those years, he also worked intensely on the translations and writings that were to be the hallmark of his legacy. Several senior disciples describe Wahid Bakhsh during that period as withdrawn, intense, and *jalali* (awe inspiring)—a far cry from the dynamic and gregarious persona he was to assume as a full-fledged *shaykh*.

In 1975 Wahid Bakhsh's *khilafat* was publicly confirmed. In typical Chishti Sabiri fashion, the impetus came from a transformative dream, as a senior male *murid* recalls:

> The year I became a *murid*, 1975, Captain Sahab saw a dream. The body of Hazrat Zauqi Shah Sahab was there, and people wanted to take it away. But instead it was brought to his house. He [Wahid Bakhsh] narrated this vision to Hazrat Shahidullah Sahab who also received some indications. He said, "You have been granted *khilafat* by Hazrat Zauqi Shah Sahab, but you have concealed it. Now the time has come that it should be announced." So Hazrat Sahab announced that he [Wahid Bakhsh] was the *khalifa* of Hazrat Zauqi Shah Sahab and could take *bay'at*. I was present at that event. Hazrat Sahab brought a turban (*dastar*) and tied it on his [Wahid Bakhsh's] head. And then Hazrat Captain Sahab came into his room and everyone came forward and congratulated him. (May 2, 2001, Bahawalpur)

This anecdote illuminates once again the fluidity and interconnectedness of hagiographic narratives within the contemporary *silsila*. In this case, a private dream is transformed into public knowledge and then recirculated through a complex network of storytelling to reaffirm the Chishti Sabiri hagiographical habitus.

Wahid Bakhsh's status as a full-fledged teaching *shaykh* was also subsequently confirmed in writing. In his last will and testament, Shahidullah Faridi writes, "Janab Wahid Bakhsh Sahab, who has been authorized by Hazrat Shaykh [Zauqi Shah], may God have mercy upon him, has initiated *halqa zikr* and guidance in Bahawalpur for which I pray may Allah bestow blessings and increase. In this context, I counsel that he should spread the *silsila* in this place only and not move from place to place as that will affect his work."[100] Here Shahidullah effectively delineates the southern Punjab as Wahid Bakhsh's personal spiritual domain (*wilayat*). In the following years, however, the *shaykh's* duties Chishti Sabiri master rapidly expanded in scope and scale.

Qualities as a Teaching *Shaykh*

During the course of my fieldwork, I compiled an expansive catalogue of oral histories from the disciples of Wahid Bakhsh. Collectively, these accounts offer unique insights into the dynamics of the master-disciple (*pir-murid*) relationship. Often conveyed with great emotion, they detail the most intimate dimensions of people's spiritual lives. Collectively, these personal narratives also reveal a detailed portrait of the *shaykh's* private and public persona that both confirms and expands the premodern paradigm of Chishti sainthood.

Like Zauqi Shah and Shahidullah Faridi before him, Wahid Bakhsh never maintained a permanent hospice (*khanaqah*). In fact, he rarely stayed in one place for more than a few weeks. Instead he traveled widely throughout Pakistan and, on several occasions, to Malaysia in order to administer directly to the needs of disciples. He also regularly attended the cycle of annual *'urs* celebrations at Sufi shrines. The *shaykh's* many devoted followers recall his remarkable energy and unwavering self-discipline, even when incapacitated by old age and sickness. The following anecdote from a family member and senior male disciple encapsulates the *shaykh's* personality. It is representative of stories I heard repeated time and again:

> Those of us close to Hazrat Wahid Bakhsh, we were not even aware that the *shaykh* followed such a strict routine. He was accessible most of the time. People used to visit him after evening prayers. He had the capacity to attend to guests until midnight, and then stay awake the whole night and do all these things [spiritual exercises]. I personally saw him do that. The first time we went to Islamabad together [to visit disciples], we started out in the morning. My car broke down three or four times on the way. It was the month of June, very hot.
>
> We reached there at almost 10 pm. We were so thoroughly exhausted that he said, "Why don't we go to bed. Just pray your night prayers. Do the required [*farz*] prayers only and go to bed." It was about midnight, and I went to bed since I was so tired. After a few minutes I opened my eyes and saw him in meditation [*muraqaba*]. It was only when morning prayers were almost over that he nudged me and said, "Your prayers are getting away." I got up. I had a full five hours of sleep, but I don't think he had slept at all after taking this whole journey which had exhausted me. And this was when he was late in his late seventies! (August 26, 2001, Lahore)

This story, like so many others I heard from the *shaykh's* many disciples, illustrates Wahid Bakhsh's indefatigable personality, as well as his unwavering discipline and piety.

With his disciples, Wahid Bakhsh was tolerant, flexible, and patient. *Murids* unanimously laud his abilities as a teacher and communicator. The *shaykh's* keen intellect, openness, and charisma attracted people from a broad range of social and cultural backgrounds. The *shaykh's* inner circle of disciples was composed largely of middle-class, educated Pakistani urbanites. Yet he also had a large following among the rural communities surrounding his hometown of Allahabad. This is reflected in an account of his funeral on April 21, 1995 that appeared in the order's English language journal *The Sufi Path*: "Thousands of people attended Hazrat Sahab's funeral. Most of us had the impression that he had known mostly intellectual people, as he was a learned scholar and theologian, and his mission was obviously to propagate Islam to educated people at home and abroad. But the villagers said that he would often sit under a shady tree and listen to their complaints, giving them spiritual and worldly advice and prayers."[101] I personally attended Wahid Bakhsh's first death anniversary in Allahabad in 1996 and again during the course of my fieldwork research in February 2001. On both occasions, these public events were well attended, drawing hundreds of *murids* from Pakistan and abroad, along with large numbers of local villagers and curious onlookers.

Like Zauqi Shah and Shahidullah Faridi before him, Wahid Bakhsh deviated sharply from the traditional paradigm in his openness toward non-Muslims. He readily accepted non-Muslims as disciples and encouraged conversion to Islam. In his public lectures and writings, the *shaykh* frequently commented on comparative religions, championing Sufism as the most

complete and efficacious mystical path. His numerous books in Urdu and
English were clearly aimed at a broad, international audience. And, in fact, he
attracted both male and female *murids* from the United States, Europe, and,
in particular, Malaysia. The following account of Wahid Bakhsh's attitude
toward non-Muslims provides a sense of why so many foreign disciples found
his teaching style attractive:

> Captain Sahab, may God have mercy upon him, never asked people about
> "religion" per se. The religion of the Sufi is the nearness of Allah. Most
> people are now restricted to very specific types of paths. They have not made
> religion open, so that everyone may come into it. In his thinking and his
> liberal mindedness, he [Wahid Bakhsh] was unique. I've never seen another
> saint like him. He would allow everyone, even foreigners, a person of any
> religion, to sit in his *zikrs*. Whenever any person who did not belong to his
> religion was sitting in his company he was given due respect. (April 28, 2001,
> Bahawalpur)

A bibliophile and avid reader, Wahid Bakhsh was conversant in a wide
range of subjects: from classical Islamic scholarship to contemporary
geopolitics, science, and Western academic scholarship on Islam. The
shaykh's personal library—now housed at the growing tomb complex in
Allahabad—offers tangible proof of his wide-ranging literary interests. The
library also reflects Wahid Bakhsh's dedication to his disciples. Among vol-
umes of classical *tafsir* (Qur'an interpretation), *fiqh* (jurisprudence), and
Sufi poetry in Arabic, Persian, Urdu, Saraiki, and Punjabi are thousands of
letters from Wahid Bakhsh' *murids*. They are stacked in piles and stored in
large bags. Although the *shaykh* traveled constantly, much of his interaction
with disciples came in the form of letter writing. A large portion of his daily
routine, in fact, was occupied with this correspondence. As disciples readily
attest, the *shaykh's* replies to their frequent inquiries were invariably thorough and prompt. In the words of a Pakistani male *murid*, "Not one letter
was left unanswered. Even when he was sick with fever, even then he was
writing letters. His wife would get angry with him and say, 'What are you
doing? You're spoiling your health. Please have mercy on yourself!' But he
did not. His family even tried to hide the letters from him when he had cancer. As soon as he received a letter, he was not at rest until he could respond
to it" (May 2, 2001, Bahawalpur).

During my fieldwork, a number of Chishti Sabiri *murids* showed me selections of their lengthy correspondence with the *shaykh*, letters that they have
carefully preserved and continue to reread. Catered to the particular needs of
each individual, these letters address an immense range of material. This
includes dream interpretation, prescriptions for spiritual practices, and
practical advice on personal and family matters (marriage, divorce, finances,
children's education, etc.). This communication was particularly important
for Wahid Bakhsh's foreign disciples. In the absence of direct, face-to-face
interaction with their *shaykh*, they depended on letters for guidance and

inspiration. According to a senior Malaysian *murid*,

> His letters were all hand written. Sometimes on one page he would write on the lines, and if he ran short of space he would write on the sides—on the left side, the right side, at the top of the page, and along the bottom edges. Everywhere! The most beautiful thing was that every time we sent a letter to him, we knew that a reply would come within three weeks. And I tell you, every day we would look forward to the postman coming. I think all the *murids* here would tell you that their hearts would be pounding. During those three weeks, each day when the postman came to the house, we would rush out! (September 30, 2001, Kuala Lumpur)

Clearly, Wahid Bakhsh was deeply involved with every dimension of his disciples' lives. The *shaykh* transmitted spiritual knowledge as well as practical worldly advice both through *suhbat* (direct, interpersonal exchanges) and the pen.

Married Life

In keeping with the paradigm of an Indo-Muslim Sufi *shaykh*, Wahid Bakhsh was also a dedicated family man. The father of four sons and a daughter, he too viewed the institution of marriage as a central pillars of Sufi spiritual practice. Much like the wife of Shahidullah Faridi, Wahid Bakhsh's spouse Maqsuda Begam was renowned for her own piety, wisdom, and advanced spiritual status. Known affectionately as Amma Jan, she too was an important source of guidance for many disciples, especially women. In interviews, numerous *murids* spoke of her penchant for dreams and visions of prophets and saints. They narrated stories of her spiritual encounters with the Prophet Muhammad, Khizr, Jesus, Baba Farid ad-Din Ganj-i Shakkar, Muhammad Ali Jinnah, Shah Sayyid Waris Hasan, and Zauqi Shah, among others. According to a senior male disciple, Maqsuda Begam was, in fact, a vital intermediary for Wahid Bakhsh: "The Holy Prophet, God bless him and grant him salvation, and all the saints of the *silsila* were very kind to her, and they would give her indications concerning the work of her husband. They would come to her in dreams or in visions, or even in person" (April 30, 2001, Bahawalpur).

Wahid Bakhsh's relationship with his wife mirrors that of Shahidullah Faridi. Disciples remember the intensity of respect and affection between them. Many female *murids* point to the *shaykh's* marriage as the source for his attitudes toward women in general. A revealing quote from a senior female disciple captures this dynamic:

> Hazrat Wahid Bakhsh, God have mercy upon him, had this capacity to relate to women's problems, their insecurities. We felt heard. We felt that he gave us a status much higher than most men do. We felt equal in a sense. With other *pirs* you feel that they're too awesome, too big, larger than life. But he didn't appear to be that way, not while he was alive. It was only when he went away that we

realized the immensity of this man. He just didn't show it, he lived a very normal life. I was not there, but I heard about what he said to his wife before he died. The man was in his eighties. Just before his death he called his sons into his room, his four sons, and he called his wife. And he told her, "Look. You have four sons to take care of you, and I have a pension that you can receive. But if at any stage you feel lonely and insecure, I give you the permission to get married again."

Can you imagine this? A man saying that here, in Pakistan? And a Sufi *pir*? His wife started laughing, of course, saying, "Who would marry me at this stage?" But I think he was giving a message to his children and to all of us. He gave so much importance to women as human beings, that I think women just naturally flocked to him. They just were drawn towards him. I have not heard of another example of a *pir* saying this to his wife. I think it's tremendous. He was a very generous man in every sense of the word: intellectually, spiritually, emotionally. It was his personality that attracted women. It attracted everybody. (November 22, 2000, Lahore)

Wahid Bakhsh had a disproportionately large number of female disciples—a notable phenomenon partly explained by his relationship with his own wife. Maqsuda Begam died in Lahore in 1997 where she was receiving treatment for cancer. She lies buried near Wahid Bakhsh within the shrine complex in Allahabad.

Miracles, Ecstasy, and Sobriety

In demeanor, lifestyle, and worldview, Wahid Bakhsh embodied the traditional paradigm of Chishti sainthood. In both his public writings and private interactions with disciples the *shaykh* championed the *shari'a* and *sunna* as the unassailable foundation of Sufi faith and practice. Wahid Bakhsh wrote extensively on Sufi ritual practice and spiritual training. As chapter 5 will demonstrate, he was especially known as a passionate defender of the Chishti tradition of *sama'*. Yet like his mentor Zauqi Shah the *shaykh* was careful to insist on the absolute necessity of maintaining sobriety and ritual propriety.

In keeping with Chishti doctrine, Wahid Bakhsh downplayed the significance of saintly miracles. "Miracles relate to a much lower level and are sometimes possible at the hands of the novices and ordinary people having a strong dose of spirituality by birth," he wrote. "But the *awliya' Allah* [Friends of God] do not like to indulge in miracles because miracles cause distraction and block the process of progress."[102] Despite this, many of Wahid Bakhsh's disciples recall tangible demonstrations of his powers of insight and knowledge. In the words of a novice male *murid*, Wahid Bakhsh's attitude toward miracles falls within the purview of prophetic precedent:

Normally Hazrat Wahid Bakhsh Sahab would never show that he could perform miracles. He said, "Our Prophet Hazrat Muhammad, God bless and grant him salvation, never performed miracles, so why should I? Who am I to do such things?" This was his opinion, and rightly so. Despite the fact that I was very

close to him and had a lot of contact with him, I never dared to ask him to perform some miracle. He told me that the holy saints can perform miracles, but
they do not. They do not find it important and that is not their motive, to perform miracles and impress people. Their goal is simply to be close to Almighty
Allah, to seek His guidance and love. (November 5, 2000, Lahore)

Lifestyle

On a personal level, Wahid Bakhsh is perhaps best remembered for practicing
what he preached. Throughout his life, the *shaykh* followed a simple, ascetic
lifestyle. Disciples recall that he ate little, slept little, and always lived in very
humble surroundings; his only material possessions of note, they assert, were
his books. Another anecdote about Wahid Bakhsh's wife provides further evidence of the intense piety and self-discipline that guided the *shaykh's* life.
According to a senior male *murid*,

> Captain Sahab, may God have mercy upon him, was very lucky to have a very
> sincere wife. She was also a favorite of the saints. When she was newly married,
> Captain Sahab needed some money for a good purpose. She offered all of her
> ornaments, her jewelry. Those were sold and given for that purpose, but she
> missed them. At night she saw a dream of Khwaja Gharib Nawaz [the saint,
> Mu'in ad-Din Chishti], may God have mercy upon him, riding on a horse. He
> was in the form of a very handsome prince, and wearing a lot of jewelry. Even
> his horse was draped in precious jewelry. He questioned her, "Do you want me
> or this jewelry?" She said, "I want you." He replied, "Then everything is all
> right. If you want jewelry, I can give you more than this. Why are you sorrow-
> ful? If you want me, I am yours. You have decided and now there is no prob-
> lem." (April 29, 2001, Bahawalpur)

Here again a private dream enters into the *silsila's* shared hagiographical narrative, serving as a vital pedagogical device. Echoing the story of Ammi Jan—
the wife of Shahidullah—Maqsuda Begam's dream of the paradigmatic figure
of South Asian Chishti Sufism symbolizes the Sufi adept's necessary surrender of worldly pleasure for spiritual gain.

Public and Political Life

Wahid Bakhsh spent fifty-five years immersed in the Sufi path. For the last
seventeen years of his life he maintained an especially demanding schedule as
both a teaching *shaykh* and public writer. Until his death in 1995, he continued to guide his own large corps of disciples while serving as the *silsila's*
chronicler and public mouthpiece. What emerges from Wahid Bakhsh's collective writings is an image of the *shaykh* as a public intellectual and polemi-
cist who thought deeply and critically about the challenges of the twentieth
century for South Asian Muslims. Beyond the principal focus on Sufi thought
and practice, his writings ask probing questions about Pakistani identity and
its relationship to Muslim unity. In the face of changing geopolitical realities,

his works seek a balance between loyalty toward the nation and a commitment to a broader, universal Islamic community (*umma*).

In the minds of prominent disciples, Wahid Bakhsh's flair for words was itself another sign of his lofty spiritual status. In the words of a female disciple and family member, his scholarly bent was nothing less than a Divine gift:

> The saints are directly guided by the Holy Prophet, God bless him and grant him salvation. The orders to write come from him directly. Once I remember Hazrat Wahid Bakhsh told me that when he was very young he went for pilgrimage to Mecca (*umra*). He was coming out of the Prophet's mosque when somebody came up to him and gave him a pen. From that day he started writing. What does that indicate? He certainly had the intellect, not everybody can write. Yet he was especially guided to do this work. (June 17, 2001, Lahore)

Chapter 3 explores Wahid Bakhsh's public and political life in detail through a survey of his literary legacy. As we will see, through his writings the *shaykh* mounted a concerted defense of Sufi thought and practice within the combative discursive space of contemporary Pakistan.

CONCLUSION

Sainthood is a profoundly social phenomena, whatever its guise and wherever its location. Holy persons are born, live, and die, but they are *made* into saints. The process of emplotting the lives of pious individuals in sacred biographies involves a complex and creative act of interpretation. Sainthood is negotiated in dynamic public discourses and then memorialized in both oral narratives and hagiographical texts. Every sacred biography is shaped by an idealized, metahistorical sacred past. At the same, it must respond to localized settings and particularized discourses. In the context of contemporary Pakistan, the public and private wrangling over Sufi doctrine and practice has effectively transformed the Sufi saint into "a kind of nodal point where these political and personal processes come together."[103] Amid a cacophony of competing voices, the *wali Allah*—the Sufi "Friend of God"—remains an enduring, if at times controversial, symbol of Muslim piety in twenty-first-century South Asia.

The sacred biographies of Muhammad Zauqi Shah, Shahidullah Faridi, and Wahid Bakhsh Sial Rabbani conform to the hagiographical habitus of Indo-Muslim sainthood. Like their premodern Chishti predecessors, these twentieth-century *shaykhs* are remembered for the depth of their religious knowledge, the rigors of their spiritual training, their unwavering commitment to both their nuclear and spiritual families, and, above all, their intense piety and sanctity. At the same time, the *shaykhs'* lives and legacies are indelibly marked by the ideologies and institutions of modernity. Their life experiences provided this trio of twentieth-century Chishti Sabiri masters with a unique perspective on Sufism and its relation to colonial and postcolonial structures of authority, knowledge, and power. Unlike their *madrasa*-trained *'ulama* counterparts, these *shaykhs* were educated in Western-style universities. They were multilingual, urban, and cosmopolitan and moved fluidly in multiple cultural complexes and epistemological universes. In the face of momentous social change, the *shaykhs* found a way to communicate Sufi teachings in modern idioms and accommodate Sufi practices to the changing realities of twentieth-century life in late colonial India and postcolonial Pakistan. Their collective legacy established a new style of Sufi leadership that now shapes the Chishti Sabiri order in the twenty-first century.

In many ways, the story of these twentieth-century Chishti Sabiri masters is not entirely unique. Other *shaykhs* from multiple Sufi orders also struggled to adapt tradition to the shifting landscape of postcolonial South Asia. With his constant travel, polemical writings, and direct political engagement, Shaykh Jama'at 'Ali Shah (d. 1951), for instance, initiated a similar model of leadership for the Naqshbandi Mujaddidi order in India. The *shaykh* actively engaged in polemical debates and founded an organization called the Anjuman-i Khuddam as-Sufiyya to "promote a mediatory brand of Sufism and to meet the attacks of Deobandis, Ahmadis, Ahl-i Hadith and Arya Samajis."[104] Shaykh Khwaja Hasan Nizami (1878–1955) did much the same for the Chishti Nizami *silsila* in India, communicating Islamic Sufism in a new idiom through his public writings, institution building, and pan-Islamic activism.[105] Yet Muhammad Zauqi Shah, Shahidullah Faridi, and Wahid Bakhsh Sial Rabbani are distinguished by their concerted efforts to root Chishti Sabiri history, doctrine, and practice in the contested landscape of postcolonial Pakistan. Chapter 3 delves deeper into the *shaykhs'* voluminous public writings—a diverse corpus of texts that valorize Sufism as the bedrock of an imagined Pakistani religious and national identity. This vision continues to inspire a new generation of Chishti Sabiri adepts who now use the instruments of mass media to communicate Sufi identity to an expanding, global audience well beyond the order's traditional South Asian milieu.

CHAPTER 3

IMAGINING SUFISM: THE PUBLICATION OF CHISHTI SABIRI IDENTITY

It is often said that the Sufi path transcends the boundaries of discursive thought and the limits of language itself. Yet Sufi masters past and present have rarely been at a loss for words. While the tradition's inner dimensions may ultimately be ineffable, Sufis have managed to produce a vast and remarkably diverse range of texts. In today's South Asia, a broad spectrum of Sufi works are written, published, and consumed. Communicated in myriad languages in both poetry and prose, Sufi works explore history, doctrine, and practice. Others enter the more mundane realm of politics and polemics. As a comprehensive system of knowledge and practice, Sufism continues to engage both inward (*batin*) and the outward (*zahir*)—the mind and the body, the individual and society, religion and politics.

This chapter explores the inscription of Chishti Sabiri identity in twentieth-century South Asia through a study of the literary legacy of three Pakistani spiritual masters: Muhammad Zauqi Shah, Shahidullah Faridi, and Wahid Bakhsh Sial Rabbani. From the outset it is important to emphasize that this trio was, first and foremost, a group of teaching *shaykhs*. As heirs to a long and storied Indo-Muslim Sufi teaching tradition, their principal loyalties, commitments, and identities centered on their primary roles as spiritual mentors. Even so, they each recognized the need to articulate the Chishti Sabiri tradition to a broader audience through public—and polemical—discourse. Evoking the *shari'a*-minded, socially engaged, reformist Sufism of their nineteenth-century Chishti Sabiri predecessors, the *shaykhs* entered the contested public sphere to stake their own claims to Islamic authority and authenticity. Like the Chishti Sabiri masters, political activists, and Deoband founders Hajji Imdad Allah and Rashid Ahmad Gangohi before them, they believed that a Sufi master must be both a paragon of moral virtue and a public spokesman for his community. In response to the shifting landscape of the late colonial and early postcolonial eras, Muhammad Zauqi Shah,

Shahidullah Faridi, and Wahid Bakhsh Sial Rabbani each searched for a resolution to the incongruities and ambiguities of South Asian Muslim identity. Defending the orthodoxy of Sufi doctrine and practice, these Sufi masters imagined and articulated an alternative Pakistani identity that was *simultaneously* Muslim, modern, and mystic.

In the following pages, I explore the role of twentieth-century Chishti Sabiri masters as public writers by highlighting the salient themes and key rhetorical strategies in select texts from their vast literary corpus. While subsequent chapters draw on the *shaykh's* voluminous writings on Sufi ritual practice, here I focus more narrowly on their political (and polemical) works. The bulk of my analysis spotlights two lengthy works by Wahid Bakhsh Sial Rabbani. Together, these texts encapsulate the overarching Chishti Sabiri project to defend Sufism as the essence of Islamic orthodoxy and a vital dimension of Pakistani national identity. I conclude with an analysis of the current Chishti Sabiri publication campaign in both Pakistan and Malaysia. Through the translation and publication of important Sufi texts—in particular the writings of its own *shaykhs*—the contemporary *silsila* uses texts to defend its history and practices from critics. At the same time, Chishti Sabiris aim to transcend the limits of language, culture, and geography and reach a new, global audience through the creative use of emergent technologies such as the Internet. I view these efforts as a striking case study of postcolonial, mass media Sufism—and yet another example of the Chishti Sabiri order's dynamic attempt to forge an alternative modernity in the twenty-first century.

MASS MEDIA SUFISM

Although the extensive writings of Muhammad Zauqi Shah, Shahidullah Faridi, and Wahid Bakhsh Sial Rabbani explore a variety of themes, they are ultimately concerned with *identity*—about what it means to be a pious Muslim, a committed Sufi, and a loyal Pakistani citizen amid the shifting global landscape of the twentieth century. The articulation of this nexus of identity is no simple thing, however. Why? Because whatever its focus and wherever its location, questions of identity are invariably contextual: enmeshed in complex, interdependent webs of signification rooted in social, historical, and cultural specificity. To state the obvious, *who* we are depends to a great extent on the *where* and *when* of our location. Identity is neither a priori nor inherited. Instead, it is imagined, constructed, and then articulated in narratives—dynamic assemblages of stories about the nature of the self and its relation to others. Whether grounded on language, race, ethnicity, or religion, identity is invariably a fluid construct. It is "relational and incomplete," always in process and under construction.[1] Individuals and communities are free to stake their own claims to identity. Yet these narratives have immediate social consequences once they are communicated in public discursive spaces to a listening—or reading—audience. As Sudipta Kaviraj notes, "Narrative is not for all to hear, for all to participate in to an equal degree. It has a self in which it originates, a self which tells the story. But that self obviously is not soliloquizing or telling a story to itself. It implies an audience, a larger self towards which it is directed, and we can extend the idea to say that the transaction of a narrative creates a kind of narrative contract."[2] In short, the expression of identity—whether personal or collective—constitutes a public, often political act.

From the printing press to cyberspace, the invention, exploitation, and dissemination of mass media technologies have radically transformed the way in which identity is experienced and expressed. Numerous scholars have explored the role of mass media in the formation of networks—whether social, political, or religious—of community. In his groundbreaking work *Imagined Communities*, Benedict Anderson documents the convergence of print technology and capitalism in the rise of the nation—an "imagined political community" bound together by a common "print language."[3] Expanding on Anderson's conclusions, Armando Salvatore argues that the pervasive shift in media intervention marks "a deeper change in the very conditions of production, diffusion and consumption of discourse." He sees this as a "transformation in the 'episteme' of an age," nothing less than a "type of change that potentially affects every discursive formation and influences the modalities themselves of defining the objects of knowledge."[4] This dynamic continues in the early twenty-first century as new forms of media continue to reconfigure the rules of economic consumption, social interaction, political discourse, and religious practice.

In South Asia, new media technologies have played a central role in contestations over the relationship between religious and national identity. In the twilight of the colonial age, India and Pakistan—and later Bangladesh— were first imagined, and then delineated, inscribed, and institutionalized. New passports and redrawn boundaries on maps were merely the final step in a prolonged and often tumultuous process of imagining the nation. Print media, radio, television, film, and most recently the Internet have all been used to reify and reinforce linguistic, religious, and communal divisions. In the postcolonial era, technologies have proved equally important in transforming imagined communities into the concrete political institutions and territorial boundaries that now divide the Subcontinent into separate nations.[5]

South Asia's diverse Muslim communities have long recognized the power of mass media as a tool to communicate their visions of religious identity. Print technology was not established in the Islamic world and among South Asian Muslims until the nineteenth century, 400 years after Gutenberg's invention of moveable type facilitated the dissemination of Martin Luther's German translation of the Bible. The explosion of religious publications in multiple formats and venues brought a new dynamism to Muslim civil society. As historian Francis Robinson notes, "By the 1820's, Muslim reformist leaders in the Indian subcontinent were busily printing tracts. By the 1830s the first Muslim newspapers were being printed. By the 1870s, editions of the Qur'an, and other religious books, were selling in tens of thousands. In the last thirty years of the century, over seven hundred newspapers and magazines in Urdu were started. All who observed the world of printing noted how Muslims understood the power of the press."[6]

This sudden influx of bibliomania among South Asia's Muslims was largely a defensive response. Muslim communities generated their own publications as a weapon in the defense of the faith against the polemical attacks of such Hindu reformists groups such as the Arya Samaj, as well as the campaigns of British colonial administrators and Christian missionaries. Diverse groups of Muslim scholars, intellectuals, and ideologues eventually capitalized on multiple media resources to forward their own agendas. This included Barelwis, Deobandis, Ahl-i Hadith, various Shi'a groups, the followers of Sayyid Ahmad Khan, and, in time, the Jama'at-i Islami. Engaging their rivals head-on, each of these movements published voluminous translations of the Qur'an, *hadith*, and premodern texts. They also wrote and disseminated original tracts in Urdu—from the legal opinions of Muslim jurists (*fatwas*) to political treatises—in an effort to voice their own messages to the reading public at large.

The cumulative effects of this barrage of publications were wide-ranging. The polemical "pamphlet wars" of the nineteenth century that pitted Hindus, Christians, and rival Muslim groups against one another cemented Urdu as the official language of Muslim discourse and identity. In the decades that followed, the expansion of mass media technologies spurred a marked rise in the prevalence of Islamist scripturalist movements, fostered the internationalization of the Muslim community, and encouraged the democratization of religious knowledge as new religious intellects entered the public sphere to challenge the traditional authority of the '*ulama*.[7] Once begun, the transformative impact of mass media on South Asian Muslim consciousness, epistemology, and politics was profound and enduring.

In postcolonial South Asia, the nation-state has never held a monopoly on the use of mass media. Instead, in competition—and at times conflict—with the state, a broad spectrum of political actors has utilized media technologies to broadcast their own discrete messages and claims to authority. As Eickelman and Anderson note, this mirrors a trend found throughout the contemporary Muslim world: "This combination of new media and new contributors to religious and political debates fosters an awareness on the part of all actors of the diverse ways in which Islam and Islamic values can be created and feeds into new senses of a public sphere that is discursive, performative and participative, and not confined to formal institutions recognized by state authorities."[8] The increasing volume and intensity of public debate has further decentered Islamic religious authority in South Asia. In an often combative competition over the mantle of Islamic orthodoxy, mass media technologies now serve a broad spectrum of religious leaders who all claim to speak for Islam.

Sufis have added their own voices to the din of Muslim social discourse. Drawing on both Arab and Ottoman evidence, Muhsin Mahdi has demonstrated that aside from state governments Sufis were in fact the main patrons of printing in Muslim countries during the nineteenth century.[9] In South

Asia, Sufi orders eagerly embraced the print revolution, adopting a variety of media as a mouthpiece to disseminate their messages. These ranged from pamphlets and glossy texts to periodicals, journals, and, more recently, digital Web sites. Contemporary Sufi publications cover an equally expansive range of genres. Vernacular translations of "classical" Arabic and Persian Sufi texts, for instance, are now commonplace. In today's Pakistan, Urdu translations of premodern Sufi masters—Sarraj, Qushayri, Suhrawardi, and Rumi—are readily found on the shelves of local libraries, bookstores, and in the stalls of Urdu bazaars. The writings of contemporary Sufi leaders are also widely available in a variety of formats—from discourses, informal lectures, essays, and biographies to practical manuals on everything from prayer and meditation practices to the use of talismans and charms for healing purposes. As Ernst argues, since many of these publications are available commercially this trend amounts to "a mass marketing of Sufism on an unprecedented scale."[10]

Mass media publications proved to be a highly effective medium for disseminating the messages of Sufi *shaykhs* to a broader public. The widespread distribution of inexpensive books to middle-class consumers opened Sufi knowledge to a vast audience—well beyond the privileged few with access to manuscripts or the intimate, word of mouth exchanges with a Sufi master. These publications gave certain Sufi masters unprecedented fame and influence. The monthly magazine *Risala-yi anwar al-sufiyya* [Magazine of Sufi Illuminations], for example, played a vital role in the propagation and popularity of the teachings of the Naqshbandi master, Jama'at 'Ali Shah (d. 1951).[11] These publications did more than alter the profile of individual masters, however; they fundamentally altered the makeup of both interpersonal relations and Sufi institutional life. In effect, Sufism was transformed from an esoteric community based exclusively on the oral instruction between master and disciple into a public institution. With new confidence and determination, Sufi orders defended their own traditions and identities against the polemical attacks of European Orientalists, Islamists, and modernists alike. As Carl Ernst notes, "The publicizing of Sufism through print and electronic media has brought about a remarkable shift in the tradition. Now advocates of Sufism can defend their heritage by publishing refutations of fundamentalist or modernist attacks on Sufism. In this sense, the media permit Sufism to be contested and defended in the public sphere as one ideology alongside others."[12] In the twentieth and now twenty-first centuries, the Chishti Sabiri order has been particularly adept at appropriating multiple forms of mass media to communicate and defend its own interpretation of Islamic tradition, piety, and practice.

CHISHTI SABIRI *SHAYKHS* AS PUBLIC WRITERS

As modern Pakistani Sufi *shaykhs*, Muhammad Zauqi Shah, Shahidullah Faridi, and Wahid Bakhsh Sial Rabbani combined spiritual pedagogy and practice with literary acumen in order to ground Chishti Sabiri Sufism in a distinctly modern idiom. Together they produced an eclectic range of texts, written in both Urdu and English. In them, the *shaykhs* valorized Chishti Sabiri identity as a defense against the tradition's Muslim critics and a barrier against Western cultural encroachment and political hegemony. Addressing a diverse Pakistani and international audience, they employed technical and scientific vocabulary in combination with mass media to demonstrate the enduring relevance of the doctrinal teachings and ritual practices at the heart of Sufi identity.

In all this the *shaykhs* were not unique. Other notable twentieth-century South Asian Sufi masters have pursued similar reformist agendas—the Chishti Nizami masters Sayyid Mehr Ali Shah (1856–1937) and Khwaja Hasan Nizami (1878–1955), for example, as well as the Naqshbandi activist, Pir Jama'at 'Ali Shah (1841–1951).[13] The combined efforts of these twentieth-century Chishti Sabiri leaders, however, constitute a marked deviation from the precedent of their premodern predecessors who largely avoided urban spaces and networks of royal patronage in favor of a life of spiritual quietism and withdrawal in rural locales. As Ernst and Lawrence note, by accepting the "challenge of mobilizing the same resources of past generations" the *shaykhs* entered the public sphere to articulate "creative responses to new realities."[14]

The contemporary Chishti Sabiri writing project envisions an alternative religious identity with Sufism as the heart of Islamic orthodoxy. The very fact that the *shaykhs* felt compelled to publicly defend Sufism's religious credentials reflects the increasing politicization of Islam in postcolonial South Asia. For South Asian Muslims, the twentieth century marks the culmination of what historian Marshall Hodgson calls the "Great Western Transmutation" (hereafter, the GWT)—the bureaucratization, rationalization, technicalization, and systemization of every dimension of human life. In the face of such momentous social changes, Muslims were forced to reevaluate their own history, faith, and practices.[15] They did so in remarkably diverse ways. As we have seen, through both education and personal experience this trio of Chishti Sabiri *shaykhs* was intimately acquainted with the institutions and ideology of the British colonial state. Through a range of essays, articles, journals, and books, they each directly and forcefully address this legacy. Their numerous Urdu translations of premodern Persian *malfuzat* texts highlight the essential continuity of the Chishti Sabiri tradition. At the same time, the *shaykh's* own original works attempt to accommodate Sufism to contemporary life while rethinking key categories of postcolonial modernity.

Throughout their writings, the *shaykhs* stake a middle ground amid the range of Indo-Muslim responses to the GWT.[16] Like a host of other Muslim modernists, they embrace science, educational reform, and independent legal reasoning (*ijtihad*), recognizing the pressing need to adapt to social change. The *shaykhs* also champion egalitarianism, civil liberties, and socioeconomic justice as essential features of the Qur'anic worldview. Yet they remain wary of Euro-American cultural and political hegemony and warn against the wholesale adoption of Western political models of liberal democracy. In line with *'ulama* traditionalists, the *shaykhs* view the Qur'an, Prophetic *sunna*, and *shari'a* as the indispensable foundation of Islamic piety and practice. They challenge the *'ulama's* exclusivist claims to interpretation, however. Islamic authority and authenticity, they assert, are ultimately rooted in *ma'rifa* (the direct, intuitive knowledge experienced through Sufi practice) rather than *'ilm* (the rational, discursive book knowledge taught in traditional *madrasas*). Like their Islamist counterparts, these Chishti Sabiri masters reject the ideology of secularization, viewing Islam as a comprehensive way of life. At the same time, the *shaykhs* critique the Islamists' exclusivist and literal interpretations of scripture, and they decry Islamists' narrow emphasis on Islam's political and ideological dimensions. Chishti Sabiris lament the spread of Wahhabi doctrine and the rise of sectarian identities and vehemently defend Sufi doctrine and ritual practices against all forms of criticism. Maneuvering between these divergent schools of thought demands a remarkable degree of flexibility and creative adaptation—a dynamic approach that itself belies the Orientalist portrait of contemporary Sufism as an intransigent, ossified relic.

In their critique of colonial and postcolonial structures of power and knowledge, the Chishti Sabiri *shaykhs* alternatively reject, appropriate, and manipulate certain key categories of modernity. Taken as a whole, the order's writing project "does not necessarily represent a rejection of modernity *per se*, but can be seen as a reconstruction of modernity according to Islamic models and motifs."[17] This hybridity is clearly evident in the *shaykhs'* portrayal of Sufism's public and private dimensions. Their writings constantly emphasize Sufism's enduring relevance as the very essence of Islamic orthodoxy. Sufism is a vital component of Indo-Muslim identity, they insist, that impacts every dimension of social life—from moral behavior and aesthetics to social and political ethics. At times, however, the *shaykhs* also characterize Sufism as a distinctly private matter—a closed, interpersonal network of knowledge and practice. This balancing act allows them to distinguish Sufi tradition from both the official Islam of the state and that of their Islamist counterparts. The *shaykhs* view both as one-dimensional and essentially political ideologies.

Muhammad Qasim Zaman traces a similar dynamic in his discussion of the contemporary *'ulama* in Pakistan. As Zaman illustrates, "The very effort to preserve Islam 'unchanged' in a rapidly changing world involves considerable redefinition of what Islam means, where to locate it in society, and how best to serve its interests. For the Pakistani 'ulama one way to serve such interests is to define Islam as occupying a distinct sphere in society and to equate the autonomy of this sphere and their own authority and identity with a textually embodied religious tradition."[18] Chishti Sabiri *shaykhs* assert a distinct, autonomous sphere of their own. They locate this space within an interpersonal network of Sufi teaching tradition. This network of knowledge and practice is communicated via the master-disciple relationship and embodied in ritual practices. Much like their *'ulama* counterparts, these Chishti Sabiri masters are primarily concerned with preserving tradition. To do so, they define Sufism as a totalizing system—a multifaceted worldview and a comprehensive way of life. In essence, the *shaykhs'* teachings characterize Sufism as a personal spiritual discipline experienced in a communal teaching network, a comprehensive moral and ethical system, and, most significantly, an essential component of South Asian Muslim history and Pakistani national identity.

Pakistan is front and center in the contemporary Chishti Sabiri imagination. Indeed, Muhammad Zauqi, Shahidullah Faridi, and Wahid Bakhsh Sial Rabbani were ardent Pakistani nationalists. They were unwavering in their support for an independent homeland for South Asian Muslims and their optimism for Pakistan's future. This too distinguishes them from their Islamist and 'ulama peers, many of whom resisted the independence movement and lamented Partition because they feared it would further divide and weaken South Asia's minority Muslim communities. In keeping with the famous hadith, "Love of the homeland is part of one's faith" (hubb al-watan min al-iman), the shaykhs' writings sacralize Pakistan as nothing less than a Divine reward. At the same time, they define the silsila as a sacred moral community antecedent to the nation-state. For these Chishti Sabiri masters, Sufi identity is rooted in genealogy, communicated in the intimate connection between master and disciple, and performed in ritual practices. Resisting co-optation by the postcolonial state and defending the Chishti Sabiri tradition in public polemical debate, the shaykhs champion Sufism as the enduring bedrock of Indo-Muslim identity.

Shaykh Muhammad Zauqi Shah drew on his personal experiences and expertise as a journalist to inscribe a new vision of twentieth-century Chishti Sabiri identity. Through education and profession, he developed an affinity for language and an appreciation for the power of print, both of which he used to voice his own opinions on contemporary political affairs. Significantly, Zauqi Shah's training as a journalist places him in the company of numerous twentieth-century Muslim reformists who also employed their acumen for the written word to forward political agendas, from Muhammad 'Abduh (1849–1905) to Mawdudi (1903–1979). As a young man in his late twenties, Zauqi Shah worked for four separate Urdu newspapers in Lahore. Between 1904 and 1906, he served as the editor of a weekly English language newspaper al-Haq, published first in Hyderabad, Sindh, and subsequently in Karachi. During this time, he was appointed to cover the Prince of Wales' tour of India. As one of six correspondents from the Indian Muslim press, he traveled with the prince's entourage from November 1905 to March 1906, writing a series of articles on various social and political issues. From August 1907 to February 1908, Zauqi Shah served a final stint as the editor of another newspaper in Karachi called al-Wakil, before resigning to embark on a series of independent business ventures.[19]

After his formal initiation into the Chishti Sabiri order in Lucknow in 1914, Zauqi Shah abandoned his career as a journalist in order to immerse himself entirely in Sufi practice. His role as spiritual teacher, however, was profoundly colored by his earlier professional experience. Throughout his long life, Zauqi Shah continued to write. In a wide-ranging series of essays, articles, and books—published in numerous forums in both Urdu and

English—he wrote on Sufi history, doctrine, and ritual practice. *Sirr-i dilbaran* [The Heart-Ravishing Secret], a comprehensive encyclopedia of Sufi terminology, is undoubtedly his magnum opus. Begun in Peshawar in 1923, this lexicon, written in Urdu, was compiled over a number of years. The text was first published by the *silsila* in 1951 and is now in its fifth edition (1985).[20] Zauqi Shah also founded a Sufi magazine titled *Anwar al-Quds* [The Lights of Holiness], published in Bombay from October 1925 to February 1927.[21] Most remarkably, the *shaykh* experimented with a new form of literary expression in *Bada u Saghir* [The Wine and the Cup]. Set in colonial Bombay, this unusual Urdu spiritual novel centers on a lengthy dialogue between the Mughal Emperor Shah Jahan and his queen, Mumtaz Mahal. The entire story is described as a metaphor for the states and stations of the Sufi spiritual path. The book was inspired by a trip to the tomb of Qazi Mahmud Darya'i in Ahmedabad in 1919 where Zauqi Shah witnessed three miracles. According to *Tarbiyat al-'ushshaq*, "This shrine confers the blessings of poetry. Yet he [Zauqi Shah] used to say, 'I am not a poet, so for that reason I began to write a novel, *Bada u Saghir*.' He was overpowered with such enthusiasm that he continued writing [the novel] while seated on a bullock cart. When he ran out of paper, he began writing on scraps of newspaper."[22] Though an anomaly in his corpus, *Bada u Saghir* is certainly Zauqi Shah's most intriguing literary contribution.

Zauqi Shah's enthusiasm for the written word was well suited to the heightened atmosphere of late colonial India. Through his writings, he transformed himself into a public apologist for Sufism. His works can be seen as an attempt to counter the discourses of British Orientalism and Islamist movements on the one hand and the anti-Muslim polemics of Christian missionaries and Hindu nationalists on the other. The *shaykh* was especially critical of the ideology of Wahhabism and the politics of the Jama'at-i Islami. He even wrote a lengthy article critiquing the views of Mawlana Mawdudi.[23] Zauqi Shah often highlighted his own spiritual connections with Hajji Imdad Allah al-Muhajir Makki and Rashid Ahmad Gangohi, founders of the Deoband *madrasa*. Yet he rejected the scriptural reformism of the movement that championed their legacy while erasing their Chishti Sabiri roots. Throughout his writings, Zauqi Shah loudly asserts the orthodoxy of Sufism. In an article entitled "Sufism"—first published in a journal *The Islamic Review* in London in 1933—he writes,

> It is wrongly supposed that Sufism has nothing to do with Islam. In fact, it is the life and soul of Islam. It is really Islam in its higher and practical aspects. It is action and the consequent realization. It is a process of purification of the soul. It is not an idle and unproductive philosophy. It is not a set of fresh beliefs in any way different from the teachings of Islam. It is not a series of secretive teachings of any fantastic nature. It is work on proper lines, and as a result of such work and the consequent purification of the soul, it is enlightenment and realization.[24]

Zauqi Shah's rhetorical defense of Sufism often involves a highly polemical engagement with other religious traditions. In numerous articles, the *shaykh* asserts the supremacy of Sufism over other mystical paths. While living in Hyderabad, Deccan, Zauqi Shah began writing an ambitious book in Urdu titled *Kutub-i samawi par ek nazar* [A Glance at the Heavenly Books]. In it he planned to compare the sacred scriptures of Christianity, Judaism, and Hinduism with the message of the Qur'an. Though he completed the sections on the Torah and the Gospels, his analysis of the Vedas and the Qur'an were never finished. Nevertheless, extracts from the manuscript were published in *Tarjuman al-Qur'an* [Interpreter of the Qur'an], a journal owned and edited by Mawlana Mawdudi, the famous Islamist ideologue and founder of the political party, Jama'at-i Islami.[25] This seems a curious choice given the *shaykh's* dim view of his Islamist counterpart. Yet as Ernst and Lawrence argue, "Despite his opposition to Maududi's authoritarianism, Zauqi essentially agreed with Maududi's analysis of the crisis facing Indian Muslims; both felt that reviving Islam through political means was absolutely necessary, but they differed considerably in their interpretation of what Islam actually meant."[26] In Zauqi Shah's view, the innermost dimensions of Islamic spiritual truth were accessible only to those who accepted the discipline and rigors of the Sufi path.

The most controversial of Zauqi Shah's polemical remarks on religion are found in *New Searchlight on the Vedic Aryans.*[27] This pamphlet was originally published in the Delhi Urdu newspaper *Manshur* in installments on June 20, June 27, and July 4, 1943. An English version was simultaneously published in the Allahabad paper *Onward* on June 14 and June 21. In this brief but highly charged text, Zauqi Shah directly responds to an article "The Arctic Home of the Vedas" written in 1903 by the ardent Hindu national politician, Lokmanya Bal Gangadhar Tilak. The *shaykh* marshals archeological, scholarly, and scriptural evidence to deduce that both the Aryan and Dravidian races were originally Semitic tribes from the Middle East. Zauqi Shah summarizes his argument in a discourse recorded in *Tarbiyat al-'ushshaq*:

> In *New Searchlight on the Vedic Aryans* I have made it clear that the Hindus and Jews have a common origin. Their customs and habits are identical. Notice how the Jews have harassed the people in Europe and America with their tricks, and the Hindus have fanned the flames of discord and corruption in India. The First and Second World Wars were both caused by the Jews. The real reason is that these people are great capitalists and owners of immense weapons factories. They actually want war so that the demand for their weapons increases and their business progresses. This is the extent of the savagery and vileness of their thinking. You will see, these people will also be the cause of World War Three.[28]

Zauqi Shah's polemic needs to be understood in the context of the confrontational communal politics of the late colonial period. In the wake of the Second World War, the *shaykh* was profoundly concerned about the future of India's Muslims in the face of an increasingly aggressive Hindu nationalism. He responds to attacks against Indo-Muslim civilization by denigrating Hindu history and identity and then conflating it with a vision of a parallel global Jewish conspiracy. As Ernst and Lawrence note, "Here Zauqi Shah regrettably opened the door to acceptance of notorious anti-Semitic propaganda, such as the apocryphal 'Protocols of the Elders of Zion,' within the Chishti order."[29] These attitudes have indeed continued. In his book *Reactivization of Islam*, for example, Wahid Bakhsh Sial Rabbani echoes this rhetoric, quoting extensively from the "Protocols" in a chapter entitled "Glimpses of a Zionist Conspiracy."[30] At times, Chishti Sabiri *shaykhs* have characterized attacks against Islam—and Sufism in particular—as part of a much larger anti-Muslim conspiracy.

Zauqi Shah's writings went hand in hand with his lifelong commitment to political activism. The *shaykh* was a fervent supporter of the campaign for an independent state for the Muslims of South Asia. He attended the first meeting of the Muslim League in Karachi in 1907 and formally joined the organization in Ajmer in 1940. He subsequently was elected vice president of the League's district and provincial administration and served as the head of the Ajmer Sirat Committee. As a member of the All India Council, Zauqi Shah attended the Muslim League's annual session in Madras on April 8, 1941, and he remained active in the organization until his death a decade later. His myriad activities resulted in a broad network of political contacts and personal friendships. Between 1937 and 1947, the *shaykh* exchanged a series of letters in English with Pakistan's future leader Muhammad 'Ali Jinnah (1876–1948).[31] This lengthy and lively correspondence encompasses a wide variety of topics. In these letters, for example, Zauqi Shah documents his involvement with the Muslim League, rails against Gandhi and the Congress Party, warns Jinnah against Hindu political designs, and makes an impassioned plea for Muslim unity. The *shaykh* concludes a lengthy letter written on February 25, 1939: "As a Sufi, let me assure you that, in spite of all their faults and weaknesses, the Muslims are going to have a brilliant future. My recent Sufistic revelations fully confirm what I have been feeling intuitively for some time—that, before long, Islam will become the only dominating force in the world. But that does not mean that the Muslims will not have to make big sacrifices. Of course, no sacrifice is too great for it. So, let us take courage and dash on. The present happenings in the world only encourage us to push forward."[32] Despite the ambiguities and dangers of the times, Zauqi Shah maintained a unwavering optimism about the future of South Asia's Muslims.

Amid his political work, incessant travels, and spiritual duties as a teaching *shaykh*, Zauqi Shah's writing continued unabated. Even as his health failed, he published a series of articles in Urdu language and English language newspapers. This included numerous essays that appeared in the Karachi paper *Dawn* in 1945 and 1946, as well as a regular column in the short-lived English language weekly *The People's Voice*, which ran for several months beginning in December 1947.[33] Zauqi Shah summarized his political views in a short Urdu pamphlet titled *Islam, Pakistan aur jamhuriyat* [Islam, Pakistan and Democracy] published in 1950. A number of his more political writings—including his reciprocal correspondence with Jinnah—were eventually compiled and published by the Chishti Sabiri order in 1949 in a volume entitled

Muzamin-i Zauqi [The Articles of Zauqi]. An English version of this book was reprinted in Lahore in 1998 under the title *Letters of a Sufi Saint to Jinnah*. Collectively, these texts cover a wide range of contemporary issues, both local and global. They include lengthy diatribes against Western civilization, liberal democracy, modernity, and secularization. Other key themes that permeate Zauqi Shah's political works are Islam's role as a comprehensive system, the potential of Pakistan as an Islamic state, and the imminent dangers of Pakistan's internal discord.

Among today's Chishti Sabiri disciples, Zauqi Shah is remembered for both his advanced spiritual status and political clout as an early Pakistani nationalist. In the words of one young Pakistani disciple, the *shaykh's* example inspired his successors as well: "I think the *silsila* and the *shaykhs* have definitely been patriotic. They were Pakistani nationalists, all of them. In the Pakistan movement, the religious political parties were largely against the creation of Pakistan. It was more the *shaykhs*, the Sufis who supported it. I know that in the *silsila*, Hazrat Shah Shahidullah, Wahid Bakhsh Sahab, all of them were extremely pro-Pakistan. Hazrat Zauqi Shah Sahab was living at a time when he simply had to take sides [on political issues]. And I think he took the side that was destined to succeed" (March 22, 2001, Islamabad).

In the introduction to *Tarbiyat al-'ushshaq*, Wahid Bakhsh Sial Rabbani pushes this argument even further. In his alternative history, Zauqi Shah is eulogized as the true spiritual founder of Pakistan. In his words, "This matter is not generally known by the people, but the elect know it: while Qaid-i Azam [Muhammad 'Ali Jinnah] was the outward founder of Pakistan, Hazrat Muhammad Zauqi Shah was its inward, spiritual founder. The fact is that from ancient times Chishti saints have played a major role in the conquest of Hindustan . . . That is why Hazrat, may God have mercy upon him, often used to say, 'Hindustan is the inheritance of the Chishtis.'"[34] As this retelling of Indo-Muslim history suggests, the Chishti Sabiri historical project deviates radically from that of its Islamist counterparts. Here Sufi saints are anything but marginalized, navel-gazing mystics. Instead, Chishti Sabiri masters are positioned at the forefront of both religious and political life. In this counterpolemic, Shaykh Muhammad Zauqi Shah continues the legacy of his spiritual ancestors—guiding and sanctifying the evolution of South Asian Islam from the eleventh-century Delhi Sultanate through the birth of the "Land of the Pure" (Pakistan) in 1947.

Zauqi Shah's successors, Shahidullah Faridi and Wahid Bakhsh Sial Rabbani, never matched their predecessor's political activism. Neither of them was as publicly vocal nor as openly involved in politics as their *shaykh*. Both, however, followed Zauqi Shah's example by taking up the pen. As teachers, writers, and publicists, they were active in the efforts to articulate and disseminate the *silsila's* identity through the mass media. As a result of their efforts, there is a remarkable continuity of practice, teaching style, and public posturing in the twenty-first-century Chishti Sabiri order.

According to the *silsila's* contemporary biographers, it was Shahidullah Faridi who inherited the Chishti Sabiri prerogative for the spiritual and political protection of the Subcontinent in the wake of Partition. Wahid Bakhsh makes this explicit: "After Hazrat Mawlana Zauqi Shah, may God have mercy upon him, his principal successor [*khalifa-i a'zam*], Hazrat Shah Shahidullah Faridi, may God have mercy upon him, received the political charge of India. The people of spiritual insight know well the apparent [*zahiri*] and hidden [*batini*] work he carried out for the politics of the country."[35] Shahidullah Faridi was renowned for his intense piety, powerful personality, and deep erudition. Given his enduring reputation as an accomplished Chishti Sabiri master, however, it is somewhat surprising the *shaykh* wrote far less than either Zauqi Shah or Wahid Bakhsh. More importantly, none of the *shaykh's* works expressly engage political matters. As I suggested previously, it is likely that Shahidullah's personal background as an Englishman and Muslim convert may have contributed to this reluctance to explicitly address the political realm. Instead, his writings focus exclusively on spiritual matters, from Sufi history and doctrine to the nuances of ritual practice. Though he was fluent in Urdu and communicated with the bulk of his followers in their native tongue, most of Shahidullah's writings were published as essay compilations in English. This includes *Inner Aspects of Faith*, *Everyday Practice in Islam*, *Spirituality in Religion*, and *The Moral Message of God and His Prophet*.[36] Beyond his own literary efforts, Shahidullah played a central role in continuing and expanding the *silsila's* publication campaign. In his last will and testament, the *shaykh* emphasizes the vital importance of the order's books and directs several senior *murids* to carry on with this important work.[37]

Though never as overtly political as his predecessor, Shahidullah remained deeply concerned with Pakistan's survival and development. His Urdu spiritual discourses, in fact, contain selective but insightful lectures on a broad range of relevant political topics. *Malfuzat-i shaykh*, for example, details the *shaykh's* views on Islamic political theory and the support of Sufis for just political rule, secularism in Europe, *hudud* punishments and social reform, Shi'ism and sectarian politics, and the spiritual duties of *jihad*.[38] The *shaykh's* own disciples recall that Shahidullah was on occasion extremely frank about his opinions of Pakistan's political leaders and their policies, particularly after the emergence of a narrow, Arab-centric Islamism under General Zia al-Haq. Yet to this day, Shahidullah is remembered more for his personal piety, charisma, and advanced spiritual status than for his contributions as a writer. A senior Pakistani female disciple draws an explicit parallel with the Prophet Muhammad to explain Shahidullah's pedagogical style:

> This is what I feel about my *shaykh*. Studying at Oxford, with such perfection in English, he could have written much more for the Western world. I have often thought about these things, because many people used to ask me, "Has he written any books?" Of course, his book *Inner Aspects of Faith* is wonderful. But you know what I feel? He was a replica of our Prophet, God bless him and grant him salvation. Our Prophet was an illiterate man. He had not written a word. People would simply come and sit with him and get converted to Islam. This *was* Islam in those days. With Hazrat Sahab [Shahidullah Faridi] it was the

same. I remember that when newcomers would come to meet him for the first time, they would sit with him. Muslims and non-Muslims too. The moment they would sit with him, they would be quiet and they would not dare utter a word. I think that was the presence that was transferred to him from the Prophet, God bless him and grant him salvation. That is why he didn't write that many books. (June 17, 2001, Lahore)

This is a statement that I heard repeated, in various iterations, during my interviews. It suggests that Shahidullah Faridi, like the Prophet Muhammad before him, was a true spiritual master who inspired anyone who met him through the sheer force of his personal charisma and piety.

THE WRITINGS OF SHAYKH WAHID BAKHSH SIAL RABBANI

Following Partition, it was Wahid Bakhsh Sial Rabbani who clearly emerged as the Chishti Sabiri order's principal spokesman and public ideologue. With boundless energy, he composed a voluminous corpus of texts, wide-ranging in scope and scale, written in both Urdu and English. The *shaykh* published numerous Urdu translations of classical Persian biographical texts, including the discourses of Farid al-Din Ganj-i Shakkar, *Maqam-i Ganj Shakkar;* Shaykh 'Abd ar-Rahman Chishti's *malfuzat, Mirat al-asrar* [Mirror of Secrets]; and al-Hujwiri's famous tome titled *Kashf al-mahjub* [The Unveiling of the Concealed].[39] Wahid Bakhsh also wrote numerous original treatises on ritual practice, as well as overtly polemical pieces in defense of the Chishti Sabiri tradition. Many of these works are now easily found in the Urdu bookstores of Karachi and Lahore. Wahid Bakhsh clearly inherited the literary mantle from his mentor. In fact, Zauqi Shah's impact is palpable in the content and style of his writings. According to a senior Pakistani *murid,* this was all by design: "Zauqi Shah started with pen and paper and finished with pen and paper, and Wahid Bakhsh carried on the work of his *shaykh.* He was assigned this work by Hazrat Shahidullah Sahab" (December 10, 2000, Karachi).

In the following pages I explore two key texts written by Wahid Bakhsh that together encapsulate the essential themes and rhetorical strategies of the entire Chishti Sabiri writing project: *Islamic Sufism* and *The Magnificent Power Potential of Pakistan.* Together, these eclectic works offer a comprehensive rethinking—an alternative vision—of Sufism's place in Islamic history and contemporary Pakistani identity. They each combine local and global discourses to argue for Sufism's orthodoxy and compatibility with nationalism and a scientific worldview. Published in both Urdu and English, these works are clearly aimed at a broad audience of educated Pakistanis, as well as potential international converts and allies. With attention to content and style, I examine these works to illustrate the Chishti Sabiri critique of Orientalist interpretations of Sufism, its rethinking of South Asian Islamicate history, and its valorization of Sufi practice as the bedrock of Pakistani national identity.

The *Shaykh* Strikes Back: *Islamic Sufism*

Islamic Sufism was first published in English in 1984 and subsequently reprinted in several editions, both in Pakistan and Malaysia. Many of its key ideas and much of its rhetoric echo Wahid Bakhsh's Urdu writings, particularly *Mushahada-i haqq*.[40] *Islamic Sufism*, although hardly unique, serves as a useful primer for the *shaykh's* wide-ranging thought. In this eclectic text, he responds directly to pervasive and persistent (mis)interpretations of Sufi history, doctrine, and practice. Marshaling an array of historical, scriptural, and scholarly evidence and brandishing a sharp polemical sword, the *shaykh* reasserts the orthodoxy of Sufism. In a spirited defense of his own tradition, Wahid Bakhsh castigates Western scholars and Islamist ideologues alike for their one-dimensional and reductive portraits of Sufi tradition. Through a wide-ranging and nuanced exposition, he challenges the assumptions, methodologies, and conclusions of Western scholars with a critical eye and sharp tongue.

Wahid Bakhsh begins his exposé by confidently asserting his own credentials as a spiritual master in the Chishti Sabiri *silsila*. Apologizing for his deficiencies in the English language, he declares, "Having been a practicing Sufi for the last forty-five years, it can reasonably be hoped that my understanding of Sufi doctrine is better than that of the competent English scholars who have never practiced this discipline but have looked at it from a distance. So it is perhaps a choice between better understanding expressed in a defective language and defective understanding expressed in better language."[41] This is an intriguing statement. Here Wahid Bakhsh defends his own intellectual turf, claiming the authority and authenticity to speak. Sufi piety, he insists, constitutes a specialized sphere of knowledge to which he has privileged access. Distinguishing himself from foreign academics whose understanding is limited to the second-hand abstractions of books, Wahid Bakhsh asserts an expertise rooted in direct, unmediated experience gained through the rigors of Sufi practice.

Wahid Bakhsh commits a third of *Islamic Sufism*'s 400 pages to a detailed critique of Orientalist characterizations of Sufism in a chapter entitled "The Myth of Foreign Influence of Sufism Exploded." The opening paragraph challenges Sufism's academic interlocutors to task for mistaking the similarities between mystical traditions as proof of outside influences on Sufism. In Wahid Bakhsh's words,

> The storm of allegations of outside influence on Sufism has been raised partly by a section of ill-informed and biased Western scholars popularly known as Orientalists and partly by a small minority of ultra-orthodox and purely exoteric Muslim theologians. Both of these groups have been badly misled by some sort of similarity between the Sufis (*awliya'*) of Islam and the mystics of Christianity, Hinduism, Buddhism, etc. They do not realize that when god is One and Truth is One, the nature of views, beliefs and spiritual experiences of various mystics are bound to be identical.[42]

In the ensuing exposition, Wahid Bakhsh offers a trenchant analysis and refutation of seven principal misconceptions of Sufism propagated by

Western Orientalist scholars. Writing in a direct and unambiguous style, he marshals evidence from disparate sources—Qur'an, *hadith*, Sufi exemplars, and even "respectable" Western experts—to bolster his arguments. I will briefly examine Wahid Bakhsh's critique, point by point.

1. "The first and foremost reason for the misunderstanding of Sufism is their [Orientalists] misunderstanding of Islam itself."[43]

Wahid Bakhsh begins with the assumption that the Christian heritage of most Orientalist scholars inherently biases them against the Qur'an and the Prophet. An objective reading of history, he insists, reveals Europe's debt to the Islamic world whose "learning, art, culture, science and civilization . . . drew Europe out of the quagmire of the Dark Ages and laid the very foundations of the era of science, culture and technology in which we are living today."[44] As evidence of Europe's debt to Islamicate civilization, Wahid Bakhsh lauds the medieval Muslim polymaths, Ibn 'Arabi and al-Ghazali, whose theology, he asserts, had a profound impact on their Christian counterpart Thomas Aquinas. Quoting liberally from the scholarly works of Philip Hitti and A.J. Arberry, Wahid Bakhsh highlights the legacy of Muslim philosophers who preserved and advanced the legacy of Plato and Aristotle while "reconciling philosophy not only with religion but with Sufic [*sic*] theosophy as well."[45] Given his overarching critique of European Orientalism, Wahid Bakhsh's reliance on Western scholarship in this context is particularly intriguing. Elsewhere in *Islamic Sufism* he quotes liberally from numerous scholars, including H.A.R Gibb, Louis Massignon, William Cantwell Smith, R.A Nicholson, Margaret Smith, and Annemarie Schimmel. The *shaykh's* eclectic selection of Western "experts" on Islam even includes an enigmatic quote from James Michener drawn from *Reader's Digest*. Clearly, Wahid Bakhsh has read widely. Yet even as he acknowledges the contributions of select Western academics, the *shaykh* insists that Muslims are fully capable of speaking for (and defending) themselves. In his view, the intellectual and cultural accomplishments of Islamic civilization stand as incontrovertible proof of Islam's sacrality and inherent superiority.

2. "The second reason for the misunderstanding on the part of the Orientalists is that, according to them, the word Sufism (*tasawwuf*) was not in vogue in the time of the Prophet of Islam and that, therefore, it is of an extraneous origin."[46]

Here Wahid Bakhsh argues that each of the Islamic interpretive traditions—including exegesis (*tafsir*), *hadith*, law (*fiqh*), theology (*kalam*), and Sufism—came to full fruition only after the Prophet Muhammad's death. Quoting numerous well-known *hadith*, he asserts that the spiritual practices associated with Sufism were also an integral dimension of faith and practice from Islam's origins. He concludes with a statement from Malik ibn Anas (d. 795) as proof that the actual word *tasawwuf* was in vogue in Islam's first century: "One who indulged in *Tasawwuf*, but did not learn *Fiqah* [*sic*] is a heretic. One who learnt *Fiqah*, but did not practice Sufism is a sinner. One who combined Sufism and *Fiqah* finds the Truth."[47] Islam and Sufism, Wahid Bakhsh asserts, are coeval and coterminous.

3. "The third reason for misunderstanding is the similarity of Sufi phrase-ology to that of Christian and Hindu mysticism and Neoplatonism."[48]

A refutation of outside influences on Sufism is a major focus of Wahid Bakhsh's apologetic, as the subtitle to his book suggests. In this section, the *shaykh* provides lengthy quotations from both A.J. Arberry and Shahidullah Faridi to assert Sufism's firm foundations in Islamic history. He vehemently rejects all allegations of outside influences from other spiritual traditions. Wahid Bakhsh returns to this theme in two later sections of the book entitled "The Strong Influence of Islamic Sufism on Hindu Mysticism" and "The Influence of Sufism on the Hindu Sects, Lingayats (Jangamas) and Siddhars [*sic*]." Quoting liberally from *The Influence of Islam on Indian Culture*, a text by the Indian scholar Tara Chand (b. 1888), he turns the Orientalist argu-ment on its head to assert the widespread influence of Sufi mystics on their South Asian religious counterparts. Wahid Bakhsh concludes with a remark-able statement:

> We have seen that giant Hindu saints, right from Sankara, Ramanuja, Ramanand and Kabir to their illustrious disciples and disciples of their disciples for so many centuries had, under the influence of the company and direct teachings and training of Muslim saints, given up most of the beliefs and doctrines of Hinduism, such as belief in idolatry, transmigration, cremation of the dead, temple worship, death ceremonies and so on. And, moreover, that they had accepted important Islamic beliefs and doctrines, such as the belief in one God and the belief in the genuineness of the Prophet of Islam, and had adopted practices of piety, austerity, righteousness and devotion, to the extent [of performing] five prayers daily, and were at the same time striving for the reconciliation of Islam and Hinduism.[49]

While these are certainly debatable claims, they nonetheless offer key insights into the logic and rhetorical strategy of Wahid Bakhsh's counter-polemic. The intensity of his defensive posturing suggests that the articula-tion of a distinct South Asian Sufi identity was among his highest priorities. In this, Wahid Bakhsh's rhetoric parallels the historical project of his con-temporary Sayyid Abu'l Hasan 'Ali Nadwi (1914–1999). This prominent religious scholar and political activist was best known for his lifelong associa-tion with the reformist movement Nadwat al-'Ulama. In his public writings and political activism, Nadwi was primarily concerned with rejuvenating the position of the 'ulama in Indian society, not with defending Sufism. Like Wahid Bakhsh, however, Nadwi's writings defend the orthodoxy of Indian Islam and attempt to document the intellectual and cultural achievements of Islam in South Asia. And not surprisingly, Nadwi was also highly critical of Islamist ideology.[50]

4. "The fourth reason for misunderstanding on the part of the critics is the pantheism of the Sufis [the doctrine of *wahdat al-wujud*] which has proved to be the greatest stumbling block for them."[51]

In this lengthy section, Wahid Bakhsh delves into the intricacies of Sufi metaphysics to elucidate one of the principal doctrines of the Chishti order: *wahdat al-wujud* ("unity of being"). Rejecting the allegations of Christian, Hindu, or Neoplatonic influences, he proclaims that there is no conflict between pure Islamic pantheism and pure Islamic monotheism. The differences between these two doctrines, he asserts, are "verbal (*lafzi*), not real (*haqiqi*)."[52] Invoking the fundamental doctrine of *tawhid*—the absolute "oneness" of God—Wahid Bakhsh attacks the conservative Hanbali theologian Ibn Taymiyya (1263–1328), for his anthropomorphic view of divinity, and he critiques both the Hindu concept of reincarnation and the Christian Trinity. In explaining *wahdat al-wujud*, Wahid Bakhsh writes, "The correct Islamic conception of God is that He is the only Being that exists and nothing exists besides Him. All things have only relative or imaginary existence like waves, bubbles and ice which are nothing but water in reality. They are water in different shapes and forms . . . According to real Islamic pantheism, everything is not God, but it is not separate from God either."[53]

Quoting from the Qur'an and such spiritual luminaries as Jalal ad-Din Rumi, al-Hallaj, Abu Yazid al-Bistami, Ibn 'Arabi, Shah Waliullah, and Ahmad Sirhindi, the *shaykh* explains and defends pantheism. A full understanding of this complex doctrine, he maintains, is accessible only through direct spiritual experience. Here again Wahid Bakhsh ridicules Western scholars for debating matters they know nothing about:

> Since pantheism is a matter of personal spiritual experience which only comes when the lower-self [*nafs*] is annihilated and replaced by the luminous spiritual self [*ruh*], it is not possible to explain it in terms of the exoteric knowledge of the scholars. But since the scholars think they are capable enough to understand everything they, when confronted with this inexplicable subtle phraseology of the spiritualists, indulge in all sorts of speculations and create a labyrinth of conjectures and guess work only to make confusion more confounded.[54]

For Wahid Bakhsh, the Sufi's intuitive, experiential knowledge eclipses the abstractions and positivism of both the Orientalists and the *'ulama*. Claiming access to both, the *shaykh* concludes by stating, "I, as a Sufi, cum orthodox Muslim theologian, reiterate that pure and unadulterated pantheism is a certainty and is supported not only by the Qur'an and *hadith* of the Prophet, but by logic as well."[55]

5. "The fifth reason for misunderstanding on the part of the Orientalists is the extreme state of maturity or perfection of the stage of baqa-bi-Allah ["remaining in God"], when control over ecstasies and raptures is so great and the seeker looks so ordinary in the midst of inner storms of fascinations and charms that it becomes exceedingly difficult to detect his high spiritual attainments."[56]

In this section, Wahid Bakhsh stresses the importance of spiritual etiquette (*adab*), arguing that the highest stages of esoteric mystical insight are properly masked by the outward display of sobriety. Evoking the example of the Prophet and his Companions, he argues that spiritual growth demands an unwavering attention to propriety and self-control. The Sufi path, he maintains, is an intimate and private affair between the seeker and God, and esoteric knowledge must be carefully guarded. Here the *shaykh* is critical of figures such as al-Hallaj who failed to maintain silence when overwhelmed by spiritual intoxication. In Wahid Bakhsh's words, "Since ecstasies and raptures are the result of weakness and smallness of one's vessel, the Sufis of the later ages who had lesser self control to suppress the storm of inner inspiration, succumbed to ecstasies and were overwhelmed and, thus, gave out their secret."[57] According to Wahid Bakhsh, Sufi decorum requires the concealment of inner spiritual attainments coupled with a dignified public demeanor. This outward comportment, he insists, lulls the Orientalist observer into concluding that Sufism is nothing more than an intellectual abstraction. According to Wahid Bakhsh, the perfected Sufi veils her/his inner spiritual mastery.

6. "The sixth reason for Western misunderstanding of Islam is that they try to judge Islam on the standards of Christianity, and the Prophet of Islam on the standards of the Prophet of Christianity."[58]

Here Wahid Bakhsh broadens his apologetic to defend Islam against the stereotypical images of the tradition's worldliness and militancy. Dismissing such allegations as shallow polemics, he argues that the Qur'an rejects the separation between church and state. In a statement reminiscent of numerous Islamist ideologues such as Mawdudi, he proclaims, "[Islam] provides a complete code of action to mankind both in the temporal and spiritual fields of activity, including politics, economics, and social behavior."[59] Championing Islam as the culmination of the Abrahamic religions, Wahid Bakhsh dismisses allegations of the Prophet's excessive worldliness. He highlights his disregard for wealth and power as ends in themselves, asserting that the Prophet's real battle was "for human rights, peace and justice in the world."[60] In denying the authenticity of the Qur'anic revelation, Wahid Bakhsh asserts, Orientalists have invariably misunderstood and misrepresented Islam's true spirit and message.

7. "The seventh reason for misunderstanding on the part of the Orientalists is some difference of opinion between the Sufis and the orthodox theologians of Islam on certain spiritual matters, which is not a peculiarity of the Muslims alone."[61]

In this final section, Wahid Bakhsh argues that in all religious traditions there is an inherent tension between exoteric and esoteric knowledge. Within Islam, however, it is a mistake to equate this friction with incompatibility. Drawing on numerous Western scholars, the *shaykh* documents the historical battles between Christian theologians and mystics as proof of a deep and lasting divide within Christianity. By contrast, he argues, Sufism is completely in line with Islamic orthodoxy. In Wahid Bakhsh's words, "Far from being antagonistic to Sufism, orthodoxy is the very basis and foundation of all spiritual endeavour, progress and development. Sufism (*tasawwuf*) is defined as a combination of four elements: *shari'at* (law), *tariqat* (inward advance), *haqiqat* (truth) and *ma'arifat* (Gnosis), and none of these are dispensable. The Holy Prophet himself was at once the greatest orthodox Muslim and the greatest spiritualist."[62] The *shaykh* goes on to assert that the Companions and most of the renowned premodern scholars of Islam—including the founders of the four schools of law (*madhahib*)—were all practicing, pious Sufis. In a rhetorical jab at his Islamist critics who claim Ahmad ibn Hanbal as their intellectual standard bearer, he asks, "[W]hen the heads of the four orthodox schools of Islam were Sufis, how could their followers in subsequent centuries take exception to Sufism?"[63] Thus, Wahid Bakhsh ends his critique of Orientalist scholarship by returning to his initial point: Sufism is fully in keeping with orthodox Islamic doctrine and normative practice.

As we have seen, the discursive landscape of contemporary Pakistan is littered with a dizzying array of competing ideological formulations associated with colonialism, economic modernization, scientific secularism, and anti-Hindu communalism. Within this bricolage, even the notion of a distinctive "Pakistani Islam"—the very rationale for the founding of the nation-state—has proved to be a highly contested signifier. As Katherine Ewing notes, "Today in Pakistan, after many years of reformist activity, there is a wide range of opinions about which activities fall within the boundaries of proper Islam and which fall outside, despite many efforts to articulate an Islam that would draw all Pakistanis together as a nation."[64] In a direct challenge to these competing discourses, Wahid Bakhsh forwards an alternative reading of Indo-Muslim history that reasserts the primacy of Chishti Sabiri identity. In essence, his reformulation champions the *continuity* of Sufi doctrine and practice—the persistence of Sufi values, rituals, and institutions—as a bastion against the erosion of Islamic values by Western materialism and secularization.

Wahid Bakhsh asserts that human beings are instinctually religious creatures. To deny the ultimate reality of God, he argues, is to deny one's own humanity. "Man's religious urge is not an ordinary thing," the *shaykh* writes. "It is his ultimate source of ethics, of morality and of his quest for the attainment of truth and reality. It is the only answer to his real and basic needs at all times and in all environments. It is an instinct, the very nature of man, and denying it can only mean disaster and destruction."[65] In Wahid Bakhsh's assessment, Western civilization undermines the centrality of religious identity and spiritual practice, replacing God with the false idols of materialism and secularism. Lamenting the current state of the world—war, social injustice, economic and political exploitation, and moral decay—he asks,

> Do people still want to be told that, as things stand, their future is dark, very dark indeed? Do they still need reformers to preach to them the virtues of honesty? Do they still require another century to learn that material progress and scientific achievements without a good and genuine moral background are capable of very great mischief? There can be no smooth and sustained progress without religion, and no religion can be true, authentic and complete unless it is comprehensive enough to furnish mankind with a complete code of life.[66]

Wahid Bakhsh asserts that Christianity has failed Western civilization by "divorcing itself from the worldly aspects of human life, from man's bodily life of physical needs and desires, [from] his economics and his politics."[67]

Christianity, in his view, is fundamentally at odds with human nature. Further, this incompatibility has hastened the marginalization of religion from modern life. In the *shaykh's* words, "Now, because Christianity has been the West's only religious experience for centuries, the Western people have grown accustomed to identifying it with religion proper and, therefore, their disappointment with Christianity has assumed the shape of a disappointment with religion proper."[68] As befits a practicing Sufi master, Wahid Bakhsh proclaims the timeless and enduring wellspring of Qur'anic revelation and the prophetic teachings accessible through Sufi doctrine and ritual practice as a remedy to this spiritual lacuna.

Islamic Sufism offers numerous expositions of Sufi doctrine. This includes a chapter on "Belief in God"; a translation of a work by Wahid Bakhsh's own *shaykh*, Muhammad Zauqi Shah, entitled "The Sufi Path"; and an essay by Shahidullah Faridi titled "The Spiritual Psychology of Islam." These introductory pieces cover a range of key concepts, including the immanence and transcendence of God; the grades of Divine Being (*muratib-i wujud*); the doctrine of *wahdat al-wujud*; the six subtle centers (*lata'if*); the duties of a spiritual guide (*shaykh*); the states (*hal*) and stations (*maqam*) of the Path; the doctrine of love (*ishq*); *fana'* and *baqa'*; asceticism; and the relationship between the lower self *(nafs)*, heart (*qalb*), and spirit (*ruh*). What is perhaps most striking about the text, however, is the marked absence of the nuanced examinations of Sufi doctrine and ritual practice so prevalent in Wahid Bakhsh's Urdu works. In the introduction he acknowledges this deficiency, stating, "In the end, I tender my apologies for an inadequate exposition of the Sufi doctrine and a weak expression of these high spiritual subjects. This is partly because of my inadequate knowledge of the foreign language and partly because of the scarcity of adequate substitutes for Sufi terminology in the English language. In fact, human language is incapable of explaining the inexplicable realities and truths of spiritualism, which can better be realized and experience than expressed in words."[69] While Wahid Bakhsh does not say so, I suspect that the relative absence of detailed attention to doctrine has much to do with *Islamic Sufism's* intended audience: educated Pakistanis and international disciples, scholars and potential converts. The text focuses principally on the outward, embodied dimensions of ritual practice by design—a distinguishing feature in the writings of many Islamic reformists, here with a uniquely Chishti Sabiri spin.

Emphasizing Sufism's roots in Islamic orthodoxy, Wahid Bakhsh devotes an entire chapter to the Five Pillars of Islam (*arkan*). Throughout, he emphasizes that strict adherence to the *shari'a* is a vital precursor to the Sufi path (*tariqa*) toward gnosis (*ma'arifa*). "So, like every other Muslim, a Sufi has to observe all the prayers and perform all the deeds of piety made obligatory in Islam," he writes. "The Sufis know by experience that the slightest deviation from the injunctions of Islam affects them adversely."[70] In a revealing passage, Wahid Bakhsh acknowledges that certain people, claiming the title of Sufi, neglect the *shar'ia*. In doing so, they give the entire tradition a bad name, adding fuel to the fire of Islamist polemical attacks on Sufism. These fakers—as opposed to real *faqirs*—he insists, deserve the strongest condemnation: "We admit, orthodoxy has been fighting some genuine battles, but these battles have been fought against those who are charlatans and pseudo-*faqirs*, who in order to fleece the simple innocent people, have appeared in different garbs and guises. Their tactics are manifold, the most common being the cult of pantheism of the Hindu type under whose cover they get rid of all the rituals of Islam, saying they are too 'intoxicated' to attend to these formalities, and in order to make their 'intoxication' appear real they resort to heavy drugs."[71] Wahid Bakhsh contrasts these "pseudo-*faqirs*" with "true Sufis" who are distinguished by their excessive piety, incessant prayers, and constant recollection of God. Since Sufism begins where orthodox practice ends, the *shaykh* asserts, Sufi ritual practice extends worship and deepens faith.

In an effort to illuminate the centrality of ritual devotions for Sufi identity, Wahid Bakhsh commits an entire chapter to the practice of *zikr*—the recollection and recitation of the names of God. In it, he explores a range of vocal recitations, physical movements, and breathing techniques, along with the resulting spiritual effects. Another chapter examines the efficacy of listening to music (*sama'*), extolling the benefits of Sufi spiritual poetry performed by a singer (*qawwal*) under the strict supervision of a *shaykh*. In addition to these distinctly Chishti Sabiri practices, Wahid Bakhsh also comments on the efficacy of visiting the graves of deceased spiritual masters (*ziyarat*)—a ritual act widely condemned by Islamists. Here he evokes numerous *hadith* in defense of the practice. Visiting shrines, Wahid Bakhsh maintains, is a powerful catalyst to spiritual development but only when complemented by a vigilant adherence to discipline and decorum (*adab*). Addressing the reader directly, he writes, "The amount of inspiration you get from *shaykh* of the *mazar* very much depends on the effort which you put in at home during the year. The more you pray, worship, fast, recite the Qur'an and do spiritual exercises and *zikr* at home, the greater is your power of reception at the shrine, which in turn serves as greater incentive for increased endeavour at home the year round. In other words, work at home and inspiration at the shrine are interdependent and supplement each other."[72] *Islamic Sufism* concludes with a series of biographical portraits of influential Sufi luminaries. This includes a discussion of such illustrious premodern Sufi masters as Hasan al-Basri, Rabi'a al-'Adawiyya, Abu Yazid al-Bistami, Sufyan al-Thawri, and Ibn 'Arabi. Wahid Bakhsh lauds these paradigmatic figures as models of Muslim piety, propriety, and orthodoxy—Sufi saints who embodied the very essence of Islamic doctrine. By evoking these premodern spiritual exemplars, the *shaykh* affirms the continued relevance of Sufi values and ritual practices for the modern age.

Throughout *Islamic Sufism*, Wahid Bakhsh asserts that the Sufi worldview is entirely amenable to rational thought and scientific inquiry. As the subtitle to his book suggests, he views Sufism itself as a "science"—a practical, rational, systematically arranged form of knowledge committed to the exploration of natural laws. In the introduction, Wahid Bakhsh writes, "Sufism and science are striving for the same destination. Science wants to know: How did the universe come into being and what is its nature? Is there any Creator?

What is He like? Where is He? How is He related to the universe? How is He related to man? Is it possible for man to approach Him? Sufism has found the answers and invites the scientists to come and have that knowledge."[73] Though he recognizes the compatibility of science and Sufism, however, Wahid Bakhsh asserts the innate superiority of the latter. Scientific exploration of the material world, he argues, has no answers for many vital dimensions of life, from morals and ethics to eschatology, metaphysics, and spirituality. In Wahid Bakhsh's assessment,

> The really advanced scientists are now beginning to realize their mistake. Faced with the impossibility of deciding metaphysical questions by means of physical research, they have to give up the childish hopes of the last two centuries that science will provide directives in the field of ethics and spirituality. They are now realizing that *science has no direct connection with man's moral life*. Science can certainly guide us to a better understanding of the physical world around us and in us, but it cannot be called upon to deliver a verdict as to the purpose of life and, thus, create a moral consciousness in us. No amount of enthusiasm for scientific thought can hide the fact that the problem of morality is *not within the scope of science*. It is, on the other hand, *entirely within the scope of religion*.[74]

As evidence of "advanced scientists" Wahid Bakhsh includes an extract from a curious article entitled "Psychic Discoveries behind the Iron Curtain," along with another selection from "a highly reputable English medium, Geraldine Cummins." These texts purport to document "scientific" proof of a spiritual energy animating the universe.[75] The *shaykh* quotes liberally from two additional sources—*The Bible, The Qur'an and Science* by Dr. Maurice Bucaille, a French scientist, and Michael Talbot's *Mysticism and the New Physics*—to illustrate the scientific contributions of Islamic society and to assert that the Qur'an is entirely compatible with the latest scientific discoveries.[76] In this rhetorical move, Wahid Bakhsh is no different from a host of other Muslim reformers and revivalists, including Jamal ad-Din al-Afghani (d. 1897), Sir Sayyid Ahmad Khan (d. 1898), Muhammad Iqbal (d. 1938), Bediuzzaman Said Nursi (d. 1960), and even Mawlana Mawdudi (d. 1941).[77] Despite his curious choice of sources, Wahid Bakhsh's point is clear. In his view, even in the face of massive societal change—from the rise of Western political power, to widespread economic and political restructuring, to the triumph of scientific rationalism—timeless, bedrock religious truths endure. When used appropriately, scientific inquiry and technological advances may refine and deepen religious knowledge, the *shaykh* argues, but they can never replace it.

On the whole, *Islamic Sufism* offers numerous insights into the Chishti Sabiri writing project. In this enigmatic text, Wahid Bakhsh Rabbani employs new idioms in a novel format to express the enduring fundamentals of Chishti Sabiri thought and practice. In form and style, the book mirrors the models of Western academia. It contains technical vocabulary, an index, bibliography, glossary, graphs, and even a color photograph of the *shaykh*. A true bibliophile, Wahid Bakhsh moves fluidly in multiple languages and diverse epistemological registers to present an old message in a new medium. In appropriating select categories of modernity (rationalism and science) and simultaneously rejecting others (Westernization, materialism, and secularization) the *shaykh* walks an ideological tightrope. Yet despite this balancing act, there is never any doubt about Wahid Bakhsh's fundamental worldview and underlying objectives. Though eclectic in style and wide-ranging in subject matter, *Islamic Sufism* is a quintessentially Sufi text designed to communicate the Chishti Sabiri tradition to a global audience.

Sacralizing the "Land of the Pure": The Magnificent Power Potential of Pakistan

Throughout their writings, Muhammad Zauqi Shah, Shahidullah Faridi, and Wahid Bakhsh Sial Rabbani champion Sufism as an alternative network of Islamic piety and practice. The vast majority of their work in fact explores Sufi doctrine and ritual performance. Yet in select writings, the *shaykhs* directly engage the realm of politics and polemics, commenting on the ideology and institutions of the Pakistani nation-state. Why? As Talal Asad argues, they have little choice: "Given that the modern nation-state seeks to regulate all aspects of individual life—even the most intimate, such as birth and death—no one, religious or otherwise, can avoid encountering its ambitious powers. It is not only that the state intervenes directly in the social body for purposes of reform; it is that all social activity requires the consent of the law, and therefore of the nation-state. The way social spaces are defined, ordered and regulated makes them all political."[78] As the 2001 Pakpattan tragedy clearly illustrated, Islamic authority and authenticity are intensely argued and debated in Pakistani public discourse. In response to the state's attempts to appropriate Sufi tradition, Chishti Sabiri writings imagine an alternative past, present, and future in which Sufi traditions—its sacred sites, its spiritual luminaries, its doctrine, and its practices—play a central role in the constitution of local and global Muslim identity.

No text more succinctly encapsulates the contemporary Chishti Sabiri *silsila's* imaginings of Pakistan and the roots of its national and religious identity than Wahid Bakhsh's massive tome: *Pakistan ki azim ush-shan difai quwwat* [*The Magnificent Power Potential of Pakistan*].[79] In this eclectic work, the *shaykh* turns his attention from the rarefied heights of *din* (religion) to the concrete realm of *dunya* (the practical, lived-in world of realpolitik). In a sweeping survey of Islamic military and cultural history, he draws inspiration and guidance from a reified portrait of a lost Golden Age. Wahid Bakhsh champions the compatibility of Islam, modernity, and mysticism as the genuine foundation of Pakistani nationhood and a bulwark against Western—and Indian—cultural encroachment and political hegemony. A critical examination of this text offers further insights into postcolonial subjectivity and its relation to religious identity, ideology, and expression.

The Magnificent Power Potential of Pakistan was first published in Urdu in 1986. It was subsequently reissued in 2000 in an English translation by one of the *shaykh's* senior disciples, Brigadier Muhammad Asghar. It is a weighty book, more than 550 pages in length in both its Urdu and English manifestations. This scale is equaled by the text's scope. Wahid Bakhsh's analysis ranges from a comprehensive analysis of early Islamic military history to a survey of Indo-Muslim culture. It culminates in a frank assessment of Pakistan's position—as the title suggests, its "power potential"—in the contemporary global order. Throughout the text, the *shaykh* utilizes a scholarly voice to place Pakistan in its historical and geopolitical context. In a subtle, subversive twist, however, he places Sufism at the very center of both Islamic thought and practice and Pakistani national identity and ideology. In Wahid Bakhsh's alternative reading of history, Pakistan is rightfully an Islamic republic rooted in Sufi piety.

The *shaykh's* political magnum opus is firmly grounded in historical context. Many of the book's parameters—and all of its polemics—are understood only against the backdrop of South Asian geopolitics in the late cold war period. It was written at a time of profound upheaval and uncertainty for Pakistan. During the 1980s, Pakistan's domestic politics were radically transformed under the military dictatorship of General Muhammad Zia al-Haq. At the same time, the proxy war in neighboring Afghanistan fought by U.S.- and Pakistan-sponsored *mujahidin* groups against the Soviets further exacerbated regional instability.[80] Writing in the midst of these turbulent times, Wahid Bakhsh frames the late twentieth century through a polarized lens. His analysis bifurcates the globe along two civilizational fracture zones: an aggressive, expansionist "West"—Europe, the United States, and, by extension, its satellite state, Israel—that perpetuates the colonial legacy in order to subvert and control the Muslim world. In Wahid Bakhsh's words, "Now that the valiant people of Asia and Africa have expelled the colonialists, they are trying to stage a comeback by weakening these countries from within. They are applying direct as well as indirect strategies, which include naked aggression, subversion, a cultural offensive, an economic aid offensive, a technical aid offensive and the so-called 'peace' offensives. The Muslims must wake up to assess and respond to these seemingly innocuous but otherwise more dangerous dimensions of threats."[81]

In surveying the contemporary global political landscape, Wahid Bakhsh inverts Orientalist essentialisms to valorize a spiritualized "East" against a godless "West." In many ways, this rhetorical move parallels the ideological formations of early Indian nationalism in its campaign of resistance against the British Raj.[82] It is a common rhetorical strategy in South Asian Islamic discourse as well. The notion of clashing civilizations is a familiar motif in the writings of the famous Indian religious scholar Sayyid Abu'l Hasan 'Ali Nadwi (1914–1999), for example. And like Nadwi, Wahid Bakhsh's notion of a chasm between East and West probably "owes more to nineteenth and early twentieth century Orientalist notions than he seems to recognize."[83]

Echoing the polemical attacks of numerous Islamists—from al-Afghani and Sayyid Qutb to Mawlana Mawdudi—Wahid Bakhsh attacks the West for its hypocrisy, cruelty, greed, and violence. In his words,

> They [Westerners] accepted what related to the physical sciences and what
> contributed towards material progress, but rejected what belonged to the
> purification of self, spiritual progress and success in life hereafter. Consequently,
> their one sided development has created a culture which is unstable, imbal-
> anced and moving on a single track. Since they rebelled against their religion,
> they have been deprived of the treasures of religious knowledge. They have jumped
> from one extreme to the other, as they have run away from absolute renuncia-
> tion and walked into the trap of absolute materialism. They have rejected
> absolute superstition but adopted absolute secularism. Their absolute hatred
> for women has been replaced by absolute sexual frivolity. They have freed them-
> selves from religion, but got into a race for material progress and national
> superiority. In their reckless pursuit of power they have stumbled, only to dis-
> cover that the weapons of mass destruction, which they claim as their proud
> inventions, are there to destroy the entire edifice of their civilization.[84]

Obsessed with power, money, and conquest, Wahid Bakhsh argues, the West
is morally bankrupt. Though technologically advanced, it has sacrificed religion in favor of science, secularism, and worldly pleasure. And it is this fatal
choice, the *shaykh* concludes, that will be the West's undoing.

In response to the West's cultural and political challenge, Wahid Bakhsh
calls upon Muslims to reclaim and resurrect their own cultural heritage.
Resistance, he insists, need not take the form of physical violence. Instead,
Muslims should mount a peaceful, spiritual campaign to attack the West
where it is most vulnerable. "The miraculous power of Islamic spirituality is
so strong that we, the Muslims, are not required to pick up swords to con-
quer the spiritual wastelands of the West," writes the *shaykh*. "Since every
heart by nature yearns for Divine love and Divine bounty, any heart with a
spiritual vacuum is absolutely defenseless against the expanding spiritual tor-
rent of Islam. The West is helpless and exposed to the ingress of the Truth.
The process of Islamic conquests in spiritually starved humanity is therefore
an eternal and continuous process.[85] For Wahid Bakhsh, a return to the lost
Golden Age of Islam presupposes a revitalization of the roots of Islamic
orthodoxy. For him, "true Islam" is found in the immutable blueprint
enshrined in the Qur'an, *sunna*, and, most significantly, Sufi tradition.

Throughout the book, Wahid Bakhsh again invokes numerous Sufi
exemplars, among them Imam Ghazali, Ibn Arabi, Junaid Baghdadi, Jalal ad-
Din Rumi, and Sayyid 'Ali al-Hujwiri. As befits a Chishti Sabiri *shaykh*, he also
lauds the early luminaries of his own spiritual genealogy, especially Khwaja
Mu'in ad-Din Chishti and Baba Farid ad-Din Ganj-i Shakkar. In Wahid
Bakhsh's eyes, these paradigmatic Sufi saints embody the Prophet
Muhammad's virtues: piety, self-sacrifice, sincerity, charity, humility, and an
unwavering commitment to social justice. As the heirs to the Prophet, the
Sufi "Friends of God" therefore offer a moral compass for Muslims and dis-
enchanted Westerners alike. According to Wahid Bakhsh, "We, the Muslims,
must realize that the Westerners themselves are alienated against the Western

civilization. They have very high hopes and high expectations from Islam. The new manifestation of religion which I have pointed to is the ever-increasing demand of the West for Sufism. *It is our first and foremost duty to offer Sufism to the West.* And in this lies the secret of our success."[86] Western civilization, the *shaykh* maintains, is ready for a fall. And it is Sufism—the heart of Islam and the essence of orthodoxy—that stands ready to fill the "spiritual vacuum."

The bulk of *The Magnificent Power Potential of Pakistan* centers on a comprehensive (and profoundly romanticized) review of Islamic military and cultural history. For Wahid Bakhsh, the martial spirit of the Muslim past offers a blueprint for societal renewal and the promise of a self-confident and assertive Indo-Muslim future. In his interpretation of history, piety was the backbone of power—military, social, cultural, economic, and political—during the zenith of the Muslim empire. Wahid Bakhsh's call for Islam's revitalization conflates religious orthodoxy—with Sufism at its center—with military might, social order, and cultural florescence. Rejecting passivity, apologetics, and defensiveness, the *shaykh* challenges Muslims to restore the dynamism of the *umma* by embracing the lessons of their own past. The neglect of Islam's original teachings and traditions, he asserts, has only resulted in doubt, weakness, and civilizational drift:

> One of the causes of Muslim decline is their indifference to and detachment from their glorious history. This book therefore brings to focus the feats of valor, operational brilliance and tactical excellence of the great captains of Islam. It also throws light on the contributions of our forefathers to science, technology, artistry, social sciences and cultural fields. The aim is to pull our Westernized and defeated minds out of their inferiority complex so that they realize that they are sparkling stars of the glorious galaxy of the Muslim civilization and culture.[87]

For Wahid Bakhsh, a thorough study of history is an essential first step toward the revitalization of Islamic civilization.

Beginning with the early community of believers surrounding the Prophet Muhammad, Wahid Bakhsh's narrative charts the rise and fall of Islamic civilization across the centuries and around the globe. His analysis moves from the *Hijra* to Medina and the military conquests of Persia, Byzantium, and Spain, to the Crusades, the fall of the Ottoman Empire, and resistance to colonial regimes. Not surprisingly, the *shaykh* gives particular attention to Muslim incursions into the Subcontinent and the subsequent rise of a distinct Indo-Islamic culture. Throughout this chronological survey, Wahid Bakhsh lauds the self-confidence, faith, bravery, and bravado of the early Muslim community. Significantly, his interpretive lens is entirely self-referential, following the thread of a sacred Muslim past beyond the purview of the West. The *shaykh's* historical project is much more than an academic pursuit, however. By returning to their roots, Wahid Bakhsh suggests, twentieth-century Muslims can build a bulwark against Western cultural encroachment and political hegemony.

To this end, Wahid Bakhsh's counternarrative also offers a spirited defense of the necessity—the orthodoxy—of *jihad*. Reciting a well-known (if disputed) tradition, he defines *jihad* as both an internal struggle against the lower self (the "Greater Jihad," or *jihad-i akbar*) and an external resistance against the enemies of Islam (the "Lesser Jihad," or *jihad-i asghar*). All Muslims, he insists, are compelled by their faith to fight against oppression, injustice, and tyranny. In another clear example of Wahid Bakhsh's eclectic mix of ideology and idioms, he invokes the Qur'an (4:74–76) to "urge the Muslims to fight for Truth and Justice, and wage Jihad for human rights."[88] Outlining the rules of military engagement, the *shaykh* asserts that armed conflict is always moderated by rules of conduct that insure discipline, moderation, and mercy. Torture, mutilation, and the killing of noncombatants, he insists, are strictly forbidden in the Muslim tradition of just war.

Acutely aware of the Western polemic against *jihad*, Wahid Bakhsh remains unapologetic. Once again, he goes on the offensive, criticizing the West for its hypocrisy and double standards. In his words,

> Some Western thinkers criticize Jihad. Their criticism is not understandable as they themselves have acquired greater wealth and power by subjugating weaker peoples, conquering foreign territories and plundering others' treasuries. Their hands are stained with the blood of many innocent and weaker nations. If enhancement of national superiority and imperialism through exploitation of weaker nations is considered legitimate by them, how do they criticize Jihad, the objectives of which are to extirpate falsehood, uphold Truth, uproot oppression, eliminate infidelity [*kufr*] and associationism [*shirk*], and wipe out all kinds of malpractices?[89]

For the *shaykh*, the rapid expansion and fruition of Islamic civilization in the past is itself a confirmation of the fruits of a just, moral struggle. He urges modern Muslims to emulate the example of their spiritual predecessors in order to reclaim Islam's original dynamism, zeal, and power.

Wahid Bakhsh's wide-ranging narrative conveys a triumphal and teleological portrait of Islamic sacred history. It culminates in an attempt to discover the origins of Pakistan in a divinely sanctioned, sacralized past. According to the *shaykh*,

> The creation of Pakistan is therefore not a fortuitous happening, or the consequence of an accident of history. It is rather a Divine reward for the centuries of sacrifices, toiling and tribulations of the *Mujahidin* of Islam. Those visionary leaders had sensed that the decline of the Ottoman and Mughal empires would spell disaster for the Muslims and their future would be absolutely dark. The Muslims had to be rescued, and an ideological state like Pakistan was a dire necessity of the time and the right answer to the prayers of the millions of oppressed human beings in general, and the Muslims in particular.[90]

A patriotic nationalist, Wahid Bakhsh asserts that Pakistan carries the mantle of the "first Pakistan," the foundational Muslim state formed by the Prophet

Muhammad and the early community of believers in Medina. Written forty years after Partition, however, his discourse is permeated by a sense of moral outrage, indignation, and loss. In the *shaykh's* eyes, Pakistan has betrayed its auspicious beginnings. Mired in poverty, nepotism, corruption, and a profound crisis of identity, the modern state has failed miserably in its mission to revive the spirit and values of the Prophet's Medina. In language that resonates with sadness and righteous anger Wahid Bakhsh writes,

> [The Muslims of South Asia], their dream was Pakistan—a Muslim state based on the ideology of Islam and a state founded on the edifice of *Nizam-e Mustafa* ["the system of the Prophet"], and a state which would be the precursor of Islamic renaissance. By the grace of Almighty Allah, the sacrifices, toiling and efforts of the Muslims led to the creation of Pakistan. A part of the dream had come true: we had a geographic entity called Pakistan, and we had to develop it into a citadel of Islam. But alas, we lost our way! We forgot the lofty ideals and objectives for which Pakistan was created. We changed our direction and we drifted away from our course—the course that would have led us to Mecca Muazzamah ["Exalted"] and Medina Munawwarah ["Illuminated"]. We are now heading towards temples, churches and abodes of idolatrous practices. We had sought to make Pakistan a fortress of Islam. But we have turned it into the center of greed, corruption, luxury, materialistic values and internal discord.[91]

Incensed by Pakistan's weakness, Wahid Bakhsh calls for immediate and comprehensive changes to combat its endemic cultural rot. In his assessment, it is only through the moral reform of the individual that social and political institutions can be revitalized. In a revealing passage, he attacks those who call for top-down structural changes in the absence of a prevailing change in the way people think and act:

> Some of our impatient politicians, who include some religious scholars as well, claim that they can reform the society only after coming to power. And that too despite the prerequisites spelled out by the tradition of the Prophet (peace be upon him). Unless the masses are reformed, pious and virtuous individuals will not come to power . . . In order to bring pious individuals to power, we need to commence our work at the grass roots level. Piety will not trickle down from top to bottom. Reconstruction of any nation is possible only if scholars, educationalists, reformers and thinkers reform the masses by interacting with them. There is a need to establish religious schools, arrange talks for the common men, write articles in newspapers, magazines and journals, write books and help in the control and eradication of crime from society. Once the society is reformed, virtuous people will emerge in accordance with the laws of nature.[92]

Islamic values and practice, Wahid Bakhsh asserts, cannot simply be codified, systematized, and enforced. Instead, they must be inculcated, internalized, and enacted. The *shaykh* calls for an educated, pious elite to lead the Pakistani masses back to their Islamic roots. And once again, he evokes the Golden Age of the early Muslim community as the eternal, universal paradigm for emulation. It is the only political model, he asserts, in which national policy and public institutions emerge directly from piety and practice.

Wahid Bakhsh outlines a host of practical reforms for Pakistan's revitalization. The restoration of the nation's foundations, he argues, is not solely a spiritual battle, but it is one that must be fought simultaneously on multiple worldly fronts. In response to ground-level realities, the *shaykh* offers a broad palate of prescriptions designed to purge Pakistan of its colonial vestiges. He calls for legal reforms to institutionalize and enforce *shari'a*;[93] educational reforms to promote science and technology while solidifying "religious literacy";[94] economic reforms to promote growth and stability while eliminating usury (*riba*) and the vicious cycle of the debt trap laid by international monetary institutions;[95] military reforms to secure internal social stability and promote a unified front of Islamic nations to resist Euro-American, Israeli, and Indian expansionism and hegemony;[96] and political reforms to institutionalize an "Islamic democracy" purged of all "Western influences" under the leadership of an educated, pious elite of select "intellectuals, scholars, thinkers and social reformers."[97] To say the least, this panoply of reforms is ambitious in scope and scale. Yet Wahid Bakhsh offers few practical details on precisely how these reforms should be implemented, institutionalized, and administered. In this sense, his vision of social reform is reminiscent of Mawdudi who "showed little interest in the actual working of institutions" and "was more concerned with abstract theoretical formulations and lessons in moral philosophy."[98]

Pakistan can never be rebuilt, Wahid Bakhsh states, if it fails to overcome the forces of internal dissolution. Regionalism and local ethnic identity politics, he says, threaten national unity, undermine political institutions, and weaken the boundaries of defense. In his words,

> We need to bury our political, religious and ethnic differences and face the enemies of Islam like a solid wall . . . Nationalist parties are raising slogans of "Pashtunistan" ["home of the ethnic Pashtuns"], "Azad Balochistan" ["a free home for the ethnic Baluchis"], and "Sindhu Desh" ["the ethnic Sindhis' country"]. But selfish motives, mutual rivalries and jealousy blind them. They do not realize that four smaller countries, which they wish to create, will be swallowed by India overnight. Their dreams of independence will be shattered and their personal ambitions ruined. When the necks are chopped off, who will wear garlands? And what use is the crown when the heads have rolled?[99]

In Wahid Bakhsh's view, the homegrown divisions of ethnic rivalry are as destructive as any external enemy.

An even greater strain on Pakistan's strength and integrity, Wahid Bakhsh suggests, is the threat of religious sectarianism: the growing specter of Sunni and Shi'a communalism. Drawing on a well-known *hadith*, he makes a desperate plea for Muslim brotherhood. The divisions within the *umma* are a blessing, he insists, promoting healthy debate and competition that deepens faith and solidifies the community of believers. The alternative—the proliferation of sectarian violence—could tear the nation apart, threatening Pakistan's very survival. Here Wahid Bakhsh is pointedly critical of Sunni-centric Islamists. He decries the spread of Wahhabi and Salafi doctrine, denouncing the exclusivity of their faith and the absolutism of their political and ideological agendas. Not surprisingly, Wahid Bakhsh levels an especially harsh critique of the Deobandi movement. "The Deobandis have deviated from the path of their prominent leaders and founders of their school of thought," he writes. "In fact, they are treading the path outlined for them by the enemies of Islam."[100] For Wahid Bakhsh, the Deoband movement has betrayed the legacy of its Chishti Sabiri predecessors by jettisoning its Sufi roots in a misguided attempt to purify the faith.

As an antidote to sectarian infighting, Wahid Bakhsh makes an urgent appeal to Pakistan's leaders to stop exploiting religion for political gain. As an Islamic republic, Pakistan's institutions and laws must encourage unity, defend minorities, and promote a shared sense of community. Although he never mentions him by name, it is clear that Wahid Bakhsh is addressing the government of General Zia when he writes,

> These differences among Sunnis, Shias, Barelwis, Deobandis, *Muqallids* [followers of discrete schools of Islamic law] and non-*Muqallids* are of a peripheral nature. They have nothing to do with the core issues of Islam on which, by the grace of Allah, the entire *Ummah* [global community of Muslims] has consensus . . . We must not worry about the sectarian differences while enforcing Islam in the country. Our constitution should permit all sects to practice religion the way they want. The Government should enforce only those clauses on which all the sects have consensus, such as prohibition of interest, laws of inheritance, prohibition of drinking, adultery, corruption and criminal procedures. Peripheral or controversial issues like visits to the shrines, *sama'* [listening to music], *ta'ziya* [Shi'a processions during Muharram], and *milad* [public celebration's of the Prophet's birthday] should be left to the individual sects.[101]

For Wahid Bakhsh, only a strong, centralized, and assertive state can protect religious freedom and preserve social order. Loyalty to the nation and a shared Pakistani identity, he concludes, must ultimately trump the parochialism of regional, tribal, familial, and sectarian identities if Pakistan is to survive in an increasingly hostile and dangerous world.

In Wahid Bakhsh's optimistic assessment, once its own house is in order Pakistan can finally realize its full potential as a central player in the twentieth century's geopolitical landscape. In a spirited call to arms, he challenges his countrymen to work together to resist the perpetuation of global neocolonialism. His strategic analysis characterizes Pakistan as a key buffer state for Middle Eastern and Asian countries alike, a counterweight to the West's hegemonic designs:

> Colonization of the entire under-developed world by the West has a lesson for all the Muslims and non-Muslims. Strong Islamic Empires did and can even now help to protect the rest of humanity from the ravages of the West . . . Although colonialism has ended and the physical size of European empires has shrunk to their native lands, they continue to dominate the international politico-economic sphere and exploit the weak nations on the basis of their industrial power, economic prosperity and military muscle . . . India and other

Asian countries must therefore strengthen Pakistan rather than weaken it. The politicians and religious clergy of Pakistan must understand the role of Pakistan in the global power structure. They must overcome mutual rivalries and get united to fight the enemies of Islam. They must remember that any weakness in Asia will promote Western hegemony.[102]

For Wahid Bakhsh, this ultimately is Pakistan's true calling: to assume the vanguard of a global Islamic renaissance. In his reified portrait of Islamic sacred history, nothing less will do if Pakistan is to live up to its name ("The Land of the Pure") and divinely sanctioned legacy as the heir to the "first Pakistan," the Prophet's Medina.

The Magnificent Power Potential of Pakistan is a unique and in many ways atypical work in a market glutted with religious literature, much of it ideological and highly polemical. Even for Wahid Bakhsh, whose literary pursuits embraced multiple genres in diverse registers, this book is an anomaly. In a critical but creative voice, the *shaykh* alternatively embraces and resists the parameters of modernity. He appropriates scientific thought, technological innovation, and the mass media. At the same time, he rejects absolute secularization, the cult of individualism, and unbridled free market capitalism and democracy—all of which he sees as distinctly Western values and institutions. Wahid Bakhsh's historical narrative draws inspiration and guidance from a reified portrait of Islam's Golden Age. Pakistan's salvation, he argues, lies in the restoration of the spirit of the early Muslim community—an ethos grounded on tolerance, discipline, order, and strength. Throughout the text, the *shaykh* seeks a middle ground between two opposing ideologies: an aggressive, exclusivist, conservative Sunni Islam (with no space for Sufism), and an absolutist, expansionist, secular West (with no space for religion). In many ways, Wahid Bakhsh's framing of Pakistan as an Islamic state, his frequent evocation of a lost Golden Age, and his outrage at social and moral decay mirror the style and substance of numerous Muslim social critics. Yet the *shaykh's* final rhetorical flourish distinguishes him from his counterparts. For Wahid Bakhsh—the most prolific of twentieth-century Chishti Sabiri masters—Sufi piety and practice are both the quintessential expression of Islamic orthodoxy and the enduring bedrock of Pakistani identity.

THE TWENTY-FIRST-CENTURY *SILSILA*: NEW MEDIA, NEW AUDIENCES

In the twenty-first century, the Chishti Sabiri order maintains a public face, even as its private networks of spiritual knowledge and pedagogy remain unbroken. Following the example of Muhammad Zauqi Shah, Shahidullah Faridi, and Wahid Bakhsh Sial Rabbani, the *silsila* remains focused on the written word and continues to publish a diverse array of texts. On both sides of the Indian Ocean, Pakistani and Malaysian disciples employ a variety of media outlets to articulate Chishti Sabiri identity for new audiences. Their efforts are led by a select group of senior *murids*—both men and women—under the guidance and supervision of Shaykh Siraj 'Ali Muhammad, the designated successor of Shaykh Shahidullah Faridi and the order's current teaching *shaykh*. At present, some fifty different texts are produced and distributed from a number of publishing houses. First and foremost among them is Mahfil-i Zauqiyya. Located in Karachi, it publishes the bulk of the original Urdu works of Muhammad Zauqi Shah and Shahidullah Faridi. Founded by Shahidullah himself, it is now administered by a senior male disciple, a man who was expressly ordered by the *shaykh* to spearhead the *silsila's* publication efforts.

From this base in Karachi, the Chishti Sabiri publication campaign has progressively spread throughout Pakistan, and beyond. Since 1989, The Association of Spiritual Training—founded by Wahid Bakhsh and administered by a number of his senior disciples—has published an English language journal titled *The Sufi Path*. Based in Islamabad, it has produced fourteen issues to date. This journal is intended for both an educated Pakistani and an international audience. Each issue contains a wide variety of materials, ranging from translations of classical Sufi texts and poetry, to selections from the writings of Chishti Sabiri *shaykhs* and prominent disciples, to various scholarly articles. In both format and content, *The Sufi Path* resembles similar publications by numerous other Sufi orders in the West. The *silsila* also maintains a number of important publishing outlets in the city of Lahore. The Sufi Foundation, founded by another senior male *murid*, published a series of translations and original writings by Wahid Bakhsh during the 1980s. This work has since continued under the auspices of Bazm-i Ittehad al-Muslimin, founded in 1984 by the *shaykh's* nephew. Beginning in 1996, Talifat-i Shaheedi, established by another *murid* of Shahidullah Faridi, has published four additional texts, three of them in English.

In addition to these "in-house" publishers, the *silsila* outsources work to several professional publishing houses in Lahore as well. Ziya al-Qur'an, for example, currently publishes two of Wahid Bakhsh's Urdu translations of classical Persian *malfuzat*; Qausin Publishers prints two key Urdu *malfuzat*; and, most importantly, al-Faisal Publishers distributes a number of Wahid Bakhsh's works in both English and Urdu. With these combined efforts, Chishti Sabiri texts are today readily available in the bookstores and bazaars of Pakistan's major cities. The *silsila's* books are also found in the myriad bookstalls that flank the country's major Sufi shrines, most prominently in the narrow lanes surrounding the tomb complex of Baba Farid, the Chishti saint, in Pakpattan.

The Chishti Sabiri order's persistent commitment to publishing raises an important question: who precisely is the intended audience? Given Pakistan's alarmingly low literacy rates—less than half of the adult population—the potential reading public is extremely limited and largely determined by education and class. As Eickelman and Anderson note, this too is a common characteristic of new Muslim media that invariably "occupy an interstitial space between the super-literacy of traditional religious specialists and mass sub-literacy or illiteracy. Their natural home is the emerging middle, bourgeois classes of the Muslim world."[103] Despite these limiting factors, Chishti Sabiris insist that their publications are not designed for mass consumption. In the words of a prominent male *murid*, "Our *silsila* is for the elite [*khas*], those who want to advance spiritually through their own efforts. Our publications are a response for the future, to preserve the teachings. It is meant for a few, not for the general public ['*am*]. For the masses who come by the thousands it is enough to know the power of the saints. As the teaching says, you do not discuss Sufi doctrine with the unlettered masses or anyone who think that this is all blasphemy" (October 3, 2000, Lahore). In explaining the utility of books, Chishti Sabiri disciples once again emphasize the distinction between the rational, discursive book knowledge of the religious scholar ('*ilm*) and the intuitive, experiential, esoteric knowledge of the Sufi master (*ma'rifa*). For the average reader with an intellectual curiosity about Sufi doctrine, the *silsila's* books offer a useful and informed point of reference. However, for the spiritual elites (*khas*)—the select few who seek the guidance of an accomplished Sufi *shaykh*—books are at best an invitation to practice.

From doctrinal tracts and ritual manuals to political and polemical works, I would argue that Chishti Sabiri texts actually target multiple audiences through particular rhetorical styles and languages. The primary readership is clearly the *silsila's* own members. *Murids* view printed texts as vital repositories of the order's collective wisdom. At the same time, books also serve as important heuristic tools. As chapter 4 will demonstrate, texts are fully integrated into contemporary Chishti Sabiri ritual practice. For individual disciples, the *shaykhs'* writings on doctrine and practice offer a critical source of inspiration and guidance along the twists and turns of the Sufi path. As a road map and a litmus test for spiritual development, books complement and clarify the oral teachings communicated via the central master-disciple relationship.

The contemporary *silsila* is obviously interested in reaching a much broader Pakistani audience as well. If not, why publish? Beyond their own community, the order's Urdu publications are aimed at a diverse spectrum of readers who are interested in Sufism, regardless of personal background. According to the senior disciple who oversees the central publishing house, Mahfil-i Zauqiyya, in Karachi, "These books are printed with the intention of spreading the word of Allah among the people. If after reading these books even one person changes his life for the better, that is more precious to us than all the treasures of the world. The focus is on the individual, not on the masses. That is what is important. The books are available to anybody. We print them not with the intention of making money, but to make them available to people at the least possible cost so that they can benefit from this as much as possible" (May 21, 2001, Karachi).[104]

Despite this openness, the volume of the order's publications is restricted by design. Typically, no more than a thousand copies of each text are printed at a time. Any profits from the sale of books are immediately rolled back into the system, making the production process a largely self-sustaining enterprise. Remarkably, no resources are committed to advertising. In the words of one *murid*, "If someone makes an effort to get these books, there are no

restrictions. But marketing is not considered helpful for spiritual development" (October 3, 2002, Lahore). Chishti Sabiris assert that the goal is to
communicate with those who are willing to listen, not to convert the critics.
Preservation of the *silsila's* historical memory, and not persuasion of Sufism's
detractors, I was frequently told, is the real motivation. As the following
quote suggests, Chishti Sabiris insist that they are not interested in prosely-
tizing or political diatribe:

> These books are not meant to be controversial. They can benefit everybody and
> anybody, whether he is from a group that accepts *tasawwuf* or one that does
> not. It is not the way of the holy saints to condemn any sect or any religion or
> any particular group of people. Proselytizing is something different altogether.
> We are spreading the word of Allah as we understand it, as our *shaykhs* have
> understood it, in the light of the Qur'an and *sunna*. They understood and
> embodied it, and we are continuing that practice. So we do not take an apolo-
> getic attitude. If you like it, fine. If you don't like it, fine. The way of the Sufis
> is to bring people closer rather than to divide them. (May 21, 2001, Karachi)

This is an intriguing statement that reveals a careful balancing act. The
Chishti Sabiris critique their conservative counterparts for mixing religion
and politics. They insist that they are beyond polemics. Yet in printing and
disseminating these texts, the *silsila* purposefully enters the contested public
sphere to stake a claim to Islamic authority and authenticity. Within the combative landscape of today's Pakistan and Malaysia, such a proactive publishing
campaign can only be seen as an overtly political act.

At yet another level, Chishti Sabiri publications target a much broader
audience, well beyond the order's traditional locus in South Asia. Following
the precedent established by Muhammad Zauqi Shah, Chishti Sabiri *shaykhs*
have each written in both Urdu and English. As we have seen, Wahid Bakhsh
in particular made an appeal to disillusioned Westerners in his writings. In the
words of one of the *shaykh's* disciples, "He [Shaykh Wahid Bakhsh] used to
tell me that in many places, people would not want to read these books. But
outsiders, people who are thirsty for this knowledge, they might see it in a
more positive way. Especially in the West, people are really longing for this.
It's missing there, so that is the reason" (September 26, 2001, Kuala
Lumpur). In keeping with this legacy, the Chishti Sabiri order now publishes
a number of texts in English. This includes both the *shaykh's* original writings
as well as several translations of their Urdu works. Following precedent, the
silsila continues to operate in multiple linguistic and cultural registers.

The growing transnational profile of Chishti Sabiri publications is most
clearly demonstrated by the concerted efforts of the Malaysian disciples—a
dynamic contingent of Wahid Bakhsh's disciples that I explore further in
chapter 4. Planting Chishti Sabiri Sufism in Southeast Asian soil, they
recently established an independent printing press in Kuala Lumpur. To date,
A.S. Noordeen Publishers has published four books: an English version of
Wahid Bakhsh's translation of *Kashf al-mahjub*, a partial translation of the
malfuzat of Shaykh Sayyid Shah Waris Hasan, an edition of Shahidullah

Faridi's *Inner Aspects of Faith*, and *Islamic Sufism*, a reprint of Wahid Bakhsh's lengthy monograph. Though modest in scope and scale, these publishing efforts are nonetheless remarkable. After all, literature of any kind on *tasawwuf* is a rarity in Malaysia where—as in Pakistan—Sufism is a highly contested tradition and a controversial practice.

Despite Malaysia's restrictive atmosphere, Chishti Sabiri publications have begun to draw a local audience. Interestingly, this has included members of other local Sufi orders. According to a senior Malaysian disciple, "There are some Sufi *shaykhs* here in Malaysia. They are actually now using these books like textbooks. When they instruct their *murids* they say, 'Buy this book.' And then they read from it. This is slowly correcting aberrations. There are no other resources because there is no strong Sufi tradition here anymore" (October 1, 2001, Kuala Lumpur). At present, the Malaysian publications are limited to English, though disciples say they intend to eventually make them available in Bahasa Malaysia, the national language. In the words of another Malaysian *murid*, "When it comes to *tasawwuf*, the Malays will look for a book in *bahasa*. To find a book in *tasawwuf* in English is something that for them is, well, strange. They don't go for it. We tried to translate them, but translating these books is not so easy. The translator must be a spiritual person. We arranged for a man in Indonesia to translate *Islamic Sufism*, but he made some mistakes. He remarked, 'I have translated the work, but I do not agree with it.' So we didn't publish it" (September 30, 2001, Kuala Lumpur).

The Malaysians have reached new ground in another vital arena as well. Since 1996 they have operated a *silsila* Web site (http://www.moonovermedina.com). Entitled Moon Over Medina: A Sufi Bookstore, this virtual bookstore offers Chishti Sabiri publications for sale to global cybersurfers on the World Wide Web. The site's main page displays a brief description of each *shaykh's* book, along with a full color photograph of its cover. A link, More on Sufism, provides short extracts from the texts, along with a pair of essays in English by Muhammad Zauqi Shah. According to the site's manager—a Malay businessman and disciple of Wahid Bakhsh who was educated in America—most of the current visitors are foreigners. In his words,

> The Web site is quite interesting. I would say the largest proportion [of visitors] are Americans. They have Christian names. When they submit their orders they use a Christian name, but sometimes when they send me an e-mail to confirm their orders some use Muslim names. I've had several orders from Switzerland, and inquiries from Europe, Canada, and Brazil. When I started there were about ten to fifteen visitors a day. It's like owning a shop, having people come in and browse every day. Now it is up to forty people a day, about 1,200 a month. But of those, only a few buy books.
>
> I added the articles [by Zauqi Shah] on Sufism to the site, and a lot of people go there to look at them. They also look at the extracts from the books. I do not accept credit cards, and that is the problem. I just wouldn't be able to cope with the volume, because I'm the only one running it. I post the books

myself—I go to the post office and collect the checks myself. It doesn't make any money, just enough to cover the fees. (October 1, 2001, Kuala Lumpur)

The Internet offers a new platform to communicate Chishti Sabiri identity to a potentially vast global audience. By launching into cyberspace, the *silsila* has joined a growing movement. In the twenty-first century, tech-savvy Muslims in diverse cultural settings are rapidly adapting to digital technology, much as their predecessors once capitalized on the advent of the printing press. As Jon Anderson notes, "They range from political activists to Sufi orders, from mobilization to witness. They both recruit and propagandize, bringing their issues into a wider, already public sphere in some cases but in others carving out a new one that encompasses or repackages existing ones, compelling dialogue by leveraging forms of communication that reshape the social field . . . Islam on the Internet is first a story of new interpreters, newly emboldened by confidence in and command of the channel."[105] While at present the Internet remains accessible only to a privileged core of educated, middle-class professionals with access to computers, it has the potential to radically transform the boundaries of public discursive space. "New forms of communication and their increased rapidity allow 'peripheries' and audiences to talk back and can infuse new life to local and regional traditions," argues Eickelman. "The new political geography of communications may actually facilitate pluralism. In the sense that symbolic and political connections across national and other political boundaries are encouraged, conventional understandings of 'external' and 'internal' become increasingly blurred."[106] In theory and increasingly in practice, the Internet expands networks of knowledge and builds new communities, unbound by physical space, gender boundaries, and national borders. For these reasons, it is a useful tool for the Chishti Sabiri order's ongoing efforts to expand its reach beyond South Asia.

In *Mullahs on the Mainframe*, Jonah Blank demonstrates how the Daudi Bohra communities of Bombay and Karachi have accommodated to the tectonic shifts of global modernity. These dynamic South Asian Shi'a, he notes, are distinguished by "the holistic nature of their modernization." They "regard modern technology (and its accompanying ease of societal communication) as something beneficial even on its own merits . . . New technologies are not adopted solely for the sake of novelty, but anything that brings the community closer—or simply makes life easier—is heartily encouraged."[107] A similar dynamic is seen among twenty-first-century fundamentalist movements—Jewish, Christian, and Muslim alike—who make use of technology to publicize their own critiques of modernism.[108] While employing the medium, they reject the message. I would argue that this is equally true of the contemporary Chishti Sabiri order. Amid the cacophonous public debates over Islamic orthodoxy, Chishti Sabiris have proved adept at using new technologies to amplify their defense of Sufi orthodoxy. In multiple locations, languages, and forums, today's *silsila* employs mass media to explain tradition, articulate identity, and expand the boundaries of community.

CONCLUSION

The writings of Muhammad Zauqi Shah, Shahidullah Faridi, and Wahid Bakhsh Sial Rabbani imagine a distinct Indo-Muslim Sufi identity: a *shari'a*-minded and socially engaged Sufism, firmly rooted in South Asian tradition but responsive to the challenges of postcolonial modernity. Throughout their diverse literary corpus, the *shaykhs* demonstrate a keen awareness of Sufism's multiple dimensions—orthodoxy and orthopraxy, doctrine and ritual, piety and politics, texts and contexts. They employ diverse rhetorical devices (the English language, scientific, and technical vocabulary) and multiple media (books, essays, and journals) to communicate Sufi tradition to a new audience (beyond the inner circle of *murids* whose training remained their primary concern). Their vision frames Sufism as the quintessential expression of Islamic orthodoxy. In the transition from the colonial to postcolonial age, the *shaykhs* mark the continuity of doctrinal teachings and ritual practices at the heart of Chishti Sabiri identity as a bulwark against Sufism's critics and a panacea for Pakistan's social ills.

In many ways, the *shaykhs'* writing project is not unique. As we have seen, their emphasis on social activism consciously mirrors the legacy of their nineteenth-century Chishti Sabiri predecessors. On a wider level, their work also recalls that of the Egyptian reformist, activist and *mufti* of al-Azhar, Muhammad Abduh (1849–1905), whose interpretation of Islamic tradition emphasized "a moral earnestness and a concern with interiorization of the faith that would have satisfied al-Ghazali."[109] The Chishti Sabiri writing project even resembles the efforts of their *'ulama* counterparts who aimed to "authoritatively represent an 'authentic' Islamic tradition in its richness, depth, and continuity" by portraying themselves as the guardians of a "continuous, lived heritage that connects to the past and the present."[110] What distinguishes the writing of this trio of modern Chishti Sabiri *shaykhs*, however, is the distinct way they conflated Sufi identity and Pakistani national identity. In their alternative reading of history, Sufism is both the essence of Islamic orthodoxy and the only viable antidote to Pakistan's crisis of identity—a middle way between the extremes of Islamism on the one hand and Westernization on the other.

These three twentieth-century Sufi masters certainly did not see themselves as polemicists or ideologues. They emphasized instead their roles as spiritual teachers, and this is how they are remembered within the Chishti Sabiri order to this day. Yet a survey of their collective writings shows that the *shaykhs* did not shy away from the mundane and messy world of politics. On the whole, their literary legacy runs counter to the prevalent Orientalist stereotypes of Sufism's devolution, rigidity, and intellectual stasis. It also confirms that Sufism simply cannot be separated from the everyday practices of social and political life.

An assessment of the contemporary Chishti Sabiri writing project raises a host of broader issues as well—far-reaching questions that continue to preoccupy postcolonial scholarship: How free is the postcolonial subject? Are nationalist and modernist discourses hegemonic, or is there still space for individual agency? At the level of embodied practice, beyond the long arm of the state, are independent, creative expressions of religious identity possible? Among scholars there has been no consensus of opinion regarding these complex issues. For some, such as Gayatri Spivak, the legacy of colonial discourse is hegemonic and therefore effectively silences the voice of the colonized subject. The subaltern *cannot* speak.[111] Other scholars have argued that no discourse is so totalizing as to erase the potential of individual agency. Though marginalized and exploited—physically, materially, and psychologically—by systems of coercion and control individuals are never fully silenced or controlled. "In historical fact, the Orient is never reduced to silence," writes Sudipta Kaviraj, "indeed, it constantly gives vent to its resentment against colonialism through an enormous range of expressions from insults, dishonesty, graft, opportunism, gossip, to social reform, political programs, mass mobilizations, movements, but also serious historical reflection."[112] According to this school of thought, there is always a gap between the ideology and institutions of the state and the localized experience of everyday social practice. As Homi Bhahbha argues, this "contradictory and ambivalent space of enunciation" allows for the possibility of creative resistance to state hegemony.[113] In this sense, the postcolonial subject remains free to reinvent her/himself.

In my view, Muhammad Zauqi Shah, Shahidullah Faridi, and Wahid Bakhsh Sial Rabbani provide further evidence of this discursive freedom. In both its scope and scale, the *shaykh's* literary legacy confirms the capacity of the postcolonial subject not only to speak—but to think, read, and write, critically and creatively, as well. In the face of pervasive social and political change, these twentieth-century Sufi masters mounted a spirited defense of Sufi tradition. As social critics and political commentators, they engaged in a creative reformulation of Chishti Sabiri identity. Their diverse writings articulate an old message in a new medium. In doing so, they demonstrate the fluidity of identity and the malleability of tradition. Today, the *shaykh's* legacy continues to guide and inspire a new generation of disciples. In Pakistan and Malaysia, Chishti Sabiris employ the instruments of mass media to inscribe and articulate Sufi identity for a new millennium.

This chapter has explored Sufism as a discursive tradition, imagined and inscribed in texts. To fully understand how contemporary Chishti Sabiri identity is expressed and experienced, however, we need to go beyond the written word. In the book's remaining chapters, I turn from the outward to the inward dimensions of Sufism in order to reveal the heart and soul of Chishti Sabiri practice: ritual practice. Focusing on the lived experiences and personal stories of individual disciples, chapter 4 examines today's Chishti Sabiri order as a teaching community centered on the intimate and intense master-disciple relationship.

CHAPTER 4

TEACHING SUFISM: NETWORKS OF
COMMUNITY AND DISCIPLESHIP

Sufis write books, some of them polemical and political. Yet the heart of the Chishti Sabiri tradition remains firmly grounded in an interpersonal teaching network centered on the fundamental master-disciple (*pir-murid*) relationship. This chapter turns from texts to ethnographic contexts to explore how knowledge is transmitted within the contemporary Chishti Sabiri order. By quoting liberally from personal interviews, I aim to allow *murids* to articulate their own experiences and understanding of the Sufi path. The words of a senior *murid*—a middle-aged, middle-class, male Pakistani who is a father and husband, a businessman and a Sufi adept—offer an appropriate entry point into this worldview:

> Our antennas are so deeply attuned to the material world that we rarely tune in to the spiritual transmitter. There is a whole world there that directly impacts this material world, what we are doing here. Allah Most High is the source of the spiritual transmission. He is on 365 days a year, twenty-four hours a day. If you want to find this frequency, you must join a Sufi order [*tariqa*]. The *shaykh* is your antenna. (October 15, 2000, Lahore)

Spiritual insight, this disciple suggests, requires the altering of perspective and the cultivation of awareness. The self must realigned toward the Divine Other. This process of self-fashioning, he insists, is most effectively channeled through a Sufi order and amplified under the tutelage of a spiritual master. In the absence of proper guidance, the message remains muted. The language in this evocative description is revealing. The abundance of technological metaphors reflects the worldview of contemporary Chishti Sabiri devotees who are fully enmeshed in the complexities and contradictions of the mundane world of twenty-first-century life. At the same time, they maintain a discursive tradition and ritual discipline that both links them to a sacralized Islamic past and sacralizes the living present.

Though marked by its distinctive South Asian roots, the Chishti Sabiri order has demonstrated a remarkable vibrancy, dynamism, and adaptability while expanding into new technological, geographical, and cultural spheres. For disciples living in twenty-first-century Pakistan, Malaysia, and beyond, the *silsila* functions on multiple levels simultaneously. In this chapter, I explore three interdependent dimensions of Chishti Sabiri identity:

1. *The silsila as a spiritual pedigree.* The Chishti Sabiri order is a spiritual community grounded in sacred history and shared genealogy. The current generation is linked to its antecedents through an unbroken chain of authority that collapses the rigid boundaries between the remembered past and the living present. Among contemporary disciples, stories about the lives of previous Sufi exemplars are memorialized in texts and continuously recirculated in a network of oral narratives. In Chishti Sabiri practice, this relationship with past masters is also confirmed through dreams and visionary experiences. Within the order's communal network, the teaching *shaykh* serves as the living embodiment of all his predecessors—the heir to the legacy of the paradigmatic Sufi, the Prophet Muhammad.

2. *The silsila as a teaching network.* Chishti Sabiri identity is forged through didactic techniques of mental and bodily discipline, a rigorous ritual praxis informed by a comprehensive epistemology and a detailed theory of subjectivity. The continuity of the order's networks of knowledge and practice rests on the hierarchical yet intimate bond between master and disciple. At the same time, Chishti Sabiri *murids* provide each other with a horizontal support system. This supplementary source of practical knowledge both complements and clarifies the vertical *pir-murid* teaching relationship.

3. *The silsila as a social nexus.* Contemporary Chishti Sabiri disciples are bound together in webs of experience and identity via their common ties to Chishti Sabiri *shaykhs.* Beyond the rigors of the Sufi path, these linkages impact every dimension of a *murid's* social life. Disciples share deep personal friendships, and extended families are connected through dynamic interpersonal networks, often cemented by marriage. These relationships are frequently passed down from generation to generation, ensuring the continuity and strength of Chishti Sabiri tradition.

Together, these interlocking networks constitute the Chishti Sabiri order as an alternative locus of Islamic piety: a Sufi spiritual brotherhood cemented in shared values, ethics, ritual practices, and historical perspective. Chishti Sabiri identity rests on a symbiotic balance between the individual seeker and the broader community of adepts. Under the tutelage of a *shaykh*, a disciple's body and mind are systematically reshaped through disciplined ritual practices. While spiritual progress ultimately depends on individual action and personal responsibility, the Sufi subject is molded within the overarching framework of a public, communal network. Even as he/she travels the inner path, each disciple benefits from the collective wisdom and support of fellow *murids*. In the end, this system of knowledge and practice engenders a private, moral self that is, at the same time, imbued with a powerful sense of a shared, communal identity.

In everyday practice, the relations between the Chishti Sabiri *shaykh* and individual *murids* are mediated by an elaborate matrix of rules of conduct that fall under the rubric of *adab*. *Adab* is a multivalent concept, pervasive yet difficult to define. It encompasses everything from etiquette and decorum to moral character and interpersonal ethics. *Adab* is both the measuring stick of propriety, civility, and sophistication and the grease that oils the machinery of social life. As historian Barbara Metcalf notes, "*[A]dab* may 'mean' correct outer behavior, but it is understood as both cause of and then, reciprocally, fruit of one's inner self. Knowing, doing, and being are inescapably one."[1] Encompassing both external codes of social behavior and the inner mechanics of personal transformation, *adab* can be thought of as both a noun and a verb.

Adab has a particular resonance in Sufi theory and practice. According to the well-known Arabic adage, "All of Sufism is *adab*" (*al-tasawwuf kulluhu al-adab*). Time and again during interviews, Chishti Sabiri disciples highlighted the distinction between outer/exoteric (*zahiri*) and inner/esoteric (*batini*) dimensions of knowledge and experience. As the science of the heart, I was often told, Sufism aims at a balance between these two realms—the cultivation of a private, moral self goes hand in hand with public displays of virtue. The semantic parallels between *adab* and *suluk* (the Sufi "path") highlight this reciprocity. At one level, *suluk* means "journey," "road," or "way." Like *adab*, however, it also connotes "behavior," "conduct," or "civility." Quite literally, the Sufi's interior journey and outward actions are inextricably intertwined.

This constant emphasis on both inner moral perfection and outward social decorum is yet another theme that links the Chishti Sabiri *silsila* with its premodern antecedents. Indeed, Sufi models of public morality and ethical practice have had a profound and lasting impact on Muslim social life across the historical and cultural spectrum of the Islamic world. As Ernst and Lawrence note, "In this sense, one should acknowledge the Sufi orders, including the Chishtiyya, as bellwethers for society as a whole. They projected not merely mystical insights for like-minded mystics, but practical points of responsible behavior, which had an ethical appeal to Muslims from numerous classes and professions in the major urban areas of the Muslim world."[2] For today's Chishti Sabiris, the rules of *adab* continue to shape their interactions with the spiritual master, with their fellow disciples, and with society at large.

This chapter explores the *adab* of contemporary Chishti Sabiri master-disciple relations through an ethnographic lens. My analysis draws upon extensive interviews with *murids* in both Pakistan and Malaysia in an attempt to answer a series of questions: Who are these contemporary *murids*? How are the networks that bind adepts to their *shaykhs* and to each other constituted? How do disciples understand and articulate their own Chishti Sabiri identity? How are tensions, ambiguities, and contradictions mediated and resolved? In what ways do these networks of knowledge and practice confirm or contradict premodern traditions? On the whole, this inquiry is less concerned with the ideals of Sufi doctrine than with the realities of everyday, ordinary Sufi practice. My aim is to trace how contemporary Chishti Sabiri *murids* themselves experience and explain the multilayered teaching networks through which Sufi knowledge is transmitted and performed. This survey of the mechanics of master-disciple relations serves as a springboard for a detailed ethnography of contemporary Chishti Sabiri ritual practices in chapter 5. For twenty-first-century Chishti Sabiri adepts, spiritual companionship and ritual performance are the bedrock of Islamic faith. In an era of momentous social change, the *silsila's* teaching networks anchor religious identity, uniting today's disciples with a shared sense of meaning, purpose and belonging.

FROM KARACHI TO KUALA LUMPUR: CHISHTI SABIRI DISCIPLES

As Chishti Sabiri teaching *shaykhs*, Muhammad Zauqi Shah, Shahidullah Faridi, and Wahid Bakhsh Sial Rabbani each led his own independent coterie of disciples. Under the guidance of Shaykh Siraj 'Ali Muhammad—the designated successor (*khalifa*) of Shahidullah Faridi and, at presently, the order's only teaching *shaykh*—the order maintains its dynamism and vitality. The *silsila* continues to adapt to Pakistan's changing cultural landscape while expanding beyond the boundaries of South Asia. While the majority of today's Chishti Sabiri disciples are Pakistani, there is a significant and growing contingent of foreigners as well: Malaysians, South Africans, and Europeans. The *silsila* is distinguished from many other Sufi orders by the numbers and prominence of its female disciples. Women are full participants in all the order's ritual activities, and select senior female disciples are renowned for their advanced spiritual status and authority. My own interviews and observations confirmed what *murids* often told me: Chishti Sabiri *shaykhs* are fully accessible to women, and treat their female disciples as the spiritual equals of their male counterparts.[3] As a collective whole, the contemporary Chishti Sabiri order is as diverse as it is dynamic. Its overall scale, however, is difficult to assess. The *silisla* does not maintain public *murid* registers, and, as disciples note, Chishti Sabiri *shaykhs* as a rule never openly talk about their followers. In the absence of verifiable data, estimates of the total numbers of contemporary disciples vary. Anecdotal evidence and my own informal calculations suggest that Chishti Sabiri *murids* certainly number in the thousands. Yet I would also suggest that it is extremely misleading to measure the order's impact by counting heads. With its diverse publications and growing interpersonal networks, today's Chishti Sabiri *silsila* has a public profile that transcends the limits of its demographic and geographic boundaries.

In everyday practice the interactions between Shaykh Siraj 'Ali and his disciples take place mostly in private sessions. As an outsider, I was not often privy to these intimate, face-to-face exchanges. Even so, I did learn a great deal about the mechanics of *pir-murid* relations during my fieldwork through extensive interviews with disciples and direct observation of the *silsila's* public rituals. This included several visits to the weekly gatherings with Shaykh Siraj 'Ali in Karachi, frequent attendance at the *zikr* circles in Lahore, and, most significantly, numerous pilgrimages in the company of *murids* to Sufi shrine complexes in Pakistan for the annual death anniversaries ('*urs*) of celebrated Chishti saints. My analysis of this rich ethnographic material also draws on the *shaykhs'* published writings as well as the personal letters that many *murids* shared with me.

Who are these Chishti Sabiri disciples? As individuals, *murids* vary in the level of their commitment to (and engagement with) the *silsila*. At the very center of the order's life is an elite inner circle of several hundred disciples that include men and women, Pakistanis as well as foreigners. They are distinguished by their dedication to the rigors of *suluk* and active involvement in the order's myriad ritual activities. Though there are prominent exceptions to the rule, this inner core fits a general profile: they are mostly educated, middle-class, urban professionals. With the exception of several female Shi'a *murids*, they are also predominantly Sunni. Despite this imbalance, Chishti Sabiris insist that Sufi allegiances ultimately trump any divisions between Shi'a and Sunni. This is a frequent mantra in the public writings and private teachings of Chishti Sabiri *shaykhs* as well. Wahid Bakhsh Sial Rabbani in particular often downplayed Islam's sectarian divisions as nothing more than divisive, political posturing. According to a female disciple of Shi'i background,

> Hazrat Wahid Bakhsh used to get angry when people talked about "Sunni" or "Shi'a." He used to say that this was just a political conflict. The reason why 'Ali was not made caliph was that he was too involved in his spiritual devotions. He was the lion of Allah. He cared nothing for the world. He was a true Sufi and was never interested in the caliphate. (November 14, 2000, Islamabad)

While highlighting 'Ali's distinct piety and lofty spiritual status, this statement essentially confirms the normative Sunni reading of Islamic history. Even so, among Chishti Sabiri *murids* there is a deep and abiding respect for the Prophet's family and a vehement rejection of narrow, exclusive sectarian identities. This is not surprising since the Chishti Sabiri order's genealogy is traced to the Prophet Muhammad via his cousin and son-in-law 'Ali.[4]

Mirroring the legacy of their *shaykhs*, the core group of Chishti Sabiri disciples is well acquainted with the instruments and ideology of modernity. *Murids* move fluidly between multiple epistemological, linguistic, and geographical universes. Many have extensive networks of family and friends living in the Arab states of the Persian Gulf, England, Canada, and the United States. While numerous disciples come from extended families with a long history of Sufi affiliations, others were introduced to the *silsila* through interpersonal networks, word of mouth, and even dreams. Shaykh Siraj 'Ali Muhammad embodies a typical pattern. A fourth generation Chishti Sabiri, he was a graduate of the prestigious Pakistani Air Force Academy. Until his recent retirement, he was also a senior international pilot for Pakistan

International Airlines. The *shaykh* is multilingual, a voracious reader, a computer expert and technophile, and well versed in contemporary social, cultural, and political affairs. He travels frequently, both within Pakistan to meet with his own Sufi disciples and abroad to visit a number of relatives currently living in both Canada and the United States.

In keeping with broad demographic patterns, the Pakistani *murids* are ethnically diverse. The order primarily comprises ethnic Punjabis and Sindhis, along with a smaller representation of Pathans from the Northwest Frontier Province. While most disciples are multilingual—fluent in various regional languages—the standard medium of exchange among Pakistani disciples is Urdu. Like Shaykh Muhammad Zauqi Shah, a significant number of *murids* are immigrants (*muhajirs*) whose families left their ancestral homes in India in the decades surrounding Partition and political independence in 1947. Prominent disciples trace their family lineages to Delhi, Bhopal, and Lucknow in particular. In contemporary Pakistan, the majority of Chishti Sabiris live and work in the vicinity of major urban centers, especially Karachi, Lahore, Multan, and Islamabad. Most—though certainly not all—disciples are distinguished by socioeconomic status, profession, and educational background. Among their ranks are educators, engineers, publishers, bankers, computer programmers, medical professionals, technocrats, and businessmen. A number of prominent *murids* have advanced professional degrees, in several cases from European and American universities. Significantly, several senior male disciples have personal and professional links to the Pakistani military—a precedent established by both Shaykh Wahid Bakhsh Sial Rabbani and Shaykh Siraj 'Ali Muhammad.

Of course, not all contemporary disciples are Pakistani. As we have seen, Chishti Sabiri *shaykhs* have long welcomed both foreign Muslims and Western converts into the fold. Among the most influential of these foreign disciples is a dynamic group of Malaysian *murids*. During my research, I frequently met these Malaysian disciples at pilgrimage sites in Pakistan. I also traveled to Malaysia for five weeks where I interacted with many of them in and around the capital city of Kuala Lumpur. With one exception—a novice female *murid* of Shaykh Siraj 'Ali—they are all the disciples of Shaykh Wahid Bakhsh Sial Rabbani. Remarkably, these Malaysian *murids* all attribute their introduction to the *silsila* to a single individual: a medical doctor from the northern state of Kalantan who joined the Chishti Sabiri order in 1979 while studying in Karachi. Following his lead, several other Malaysian students who were at the time studying in Pakistan also joined the *silsila*. Over time this interpersonal network has steadily grown, and today there is a core group of nearly one hundred Malaysian disciples.

During his lifetime, Wahid Bakhsh maintained contact with this group via an active correspondence. He also traveled to Malaysia on two occasions late in life—in December 1990 and August 1994—visiting his disciples for several weeks on each visit. Since the *shaykh's* death in 1995, the Malaysian *murids* have maintained this connection. They continue their own *zikr* circles in Kuala Lumpur, and many of them travel frequently to Pakistan and India for pilgrimage. As we saw in chapter 3, the Malaysian's publication efforts have proved instrumental in spreading the Chishti Sabiri message across the Indian Ocean and into cyberspace. Overall, the order's spread into Southeast Asia signals an important shift in its makeup and modus operandi. While the Chishti Sabiri *silsila* has always adapted to change, its transplantation into entirely new geographical and cultural contexts marks a radical break with historical precedent.

Like their Pakistani counterparts, the Malaysian *murids*—both men and women—are mostly well-educated, middle-class, urban professionals. While the majority are ethnic Malay Muslims, their numbers include a significant contingent of Chinese and Indian converts. Most Malaysian disciples are multilingual, though with their *shaykhs* and Pakistani peers they normally speak English. This plurality prompts a series of further questions: Why would a Pakistani subbranch of a distinctly South Asian Sufi order appeal to Southeast Asians? How do these Malaysian *murids* make sense of the centrality of Pakistan and a Pakistani identity in their *shaykh*'s writings? Does the physical distance—to say nothing of the cultural and national divisions— never present a problem? In interviews, Malaysian *murids* invariably respond to such questions by insisting that the personal bond with Shaykh Wahid Bakhsh and their fellow *murids* ultimately transcends all other boundaries. In the words of a senior Malaysian disciple,

> He [Wahid Bakhsh] was our guide, a spiritual master. He guided people to God, through love and by taking a deep interest in them. It never mattered that he was Pakistani. There was never any doubt about that at all. He was just a teacher. He worked towards attracting people to God. There was no politics. (September 27, 2001, Kuala Lumpur)

This is an apt summation of the Sufi *pir-murid* relationship. It suggests that even as the *silsila's* transnational reach expands, the fundamental bond between master and disciple continues to cement Chishti Sabiri identity.

From Karachi to Kuala Lumpur, the background of contemporary Chishti Sabiri stands in sharp contrast to the prevalent stereotypes of Sufi practitioners. On both sides of the Indian Ocean, the critics of Sufism often dismiss the tradition as a backwater for marginalized, rural, and uneducated Muslims in an attempt to denigrate Sufi allegiances and practices. A closer look at today's Chishti Sabiri *silsila*, however, presents a different picture altogether. In both Pakistan and Malaysia, *murids* highlight the centrality of their Sufi identity in their busy, complex lives. Disciples emphasize the importance—and difficulty—of balancing the mundane demands of the world (*dunya*) with the rigors of religious practice (*din*). In the words of a young Pakistani *murid*,

> Islam is the only religion that balances your religion and your earthly life. This means that you must be a responsible family member, give attention to your family, earn a good livelihood, a reasonable livelihood—and, at the same time, observe your religious duties. [Christian] priests spend most of their lives confined to churches. A monk remains a monk until the day he dies. In fact,

those religions are very strict, unlike Islam. In Islam it [monastic life] is strictly forbidden. (November 8, 2000, Lahore)

For today's Chishti Sabiris, it is precisely the imperative for a direct engagement with ordinary, everyday life that distinguishes Islam from other faiths and Sufism from other practices.

Chishti Sabiris view the balancing of *din* and *dunya* as a central marker of their Sufi identity. Even so, they openly acknowledge that juggling the demands of worldly life and spiritual devotion is no simple matter. In both Pakistan and Malaysia, I often heard *murids* voice common concerns—from long hours at the office, to the increasing demands of time, money, and family life, to incessant worries about political instability and economic uncertainty. Chishti Sabiri teachings encourage disciples to approach these struggles as a form of religious practice. According to Shaykh Wahid Bakhsh, worldly troubles are in fact an essential part of Sufi training. In a personal letter to a female disciple in Malaysia, the *shaykh* writes,

> Nothing happens in the world without the will of Allah Almighty. Worries and difficulties are thrown in our way as tests and trials by the great taskmaster, not to harm us but to purify us and elevate us. He wants us, His near ones and dear ones, to develop strong characters and the utmost patience to be able to climb upwards. He tries us by hardships, difficulties, poverty and disease. He takes us to the bursting point, but does not allow us to burst . . . These are His ways of loving His dear ones. The great *shaykhs* love and welcome this harshness on the part of Divine Beloved.[5]

The path to God, Wahid Bakhsh insists, goes straight through the world; there are no shortcuts. The world may be seductive or destructive, but spiritual wisdom is impossible in the absence of patience, endurance, and equanimity.

Disciples often point to the example of the Prophet Muhammad when discussing the balance between *din* and *dunya*. As the paradigmatic Sufi, the Prophet's example of engaging the world as an exercise of spiritual discipline is instructive. In the words of a young disciple, a French convert who married the granddaughter of Shaykh Wahid Bakhsh and who now lives with his family in Karachi,

> We are not *sadhus* [Hindu ascetics], doing twenty-four hours of meditation a day. We have to manage this life. We have to go to work, and afterwards we have to give time to our children and wives, as the Prophet Muhammad, God bless him and grant him salvation, showed us. You cannot just come back from work and go to the shrine or remain in meditation. That is not correct, and it is not the Sufi path (*suluk*). *Suluk* is the entire thing, you see. It involves *dunya*—making money, taking care of your family, meeting with people. And it is also ritual worship (*'ibadat*), your prayers, your meditation, your *zikr*. All these things together are *suluk*. It is these things that bring you near to Allah. The point is to struggle. (September 2, 2001, Karachi)

Murids also look to the *shaykhs* of their own *silsila* for guidance and inspiration in their daily lives. Stories of Chishti Sabiri masters as well as other famous premodern Sufi luminaries are constantly circulated among disciples. According to a female Pakistani *murid*, the *shaykhs'* lives exemplify Sufi piety and social etiquette in action: "In Islam you must fulfill all your obligations, all your duties in this world, in a very proper way. All these saints, Hazrat Waris Hasan Shah Sahab, Hazrat Zauqi Shah Sahab, Hazrat Shahidullah Sahab, Hazrat Wahid Bakhsh, Hazrat Siraj Sahab, they all did their jobs, they went to schools and universities. And besides fulfilling their worldly duties, their religious discipline (*'ibadat*) was something beautiful, a bond between them and God. They really practiced what they preached" (June 17, 2001, Lahore).

Nowhere is this emphasis on balancing *din* and *dunya* more apparent than in the prevailing Chishti Sabiri attitude toward education. Disciples often distinguish between rational, discursive, worldly knowledge (*'ilm*) and the intuitive, experiential knowledge (*ma'rifa*) gained through the rigors of spiritual practice.[6] Both are seen as absolutely essential for an individual's overall development. The coupling of practical, technical knowledge with the rigors of Sufi training is recognized as a key component of the *shaykhs'* teachings. As a result, disciples typically encourage their own sons and daughters to pursue a secular education while maintaining their religious devotions. The children of a number of prominent Chishti Sabiri adepts have in fact been encouraged to pursue their studies in Western universities. Many have gone on to advanced degrees in engineering, computer science, accounting, and finance, both at home and abroad. Disciples recognize the secular university as the bastion of *'ilm*, a place to develop the practical, professional skills needed for worldly success. *Ma'rifa*, by contrast, is preserved and perpetuated only through the networks of knowledge and ritual practice maintained under the watchful guidance of a Sufi *shaykh*.

When asked, most Chishti Sabiri disciples acknowledge the merits of a more traditional religious education. They view the *madrasa* as an important symbol of Muslim identity—the bastion of the long history of intellectual and scholarly rigor in Islamic civilization. *Madrasas* serve a vital social function as repositories of religious learning and social welfare centers, disciples insist. Even so, following the precedent of their own spiritual mentors, contemporary Chishti Sabiri disciples do not typically attend *madrasas* themselves. The words of a highly respected Pakistani disciple—a man who studied for a doctoral degree in engineering in the United States and whose daughter attended university abroad—are revealing:

> Hazrat Wahid Bakhsh once remarked that we would have lost our entire religious education system to Western education had it not been for these *madrasas*. A *madrasa* is suitable for a religious education, for producing *hafiz* [experts who have memorized the Qur'an], to ensure that the mosques are run and that people learn *hadith* [traditions about the Prophet Muhammad]. *Madrasas* are popular because the have-nots of the community

send their children there for food, shelter, and education. There is a steady stream of students coming in. They cannot do anything else. Either they work as tea stall boys or auto shop boys. Some parents think they should study, and maybe take it up as a profession by becoming a preacher at a local mosque. But this is not encouraged for people who are in the *silsila* and mostly come from middle-class, educated families. (August 26, 2001, Lahore)

There is, as this quote suggests, an underlying elitism to Chishti Sabiri views on education and the pursuit of knowledge. The *madrasa* is viewed as an appropriate outlet for training in the traditional Islamic sciences, particularly for the socially marginalized who lack other career options. For those with privileged access to the teachings of a Sufi *shaykh*, however, *madrasa* training is seen as superfluous.

Significantly, there is a prominent exception to this general rule. Chishti Sabiri *shaykhs* typically encourage their non-Pakistani disciples to study for a short period in a *madrasa*. This has been the case for Western converts and foreign Muslims alike. For these newcomers, a short stint in *madrasa* is seen as an invaluable tutorial on the basics of Muslim history, theology, and religious life—a necessary prerequisite for entry into the rigors of the Sufi path. This practice was firmly established by Shaykh Shahidullah Faridi who drew a large number of foreigners into the order in Karachi during the 1970s. According to one of the *shaykh's* European disciples, "When you convert to Islam, the first thing the *shaykh* tells you is to learn Arabic, *hadith*, and *fiqh*. It is meant to guide you, so that you know what to do in various aspects of life. This is the only thing they want. They don't want you to become an *'alim* [religious scholar]. If you do become one, wonderful. If you can use this knowledge, why not? But the main aim of sending you to *madrasa* is simply to guide you in life" (September 2, 2001, Karachi).

Amid all its diversity, the contemporary Chishti Sabiri order is a distinct corporate institution—a moral community, united by the rules of *adab* and the discipline of ritual practice. Despite their significant individual differences, Pakistani, Malaysian, and foreign *murids* share a deep sense of collective identity. This bond is communicated through a common set of values and a standard code of behavior. In both public and private settings—at home, at work, or among their fellow *murids*—Chishti Sabiri men, women, and children are taught to carry themselves with a particular style. *Adab* impacts their physical comportment, the manner of their dress and speech, and in the way they interact with others. In the succinct words of a prominent Pakistani disciple, "Everyone in this *silsila* carries the stamp of the group, regardless of their own personal background" (October 7, 2000, Lahore). This pervasive ethos emerges from the central axis of Chishti Sabiri identity: the master-disciple relationship. As the living heir to the *silsila's* spiritual ancestors and the Prophet Muhammad himself, the Chishti Sabiri spiritual master leads by example. In the end, it is the teaching *shaykh* who initiates novice disciples into the *silsila's* networks of knowledge and practice.

THE SUFI MASTER-DISCIPLE RELATIONSHIP

Sufi epistemology emerges from a Qur'anic worldview. Invoking the Qur'an (57:3), Sufis describe God as "the first, the last, the outer, the inner." Sufi theorists have long distinguished between the outward (*zahir*) and inward (*batin*) dimensions of reality. A well-known Sufi formula uses a threefold rhyming structure to distinguish between the outward form of Islamic law (*shari'a*), the inner approach of the Sufi path (*tariqa*), and the ultimate reality of God (*haqiqa*). As Ernst notes,

> This kind of rhetorical formula permitted Sufis to position their distinctive practices as the internalization of the external rituals of Muslim religious life. Sufism was a way to proceed from ordinary external life to find the inner reality of God. This hierarchical grading of reality amounts to a theory of esotericism; as the Qur'an states (39:9), "Are those who know equal to those who do not know?" It is important to recognize that this pervasive metaphor of inner reality and knowledge requires the external forms of religion to make any sense at all. The self-articulation of Sufism in this way presupposed the norms of Islamic tradition at the same time that it pointed beyond the limitations of those conventions.[7]

Shari'a, tariqa, and *haqiqa* represent hierarchical yet interdependent levels of awareness and experience. This typology, in turn, mirrors the Sufi adept's inner journey toward self-realization, a path that grows narrower and steeper as it approaches the goal: the existential experience of the oneness of God (*tawhid*).

Sufi training aims at nothing less than the remaking of the self. Its ritual practices are designed to subdue the ego while purifying the body, mind, and heart. In this system, spiritual growth is measured by both inner states of awareness and outer displays of pious behavior. According to a well-known tradition of the Prophet Muhammad, "The *shari'a* are my words [*aqwali*], the *tariqa* are my actions [*a'mali*], and the *haqiqa* is my interior states [*ahwali*]."[8] Early Sufi theoreticians translated their own spiritual experiences into a sophisticated and nuanced psychology based on a tripartite division between the *nafs* (the "soul" or lower "ego-self"), *qalb* ("heart"), and *ruh* ("spirit"). This tripartite paradigm emerged with the Qur'anic commentary of Ja'far al-Sadiq (d. 765) and was later appropriated by such spiritual luminaries as al-Muhasibi (d. 857), Abu Yazid al-Bistami (d. 877), al-Hakim al-Tirmidhi (d.~905), al-Junayd (d. 910), and al-Qushayri (d. 1074). These Sufi theorists described the arduous path to gnosis as the experience of various states (*hal*, plural *ahwal*) and stations (*maqam*, plural *maqamat*). In classical Sufi doctrine, *ahwal* are understood as sudden flashes of insight and clarity. These moments of illumination are gifts from God. They stand in contrast with *maqamat*: a series of discrete psychological and ethical qualities that the adept attains only through his/her own determined efforts. The Sufi spiritual journey is not for the faint of heart. Progress demands absolute sincerity (*ikhlas*), unwavering patience (*sabr*), relentless striving (*mujahida*), and, most importantly, boundless love (*'ishq*). For a select few, the journey culminates in the states of *fana'* (annihilation of self) and ultimately *baqa'* (permanence in God).

Chishti Sabiri *shaykhs* echo these classic formulations on Sufi psychology and *suluk*. In an essay entitled "The Spiritual Psychology of Islam" Shaykh Shahidullah Faridi adopts an informal idiom to liken the spiritual heart (*qalb*) to the ruler of a country. This king is advised by two combative ministers: a saintly and ascetic man of God (*ruh*); and a greedy, proud, and cunning man (*nafs*), obsessed with the fame, wealth, and defense of the country. In the *shaykh's* words, "Man, who is the ruler of his own little kingdom, has to choose between the admonition of the unworldly and God-oriented spiritual soul [*ruh*] and the urging of the concupiscent self [*nafs*], and find the way to justice in which the rights of both are maintained. This choice leads to a resolve, and the resolve displays itself in outward action."[9] Shahidullah's metaphor outlines the contours of spiritual *jihad*, highlighting the central role of human free will in the Sufi quest. In this system, human beings are morally responsible for their own actions; in the end, the decisions individuals make dictate their fate in this world and the next.

Chishti Sabiri *shaykhs* also distinguish between multiple gradations of knowledge and experience. Drawing on a familiar typology, Wahid Bakhsh Sial Rabbani traces three distinct levels: *'Ilm al-yaqin* (cognitive knowledge), *'Ayn al-yaqin* (sensory knowledge), and *Haqq al-yaqin* (true, or intuitive, knowledge). In the *shaykh's* words, "The difference [between them] can be explained by the analogy of the degrees of faith or belief in fire. One who has not seen fire can be told that it burns. His belief in fire or its burning quality would be of the category of belief through the law of evidence. It is known as *'Ilm al-yaqin* in Islam. If he sees with his own eyes fire burning wood, his belief in fire would be of the degree of *'Ayn al-yaqin*. But if he puts his hand in the fire or walks into it, the degree of his belief in the fire would be of the highest order called *Haqq al-yaqin*."[10] As Wahid Bakhsh illustrates, these represent hierarchical but interdependent levels of knowing, experiencing, and being. In order to put theory into practice, however, the Sufi novice needs guidance. Given the rigors of the Sufi path, no one can hope to complete the rigorous spiritual journey (*suluk*) alone. In fact, spiritual dilettantism is considered extremely dangerous, if not deadly. Only an accomplished spiritual master can provide the wisdom, direction, and structure needed to propel the Sufi seeker (*salik*) toward self-transcendence and intimacy with the Divine Beloved. In the end, the *salik* needs a *shaykh*.

The Qualities of a True *Shaykh*

In his famous book, *Bihishti Zewar* [Heavenly Ornaments], Maulana Ashraf 'Ali Thanawi (1864–1943)—a Chishti Sabiri *shaykh* and a key figure in the history of the Deoband *madrasa*—offers spiritual aspirants the following advice:

> If you intend to become a disciple, you should look for certain qualities in a master. Do not become a disciple of anyone who lacks them. First, the master should know the points of religion and be acquainted with the *shari'at.* Second, his beliefs should in no way oppose the *shari'at* . . . Third, he should not practice *piri-muridi* for food and a living. Fourth, the prospective *pir* should himself be the disciple of someone who is regarded as venerable by good people. Fifth, good people should regard him as good, too. Sixth, his teaching should cause love and enthusiasm for religion to grow. This can be ascertained from seeing the state of his other disciples. If among ten disciples five or six are good, you can judge him to be a master with spiritual power; do not worry about one or two being bad. You have heard about the spiritual power (*tasir*) in elders. It is this. Do not look for other kinds of power—for example, the power to say something and make it happen; or to remove sickness by breathing on someone; or to make a wish come true by preparing an amulet; or to make someone feel agitated through direction of the *pir's* attention (*tawajjuh*) toward that person. Never be deceived by these powers. The seventh important quality is that the master's religious counsel should not be swayed by his disciples' concerns but should stop them short in anything wrong.[11]

Ashraf 'Ali Thanawi's criteria set the standard for the Chishti Sabiri revivalist milieu of the nineteenth and twentieth centuries. It also resonates with the *silsila's* contemporary teachings. Chishti Sabiri writings offer abundant advice on the qualities of a proper *shaykh.* In *Tarbiyat al-'ushshaq,* for example, Zauqi Shah submits his own list of prerequisites for sound spiritual guidance. A *shaykh* should follow the *shari'a;* he should have a deep connection (*nisbat*) with the potential *murid;* he should effect a positive and lasting change in his committed disciples; and he should influence the heart (*qalb*) of anyone who spends time in his company. "If these signs are present," Zauqi Shah asserts, "one should become a disciple without hesitation."[12] While the times change, the requirements for proper spiritual guidance do not.

A Sufi master is the bridge between the abstraction of theoretical knowledge and the concrete, visceral, and transformative power of direct experience. Though book knowledge is useful, it has its limits. For Sufis, it is the *shaykh* who demonstrates how to put thought into action, bridging the gap between theory and practice. In the words of Shaykh Shahidullah Faridi,

> The theoretical knowledge derived from books cannot be, and was never designed to be, a substitute for association with those experienced travelers who have completed their journey along the road and reached their goal, and have now returned to guide others on the same way. The Book of Allah itself was not sent alone; it was sent through the medium of the Prophet who was at the same time its conveyor, its commentator and its living interpretation. It was moreover he, who by training and instructing them in the light of the Book, purified his companions and elevated them to the heights of Godliness . . . This is the principle which is followed in the system of teaching of the Sufis; theoretical knowledge has to be quickened to life by association with a man of God, and the road ahead cannot be traversed without the guide.[13]

Just as the Prophet Muhammad embodies the Qur'anic message, so too does the *shaykh* embody the Sufi path. Disciples learn directly by living in his company, by listening to his words, and by observing him in action. For all Muslims, of course, the Prophet serves as the perfection of piety. He is, as the Qur'an (33:21) states, the *uswa hasana* (the "beautiful model"). For Sufis, the Prophet is also the paradigmatic *shaykh*, the starting point in the chain of spiritual authority. For Chishti Sabiris, the parallels between the living Sufi masters and the Prophet are more than metaphorical. Disciples expressly link the power and authority of their *shaykhs* with their unique relationship with the Prophet Muhammad. "They are the '*Ulama-i Rasikhin*," writes Zauqi Shah, "the learned people firm in their knowledge, and they have the distinction of being recognized as heirs to the Holy Prophet."[14]

This chain of spiritual power and authority is made explicit in Chishti Sabiri ritual practice. The relationship with the *shaykh* provides intimacy with the Prophet and ultimately with God. Through obedience and ritual discipline, the Sufi disciple's ego is first dissolved in the *shaykh* (*fana' fi al-shaykh*), before becoming annihilated in the Prophet (*fana' fi al-rasul*) and, eventually, God (*fana' fi Allah*). According to Shahidullah Faridi, "Dependence of the Shaykh is of course more in the beginning when the novice is making his journey along the unfamiliar road. As he approaches the end of it, the personality of the Shaykh dissolves into that of the Noble Prophet (may Allah bless and keep him), who is the Guide of guides, and then finally into that One and Single Being who is the Author of all beings, the Creator."[15] Only a perfected spiritual master (*shaykh-i mukammil*) who has traversed the terrain himself can steer the disciple through the twists and turns of this path. Effaced of individual ego, the *shaykh* serves as the embodiment of *shari'a*, the living reflection of the Prophet, and, ultimately, the key to unlock the mysteries of God. As Zauqi Shah explains,

> A *shaykh* has achieved annihilation in the essence of both the Prophet, God bless him and grant him salvation, and God Most High. For this reason, when someone reaches the state of annihilation in the *shaykh*, he will immediately receive annihilation in the Prophet and annihilation in God. If a glass of water is poured into the ocean where does it go? This water is absorbed (*fana'*) into the ocean.[16]

Contemporary Chishti Sabiri disciples see their own spiritual masters as living conduits to Islam's sacred past. They frequently explain this dynamic by drawing explicit parallels between the contemporary *silsila* and the early Muslim community surrounding the Prophet Muhammad in Medina. As a novice Pakistani disciple explained to me,

> Your immediate attachment is to your *shaykh*. It is like the Prophet with his Companions. You have to give your *shaykh* the same kind of respect. When he is speaking to you, there is no question that it is divinely inspired. There is a chain that links you to the Prophet, God bless him and grant him salvation, and through him to each of the *shaykhs* and ultimately to Allah. This is why the most

important thing a disciple possesses is the spiritual genealogy (*shajara*). If there is a manual to Sufism then it is the order's *shajara*. It is a tree, that's the literal translation, a genealogical table. Knowing the pedigree of your *silsila* is extremely important. You are supposed to be in touch with each of those *shaykhs* through spiritual contact. You seek guidance from each of them through *muraqaba* [contemplation]. And the Prophet, God bless him and grant him salvation, as well. These linkages are extremely important. (March 22, 2001, Islamabad)

As this quote illustrates, for twenty-first-century Chishti Sabiris genealogy is no mere abstraction. It is the lifeblood of spiritual power and authority.

Given the crucial importance of a spiritual master, how does an aspiring Sufi find a true *shaykh*? Among Chishti Sabiris, the stories vary widely. For the significant number of *murids* who come from families with a long history in the *silsila*, the connection with the master was formed in childhood and then deepened over time. According to a Pakistani female disciple, "I had known him [Shaykh Shahidullah Faridi] since early childhood. My mother and my grandmother always talked about these two brothers who had come from England. There was an intense love and emotion we all had for him. To this day, the love I have for him is more intense than that for my father, my brothers, my sisters, all my children. I've turned fifty now. This love has grown more and more with each passing day. I think it's really the love of Allah" (June 17, 2001, Lahore). Within mutligenerational *silsila* families, *adab* is learned first through observation and then direct participation. Parents introduce their children to the rules of decorum from an early age, and as they mature young disciples are gradually drawn into the order's symbolic universe and diverse ritual practices. As a Pakistani *murid* attests, the bonds with the Sufi master run as deep as those of blood:

I hope my sons will become *murids* and that their generation will also be associated with this *silsila*. Now my sons, they know the etiquette [*adab*]. They kiss Hazrat Siraj Sahab's hand. I didn't teach them that, but they know it. All the *shaykhs* have always been very kind to all of us. Everybody who came into contact with them received the same treatment from them. I would say that whatever we have achieved so far is because of the guidance of our *shaykh* and his *khalifa*, Hazrat Siraj Sahab. Everything: worldly things, personal things, spiritual things. All these things have been through their guidance and their prayers for us. Otherwise, a person without a teacher or a leader or a guide can be lost anywhere. (March 24, 2001, Islamabad)

Chishti Sabiri families take immense pride in their *silsila* affiliations and their personal relationships with the *shaykh*, and they take great care to ensure that this bond is passed down from generation to generation.

The majority of today's Chishti Sabiri disciples did not inherit their *silsila* connections, however. Many were first introduced to their *shaykh* by word of mouth via interpersonal networks. As chapter 5 will demonstrate, others were led to a spiritual master through dreams. Yet for most contemporary *murids*, spiritual companionship and guidance with the *shaykh* was the culmination of a long (and often arduous) search. Journeying for spiritual guidance is a common trope in Sufi hagiography. In narrating their own stories, many Chishti Sabiris describe the challenges and difficulties of finding a suitable spiritual mentor. Often it involves a paradigmatic quest in which the seeker travels widely, meeting with many potential masters before finally discovering the elusive connection with a spiritual guide. A young Pakistani male *murid* explains the logic of this process: "If you're searching for a *shaykh*, you have the right to be selective. But you go and spend time with any number of *shaykhs*. You meet with them, you see what sort of people are associated with the *silsila*. Is there anything going on there which appears to be against *shari'a*? If there is, you ask for clarification about why this is happening. There is a whole process of elimination, and only then choose your *shaykh*. In the end, you meet the person who is destined for you" (March 22, 2001, Islamabad).

Chishti Sabiri disciples frequently point to the legacy of Shaykh Shahidullah Faridi—an Englishman, a convert, and, in the end, a Sufi teacher of the highest rank—as the preeminent example of the sacrifices and potential rewards of the spiritual journey. Shahidullah's remarkable story of a protracted search for spiritual guidance is echoed in the account of a young novice, the French convert, who now lives in Karachi. After traveling widely in Asia in search of spiritual wisdom, this young man ultimately found a deep personal connection with Shaykh Wahid Bakhsh. There was, he suggests, an immediate connection that made him desperate for initiation in the *silsila*. Yet as a new convert to Islam he was filled with questions and eager for tangible proof that Wahid Bakhsh was a true spiritual master. In an interview, he recalled his first encounter with the *shaykh*:

> I asked him [Wahid Bakhsh] to show me a miracle because I'd heard about fake *pirs*. Not that I thought that Hazrat Sahab was a fake *pir*, but I knew that some people had been shown a miracle. So I asked him. And he told me, "We are not here for that. This will keep you from coming near to Allah." For a week I kept asking for initiation (*bay'at*) from Captain Sahab, but he refused, telling me, "You've got an Indian visa in your pocket. Go to India and look around. You will find holy men all over the country. Meet with them and when you return, come to me." In my heart I knew he was a good person. I was desperate to receive *bay'at* from him and he finally agreed. I met Hazrat Captain Wahid Bakhsh, may God have mercy upon him, and it is to him that my heart was attracted. I came to know afterwards that these things are already planned, the love you have for your *murshid*. It is a natural process in the system of Allah. (September 2, 2001, Karachi)

As this account demonstrates, Chishti Sabiri disciples believe that the relationship with the *shaykh* is preordained. While novices are expected to test a potential spiritual suitor, the offer for guidance is not guaranteed. The audacity of this young man's request for a display of miracles is nonetheless remarkable. Yet, in the end, he is won over by the sheer force of Wahid

Bakhsh's personality—his openness, encouragement, and kindness. More than twenty years later, the Frenchman remains in Pakistan, immersed in Sufi practice.

Once formed, the personal bond between Sufi master and disciple is as intimate as it is intense. Not surprisingly, Chishti Sabiri *murids* often characterize this connection as the single most important relationship in their lives. In interviews, disciples spoke openly with me—often at great length and with intense emotion—about their own experiences with their *shaykhs*. A *murid's* relationship with a Sufi master impacts every dimension of his/her personal, professional, and spiritual life. For Chishti Sabiris of all backgrounds, it is a bond that shapes their worldviews, directs their actions, and frames their basic sense of self-identity. Significantly, it is precisely this kind of unwavering devotion to Sufi masters that has led some critics to question Sufism. In the past, Sufi masters have been feared as much as respected because of this intense devotion of their followers. Chishti Sabiri *murids*, however, maintain that the dedication to the master is not unconditional. Every *shaykh's* status is dependent on the power of his personal charisma, the depth of his piety, the righteousness of his actions, and the strength of the genealogy that links the master to the authority of the Prophet Muhammad. Though Sufi discipleship ultimately demands personal surrender, devotion, and an unwavering faith in one's spiritual guide, Chishti Sabiri disciples insist that love for the *shaykh* is not blind.

Formal Initiation (*bay'at*)

The relationship between the Chishti Sabiri novice and the teaching *shaykh* is consecrated through *bay'at*: the ritual ceremony that marks formal initiation into the order. With *bay'at*, the Sufi aspirant is transformed into a *murid*—a full participant in the *silsila's* teaching network and corporate identity. The ceremony itself is simple yet symbolic. With prayers and invocations, the novice acknowledges the absolute authority of the *shaykh* and pledges obedience and submission to him. This custom has deep roots in Muslim culture. In pre-Islamic Arab society, *bay'at* was the traditional way of pledging allegiance to a tribal chief. More importantly, the ceremony recalls the public oath of allegiance that Muhammad's followers pledged to him at Hudaybiya in 628.[17] According to the Qur'an (48:10), "Those who swear allegiance to you [Muhammad] actually swear allegiance to God. God's hand is over their hands." Echoing this covenant, the Chishti Sabiri *bay'at* ceremony formally links the Sufi disciple with the teaching *shaykh* and, by extension, the spiritual grace and blessing of the order's chain of spiritual luminaries. Shahidullah Faridi explains the importance of this ritual:

> *Baiat* [*sic*] is a firm pact, and whoever makes it should make it with this awareness. It is a pact not only with the Shaykh, but with all the saints of the *silsila* and through them with the Prophet of Allah (may Allah bless and keep him), and ultimately with Allah Himself . . . When the *murid* makes his allegiance to

his *shaykh*, he follows this precedent [the oath of allegiance to the Prophet]; in fact, if the limitations of time and space are ignored, he really makes the very same pact as the Noble Prophet's companions. We cannot physically pay allegiance to the Noble Prophet (may All bless and keep him), but when we give our hands to one whose spiritual tree reached up to him, it is in reality the same thing.[18]

Chishti Sabiri *bay'at*, in essence, symbolizes a spiritual rebirth. It is an affirmation of intention, a confirmation of loyalty, and a pledge to honor the *silsila's* antecedents.

It is significant—if somewhat paradoxical—that Chishti Sabiri *bay'at* simultaneously inducts disciples into numerous Sufi orders. According to a highly respected senior disciple, "The masters of our order give initiation in four *silsilas*. When the initiation ceremony takes place, the disciple says, 'I take *bay'at* at the hands of my *shaykh* in the Chishtiyya Sabiriyya and Nizamiyya, Suhrawardiyya, Qadiriyya, Naqshbandiyya.' These are the primary orders, and we take *bay'at* in all of them. The teachings [and practices] are that of the Sabiriyaa *silsila*, but we receive the blessings [*barakat*] of all four *silsilas*" (September 1, 2001, Karachi). This open, inclusive notion of spiritual authority reflects a well-established historical precedent. It was in fact common practice for premodern Chishti Sabiri masters—the nineteenth-century reformist and Deoband founder Hajji Imdad Allah, for example—to accept initiation into multiple Sufi orders. For the majority of today's disciples, however, these connections with multiple *tariqas* are largely symbolic. In contemporary practice, the *silsila's* identity is exclusive and its ritual practices are tightly controlled. Once they have taken *bay'at*, disciples are strongly discouraged from seeking spiritual advice outside the insulated boundaries of the *silsila*. In the words of a highly respected, elder *murid*,

> There are so many branches to the Chishti *silsila*. Just here in Karachi there may be three or four hundred branches. There are many Chishti Sabiris too—some branches have been merging. We do not maintain contact with them at all. We do not mix with anyone. Once you become a *murid*, you stay in one place, in one *silsila*. You don't go around with others. Before you're a *murid*, it is alright to visit other *silsilas* though, and other *shaykhs*. (December 15, 2000, Karachi)

Why this marked change in attitude and practice? Why this break with the *silsila's* own traditions? Significantly, Chishti Sabiri disciples explain this exclusivity as a necessary response to the corruption and dangers of the modern age. In an increasingly unpredictable world, I was frequently told, a firm commitment to a single guide and a single path offers the best hope for moral guidance and spiritual protection. Disciples point especially to the persistent dangers of falling under the influence of ideologues and unqualified religious leaders. There is a widespread sense that the *silsila's* rigid boundaries eliminate the potential distractions, doubts, and damage of both unsound guidance and spiritual dilettantism. Given the temptations and uncertainty of twenty-first-century life, disciples view total allegiance to a single *silsila* as a prerequisite for spiritual progress. In the words of a prominent female *murid*,

> Spiritual progress is hastened by focusing energies on one *shaykh*, one *silsila*. You really need a living *shaykh* for it [spiritual development]. You would be surprised—if you don't go to different places, to different *shaykhs*, if you stick to just one, then you progress really quickly. The problem for most people is that they try to go to different places to benefit. There is a great loss in this. (June 17, 2001, Lahore)

Although exclusive affiliation is encouraged, Chishti Sabiri disciples do recognize the legitimacy of other Sufi paths and respect the *shaykhs* of other orders. During interviews I discovered that many *murids*—especially elder disciples with established family connections to the order—have a thorough knowledge of the history of Sufism well beyond the cultural landscape of South Asia. As we have seen, disciples read and discuss the writings of spiritual masters from other Sufi orders, both premodern and modern. There is, in short, a pervasive appreciation of the multiplicity of Sufi traditions. A novice male disciple explained this to me in a revealing fashion: "In very simple terms, the *awliya' Allah* are like data that is available on a computer. For example, if you come to Lahore it's the same data available on a computer in Karachi or Multan. When you turn on a computer it's the same data. It [sainthood] is like that. There's no difference as such, they all guide you. It's the same concepts, the same issues. It is like the Internet, you log on from anyplace and the same information is available" (November 4, 2000, Lahore).

This technological metaphor is, once again, an important indication of the educational background and worldview of many twenty-first-century Chishti Sabiri disciples. Here spiritual power is likened to computer software—it is transferable, universally communicable, and widely accessible. Yet even as *murids* acknowledge the reality and viability of other spiritual paths, they are equally resolute in maintaining boundaries. They insist that each Sufi order's teachings and practices are distinct and that individual *shaykhs* are powerless to help others outside their fold. "We should never compare saints, they all have individual duties," a female *murid* assured me. "But if you're in a Sufi order, you must follow only the *shaykhs* of that *silsila*. You can only receive spiritual blessing (*faiz*) from your own *silsila*. Other *shaykhs* don't even want to meet you. They can only say, 'there's nothing we can give 'you'" (November 14, 2000, Islamabad).

The stories that Chishti Sabiri disciples tell about their own experience of *bay'at* are remarkably diverse. Some *murids*, for example, spent a great deal of time in the company of their *shaykh* before obtaining formal initiation into the order. One of Wahid Bakhsh's disciples was surprised to learn that *bay'at* was a prerequisite for spiritual training. "In fact, it took me some time [to take *bay'at*]," he told me. "I didn't know it was necessary. I just thought, 'I'm his *murid*.' And I stayed that way, I think, for a year or two until someone told me that I had to do something else. Someone else told me. They said, 'You have to physically take *bay'at*.' I said, 'Really? I'm already his *murid*.' And this person said, 'No, it must be done.' There is a specific time and date to become a *murid*" (November 4, 2000, Lahore). At the opposite end of the spectrum are those *murids* whose initiation seems to have been utterly spontaneous, the result of a sudden and an overwhelming desire. A senior male disciple, for example, recalled driving down the street in Karachi one day in 1975 when he was suddenly inspired to turn toward the home of Shaykh Shahidullah Faridi. In his words, "When I arrived, I met him and said, 'I don't know much about *bay'at* or the *silsila*, but I have a very strong attraction to you and want to be with you.' Hazrat Sahab just smiled and said, 'Yes, it's like this.' I still can't believe how he managed to get me in the *silsila*. It was his kindness and grace. I was at that time absolutely ignorant, yet he knew I would come to understand" (September 27, 2000, Lahore). Wahid Bakhsh's Malaysian disciples represent another model altogether. Distanced from the *shaykh* by the span of the Indian Ocean, most of them took *bay'at* by letter, pledging their oath of allegiance with a signature long before they had even met the *shaykh* in person (interview: October 3, 2001, Kuala Lumpur).

Regardless of gender, nationality, or personal background, however, Chishti Sabiris agree on one thing. They all mark *bay'at* as a crucial hinge moment—a life-altering event that changed forever the trajectory of their lives. Individuals remember and celebrate *bay'at* as an experience of personal transformation, a spiritual rebirth. The testimony of a female Pakistani disciple of Shaykh Wahid Bakhsh Sial Rabbani is typical:

> I first met him in 1993. He came in for the evening prayer. He was this tall, thin, stern-looking man. He came in and he glanced at us, the congregation. There were maybe seven or eight women in the room. After prayers, I was introduced to him. I told him that I'd had some spiritual experiences since childhood. So he took me aside and spoke to me. And while he was speaking to me, it seemed like he was looking inside me and I was filled with this white light. I felt very safe, very comfortable. I was very impressed with him because he was very simple, very austere. This was just two years before he passed away.
>
> I met him consecutively for the next three days, and I decided to ask for *bay'at*. I knew that this was a special person, and I wanted him in my life. I knew about *bay'at*, but I didn't know exactly the ramifications of it. I just decided that whatever it was, I wanted to be associated with him spiritually. So I took *bay'at* from him. We were together for maybe three or four days in Islamabad, he was staying there. When he left and went away, I felt as if I was in a trance. I was transformed. I remember I left him at maybe four o'clock, and for the next couple of hours I just sat in my room, transfixed. I felt that I was in the presence of God. If you are with a capable *shaykh*, then he does take you there. I think that what he was showing me was how far I could go [in *suluk*]. (March 22, 2001, Islamabad)

This account, narrated with great emotion, is representative of the many stories I heard from Chishti Sabiris, men and women, young and old alike.

For this young woman, Wahid Bakhsh's personal charisma and pious demeanor made an immediate and lasting impression. She remembers the *shaykh's* power as a tangible, physical force, a magnetic pull that created an immediate and intense desire for discipleship.

Perhaps the most remarkable narrative of personal transformation that I heard during my interviews came from Wahid Bakhsh's first Malaysian disciple, a medical doctor now living in Kuala Lumpur. He arrived in Pakistan in 1978 and immediately enrolled at a local *madrasa* in Karachi. Through personal contacts, he was eventually introduced to the *silsila* and frequently attended the *zikr* circles led by Shaykh Siraj 'Ali Muhammad. Yet despite frequent requests, he was not formally initiated into the Chishti Sabiri order. His growing desperation for spiritual guidance culminated with a pilgrimage to Pakpattan for the annual death anniversary (*'urs*) of saint Baba Farid ad-Din. It was a trip that would profoundly alter the direction of his life. For Chishti Sabiri *murids* in Pakistan and Malaysia, his story clearly demonstrates the intimacy and intensity of the master-disciple relationship. I heard it circulated on numerous occasions among diverse groups of disciples. Though it is now part of the *silsila's* collective memory, the story is best told in the disciple's own words:

> One day, I heard that the *murids* were going to go to Pakpattan Sharif. I was told that in Pakpattan nobody's requests are rejected, so I packed my bags and followed the group. It was the *'urs* of Baba Farid. There I met a dervish, an English dervish, walking around inside the shrine, searching for a *shaykh*. Neither of us were disciples. On the final days of the *'urs*, I still had not received discipleship. I was disappointed and frustrated.
>
> I went down to the shrine and joined a group reciting Qur'an. Suddenly, I received some illuminations [*kashfiyyat*]. I fell down. People carried me to Captain Wahid Bakhsh's hut, outside the shrine. I sensed that I was unconscious, but I could still hear people talking around me. They were saying, "He has had a heart attack!" Captain Sahab came and blew his breath on me. While I was unconscious I saw something. I experienced something very beautiful. Then I awoke and described what had happened. Captain Sahab agreed, "Yes. This is what happened. You do not have a *shaykh*, but you have a great deal of concentration. You are open to these things, but you don't have a filter. A *shaykh* is a filter."
>
> The following night, there was a *sama'* [musical assembly] scheduled, but he told me that I should not attend. He said, "It's too much for you. But tomorrow, if you see something in a dream, then come to me." The following day I returned early in the morning and waited for him. Captain Sahab asked, "Did you see anything?" I said, "No, sir. But please, I want to become your *murid*!" He said, "Ok, make *wudu'* [the ritual washing for prayer]." I became his *murid* right then and there. This was in 1979. At that time Captain Wahid Bakhsh had not yet started taking *murids*. I was the first. (October 6, 2001, Kuala Lumpur)

This testimonial offers a particularly striking example of the transformative power of *bay'at*. Here the aspiring disciple experiences a desperate desire for spiritual guidance, culminating with a mystical out-of-body experience at the shrine of one of the Chishti order's most renowned saints. In the midst of the chaos, Shaykh Wahid Bakhsh appears to restore order, bringing the man back to normal consciousness and confirming the verity of his spiritual experience. The anecdote ends with a resolution: the desperate longing for spiritual guidance is finally rewarded with formal initiation at the feet of a spiritual master. Though far from typical, this story conforms to a general pattern described by many Chishti Sabiri disciples. It also attests to the power of persuasion. In time, this private experience became public knowledge, inspiring a number of other Malaysians to join the *silsila*. To a large extent, the Chishti Sabiri order's growing foothold in Southeast Asia can be traced to this singular ecstatic experience at a rural Sufi shrine in Pakistan almost three decades ago.

Vertical Pedagogy: The Chishti Sabiri *Shaykh* as Spiritual Teacher

The Chishti Sabiri *shaykh*—past and present—guides his followers through the intricacies of Sufi ritual practice while instructing them in the nuances of doctrine, morals (*akhlaq*), and etiquette (*adab*).[19] In this teaching system, the *shaykh's* authority is absolute and his orders are not to be questioned. He carefully monitors the adept's evolution through myriad spiritual states (*hal*) and stations (*maqam*), alternatively expanding or restricting the *murid's* activities to facilitate spiritual growth. As a spiritual intermediary—the heir to the Prophet himself—the *shaykh* is seen as a vital buffer from the overwhelming power of spiritual energy (*faiz; baraka*). In *Tarbiyat al-'ushshaq*, Zauqi Shah employs the familiar Sufi metaphor of cooking to explain the relationship between a novice and master. In his words, "If a piece of meat is placed directly into the fire it will immediately burn up. But if it is placed in a pot of water and the pot is then placed over the fire, the meat will be saved from burning and will cook properly. A *shaykh* is a buffer, just like the pot and water. As long as a seeker is deprived of a *shaykh*, he will remain in a [vulnerable] state and cannot progress. If the proper connection with a *shaykh* is made, however, than progress begins automatically."[20] As this metaphor suggests, the relationship between master and disciple is asymmetrical. In Chishti Sabiri practice, the flow of knowledge and power is top-down and unidirectional: the *shaykh* leads and the *murid* follows. Once again, Zauqi Shah provides a clear rationale for this vertical pedagogy:

> You need the services of one who knows—a Teacher, a Sheikh, or a Murshid—call him by whatever name you please. The initiative must come from him. He initiates you into the mysteries of the Unseen. He chalks out a course of action for you. He brings the Unseen with you into harmony with the Unseen without. He keeps a constant watch over you, and saves you from slips and pitfalls. He acts as a medium between the high and the low, between the Deity and humanity, between where you are and where you ought to be, or in plainer language, between you and your God. So the Sheikh or Murshid is an indispensable necessity in the spiritual emancipation of man.[21]

In this system of spiritual pedagogy, the Sufi subject remains under the constant gaze of hierarchical authority.

Sufi learning is oral and aural. Knowledge is transmitted directly from master to student by word of mouth. Over the centuries, Sufi masters developed a distinct vocabulary to communicate the wisdom and experiences of the mystical path.[22] As a result, Sufi lexicons reveal a sophistication and nuance that matches the complexity of the tradition's theories of human psychology, physiology, and ritual performance. As in the *madrasa*-based system of the Islamic religious sciences, Sufi teaching focuses on interpersonal interaction. Direct, face-to-face encounters with the *shaykh* spur the disciple's ability to remember and internalize the master's words. Significantly, this teaching is not limited to discourse. There is, in fact, a fundamental understanding of the limits of language. In the intimate exchange between Sufi master and disciple, the *shaykh* also teaches through his actions. Disciples, in turn, are expected to listen and observe—and then model their own behavior accordingly. Summarizing this relationship, Arthur Buehler notes,

> Pedagogically, the shaykh instructs through example and personal conduct; much of a seeker's learning involves conscious behavioral modification and unconscious modeling (and subsequent internalization) of one's spiritual guide . . . If the metaphor of a disciple's spiritual growth is a journey, then the shaykh functions as both the guide for the perilous trip through unknown territory and as the teacher of the exercises necessary to proceed on that voyage. Using the metaphor of transformation for the disciple's spiritual journey implies other relationships which involve both father-son, physician-patient, and beloved-lover roles. In actual practice, each spiritual director uses a comprehensive array of behavioral and psychological strategies to enact these changes.[23]

While Buehler's research focuses on the Indian Naqshbandi-Mujaddidi *silsila*, his comments also provide an apt summation of contemporary Chishti Sabiri pedagogy.

Sufi training involves a delicate, organic process of what anthropologist Frances Trix labels *attunement*, "an increasing coordination of the heart of the *talib* [student] and *murshid* [guide], with 'heart' understood as the seat of higher faculties of perception."[24] In Chishti Sabiri practice the interchange between master and disciple is remarkably flexible and malleable. Instruction is also highly personalized. The Sufi master shapes his words and adapts the training regimen to fit the specific needs and capacities of each individual disciple. "The *shaykh* has a personal, exclusive relationship with every *murid*," a senior Pakistani devotee explained. "He may say one thing to a *murid* that is not said to others. For every *murid* he has a different platform. It is this connection that matters most" (October 13, 2000, Lahore).

In the initial stages of a disciple's spiritual training, the *shaykh* tends to be proactive, often intervening directly and forcefully to spur the novice's development. Independence and autonomy increase, however, as the disciple progresses along the spiritual path. An advanced male *murid* explained this dynamic to me:

> When you start on the Sufi path [*suluk*] you are like a blind man. You have no knowledge of anything. So you are told certain things. The *shaykh* tells you to do this, this, and this—without explaining the whole process to you. In time, once a *murid* has some experience, then he will come to the *shaykh* and say, "I have experienced this." Then the *shaykh* will say, "Ok, now do this." So the *shaykh* takes him through the course. That course is only given to people who actually step in for *suluk*. Every *murid* is not a *salik* [a traveler on the Sufi path]. Every *murid* does not go through the same experiences, nor is he given the same spiritual exercises or daily prayers. Only a select few do *suluk*. It differs according to the individual's temperament, you see? For example, somebody can stay awake at night very easily, while another person dozes off after nine o'clock. The *shaykh* makes allowances for that. The *shaykh* knows how to go about it. (September 1, 2001, Karachi)

As this quote suggests, Chishti Sabiris view this pedagogical system as a spiritual meritocracy. They acknowledge that not every *murid* is capable of the disciple and sacrifices required of *suluk*. Even for those who are willing to immerse themselves in the rigors of Sufi practice, the experience is not uniform. While certain *murids* progress quickly, others are forced to struggle at every stage of the path.

Through frequent interaction and direct observation, the Chishti Sabiri *shaykh* gauges the progress of each individual disciple. On the basis of his intuitive knowledge and keen sensitivity to the disciple's character and temperament, he prescribes a variety of spiritual disciplines in order to spur higher states of consciousness. According to Chishti Sabiri teachings, a *murid's* progress depends on the master's powers of spiritual attention (*tawajjuh*). According to Shaykh Shahidullah Faridi,

> The qualified Shaykh possesses as a gift of God the power of transference of spiritual qualities; a kind of outpouring (*faiz*) from the always full vessel of his heart. By means of this power he is continually aiding the *murid* in the development of his inner potentialities, correcting his aberrations and supporting his efforts in the proper direction. This spiritual action has been compared to the mother giving milk to the child, the physical outpouring of nourishment which makes possible his growth and development.[25]

Shahidullah's metaphor highlights the absolute ignorance and helplessness of the Sufi novice. At the beginning of the journey, the *murid* is utterly dependent on the wisdom and compassion of the spiritual guide. The remaking of the self therefore presupposes a total and complete surrender of personal will and an unwavering faith in the wisdom of the teaching *shaykh*.

In Chishti Sabiri writings, the Sufi master is frequently likened to a physician caring for a sick patient. He alone recognizes the root cause of the disease and possesses the remedy for its cure. The patient, however, must first want to be healed and trust the doctor enough to submit to his care. "The personal element is an important factor in the dissemination of *tasawwuf*," writes Zauqi Shah. "Mere book knowledge leads one nowhere. A sick man stands in need of both the physician and the prescription. Very often, he stands more in need of the physician than of the prescription. Unless there is some competent physician to administer the prescription properly, the prescription remains useless."[26] In a personal letter written to a female Malaysian *murid*, Shaykh Wahid Bakhsh adopts a similar idiom in order to explain his own duties as a teaching *shaykh*:

> I as religious teacher do not declare a wrong to be a right. Nor do I ask you to stop the wrong acts if I know you cannot comply with my order. What I do is to work with the causes of the disease and relieve the cause so that the disease is cured. In our spiritual treatment we treat the cause and not the symptoms of the disease. When the cause is removed, the symptoms disappear. But if the cause is not removed, the disease gets complicated and is never cured. You will see, God willing, how this spiritual therapy works, and works without determent to your business or profession. So go on as you are, and Allah Most High will definitely help you because your intention is good.[27]

Thus, the *shaykh* serves multiple roles in the Chishti Sabiri pedagogical system: he is a teacher, mentor, translator, healer, advisor, and disciplinarian. Caring for the spiritual lives of disciples, however, is no easy task. This is seen in a revealing discourse by Zauqi Shah in *Tarbiyat al-'ushshaq*. In a conversation recorded on October 3, 1941 (11 Ramadan, 1360), a disciple invites the *shaykh* to listen to a Ramadan Qur'an recitation broadcast on the radio from Egypt. Zauqi Shah reluctantly declines the offer, claiming that his energies are limited:

> Some other time. I am too tired. I have grown old. The days of my youth when I used to enjoy spiritual exercises [*mujahida*] have gone. It is now time for meditation. I did not sleep at all yesterday. Today is Thursday, so I will not sleep again. I have to do a great deal of work for the sake of you people. Whatever spiritual duties you are assigned to carry out I have to do myself. After I extract the spiritual essence, I transfer it to you through spiritual attention [*tawajjuh*]. A *shaykh* is necessary for this very reason. Otherwise, everyone could become a saint [*wali Allah*] just by reading books! A *shaykh* has to do an immense amount of work on your behalf.[28]

Here Zauqi Shah lets down his guard to gently remind his disciple that a Chishti Sabiri *shaykh* carries a weighty burden.

The Etiquette of Discipleship

The fundamental spiritual connection between Sufi master and disciple is rooted in desire (*irada*). The disciple, or *murid*, is literally the "one who desires"; the object of his/her longing, is the *murad*—another term for the Sufi master meaning "the one who is desired." The Sufi system of spiritual teaching is based on a benign authoritarianism: the master leads and the disciple follows. Given the inherent dangers of the path, a *murid's* submission is viewed as a vital precursor to spiritual growth. In exchange for nurturing along the spiritual path, the *murid* is expected to demonstrate a selfless loyalty and unwavering trust in her/his spiritual guide.

Chishti Sabiri pedagogy—both past and present—rests on the cardinal values of etiquette and propriety. The master-disciple relationship, in other words, is mediated and facilitated through *adab*. As a comprehensive code of moral conduct, *adab* molds character, conditions behavior, and shapes social interaction. For individual disciples, *adab* also ameliorates doubt and ambiguity. *Murids* follow the lead of their *shaykh* in the faith that the path is well marked and that sacrifice and persistence will ultimately be rewarded. In *Bihishti Zewar*, Ashraf 'Ali Thanawi outlines the parameters of *adab* for his female readers who aspire to join a Sufi *tariqa*. His thirteen rules of proper moral conduct are, in essence, corollaries of a single primary imperative: "Respect your master sincerely."[29] Twenty-first-century Chishti Sabiris adhere to the same preconditions for spiritual transformation, beginning with this essential mantra.

Respect for the *shaykh* is the essential prerequisite for *suluk*. The Sufi aspirant's spiritual potential, I was often told, completely depends on the nature of her/his bond with the *shaykh*. This relationship is founded on certain key virtues: humility, deference, trust, and love. In outlining the rules for the "training of the lovers" (*Tarbiyat al-'ushshaq*), Shaykh Zauqi Shah explains the logic of the *pir-murid* bond:

> In order to receive the spiritual blessings [*faizan*] of the *shaykh*, two things are necessary. First, they [master and disciple] must establish a straight connection. There should be no knots, tension, or breaks in this link from either the *murid* or the *pir*. Secondly, when something is poured from one vessel into another, the larger vessel is held high and the receiving vessel is kept low. Without these two conditions, it is impossible to receive spiritual blessings. Those people who say that the *pir* makes his *murids* worship him do not understand that if the vessel that gives is not held higher then nothing can be received from it. These are the etiquettes [*adab*] of this path, and it is extremely important to act on them.[30]

Upon entering a Sufi order, a *murid* relinquishes personal autonomy, abdicating selfhood to the will of the *shaykh*. A Sufi disciple's obeisance must be total and uncompromising. In the famous words of the Chishti luminary Shaykh Nizam ad-Din Awliya', "The adept conducts himself like a corpse in the hands of the washerman. That corpse asks no questions. It does not move on its own. It responds to every wish and to every initiative of the washerman. This is the third state of trust. It is the highest, and its attainment represents a lofty spiritual station for the Sufi adept."[31] Ideally, the Sufi novice is like a piece of clay—passive and malleable—in the hand of the master spiritual potter. It is important to note that the logic and mechanics of the Sufi paradigm diverge radically from Western psychology and theories of the self. As Katherine Ewing argues, "Psychoanalytic theory has embedded within it an ideology of independence as a sign of maturity. Sufi theory and Islam, in contrast, rest on an ideology of maturity manifested in submission and relationship."[32] According to Sufi theorists, everything depends on the initial act of complete surrender to the will of the spiritual guide. A *murid* must submit before she/he can be reformed and remade.

In interviews, Chishti Sabiri disciples frequently stressed the importance of following the *shaykh's* advice on all matters, both spiritual and temporal. This is, they cautioned, sometimes easier said than done. On occasion, the master's recommendations conflict with a *murid's* own desires, leaving the disciple with a difficult choice. The story of Wahid Bakhsh's French disciple illustrates this point. In his words,

> I only stayed in Pakistan because my *shaykh* told me to. He said, "You ought to go to Karachi, to the Islamic Center. You should learn Qur'an and Arabic at the *madrasa*." Most of the foreign disciples from the time of Hazrat Shahidullah Faridi, may God have mercy upon him, used to go there. I was there for three years. It was not easy for the first year. I kept writing to Hazrat Sahab, saying "I don't want to study in this *madrasa*. I just want to travel. It was my life for four years, so how can I stick to one place?" For me it was inconceivable to stay in the *madrasa*. But each time he replied to me, saying "It is good for you to stay there. You must stay there for your *suluk*." So I accepted his orders. (September 2, 2001, Karachi)

Some *murids* are asked to make profound changes to their lifestyle, changes that impact not only themselves but also their families and friends. In such circumstances, acquiescence is only possible with the firm faith that the *shaykh* knows best and that no decisions are made without a deeper purpose, even if the disciple cannot see it for himself.

However, this does not mean that Chishti Sabiri disciples have no voice or that their thoughts, ideas, and opinions are ignored. In practice, the teaching *shaykh* often encourages input from his *murids*, consulting with them before making decisions on important matters. Even so, obedience is stressed as the safest and surest path to spiritual development. A senior Malaysian disciple explains the necessity of *adab*:

> If you really want to undertake this training *adab* is very important. It has a very positive influence, it keeps everything under control. Otherwise something can come into your head, and you begin to listen to your own voice. Then you have problems. One's success depends on *adab* to a great extent. I know this from experience. Whatever your *shaykh* says, make it final. That doesn't mean that our *shaykhs* do not want to listen. You can express anything to them. You can express your views. The *shaykh* will look into it and then he'll advise you. In the end though, he is your master and you are the student. Our training is based on this: you must always think of yourself as a nobody. You get into serious problems when you think you are the center of everything. So you follow whatever the *shaykh* prescribes. You may question it, but you do not argue. The *shaykhs* are very reasonable though. They never force anything on you. (September 27, 2001, Kuala Lumpur)

For Chishti Sabiri disciples, the *shaykh* is the paradigmatic moral exemplar. The master sets the standard for conduct, decorum, and piety; *murids*, in turn, aim to model their behavior on his example. Disciples are cautioned against blindly aping the master's actions, however. In *Tarbiyat al-'ushshaq*, Zauqi Shah illustrates this important point through a teaching story. His lesson comes in a discourse appropriately entitled "The Difference between Obedience and Imitation":

> The *shaykh's* orders should be obeyed, but all of his actions should not be imitated without thought or understanding. The master's spiritual station [*maqam*] is different, and he acts according to his own station. There was once a saint who ordered one of his disciples to busy himself in a corner of a mosque while he was occupied elsewhere in the mosque. Another Sufi master was present in the same mosque at the very same time. The saint had been struggling with a problem. In order to solve this difficulty he lied down for some time and focused his spiritual attention on the Prophet of God, God bless him and grant him salvation. Seeing his *shaykh*, the *murid* imitated him. He also lay down, and subsequently fell sound asleep. After some time, the saint got up and prepared himself for prayers. The other Sufi master had been watching all these events the entire time. He got up and kicked the sleeping *murid*, saying, "Wake up and go pray your *namaz* without ablutions [*wudu*] too!" The *shaykh* should not be imitated in everything, although any order you receive from him should be acted upon.[33]

In this story, the Sufi disciple mistakes meditation for slumber, embarrassing both himself and his *shaykh* in the process. Zauqi Shah employs this anecdote to illustrate the dangers of outward action in the absence of inward knowledge.

The moral of this lesson is not lost on today's Chishti Sabiri disciples. *Murids* view their *shaykhs* as blueprints for moral living. They look to the Sufi master for guidance on all matters, spiritual and temporal alike. At all times, however, disciples are cautioned to remain mindful of their relative status. As an accomplished spiritual guide, the *shaykh* may think, talk, and act in ways that appear contradictory or confusing, even irrational. Echoing Zauqi Shah's message, a senior male disciple told me, "We can't compare our lives to theirs [the Sufi masters]. We can only take lessons from their lives. An extremely important teaching in *tasawwuf* is something that all *shaykhs* tell their disciples: 'Do what you're told to do! Don't try to copy exactly what your *shaykh* does.' That, in fact, is your training, that is your main work. You do what you're told to do, you fulfill those obligations" (September 1, 2001, Karachi). Disciples therefore are encouraged to trust the master and to follow his guidance to the letter, without passing judgment on his actions.

Thus, Chishti Sabiri pedagogy presupposes the *murid's* complete obedience to his/her *shaykh*—the voluntary abdication of subjective will and ego to the spiritual mentor. This is the ideal. In everyday practice, however, the dynamic and intensely personal relationship with a Sufi *shaykh* requires a careful and constant balancing act. It is the *shaykh* who guides the novice disciple along the path, but spiritual growth is impossible in the absence of the Sufi adept's abiding determination, discipline, and resolve. "These are not things that you just go and get for the asking, you have to strive hard for them," a high-ranking male disciple told me. "If a *salik* has perseverance and diligence, if he is hardworking, then if he wants to know about the path he will come to know about it. A *shaykh* will only tell a person who he feels has the capacity to understand and contain that knowledge. Otherwise it will not be divulged" (May 21, 2001, Karachi). Chishti Sabiri pedagogy, in short, asserts that spiritual development is never simply awarded. It must be earned.

There is, to be sure, an inherent tension between these dual imperatives of acquiescence and action. In everyday practice, each *murid* must learn to navigate between absolute submission to hierarchical authority and an enduring imperative for individual action and moral responsibility. But how? I often asked disciples this very question. One of the most cogent answers came from a senior Pakistani *murid*. When asked to explain the adage that a Sufi disciple must be "like a corpse in the hands of a washerman" he replied,

> This statement does not mean inaction on the part of the *murid*. This surrender implies total obedience, but not sitting idle. You must be very active in total obedience, like a good servant. Your submission is such that if the *shaykh* sends you one hundred times to the store to fetch something, you happily do it a hundred times. That is being "like a corpse." Whatever the *shaykh* utters, whatever he prescribes, you do it with full enthusiasm. Actively striving, that's the essential part. This still implies individuality. You never question the *shaykh's* utterances. Whatever he says, you obey. This is for God, and it has to be done. This is found in the Qur'an. When the Prophet used to ask something of the Companions, if somebody did not do it with enthusiasm, there was admonishment. Among *murids* you find varying types of behavior. There are some who are very alert, anticipating the *shaykh's* timing. And then there are some who are lazy, who do things halfheartedly. (March 16, 2001, Lahore)

This response encapsulates a prevalent view among Chishti Sabiri disciples. Regardless of their personal background and level of experience, *murids* recognize that the Sufi path is as narrow as it is long. There is, they assert, simply no way around one basic fact: *suluk* requires hard work, dedication, and personal sacrifice. "You must work very hard on your own," a female Pakistani disciple assured me. "This is the Chishti philosophy" (February 26, 2001, Lahore).

This emphasis on personal responsibility and self-reliance is doubly important in an environment where Chishti Sabiri ritual practices are increasingly pursued in isolation. Although today's twenty-first-century *murids* still consider direct contact with the *shaykh* invaluable, in everyday practice it is a rare occasion. In Karachi, the order's current teaching *shaykh*, Siraj 'Ali Muhammad, leads weekly *halqa* (communal *zikr* sessions) on Thursday evenings. The *shaykh* also hosts an informal public question-and-answer lecture session (*dars*) at his home on Sunday mornings. Disciples who live in other parts of Pakistan—and beyond South Asia altogether—are rarely able to attend these gatherings. For them, access to the *shaykh* necessarily comes via other venues. For many, companionship with the *shaykh* (*suhbat*) is limited to either infrequent visits to Karachi or the annual communal pilgrimages to Sufi shrines. In the interest of more regular communication, a significant number of *murids* also find "virtual guidance" in cyberspace. As a technophile and Internet aficionado himself, Shaykh Siraj regularly offers advice on both temporal and spiritual matters via e-mail. This new form of digital discipleship is yet another striking example of the *silsila's* fluid incorporation of modern technology into Chishti Sabiri networks of knowledge and practice. Significantly, disciples mark the increased emphasis on individual action and adaptive use of new formats for communication as a necessary response to changing times. In my view, these salient modifications to traditional pedagogy also demonstrate how Chishti Sabiris have accommodated Sufism to modernity—an important point that I explore further in the next chapter.

Within the *silsila's* teaching network, how exactly do Chishti Sabiri disciples learn? What are the mechanisms for transmitting Sufi knowledge? As spiritual teachers, Chishti Sabiri *shaykhs* often employ stories and parables as heuristic devices. In their public and private meetings with disciples, they impart practical moral lessons through both personal anecdotes and narratives of past spiritual luminaries. The mechanisms for transmitting esoteric knowledge are hardly unique to Sufism. Numerous teaching traditions in diverse religious worlds focus on precisely this sort of direct, interpersonal, oral exchange between master and disciple. Anthropologist Kirin Narayan's insights on storytelling as a medium for religious instruction in a contemporary Hindu religious community are equally applicable to today's Chishti Sabiri *silsila:*

> When disciples gather around a religious teller, they listen with an intensity and a desire to be edified, not only entertained. The cross-cutting points of view and ambiguity with a story can generate multiple meanings, and so audiences may take away different interpretations of what is being told and why. Listeners who screen these stories with the expectation that they will provide counsel, actively appropriate meanings that speak to their concerns and conflicts. Listening to a religious storyteller, believers find illumination for their disparate paths. Story worlds are compelling precisely because they relate back to everyday life.[34]

Chishti Sabiri *shaykhs* too construct rich "story worlds" to illuminate the complexities of Sufi theory and practice. *Murids*, in turn, listen to these narrative performances with rapt attention, knowing that the master's every word is imbued with deeper meaning.

Many of the Chishti Sabiri rules of *adab* expressly focus on the art of listening. Ritual propriety dictates that disciples must sit passively and speak as little as possible in the presence of the *shaykh*. Silence, disciples suggest, demonstrates an attentiveness, humility, and respect for the status of the master.[35] In any exchange with the *shaykh*, the impetus for conversation and questions should come from the spiritual master. In the words of a senior male disciple,

> The novices tend to question the *shaykh* more, converse more. The experienced *murids* keep quiet and listen. They [advanced disciples] are in attendance, in submission. They do not intellectualize the discussion or think that a lecture is being given. Many times the *shaykh* does not say anything. After a half hour he will say, "let's disperse." It's not that nothing happened in that half hour when everybody was keeping quiet. That's why the *adab* is that you should really not initiate a discussion. You should not ask questions or try to control discussion or give it a direction. That is against etiquette. (March 16, 2001, Lahore)

As this testimony suggests, in Chishti Sabiri pedagogy even silence is instructive. When sitting at the feet of the *shaykh*, the most important thing is companionship (*suhbat*), not conversation.

Disciples stress that a perfected Sufi *shaykh* possesses powers of mental insight and discernment that make all talk superfluous. In interviews, *murids* frequently recalled moments when their questions were answered by the *shaykh* without being asked. The reflections of a senior Pakistani male *murid* are instructive:

> Many times a question has occurred in my mind and immediately the *shaykh* answers that question, without having been asked. This is a common experience. Almost everyone has experienced this, I think. This is the reality of the Unseen entering the phenomenal world. I used to argue and ask questions. Now I understand that it was egoism that caused me to do those things. Sometimes I still get worried when I don't ask anything. I worry that he [the *shaykh*] might be thinking that I'm no longer serious. So then this fear comes. Am I sliding backwards because I don't ask anything now? Sometimes you really doubt your progress—if you don't feel anything, when initially you used to feel a lot. Many *murids* have these doubts. But now I just sit in silence. No state is constant. This is called expansion [*bast*] and contraction [*qabz*]. (March 16, 2001, Lahore)

Along the Sufi path, I was often told, moments of insight and clarity are followed by periods of darkness and doubt. Spiritual development is therefore marked by a deepening sense of trust—a faith that answers will come, that doubts and ambiguities will be resolved in time. Amid this constant ebb and flow, patience is essential and silence is golden.

The etiquette of Chishti Sabiri discipleship also addresses a *murid's* bodily comportment. Here too there are certain basic rules that all disciples are expected to follow. *Adab* requires that disciples stand whenever a *shaykh* enters or leaves an assembly, for example. When sitting in the master's presence, *murids* position themselves physically lower than the *shaykh*. Similarly, they are careful to avoid pointing the soles of their feet at the *shaykh* or turning their back on him at any time. When disciples do engage the *shaykh* in conversation they refrain from laughter, speak in a quiet voice, and avoid direct eye contact. These rules of decorum are common to Sufi orders throughout South Asia—the legacy of premodern Persian court culture.[36] Beyond these standard customs, Chishti Sabiris are also expected to be in a state of ritual purification whenever they enter the *shaykh's* presence. Wahid Bakhsh explains the rationale for these strict rules of decorum by recalling the teachings of his own mentor:

> Hazrat [Zauqi Shah], may God have mercy upon him, often used to say that a person should perform the ritual washing [*wudu*] before presenting himself to the blessed saints because their companionship is a form of worship. He used to say that one should not perform supererogatory prayer [*nawafil*] before entering the *shaykh's* presence. Instead, he should only do his obligatory prayers [*farz*] in accordance with the example of the Prophet Muhammad [*sunna*]. The reason for this is that companionship with a saint is by law optional [*nawafil*]. He [Zauqi Shah] declared that, like the Ka'ba, a perfected human being [*insan-i kamil*] is a manifestation of God. The rank of the perfected human being, however, is much higher than that of the Ka'ba. On one occasion a disciple was standing in front of Hazrat with his hands folded [as a sign of respect]. Someone objected to this, saying it was improper to stand before anyone other than God with folded hands [as in prayer]. On hearing this, Hazrat responded, "He should have been asked whether he would stand with folded hands in front of the Ka'ba. After all, isn't the Ka'ba also other-than God?"[37]

The use of legal language in this passage is significant. It is illustrative of how Chishti Sabiris couch their own Sufi practices in the idioms of mainstream, normative Islamic practice. This anecdote also confirms once again the fundamental belief in the legality and sanctity of sainthood. As the embodiment of *sunna* and the living link to God, Zauqi Shah suggests, the Sufi *shaykh* is deserving of the highest degree of honor and respect.

While the stories individual Chishti Sabiri disciples narrate about their experiences with Sufi masters vary, they share one common theme: an intense, overwhelming love for the *shaykh*. To a large extent, love ('*ishq*) is the foundation of the entire system of Chishti Sabiri doctrine and practice. *Murids* describe this love for their *shaykh* as the manifestation of love for the Prophet Muhammad and ultimately for God. Shahidullah Faridi explains this connection:

> Because the Shaykh combines in himself the outward observance (*shariat*) with the inner enlightenment (*tariqat*) and is one of the specially guided ones sent by Allah to call to the path of His Prophet (may Allah bless and keep him), admiration stimulates the pupil to emulate him, and the inspiration of his example urges him forward on the path. When admiration deepens and is transformed into love, then all other incentives are merged into this one great attraction. The relationship with the guide of love and respect provide him with all his disciplines, enthusiasm, spirit of emulation and keenness to reach the goal, and becomes the main stepping-stone to success in achieving nearness to Allah.[38]

Given the intensity and intimacy of the master-disciple relationship, Chishti Sabiri *murids* speak about their *shaykhs* in the most emotive of terms. They recall the interactions with their spiritual mentors in exacting detail, remembering conversations and events that happened years, even decades, before.

With remarkable consistency, Chishti Sabiri disciples characterize their connection with the *shaykh* as the most important relationship in their lives, eclipsing all others. "He was my father, my friend, my teacher," a Malaysian male *murid* assured me when asked about Wahid Bakhsh Rabbani. "There was just no one else like him in my life" (October 6, 2001, Kuala Lumpur). Not even the ties of family and friendship, disciples say, compare to this bond with the Sufi master. In the words of a novice *murid* of Shaykh Siraj 'Ali recorded at the death anniversary ('*urs*) of Wahid Bakhsh Sial Rabbani,

> I always find myself always thinking about my *shaykh*. This attraction is amazing. It's a true miracle. I never met Hazrat Shahidullah or Hazrat Wahid Bakhsh, may God have mercy on them. I have never met a *shaykh* besides Hazrat Siraj Sahab. Yet here I am traveling all this way to go to the '*urs* in a village, Allahabad. Why? There is simply this strong attraction. I can't explain this, even to other Muslims. You don't feel this way with any other people—not your family, not with your wife. This attraction makes sense with your family, your parents, people you know so well and see everyday. But this attraction to a *shaykh* is the real miracle. It is just so helpful in life to know there is always someone you can turn to for help. (February 13, 2001, Allahabad)

For Chishti Sabiri disciples, it is only the strength of this bond with the master, rooted in love, which makes it possible to endure the sacrifices and burdens of the Sufi path. Moreover, this relationship transcends time and space—even beyond physical death. According to Chishti Sabiri doctrine, a *shaykh's* spiritual powers only increase after death. "The Sufi saint is like a sword unsheathed upon his death," a male Pakistani disciple told me. "In life they must strictly follow the *shari'a*. But once they have passed the threshold, God puts no limits on their powers" (October 22, 2000, Lahore).[39] The boundary between this world and the afterlife, *murids* insist, is porous for a perfected Sufi master. *Tarbiyat al-'ushshaq* records a moving conversation on this subject. On September 1, 1942 (20 Sha'ban, 1361), Zauqi Shah held an emotional gathering with his followers. In this exchange, the *shaykh* prefigures his own death, even as he assures his disciples of guidance from beyond the grave:

> Hazrat [Zauqi Shah] had fallen ill. He said, "This body gives me a great deal of pain. It is nothing but a cage. I will be happy when the time comes to get ride of it; at that time I will finally be free. That day will be a day of great celebration." The slave [Shahidullah Faridi] said to him, "You will be happy, but we will not. Our future will be uncertain." The *shaykh* replied, "There will be no change in the teaching (*ta'lim*). It will continue despite the physical separation. In fact, the teaching from there [beyond the grave] will be on an even wider scale." I then said, "Even so, there will be no possibility for conversation and

clarification on small matters." He replied, "Even that is possible. That door will remain open as well."[40]

During my interviews, many disciples confirmed the continuity of this living connection with a deceased spiritual master. Drawing on their own personal experiences, they described how the *shaykh* continues to provide protection and succor in times of personal crisis and spiritual doubt from beyond the grave. A male Pakistani disciple describes this by referencing the Qur'an:

> The most important thing is that the *murid* should be satisfied that he has a real connection with the *shaykh*. During periods of turmoil and difficulties, he sees his *shaykh*. They come to you only when you're in trouble. Otherwise they are too busy with other matters. They appear in times of grave trouble, when you really need them, when you're absolutely helpless. They come and tell you, "Do not worry, we are with you." These are living souls, you see. This is a living connection. These are the people about whom Allah says in the Qur'an [3:169], "Do not think that those who have died in the way of Allah are dead. No, they are living, finding sustenance in the presence of their Lord." (September 1, 2001, Karachi)

More poignantly, several disciples recalled the miraculous appearance of their own spiritual guide in moments of distress and personal tragedy. For others, the relationship with the deceased *shaykh* manifests in more subtle ways. "The presence of a *shaykh* increases after he is gone. I feel that strongly," a female disciple explained. "Since his [Shaykh Wahid Bakhsh's] death, the pull towards him in every passing year is growing. When I pray, I always sense that he is there. He has become an integral part of my thought processes. I feel that he is now my conscience. There is still so much love" (February 26, 2001, Lahore). As these testimonies affirm, the relationship with the teaching *shaykh* is central to the social and spiritual lives of contemporary Chishti Sabiri *murids*. Experienced through companionship and through love and devotion, it is an unbreakable bond that transcends and ultimately transforms death itself.

CHISHTI SABIRI TEXTS AND TEACHING NETWORKS

While the transmission of Chishti Sabiri knowledge ultimately rests on the face-to-face exchange with the teaching master, there are additional resources that disciples draw upon for clarification and reinforcement. Selective texts provide an especially important supplemental source of guidance, inspiration, and edification. The text par excellence for Chishti Sabiris—as for all Muslims everywhere—is the Qur'an. *Murids* recite it constantly, quote from it in daily conversations, and discuss its meaning in private and public forums. For insights regarding the specifics of Sufi doctrine and ritual practice, however, they also turn to the literary legacy of past spiritual masters. In both Pakistan and Malaysia, Urdu and English translations of classical Sufi works are read, discussed, and reread. The writings of Sayyid 'Ali ibn 'Uthman al-Hujwiri (d. 1074), Abu Hamid Muhammad al-Ghazali (d. 1111), Ibn al-'Arabi (d. 1240), Shihab ad-Din Abu Hafs 'Umar al-Suhrawardi (d. 1234), and Jalal ad-Din Rumi (d. 1273) are especially popular. The reading and interpretation of the words of such premodern Sufi luminaries play a central role in the transmission of Chishti Sabiri knowledge. In a very real sense, books bind today's disciples to their spiritual predecessors.

Contemporary Chishti Sabiri *shaykhs* purposefully employ premodern Sufi texts as teaching aids. On occasion they explicitly order their disciples to read certain books, and they often discuss these texts with *murids* in teaching circles. The pedagogical importance of Sufi writings is illuminated in an exchange between Zauqi Shah and his circle of followers recorded in *Tarbiyat al-'ushshaq*:

> Hazrat [Zauqi Shah] gave us a lesson on Imam Ghazali's book, *Tibb-i Jismani o Tibb-i Ruhani* [*Bodily Medicine and Spiritual Medicine*]. When the lesson was finished, Hazrat Shah Shahidullah Sahab said, "This should be read two or three times." Hazrat replied, "It should be read ten times. The writings of the noble saints [*awliya'-i kuram*] provide the same kind of blessing as the Qur'an which offers new meanings and disclosures each time it is recited. In reading it over and over, new dimensions are revealed. This is because the perfect human being [*insan-i kamil*] is the representative [*khalifa*] of God Most High. A saint's writings match his lofty state."[41]

As Zauqi Shah illustrates, the writings of renowned Sufi masters offer an invaluable wellspring of supplemental knowledge. Rooted in personal experience, the works of premodern masters complement and deepen the oral teachings *murids* receive at the feet of their own *shaykhs*. In effect, Sufi hagiographies offer a ready made blueprint for *adab*. As a senior male Pakistani disciple notes, "We learn about etiquette through observation and guidance, through word of mouth. You certainly don't get a manual on what to do and not do with your *shaykh*. But there are obviously traditions about the Prophet, the pious caliphs, and the Imams on how to conduct yourself. Every *shaykh* has spoken about it as well. Whatever they have taught is recorded by their disciples or successors in the form of spiritual discourses [*malfuzat*]. So guidance also comes from reading" (March 22, 2001, Islamabad).

The *malfuzat* of the major saints of the Chishti tradition are among the order's most popular and revered literary resources. The spiritual discourses of the renowned thirteenth-century luminary Shaykh Nizam ad-Din Awliya' play an especially important role as teaching aids. Both the famous *malfuzat*, *Fawa'id al-Fu'ad*, and a less-known and more enigmatic version, *Nizami Bansari*, are widely circulated and often discussed among today's disciples. *Nizami Bansari* is a particularly intriguing text. In florid prose, the book recounts a broad range of stories about Shaykh Nizam ad-Din that both echo and amplify the moral lessons and biographical data recorded in the classic

Fawa'id al-Fu'ad. The oldest extant version of *Nizami Bansari* was published in Urdu by the Indian Chishti Nizami activist and bibliophile Khwaja Hasan Nizami (1878–1955).[42] According to Nizami, the original text was composed in Persian and compiled by a contemporary disciple of Nizam ad-Din: a Hindu prince from the Deccan named Rajkumar Hardev. Although this is a tantalizing possibility, it is also impossible to verify since no record of either the original Persian text or its elusive author exists. In the absence of such tangible evidence, it is possible to speculate that the book may have been the product of Khwaja Hasan Nizami's own prodigious imagination. Regardless of its historical authenticity, however, contemporary Chishti Sabiris view *Nizami Bansari* as an authoritative account of the Sufi master-disciple relationship. The *silsila* has published an edition of Nizami's Urdu text and, more recently, a new English translation entitled *A Diary of a Disciple of Nizamudin Aulia* [*sic*]. In consulting the book for insights on Sufi doctrine and practice, today's disciples highlight distinct parallels between the moral lessons of Shaykh Nizam ad-Din and their own contemporary spiritual masters.

For today's Chishti Sabiris, the books that matter most are the *silsila's* own publications—from the discourses of its twentieth-century *shaykhs* to their own myriad doctrinal works. Collectively, this diverse corpus of texts preserves the teachings of Muhammad Zauqi Shah, Shahidullah Faridi, and Wahid Bakhsh Sial Rabbani for a new generation of Chishti Sabiri followers. Most of the *shaykhs'* works are now readily available in printed editions and widely distributed through the *silsila's* publication networks in both Pakistan and Malaysia. Published in both Urdu and English, these books are increasingly accessible to a broad, international community of readers. As we have seen, Chishti Sabiri masters were keenly aware of the power of the printed word. They viewed texts as both pedagogical aids for their followers and as polemical tools to counter pervasive misconceptions about the Sufi tradition. Wahid Bakhsh Sial Rabbani in particular was determined to write for a broad audience in a simple, accessible style. As a senior Pakistani disciple illustrates, the *shaykh* hoped to inspire and to edify multiple audiences:

> These books offer guidance on many questions. They are written in simple Urdu and English. That is very important. I remember I once asked Hazrat Wahid Bakhsh, "You have told me to read books. I've tried to read them, but most are written in such difficult Urdu that I've not been able to understand. They do not keep my interest." He said, "That is exactly what I am doing, trying to translate into simple Urdu so that more people can read and understand." He wrote his books especially for his *murids*. We are duty-bound to read them. I think he was also upset about a lot of the criticism and incorrect concepts that have developed about Sufism. He wanted the general public to understand the real meaning of Sufism. (November 4, 2000, Lahore)

Contemporary Chishti Sabiri masters clearly understand the utility of texts. For them, books preserve the order's collective memory. At the same time, they serve as signposts to guide the individual seeker's journey along the Sufi path. In his personal will, Shahidullah Faridi made this aim explicit: "The books that have already been published have instructions by the saints of our *silsila* which must be read and kept in mind by all in the *silsila*."[43] In keeping with this directive, Chishti Sabiri texts are fully integrated into the practice of Sufi pedagogy. As vital teaching aids books serve as a primer for novices and a reference guide for advanced *murids*. Disciples of all ages and backgrounds consult the order's publications for practical advice regarding their own spiritual experiences. Significantly, *murids* insist that the *silsila's* books should be read in a particular order, a sequence that mirrors the progressive stages of the Sufi path. A senior Malaysian disciple explains this rationale:

> Hazrat Wahid Bakhsh used to say that everything you need to know you can find in these letters and books. I have found that to be true. These books are for us, the *murids*. Look at the sequence of the books. They are like the journey itself: from *fana'* [annihilation of the self] to *baqa'* [permanence in God]. *Islamic Sufism* comes first. He [Wahid Bakhsh] brings us through the basics in *Islamic Sufism*. It is the primer and we all read that. Then you have books like *A Guide for Spiritual Aspirants* [the *malfuzat* of Shah Sayyid Waris Hasan]. It is a deeply spiritual book. Then you go still deeper with *Kashf al-mahjub* [a translation of the Persian classic by al-Hujwiri]. That delves into all the deeper levels of Sufism. Then you come back to earth, back to the world. This book [Wahid Bakhsh's *Immense Power Potential of Pakistan*] is the culmination. It brings us back to the reality of the world and shows us what is involved there. (October 1, 2001, Kuala Lumpur)

For *murids*, the act of reading constitutes a form of conversation. Much like the intimate, personal exchanges with the *shaykh*, texts have the potential to provide immediate answers to vexing questions. "You may not believe this," a female Pakistani disciple assured me, "but often when I open a book the answer to my questions appears. I think that the message is given to you, one way or another. Guidance may come through a dream, directly through your *pir*, through somebody's remark, or in a book. I believe it is the *shaykh* working behind the scenes. That is why I now consult books more and more" (February 26, 2001, Lahore). While not all disciples experience such miraculous guidance, *murids* readily agree that texts do amplify and clarify the lessons of the master-disciple relationship. And since the printed word is permanent, disciples find in books a constant, renewable source of supplementary knowledge and insight.

Many Chishti Sabiri *murids* find yet another wellspring for spiritual guidance in letters. Twentieth-century Chishti Sabiri *shaykhs*—in particular Wahid Bakhsh Sial Rabbani—maintained a long and detailed correspondence with their disciples who they were not able to meet with regularly in person. During my interviews, several disciples shared selections from their personal letters with me. Without exception, they are poignant and personalized, containing a wealth of advice on both spiritual and worldly matters. The contents range from detailed explications of doctrine and Islamic law, spiritual exercises, and dream interpretation to more mundane advice regarding family relationships, professional, and educational decisions. Not surprisingly, these personal letters are treasured as heirlooms. They are constantly read and reread and often shared with fellow disciples. Many *murids* take great pains to preserve this correspondence with their teacher. A Malaysian disciple, for example, has gone so far as to laminate her letters from Wahid Bakhsh Sial Rabbani and store them in bound notebooks. On Wahid Bakhsh's recommendation, she has photocopied selections from this collection and distributed them among her fellow *murids*. The circulation of personal letters is, in fact, a relatively common practice among disciples on both sides of the Indian Ocean. According to another female Malaysian disciple,

> Every time you reread the letters and the books, it brings out new meanings. [A senior Pakistani female disciple] sent us photocopies of her letters from our *shaykh*. I found a lot of answers from there, questions I wanted to ask but never asked. It was all in those letters. We [Malaysian disciples] all used to share letters—general things that we could share. Personal, private things you do not share. We would photocopy sections. Sometimes our *shaykh* specifically told us to show a letter to this or that person. In rereading these letters you find inspiration and answers. We have a whole stack of them from our brothers and sisters that we photocopied in the late 1980s. (October 3, 2001, Kuala Lumpur)

By exchanging their personal letters Chishti Sabiri *murids* facilitate and perpetuate the teaching process, communicating the *shaykh's* spiritual wisdom to a continuously expanding audience even in his absence.

Chishti Sabiris view texts as invaluable pedagogical tools. They are quick to stress, however, that real meaning and deeper knowledge of Sufi books are ultimately unintelligible to an outside, uninformed reader. The writings of Sufi masters, disciples insist, are fully accessible only to adepts—those whose reading is guided and nuanced through direct interaction with a living Sufi master. "*Tasawwuf* is not to be found in books," writes Zauqi Shah. "The saints have written them merely as a guide for experts in the art of Sufism. Commoners can receive no benefit from them. After all, what could a layman possibly understand from reading a book of medicine? For this very reason *Shaykh al-Akbar*, Hazrat Ibn 'Arabi declared, 'It is forbidden for the uninitiated to study my books.'"[44] In the absence of guidance, the reading of Sufi texts is little more than spiritual voyeurism.

To emphasize this central point, an elder Pakistani disciple narrated the following anecdote communicated to him by Shaykh Wahid Bakhsh: "I recall Captain Wahid Bakhsh Sahab saying, 'Once I was passing along the street near Baba Sahab [the tomb of Baba Farid ad-Din Ganj-i Shakkar in Pakpattan], and I thought, 'Baba Sahab has not left a large number of books for us to read.' At that moment a voice came to me; it was the voice of Baba Sahab. He said, 'You are my books!' You see, the *shaykhs* are the living books. Whatever you receive from them you cannot get from books" (April 30, 2001, Bahawalpur). In this story, Wahid Bakhsh's mystical encounter with the saint of Pakpattan conveys a simple but clear message. For a twentieth-century Sufi master obsessed with writing, the vision of his renowned thirteenth-century predecessor illuminates the superiority of experiential wisdom over abstract, theoretical book knowledge. It is a lesson that is not lost on contemporary disciples. Time and again in interviews Chishti Sabiri disciples repeated a common theme: there are simply no shortcuts along the Sufi path. No book can replace the face-to-face interchange with the spiritual master, they assert. And no amount of reading can substitute for the rigors of ritual work and the transformative power of experience. In the words of another senior Pakistani *murid*, "*Suluk* is a very detailed and difficult thing. It is not something that can be done by reading books! It is a way of life and it is a discipline that you must inculcate in yourself. Above all it is an intention [*niyyat*] which you have to make. These books make references to certain situations and certain experiences that may not be elaborated [by the teaching *shaykh*]. These books are a help for completing *suluk*, but they are not a substitute for it" (May 21, 2001, Karachi). For today's disciples, the order's books effectively enshrine a distinct Chishti Sabiri canon, preserving and perpetuating the *silsila's* collective wisdom and corporate identity. For the uninitiated, however, texts are at best invitations to Sufi practice.

Horizontal Pedagogy: Disciples Teaching Disciples

Another vital outlet for the acquisition of knowledge is found in a horizontal teaching network that allows Chishti Sabiri disciples to learn directly from their peers. This interpersonal nexus further complements and clarifies the fundamental vertical master-disciple relationship. Though the progress of each disciple ultimately depends on personal effort, *murids* provide their spiritual compatriots with a vital spiritual support system. In private and public settings, disciples share experiences; clarify doubts, ambiguities, and anxieties; and participate in collective ritual activities. Beyond the face-to-face interaction with the *shaykh*, in fact, *murids* learn a great deal about the rules of *adab* by observing and listening to one another. Novices in particular look to senior disciples as repositories of wisdom and the embodiment of tradition. According to a young male disciple from Pakistan, "*Adab* is practice. You learn by observing, by meeting your *pir-bhais* ['brothers of the master,' or fellow disciples] who are older than you and who have more experience. They know things about the *masha'ikh*, what they used to do. They know everything, even the *shaykh's* favorite sweets, the color of his clothes. So *adab* is learned by meeting these *murids* and by asking them questions. It's a lifetime of discovery with people" (September 2, 2001, Karachi). In this Sufi spiritual meritocracy, authority comes with experience.

The Chishti Sabiri horizontal teaching network provides a safe, supportive, and informal forum for disciples to ask questions and clarify matters that they may hesitate to put before the *shaykh*. As with the sharing of personal letters, disciples continuously circulate stories. Memories of interactions with the *shaykh* form a vital dimension of each disciple's life history and sense of personal identity. And these private stories, in turn, are communicated to others in various public forums in the interest of edification or clarification. Over time, these personal narratives form an integral part of the *silsila's* collective memory.

There is a striking fluidity to these oral narratives. When discussing the nuances of Sufi doctrine and practice, disciples quote from their *shaykhs*, from each other, and even from texts in order to elaborate their points. In these accounts, the original source is often ambiguous or altogether erased. Disciples often begin with an open-ended sentence, such as "Someone had a dream that . . . ," "In a text I read, a *shaykh* declared that . . . ," or "I have been told that . . . ." The anonymity of authorship emphasizes the moral message over and above the identity of the messenger. It is also indicative of a pervasive tendency for *murids* to abstract themselves out of the story. In keeping with the dictates of *adab* and its emphasis on the virtues of self-abnegation, disciples are constantly attuned to hierarchy. They are careful to avoid appearing boastful and are especially wary of making claims to spiritual experiences that they may not fully understand. In the words of a senior Pakistani disciple,

> People normally will not relate their own experiences. That is a prerequisite. The exception is for the purpose of education, or teaching or guidance. Nobody should say, "I had this experience" or "I saw the Prophet, God bless him and grant him salvation, in my dream." No! He will say that "somebody" saw it. You do not attribute it to yourself in public. That is modesty. And that is the teaching of the *mashai'kh* of our *silsila* as well. The biggest enemy is your ego [*nafs*]. Whatever augments your ego must be crushed. That is the most difficult thing to do. (September 1, 2001, Karachi)

As this quote suggests, Chishti Sabiri teachings consistently emphasize both the importance of humility and the danger of spiritual pride.

By drawing on each other's collective wisdom and experience, *murids* gain invaluable insights into the order's institutional history, doctrinal teachings, and ritual practices. Among the most important venues for these interpersonal exchanges are the annual pilgrimages to Sufi shrines for the death anniversaries (*'urs*) of the *silsila's* major saints. Pilgrimage punctuates the Chishti Sabiri ritual calendar. During the *'urs* commemorations, disciples live together for an intensive week of spiritual immersion and collective ritual practice in the company of the teaching *shaykh*. As Shahidullah Faridi notes, "Another big advantage of attending the *'urs* is to learn the etiquette [*adab*] in group association."[45] During the days of the *'urs* retreat, disciples can be found sitting together in small groups between the organized periods for prayer and ritual disciplines. While sharing tea and food, they exchange personal experiences and narrate stories about past spiritual masters and the teachings of their own *shaykhs*. In the words of a young Pakistani male novice,

> A lot of guidance comes indirectly through these group activities. I missed three or four *'urs* because of my job. The *'urs* in Allahabad [the shrine of Wahid Bakhsh Sial Rabbani] was one of the first *'urs* I have been to in two years. I was

amazed at the amount of things I picked up, and realized I was missing, just by living with the other *murids*. If a *murid* had sat with the *shaykh* three years ago and heard him say something, he would narrate that. Or someone would say that he read something in a book and then discussed it with the *shaykh*, and his interpretation was this or that. We keep learning in this way. (March 22, 2001, Islamabad)

The annual pilgrimage cycle offers vital opportunities for Chishti Sabiris to benefit from the knowledge and experiences of their peers through a complex nexus of storytelling.

The day-to-day life of the Chishti Sabiri community is marked by an atmosphere of genuine camaraderie. This is not to suggest, however, that *murids* do not experience moments of confusion and conflict. They do. During the course of my fieldwork, I heard numerous disciples complain about backbiting, petty squabbling, and competition among their peers. On several separate occasions, female *murids* voiced feelings of alienation and marginalization, frustrated with what they perceived as entrenched patriarchal practices within both the *silsila* and society at large. More commonly, disciples—male and female, Pakistani and Malaysian—expressed anxiety about the difficulties of balancing their Sufi practices with the demands of their worldly lives. Novice disciples in particular seem particularly aware of the gaps between the ideals of doctrine and the realities of everyday practice. They worry that they will not be able to maintain the discipline and dedication required of the serious *salik*. They also struggle to make sense of their own spiritual experiences, at times overwhelmed by feelings of inadequacy and indecision. These moments of ambiguity demonstrate, as Catherine Bell suggests, that religious beliefs are often unstable and "even the basic symbols of a community's ritual life, can be very unclear to participants or interpreted by them in very dissimilar ways."[46]

As an outsider I was not often privy to confessions of confusion—but I heard them enough to conclude that such moments of dissonance are significant. Though difficult to measure, they suggest that a pervasive and deepseated ambivalence about Sufi identity underlies daily life in contemporary, postcolonial Pakistan and Malaysia. This is not surprising since in both countries, the twenty-first-century Sufi subject is assaulted with multiple, competing social, cultural, and political ideologies. For Chishti Sabiri disciples, these pervasive tensions are further exacerbated by social environments in which Sufi piety and practice is increasingly controversial. Katherine Ewing traces this ambivalence in her ethnography of popular Pakistani Sufism. In her assessment, "Many highly educated Pakistanis who regard themselves as modern, rational, and professional are also caught between ideologies, inconsistent in their self-representations, uncertain about how to articulate their relationships to Islam and to modernity. Many are drawn to Sufism and yet avoid identifying themselves as Sufis. Their conversations about Sufism display an ambivalence and show evidence of intense conflict."[47]

On several occasions, I noticed a similar dynamic among Chishti Sabiri disciples. *Murids* are noticeably wary of announcing their Sufi affiliations to strangers, and consciously avoid arguments over Sufism in the home, at work, and in public spaces. In private—and among their fellow disciples—however, Chishti Sabiris wear their *silsila* affiliation with immense pride. It is at the very core of their self-identity. Within the bounded confines of the *silsila*, what is perhaps most striking is the relative *infrequency* of dissonance and disruption between *murids*. In both theory and practice, the order's vertical (*pir-murid*) and horizontal (*murid-murid*) teaching networks promote a culture that minimizes and ameliorates doubt and discord. Beyond the spheres of work and family, disciples spend a great deal of time together—in both formal worship and informal social interaction. They communicate mutual respect and a deep affection for each other through their language, gestures, and bodily comportment. Disciples share a common vocabulary to articulate their experiences, and they express remarkably uniform definitions of identity and selfhood. At every turn, the *silsila* places great stress on fostering and preserving communal harmony. Etiquette and social propriety are highly valued—and actively cultivated.

These virtues, of course, are at the very core of Sufi *adab*. In fact, Chishti Sabiri *shaykhs* define an ethic of cooperation and mutual respect among *murids* as a religious duty. It is also seen as a manifestation of prophetic *sunna*. In his final will and testament (*wasyat nama*), Shahidullah Faridi makes this explicit:

> It is therefore necessary that each one considers himself in service to the others and to try to give comfort to his brothers in every way. Any kind of selfish behavior, grouping, envy, quarreling, or not talking to one another is against the etiquette of society and must be abstained from strictly. Huzoor (S) [the Prophet Muhammad], chief of God's creation, has said, "become the true servants of your Lord and brothers" (*kunu ibadallah ikhwana'*). The Prophet of Allah has also proclaimed that one who is not respectful to the elders and compassionate to the young is not one of us. Therefore it is obligatory on the elders of the *silsila* to treat the young with loving kindness and attend to improve and guide them. In the same way it is necessary for the young to treat the elders with regard and respect.[48]

This constant emphasis on social propriety and decorum permeates every dimension of Chishti Sabiri social interaction. The love that *murids* express for their *shaykhs* is mirrored in the experience of friendship and intimacy between fellow disciples. In the words of a senior female Malaysian disciple, "My love for them [*murids*] is sometimes greater than my love for my children. We have strong ties, mothers and children, yet even that is no comparison to this love! The love of my *pir*-brothers and sisters is an expression of the love for my *shaykh*. And love for my *shaykh* is love for Allah" (October 6, 2001, Kuala Lumpur). In the final analysis, it is the strength of these bonds of fellowship that ultimately cements the Chishti Sabiri *silsila* as a coherent, corporate institution—a network of piety and practice that endures even as it continues to adapt to changing times.

CONCLUSION

Twenty-first-century Chishti Sabiri Sufis preserve a distinct discursive and
ritual tradition. As their spiritual ancestors before them, they do so within a
bounded moral community that is firmly centered on the master-disciple
teaching relationship and mediated by established rules of etiquette. The
worldview of these modern Sufi subjects is rooted in what Dipesh
Chakrabarty calls "the temporal heterogeneity of the 'now.'"[49] Today's disciples effectively live within two interdependent spheres: a "historical now"
and a "sacred now." From the perspective of the "historical now," *murids* live
and work amid the shifting landscape of postcolonial Pakistan and Malaysia.
As members of extended family networks, economic consumers and produc-
ers, and citizens of modern nation-states, they are fully immersed in the social
practices of the everyday, lived-in, mundane world. They mark the trajectory
of their daily lives by secular time—the chronology of positivist history, measured by the calendar and the clock. Yet at the very same time, Chishti Sabiri
disciples engage a transhistorical "sacred now" that is no less concrete, tangible, and real. As pious Muslims and spiritual seekers, they live within a
thoroughly sacralized universe that impacts every dimension of their public
and private selves. In this world, time and meaning are subject to different
rules altogether. Within the "sacred now," disciples orient themselves within
a teaching tradition that binds them directly to the timeless, transcendent
moral authority of the Prophet Muhammad. In effect, this temporal simul-
taneity is an experience that positivist history simply does not have the vocabulary to explain or the tools to measure. As Chakrabarty illustrates, this
ontological "now" collapses the logic of secular space and linear time, erasing
the rigid boundaries between the remembered, sacred past and the lived-in
world of everyday practice.[50]

For today's Chishti Sabiri disciples, it is the teaching *shaykh* who provides
the tangible link to Islam's sacred past. As the heir of the Prophet, the Sufi
master serves as the embodiment of *sunna*, the standard bearer of *adab*, and
the arbiter of *shari'a*. In the words of a senior Pakistani *murid*, "Our *shaykh*
is a *mujtahid* [a legal scholar] for us. Whatever he says, that is *hadith* and that
is Qur'an. We never ask, 'From where did you get this?' Whatever he receives,
he receives from the Holy Prophet, from his lineage. If his teachings are
against the traditions or against the Holy Qur'an, then he is no *shaykh*, even
if he can fly in the air or walk on water! If he is against *shari'a*, against *sunna*,
against the Qur'an, then we will never follow him" (April 28, 2001,
Bahawalpur). The intense and intimate relationship with the spiritual guide
provides Chishti Sabiri disciples a shelter from the corrupting influences of
the world, even as they continue to engage that world. As a living symbol of
Islamic piety in practice, the *shaykh* signifies the possibility for spiritual transformation amid the incongruities and inconsistencies of ordinary life.

Within the contemporary Chishti Sabiri *silsila*, spiritual training remains
centered on an interpersonal teaching network that favors direct experience

over abstract theorizing. For disciples, the transformative encounter with the spiritual master initiates a process of *deconstruction*. In Sufi practice, the disciple learns to reconstitute the bodily and mental practices that bind him/her to the world in pursuit of the deeper dimensions of intuitive, experiential knowledge. In Zauqi Shah's words, "We spend a good deal of the earlier portion of our life in physical bondage. Our libraries and laboratories only tighten the bond. Even independent thinking creates fresh chains for us. The moment we come into contact with the Sheikh [*sic*], we enter upon a new era of liberation. The ties are loosened, the chains broken, and the journey begins. From the seen, we gradually move on to the unseen and, after plunging into the fathomless depth of the Unseen, we revert to the seen to complete our course."[51]

This inner journey from *shari'a* to *tariqa* to *haqiqa* demands a careful balance between acquiescence and action. The Sufi novice submits to the *shaykh* "like a corpse in the hands of a washerman" even as she/he cultivates self-awareness through personal discipline, sacrifice, patience, and love. The seeker does not walk the path alone, however. Chishti Sabiri networks of knowledge and practice are communicated and experienced through a broad network of teaching relationships. In face-to-face companionship with the *shaykh* and the community of believers, the *murid's* body, mind, and soul are gradually refashioned. The ultimate aim is the total transformation of a secular, heteronomous self into a sacralized, moral Muslim self. Within this system, Chishti Sabiri pedagogy is primarily oral and aural. Disciples learn from each other via a complex, symbiotic nexus of stories that reinforces and refines the central *pir-murid* relationship. Nevertheless, disciples insist that discourse and language have their limits. In the end, Sufi doctrine must be interiorized through the direct experience of ritual practice. An ethnography of the embodied ritual performances at the center of contemporary Chishti Sabiri identity is the subject of chapter 5.

CHAPTER 5

EXPERIENCING SUFISM: THE DISCIPLINE OF RITUAL PRACTICE

Amid the shifting social and political landscape of twenty-first-century Pakistan and Malaysia, ritual practice anchors Chishti Sabiri identity. The Sufi path (*suluk*) couples a distinct model of human psychology with practical techniques for self-transformation. In an informal, introductory letter written to a female Malaysian disciple, Shaykh Wahid Bakhsh Sial Rabbani outlines the Sufi model of the self and details how religious knowledge is experienced and actualized through ritual performance. His words encapsulate the Sufi spiritual journey, both in theory and in practice:

> I will tell you some of the basic spiritual exercises which will, if God the Most High wills, enable you to get spiritual knowledge and also keep you from evil influences. But before I go any further I would like to tell you something about the reality of man. Every man and woman is a combination of a body and soul. The body is of earthly origin and has a tendency to pull you downwards. The soul is of Divine origin, as shown by Allah in the Holy Qur'an. Therefore it has a tendency to pull you upwards to Divine nearness. Human life is therefore the name of a constant struggle, a tug of war, between the two forces: the beastly force, called *al-nafs al-ammara bil-su'* in the Holy Qur'an, and the spiritual force called *al-nafs al-mutma'inna*. If the lower self or beastly self gets stronger and overpowers the spiritual self, one is ruined. If, however, the spiritual self overpowers the beastly self, one is successful and realizes his true destiny of reaching Divine nearness and presence which is also called "salvation."
>
> Now all the Islamic teachings—prayer, the fast, Hajj, charity—are meant to strengthen the soul and weaken the lower self. In order to accelerate the pace of progress, spiritual masters have prescribed a spiritual path comprising some extra struggles (*mujahada*). This extra worship has been urged in the following *hadith* of the Holy Prophet, God bless him and grant him salvation: "Allah says: When my servant wishes to come closer to me by additional worship, I love him and come so close to him that I become his eyes, and he sees by me, I become his ears, and he hears by me, I become his hands, and he works by me, I become

his feet and he walks by me, and I give him whatever he desires." Now what is that extra worship? It is a combination of *zikrs*, prayers, *awrad* [supplications] and other exercises that strengthen the spiritual force in man and weaken the beastly forces.[1]

By invoking the Qur'an and the legacy of the Prophet, Wahid Bakhsh portrays Sufism as a natural extension of the orthodox ritual requirements incumbent on all Muslims (*'ibadat*). Sufi rituals do not replace normative practice, the *shaykh* suggests; they expand and deepen it. Like any pious Muslim, the Sufi adept begins with a strict adherence to the *arkan*. These five fundamental "pillars" of faith are then supplemented with a regimen of extra-canonical Sufi rituals expressly aimed at taming the ego. The particular rigors of Sufi ritual, Wahid Bakhsh asserts, involve a conscious and deliberate remaking of the self. The starting point for the Sufi path of purification is the source of human frailty: "the soul that commands evil" (*al-nafs al-ammara bil-su'*; Qur'an 12:53). Through repentance and renunciation the spiritual seeker attempts to tame the ego's base instincts and voracious appetites. With patience and determination, worldly desires are gradually replaced with an insatiable desire for God. The Sufi is aided in this quest by an activated conscience that oversees and guides his/her actions, "the blaming soul" (*al-nafs al-lawwama;* Qur'an 75:2). This entire process of self-refashioning is spurred by the rigors of ritual discipline. Under the guidance of a teaching *shaykh*, the adept voluntarily submits to a host of supererogatory practices (*awrad*) designed to mold the body, sharpen the mind, and purify the soul. For the intrepid disciple, the reward is self-awareness and a pacified soul that serves as the vehicle to salvation. In the words of the Qur'an (89:27–30), "Soul at peace [*al-nafs al-mutma'inna*], return to your Lord, both pleased and pleasing [me]; enter among my servants, and enter my paradise!"

Borrowing from Foucault, it is useful to describe Sufi ritual practices as "technologies of the self."[2] For Chishti Sabiris, true knowledge about the nature of the self and its relationship to God is not found in abstract philosophizing or the academic parsing of legal and theological debate. Instead, spiritual progress demands work. The word *mujahada* (spiritual "striving") comes from the same Arabic root as *jihad*. For Sufis, *mujahada* centers on a retinue of rituals—techniques for mental concentration, combined with physical postures—that together create religious experience and communicate religious truth. These prescribed ritual acts offer the Sufi adept a tangible, tactile, and immediate source of knowledge. In Chishti Sabiri practice, rituals are taught to individual disciples by the teaching *shaykh* and subsequently reinforced and rationalized through a social network of learning.

The locus and focus of Sufi ritual techniques is the physical body. Ultimately, understanding comes only from *doing* because "what is done with the body is the ground of what is thought and said."[3] Within the Sufi pedagogical system, the body serves both as a medium for knowledge and the primary tool for the remolding of the self. In the words of Shaykh Muhammad Zauqi Shah, "A vigorous body and a powerful soul, although quite valuable in themselves, are not the objects of life. They are only means to an end. The body is merely an instrument to the soul. The soul is the agent of the 'I' dwelling within, and this 'I' again is an echo of the Real, Genuine, All-perfect 'I' which dwells neither within nor without, dwells nowhere and dwells everywhere and is the only existing Reality before whom everything else dwindles into a mere shadow."[4] By surrendering to the will of a spiritual master, the Sufi disciple learns to rehabituate the self through a program of rigorous and routinized ritual practice. Through the disciplining the body, the ego is gradually transformed and ultimately transcended. In keeping with the famous prophetic *hadith*, "die before you die," the ultimate aim is to reshape the acculturated, socialized, secular self into a sacralized, moral Sufi subject. As Scott Kugle notes, "By advocating that one die to one's own self, mystics loosen the habitual bonds that bind the self to the socially constituted body. This provides a space and freedom to re-discipline the body, to train it in a new set of stances, a new pattern of postures, a new repertoire of gestures. In short, mystics offer a method of acquiring a whole new bodily habitus, a new ground of being, driven not by selfish desires but rather by the embodiment of virtues."[5] For Chishti Sabiris, ritual serves as the primary vehicle for the interiorization of knowledge. Ritual practice, in other words, is the key to spiritual perfection.

Twenty-first-century Chishti Sabiri disciples remain connected to Islam's sacred past through genealogy, networks of knowledge, and a nexus of embodied ritual practices. *Murids* view these spiritual resources as the direct legacy of the Prophet Muhammad. For them, the Sufi path is a timeless, universal teaching—as relevant today as it was in the seventh century. At the same time, they also understand that the tradition cannot remain static. Since Sufism does not exist in a hermetically sealed vacuum, disciples acknowledge, it must respond and adapt to social change if it is to survive.

Today's Chishti Sabiris look back on their premodern predecessors with a palpable sense of envy and nostalgia. They regretfully accept, however, that the days of the traditional *khanaqah*—the premodern Sufi lodge memorialized in classical texts—have come and gone. I asked a senior Pakistani male disciple if the *khanaqah* was an institution that could function in the modern world. His response reveals how many Chishti Sabiri disciples think about the weight of tradition in the context of their own twenty-first-century lives:

> Is the *khanaqah* relevant in the modern world, could it function now? That is an important question. I think that the saints have concluded that it is not possible now—because of the requirements of the times, the requirements of jobs, with everyone living such a fast pace of life. This is how Sufism deals with the modern age. The thing which is emphasized is not to give up your spiritual exercises, even as you remain fully engrossed in the day-to-day workings of the modern world. That's the message for every *murid*, whether he is in business, an engineer, or an army officer. In previous times people had to do a lot of spiritual work (*mujahada*) to get a little [spiritual growth]. Today, even staying away from watching television is a form of *mujahada*. (August 26, 2001, Lahore)

This quote typifies the constant refrain among contemporary disciples that changing times demand a new approach to Sufi practice. Embracing a form of *ijtihad*—independent reasoning—today's Chishti Sabiri order has developed a range of practical strategies to negotiate change and accommodate Sufism to the ground-level contingencies of everyday life in the twenty-first century. In the succinct words of the same disciple, "Our *silsila* represents compatibility with modern life" (August 26, 2001, Lahore).

This chapter examines how contemporary Chishti Sabiri identity is experienced and expressed through the discipline of ritual practice. Here I focus on ethnographic contexts over doctrinal texts. My analysis is concerned less with theological and polemical debates than with documenting how today's Chishti Sabiri disciples actually experience and explain the ritual techniques that cement their Sufi identity. Drawing on extensive interviews, I highlight the stories that *murids* tell themselves and each other about the methods and meanings of the Sufi spiritual journey. With attention to both private and public realms, I also chart some of the strategies that disciples employ to integrate *suluk* into their complicated lives. In short, this chapter traces both the continuities and changes in postcolonial Sufi praxis. To do so, I focus on the three ritual complexes at the very heart of Chishti Sabiri identity: dreams and dream interpretation, the daily rituals of remembrance, and the annual cycle of pilgrimage networks and musical assemblies at Sufi shrines.

DREAMS AND DREAM INTERPRETATION

Sufi ritual practice takes place at diverse times and in myriad locations. It even extends into the dream world of sleep. For Muslims both past and present, dreams are much more than nocturnal hallucinations. As a medium for both revelation and inspiration, they impart vital ontological, epistemological, and spiritual truths. In the words of the famous fourteenth-century historian Ibn Khaldun (d. 1406), "God, therefore, created man in such a way that the veil of the senses could be lifted through sleep, which is a natural function of man. When that veil is lifted, the soul is ready to learn the things it desires to know in the world of Truth. At times, it catches glimpses of what it seeks."[6]

Sufi dream theory draws on a rich premodern heritage. Even so, its logic and practice diverges sharply from the classical science of Islamic dream interpretation (*ta'bir*).[7] Whereas *ta'bir* aims to translate the imagery of dreams in order to forecast the future, Sufis cultivate dreams as spiritual tools and catalysts for spiritual growth. As flashes of ultimate reality (*bushra*), dreams offer a litmus test for a Sufi's spiritual potential by measuring "the dreamer's gradual ascent within his inner self and, correspondingly, within the macrocosm."[8] The hagiographies of Sufi masters abound with stories of the dreams and visions of saints, the Prophet Muhammad, or even, on rare occasion, God. In the case of select spiritual luminaries, these accounts reach the level of the sublime. There is perhaps no better example of this than the Persian Sufi master Ruzbihan Baqli (d. 1209) who preserved his extraordinarily visionary experiences in a unique spiritual diary titled *The Unveiling of Secrets* (*Kashf al-asrar*).[9]

Dreams and dream interpretation play an essential role in the daily practice of contemporary Chishti Sabiri pedagogy. In a personal letter addressed to a female disciple, Shaykh Wahid Bakhsh Sial Rabbani invokes the traditional paradigm and taxonomy of Islamic dream theory. At the same time, he goes further to distinguish it from its Western, scientific counterpart:

> The psychologists know only one kind of dream, those which result from ideas or desires in the sub-conscious mind. But actually there are other kinds. Broadly speaking, the dreams are of two categories according to spiritualism: *rahmani* and *shaitani. Rahmani* dreams are from God and *shaitani* dreams are from Satan. The way to distinguish the first from the second is that the former are not against Islam, while the latter are against *shari'a*. Sometimes the *shaitan* speak in terms of *shari'a* and then gradually try to mislead us.[10]

In Chishti Sabiri practice, dreams mirror the interior states and stations of *suluk* itself. Following a typology outlined by anthropologist Katherine Ewing, we can distinguish between three distinct categories of Sufi dreams: "dreams of initiation," "spontaneous dreams," and "induced dreams."[11]

The spiritual connection between a Sufi master and disciple is often first revealed in a dream. "The relationship between *shaykh* and disciple has not so much to be established as to be recognized and cultivated," notes Valerie Hoffman, "and a major way in which such relationships are recognized is through dream-visions."[12] The theoretical foundation for dreams of initiation lies in the widespread belief that *shaykhs* and their disciples are bound together in a primordial relationship. This idea echoes the Qur'anic narrative of the Primordial Covenant (7: 172), the event that assures that knowledge of God is inscribed into the very souls of human beings. In the words of Shahidullah Faridi, "The truth is that this matter is pre-ordained, just as it is pre-ordained that a child will be born into a certain family. You do not choose who should be your mother and father, it is already decreed by Allah . . . The choice of a spiritual guide (*shaykh*) is a similar case. It is already decreed from eternity from who you will receive your portion."[13]

Sufi dream theory marks initiation dreams as the interface between a passive dreamer and an active human agent of the Divine will, the *shaykh*. It is the Sufi master who takes the initiative in this relationship, responding to the dreamer's innermost desires by appearing to him/her in the world of sleep. Not surprisingly, the experience of an initiatory dream makes an immediate and lasting impact on the dreamer's self-identity, often with enduring consequences for his/her spiritual life and social relationships. In interviews, a number of Chishti Sabiri disciples narrated such dreams to me. One of the most intriguing accounts came from a senior Malaysian *murid* of Chinese ethnicity. This man's original conversion to Islam was inspired by a vivid initiatory dream. It is an event that he still recalls with great emotion:

> I was brought up in a Taoist family. We prayed to every deity that you could imagine. As I grew up I also followed a Hindu priest. Then I met my wife. She was a Christian, a very staunch Christian, and I nearly followed her into

Christianity. But somehow or other I did not. Allah is very kind. I have a lot of Malay Muslim friends who talked with me, and guided me along. I believed in the concept of one God, even when I was young. I did some comparative studies and thought a lot about it.

Before I embraced Islam, I had a dream. I dreamt of Nabi Issa [Prophet Jesus], peace be upon him. He was wearing white robes, and floating in the sky. Many people were standing on the ground. I was standing there too. Then he called out, "Anyone who wants to be saved, kneel down." So I knelt down. After I had this dream, I spoke to many people. The Christians said, "You are a Christian!" When I spoke to Muslims they said, "Thank God! He is also a Prophet of Islam. This is a very clear indication that you should embrace Islam." So I embraced Islam, together with my wife. (October 1, 2001, Kuala Lumpur)

This narrative offers a striking example of the transformative power of dreams. Here a vision of Jesus precipitates a change of faith, the culmination of a long search for spiritual guidance that traversed a pluralist cultural and spiritual landscape. In Chishti Sabiri practice, dreams change lives.

Ewing's research on popular Sufism in Pakistan suggests that Sufi initiatory dreams are often preceded by a profound sense of longing (*shauq*) on the part of the spiritual aspirant. This desire typically culminates in a dream in which the adept is introduced to his or her *shaykh*, forging a bond that is subsequently formalized during a face-to-face meeting in the waking world.[14] Among contemporary Chishti Sabiri *murids* too this seems to be a remarkably common experience. A senior Pakistani disciple recounts a dream of Shaykh Shahidullah Faridi that led to a face-to-face encounter with the *shaykh*:

> Somebody gave me a copy of *Tarbiyat al-'ushshaq* [the spiritual discourses of Shaykh Muhammad Zauqi Shah]. One day when I was reading it, I fell asleep. I dreamt that I was standing near a pond in a beautiful garden, and there was a very holy person there. He was very good-looking. He was the true copy of a photograph [of the *shaykh*] I had seen. I thought, "He is Hazrat Shahidullah." I dreamt that I was meeting him. [After awaking] my younger brother told me, "Today Hazrat Shahidullah Sahab came here and gave you some books." I said, "Where is he staying?" [He then proceeds to meet the *shaykh*] He was standing in the very same spot that I had dreamt about. I quietly walked to him and said, "Sir, are you Hazrat Shahidullah?" "Yes," he replied. I introduced myself. That evening everyone became his *murid*, my wife, my daughter, and my sons. (March 24, 2001, Islamabad)

This single dream had immediate and lasting consequences for this disciple and his extended family, all of whom remain prominent members in the order to this day.

Such miraculous stories are not uncommon among Sufi disciples. Chishti Sabiris understand initiatory dreams as a bridge between desire and discipleship. Unanticipated and unpredictable, they are a place where all things are possible. For a male Malaysian disciple, an unfulfilled desire for *bay'at* with Shaykh Wahid Bakhsh Sial Rabbani resulted in a surprising Uwaysi-style initiation at the hands of Shaykh Shahidullah Faridi:

> In the first letter that I wrote to my *shaykh*, before I became a *murid*, I wrote
> about my dreams. I wrote down about thirty dreams, I wrote everything. He
> [Wahid Bakhsh] replied, "You have so many dreams. I will just touch on some
> of the important ones." And then he interpreted some of those dreams. I wrote
> to him again and said, "I want to be your *murid*." That night I dreamt of
> Hazrat Shah Shahidullah Faridi, may God have mercy upon him. He was sitting
> at a round table along with three more persons. I walked up to him at the table
> and he just turned around and held my hand. He shook my hand. I took *bay'at*
> with him in the dream. I had never met him, but in the dream it was him, a
> British man. Maybe I dreamt of him because Hazrat Sahab was a convert, and
> I am also a convert. So that's the reason he appeared, to accept the *bay'at*.
> According to the *shaykhs*, it is the same thing [taking initiation in dreams or in
> person]. (September 30, 2001, Kuala Lumpur)

This account is remarkable for its fluid symmetry. This disciple is first drawn
into Wahid Bakhsh's orbit by the *shaykh's* reputation as an interpreter of
dreams. From an informal exchange of letters, to an enigmatic vision of discipleship with Shahidullah Faridi, to a formal relationship with Wahid
Bakhsh—this story blurs the boundaries between the lived in world of everyday life and the sacralized, liminal space of the dream. For Chishti Sabiris
both realms of experience are interconnected and equally real.

Given their impact, dreams of initiation hold an especially prominent place
in the personal history of many Chishti Sabiri *murids*. Disciples view such
visionary experiences as an invaluable source of guidance and inspiration.
Long afterward, they point to the dates and details of initiatory dreams as life-
altering experiences—hinge moments that radically transform their perception
of reality as well as their own sense of identity. As Ewing notes, "The dream
thus becomes a pivot in terms of which the dreamer reorients his life. The
experience of finding one's *pir*, validated by a dream, becomes encapsulated in
a 'story,' a relatively fixed narrative that, in turn, may be used in the organization of a self-representation, to the extent of constituting a new social
identity."[15] When dream narratives are communicated to other disciples, they
also become part of the Chishti Sabiri *silsila's* collective memory. In this sense,
Sufi dreams are both personally transforming and collectively edifying.

In Sufi theory, a "spontaneous dream" serves as an effect, sign, or symptom of the relationship between an individual's spirit (*ruh*) and soul (*nafs*).
In the formative stages of the Sufi path, the adept's *ruh* is often described as
clouded and opaque, making the reflection of the spiritual realm a virtual
impossibility. As the disciple continues to "clean away" impurities through
ritual discipline, however, dreams increasingly come into focus. In this sense,
spontaneous dreams reflect the Sufi subject's inner spiritual state.
Muhammad Zauqi Shah explains the significance of visionary experiences in
Tarbiyat al-'ushshaq:

> Here [in this world] every person receives divine disclosures according to their
> own capacity. As [the Persian couplet by Amir Khusrau], "What wondrous

place I found myself in last night" [*che manzil bud shab jay keh man budam*]
illustrates, there is a new assembly [*mahfil*] at every spiritual station [*maqam*].
There is only one truth, but because people's capacities differ there are
differences in divine disclosures as well. In the same way, a single truth is
revealed in a dream [*khwab*], but it is manifested to different people in different
languages and diverse ways. Hazrat 'Umar, may God be pleased with him, said:
"Dreams are the language of God." For this reason, to relate a dream falsely is
to slander God.[16]

Spontaneous dreams are therefore both a mark of spiritual attainment and
a measure of spiritual aptitude. Yet as Zauqi Shah suggests, the real meaning of dreams is often not self-evident. For this reason, dreams must be
interpreted.

In her research among Sufi groups in contemporary Egypt, Valerie
Hoffman notes that visionary experiences sometimes substitute altogether
for ordinary personal contact with a *shaykh*. As a result, Hoffman argues,
dreams and visions provide an especially important outlet for women and
others who would otherwise have little opportunity for direct social interaction with a spiritual mentor.[17] This is demonstrably not the case among
Chishti Sabiri practitioners, however. Chishti Sabiri *adab* dictates that disciples must narrate their dreams directly to their spiritual mentor. This imperative is itself nothing new. In *Bihishti Zewar*, for example, the revivalist *shaykh*
Ashraf 'Ali Thanawi (1863–1943) admonishes his readers to avoid publicly
recounting their spiritual experiences: "Do not tell anyone other than your
master if, through the blessed power of reciting the name of God [*zikr*], you
attain a good spiritual state in your heart, witness good dreams, or experience
a voice or light in a waking state."[18] This same advice is echoed by contemporary Chishti Sabiris. In the words of a male Pakistani *murid*, "Hazrat
Wahid Bakhsh once told me, 'These dreams and this guidance given to you
is, in fact, guidance from Almighty Allah. It's just like if a close friend of yours
tells you a close secret and then you go and disclose it to others. That friend
of yours, he wouldn't like it and it will take you quite awhile to get his confidence back.' If you tell these secrets then, sorry, no more secrets for you"
(November 7, 2000, Lahore). Chishti Sabiris view dreams as a form of
communication with God, a personalized message that is decidedly not for
public consumption.

In his vital role as dream interpreter, the Chishti Sabiri *shaykh* listens as
the devotee narrates his/her own dream experiences in detail. Through a
careful analysis of the content of these nocturnal visions, the master gains
deep insights into the disciple's progress along the path. While the content
of dreams is individualized—reflecting differences in background and personal experience—there are certain common tropes. As with the traditional
Islamic science of *ta'bir*, the language and imagery of Sufi dreams provide
vital clues for deciphering its underlying meaning. As Wahid Bakhsh
elucidates in a personal letter written to a female Pakistani *murid*, the
signs and symbols of a spontaneous dream correspond to the individual's

psychological and spiritual states:

> Sometimes apparently good dreams are really bad, and the bad ones are good. For instance, being drenched in water, wading or struggling in water, even being drowned in water is always good. It means purification. If someone sees himself naked in a dream it is good. It means veils will be lifted and we will come across reality. Being kissed or embraced in the dream is good; it means getting spiritual or material benefits. Being garlanded in a dream is not good. It may mean death. Seeing fire is bad. Seeing wild animals in dreams is good because the wild animals are the *nafs* [the lower, concupiscent self]. It is good to see them because Allah has given him enough purification to be able to see the evils of his own *nafs*. Being married is sometimes good, sometimes bad. Marriage for a spiritual man is union with God. Seeing teeth falling out is bad—it means troubles. Being bit by a dog means wealth is to come, especially if it is a mad dog. Seeing filth or being covered with filth means wealth. Seeing oneself dead is good for the spiritual aspirant. It means he is to reach the status of annihilation in God (*fana fi Allah*). Seeing yourself ill in dreams may mean that you will receive more purification. Praying in a dream means you will perform Hajj. Seeing holy men or holy places in a dream is good. It means purification. Seeing the Holy Prophet, God bless him and grant him salvation, is a great blessing. It is said in a *hadith* that he who sees the Prophet, God bless him and grant him salvation, in a dream, sees him in reality as in life. So please do not get worried over apparently bad dreams. You should refer your dreams to me for interpretation.[19]

This long list of dream imagery and their corresponding meanings is reminiscent of the logic and style of medieval Islamic dream manuals. It is important to notice, however, that Wahid Bakhsh's typologies have predominantly spiritual ramifications. For the *shaykh*, a dream's signs and symbols reflect the inner, psychological states of the dreamer. As such, they reveal a disciple's piety and spiritual potential. Wahid Bakhsh also emphasizes that spontaneous dreams of the Prophet Muhammad are particularly auspicious. The famous *hadith* that he invokes authenticates a visionary experience of the Prophet prima facie: "Whoever has seen me has seen me truly, and Satan cannot take my form."[20] This entire passage establishes Wahid Bakhsh's authority as a spiritual guide and an expert interpreter of dreams, and the *shaykh* ends his letter with an offer of further guidance.

During the course of my interviews, several Chishti Sabiri *murids* described their own visions of the Prophet Muhammad. They did so with a particular awe and reverence. The content of these narratives varied widely. Disciples described visions of the Prophet appearing in an array of settings and dressed in a variety of clothes, most often with a black beard. An account by a female Pakistani disciple is typical: "When I saw him in a dream, he was dressed like a Pathan with a turban and a *shalwar kamiz*. I asked him, 'Are you the Prophet, peace be upon him?' He just smiled. When you see him, you just know it is him. Another time I saw him in a vision. He was standing outside a tent, wearing black, a black turban, and black clothes. He was handsome, and had this radiant smile on his face" (March 22, 2001, Islamabad). Regardless of the details of context or content, *murids* empha-size that the Prophet's appearance sanctifies a dream. Significantly, many disciples also interpret these experiences as an affirmation of the guidance and protection offered by the extended *silsila*. In the words of a female Malaysian disciple of Wahid Bakhsh,

> The more I interacted with him [Wahid Bakhsh], the more dreams came. In one dream, I was in a place that was full of *shaitan* [demons] and *jinn* [spirits]. I did not know which house to go into for protection. When the time for evening prayers came, suddenly the footsteps of *Rasul*, God bless him and grant him salvation, appeared. They just lit up. I just had to step on them, put my feet on these steps illuminated on the street in the night. I did not see the Prophet, only his footsteps. I followed them and I was safe from all the *shaitan* and *jinn*. They could not touch me. The footsteps we follow are correct. (October 3, 2001, Kuala Lumpur)

A vision of the Prophet transformed this woman's spiritual life, confirming that she was on an established spiritual path sanctioned by both *shari'a* and *sunna*.

While visions of the Prophet are cherished, they are also exceedingly rare. Chishti Sabiris assert that guidance in spontaneous dreams more often comes directly from one's own *shaykh* or, by extension, the *mashai'kh* of the Chishti order. Especially in times of doubt or need, lucid dreams of Sufi masters—both past and present—provide clarity and comfort. In the words of a female Pakistani *murid*, "Sometimes in dreams, the *shaitan* can divert you. But they cannot take the form of a *shaykh*. This is where *bay'at* helps you, because the *shaykh* is in control. Most of the spiritual dreams we have are in the form of the *shaykh*. If we need guidance or help, it comes [in a dream] in the form of your *shaykh*" (June 17, 2001, Lahore). Significantly, spontaneous dreams of the spiritual master continue even after the *shaykh's* death. *Murids* high-light the unbroken continuity of dreams as further proof that a Sufi master's power and blessing (*baraka*) transcend the limits of space and time. In the words of a female disciple of Shaykh Shahidullah Faridi, "I have a powerful connection with him, in my dreams, all the time. This has helped me throughout my life. The guidance towards Allah I felt all along, though I had not physically been with him [Shahidullah Faridi]. I don't think you need to see your *shaykh*. When you have the *shaykh* in your heart, he is always there for you" (June 17, 2001, Lahore). As this quote suggests, Chishti Sabiri dis-ciples view spontaneous dreams as evidence of the enduring connection with the Sufi master. The insights transmitted in the threshold space of dreams serve as signposts on a disciple's journey toward God. Along this pathway, the *shaykh* fulfills multiple roles, serving as a moral exemplar, a spiritual guide, and an interpreter of dreams.

Chishti Sabiri disciples also actively cultivate dreams. These "induced dreams" are most often used to resolve worldly problems. One such tech-nique known as *istikhara* involves the recitation of a litany of special prayers in prescribed locations—often in a mosque or the vicinity of a saint's shrine—with the expectation of an answering dream. This too is an ancient practice.[21] Like initiatory dreams, induced dreams are specifically aimed at the dreamer. And once again, their meaning and import is ultimately accessible to the teaching *shaykh* who interprets them. In *Malfuzat-i shaykh*, Shaykh Shahidullah Faridi details the correct performance of this ritual: "After the evening prayer, one should declare the intention [*niyyat*] to perform *istikhara* while keeping the desired goal in mind. Recite *Durud Sharif* [a benediction for the Prophet and his descendants] before and after, and recite *Du'a-i Qunut* ['supplication said standing'] seven times. Then go to sleep. If you are unable to fall asleep, then continue reciting *Du'a-i Qunut* until sleep comes. If God Most High wills, you will receive an answer in a dream [*khwab*]."[22]

Chishti Sabiri *murids* typically perform *istikhara* on Thursday or Sunday evenings. I was told that this technique is particularly useful for guidance and clarity regarding such important matters as marriage, education, financial matters, and employment. A senior Pakistani disciple, for instance, turned to *istikhara* to help him resolve a vexing career decision. Faced with a job offer that promised higher pay but more responsibilities, he was deeply concerned that it might also have a deleterious impact on his daily spiritual devotions. In his words, "This might work out, but from a spiritual point of view nothing should be disturbed. Of course, I will do *istikhara* and if it is negative I will not make the change. Decisions made with the rational mind alone, even when they are sincere, can be destructive. It [*istikhara*] is like consulting God. You offer prayers and supplication [*du'a*] and go to sleep, hoping for a dream" (April 25, 2001, Lahore). By inducing dreams, Chishti Sabiri *murids* attempt to proactively resolve the ambiguities and indecisions of their daily lives.

Regardless of their form, Sufi dreams serve a dual function: they inspire the adept and simultaneously provide the *shaykh* with a barometer to assess the disciple's progress. After interpreting a dream, the spiritual master assigns a regimen of spiritual exercises in an attempt to "lead the disciple to new spiritual growth and to point out and thus bring under control the areas in which the disciple's soul (*nafs*) is dominant and needs to be exposed."[23] At a certain point in a *murid's* spiritual development, however, dreams threaten to become a distraction. Intriguingly, disciples note that while visionary experiences are prevalent in the early stages of *suluk* they often decrease in frequency and intensity over time. A senior Pakistani *murid* argues that this too has a purpose: "The unveilings [*kashf*], dreams, and visions are sometimes veiled. Why? So they [Sufi adepts] will not be distracted by them. These things will only slow them down. When you travel by foot, if you stop along the way to look at the flowers and other things you might forget your goal, or you will reach your destination very late. But if your eyes are closed, you just keep on running. You cannot see whatever is in the way. If you run fast, you will reach your destination quickly" (May 2, 2001, Bahawalpur). Amid the complexity and ambiguity of modern life, Chishti Sabiris view dreams as a window to the eternal and unchanging realm of divinity. Dreams illuminate the way. Even so, the spiritual seeker must still traverse the long and winding Sufi path in the light of day—awake and alert, in full consciousness and with clear intention.

THE DAILY RITUALS OF REMEMBRANCE

As we have seen, a Chishti Sabiri disciple's connection with the teaching *shaykh* is cemented with *bay'at*, a bond that ensures blessings, protection, and guidance. And by joining the moral community of the *silsila* a novice *murid* gains immediate access to the order's teaching networks and support system as well. Entry into this web of relationships is no guarantee of wisdom, however. In fact, the inner journey from *shari'a* to *tariqa* to *haqiqa* demands a great deal more from the Sufi adept. For spiritual advancement, each *murid* must voluntarily accept the discipline and rigors of *suluk*. The decision to take up the practice of *mujahada* (spiritual "striving") is not taken lightly, for while the potential rewards are significant so too are the requisite sacrifices. Disciples recognize that ritual practice teaches humility, patience, and thankfulness. At the same time, they also emphasize that the Sufi path is a serious commitment made possible only by the seeker's deep desire for knowledge and an abiding love for God. In the words of a senior Pakistani *murid*,

> Fasting, abstention, spiritual exercises, and even controlling the speech—all this depends on how quickly you want to gain the results. It depends entirely upon you. If you wish to do it, you will be encouraged to do it by the *shaykh*. But the times are such that there are very few people who want to do it, or have the time and strength to do it. Allah, in his infinite mercy, has made things easier for us. He says, "If you take one step, I'll take two steps. If you start walking, I'll come running to you." Our *shaykhs* say that the fastest way to get there is to follow two things: sincerity (*ikhlas*) in your worship (*'ibadat*) and sincerity (*khulus*) in dealing with your fellow human beings. Sincerity is everything. (September 1, 2001, Karachi)

Discipline, determination, and absolute sincerity are the essential prerequisites for spiritual growth—and it is only a select few who are prepared for the long and arduous journey.

Today's Chishti Sabiri disciples assert the fundamental continuity of Sufi doctrine and practice, even as they find ways to accommodate change in their spiritual lives. Given the weighty demands of contemporary life, *murids* assert, progress along the path increasingly rests on the individual's attention to his/her own spiritual homework. In daily practice, Chishti Sabiris perform the majority of their spiritual exercises (*awrad*) in isolation. Disciples receive instructions directly from the teaching *shaykh* and do not typically share information regarding their own daily routine with others. "*Suluk* is much more isolated now," a senior Pakistani disciple explained. "I don't know what my *pir bhai* ['brother of the Sufi master,' a fellow *murid*] is doing, and he doesn't know what I am doing. We don't ask each other, 'Do you do *zikr* 5,000 times, 7,000 times, or 10,000 times a day?' In fact, you are discouraged from discussing these things. But the *shaykh* knows what every *murid* is doing. He tells you exactly what practices to follow. It's all individual instruction" (August 26, 2001, Lahore).

Significantly, disciples mark this increased emphasis on individual practice in private spaces as a significant break from Chishti Sabiri tradition, a necessary concession to the demands of twenty-first-century life. This increasing focus on individualization presupposes an unwavering self-discipline. The Sufi adept must remain diligent and determined to maintain the daily regimen of spiritual devotions, performing the prescribed rituals in spare moments. Disciples suggest that the immense challenge of integrating *suluk* into modern life has also prompted Chishti Sabiri *shaykhs* to close ranks, restricting the numbers of disciples. Speculating on the meaning of these changes, a young Pakistani male *murid* told me,

> I think some methods have been modernized by the *shaykhs*. Whenever the *murid* has free time, he has to work, focusing on acts of worship ['*ibadat*] and spiritual striving [*mujahada*]. Now you only have to work part time instead of the whole day. Maybe that is why the *shaykhs* do not like to expand [the *silsila*] too much now, because of the low quality of disciples! They are very selective, and once you're in you are supposed to keep in very close touch with them. I think that is how they balance things. Early on, disciples could come to the *khanaqah* and stay there, so they would stay in close touch in any case. They were protected from all kinds of evil. So maybe that is the reason why the *shaykhs* have smaller circles now. (May 23, 2001, Karachi)

This is an intriguing statement that echoes a central theme I often heard expressed: the Chishti Sabiri order continues to respond to the changes and challenges of the modern age with pragmatism and adaptability.

Today's Chishti Sabiris talk frankly about the never ending struggle to balance *din* (religion) and *dunya* (worldly life). To say the least, the Sufi path demands a remarkable commitment of time and energy. *Murids* are encouraged to remain fully engaged with the world—attentive to both their families and their jobs—even as they increase the duration and intensity of their Sufi practices. This juggling act, however, often requires difficult choices in a disciple's personal and professional life. "A serious person on the Sufi path is recommended to do spiritual work [*mujahada*] four to five hours a day, in addition to their job and daily routine—two to three hours in the morning after morning prayers and one to two hours after evening prayers," a senior Pakistani *murid* told me. "It is all a matter of your intention [*niyyat*]. It all comes down to your seriousness. A student preparing for A-levels [university exams] studies this much. But it affects your ability to socialize. You are cut off from outsiders, even family" (October 30, 2000, Lahore).

Chishti Sabiris negotiate the demands of *din* and *dunya* through a careful attention to time management. Indeed, *murids* are hyperaware of the clock. It marks the passage of the workday, punctuated by the daily prayers that occur five times a day. In between, disciples must find a time and place for their Sufi devotions. Maintaining this rigorous schedule is no easy task. As a senior Pakistani *murid* attests, it is a constant struggle to manage these responsibilities:

> Most of us who work try to get things done [spiritual exercises] before we go off to the office. That is the main block of time you have, a three-hour block in the morning. And in addition to that, one or two hours in the evening, especially between the afternoon and night prayers. That really is the time [to perform *mujahada*]. If you miss out, it is very difficult to catch up. So those who are serious cannot even go for morning or evening walks. Either you walk or you sit [in prayer and meditation].
>
> The morning spiritual exercises are very important. Many people sit until *ishraq* [a supererogatory prayer after sunrise]. In winter especially, *ishraq* is very close to office time. In the summer you may get some more time. But then in summers the nights are short, so you depart for the office about half an hour after *ishraq*. You always have to be fresh enough for the office work. This is the struggle that we face. Even if your office staff complains about your work, you still cannot neglect your prayers. No excuses can be put on religion's shoulders. You cannot avoid working because you are engaged in religious activities. (August 26, 2001, Lahore)

Chishti Sabiris view this struggle to combine *din* and *dunya* as the most important test of a Sufi's piety and faith. To live in the world, but to not be consumed by it, to remain ever mindful of God in the midst of the chaos of mundane existence—this is the true measure of spiritual attainment. And for today's Chishti Sabiri disciples, the daily rituals of remembrance—prayer, *zikr*, and *muraqaba*—are the real proving ground for this spiritual *jihad*.

Meditative Prayer and the Spiritual Body

When a Sufi aspirant receives *bay'at* and formally joins the Chishti Sabiri order, she/he receives a copy of the *silsila's* official handbook. Compiled by Shaykh Muhammad Zauqi Shah, this slim text is entitled, *Shajara tayyaba ma'a awrad aur waza'if* [The Exalted Spiritual Genealogy with Devotional Exercises and Daily Prayers]. This book is distributed to all disciples and is not available for public consumption. In essence, it offers a primer for *suluk*. As the title suggests, the text contains copies—one of them in verse—of the *silsila's* spiritual family tree (*shajara*). Beginning with the current teaching *shaykh*, this genealogical record traces the order's lineage of spiritual masters back to the Prophet Muhammad. The handbook also provides a list of general precepts (*hidayat-i 'am*) that outline the dietary practices, rules of decorum (*adab*), and supererogatory prayers (*nawafil*) required of each *murid*. The bulk of this text, however, focuses on the heart and soul of Muslim devotion: prayer.

A typical Sufi prayer manual, the *Shajarah tayyaba* outlines particular *suras* from the Qur'an for *murids* to recite on specific occasions, along with a host of prayers of supplication (*du'a*) and prayers of blessing (*durud*). These are divided into subcategories: the requisite daily prayers (*waza'if*) and devotional exercises (*awrad-i rozana*), recitations for Friday prayers (*ma'-mulat-i jum'a al-mubarak*), and annual recitations tied to the Muslim lunar calendar (*ma'mulat-i salana*). With its attention to detail, the *shajarah* confirms that prayer is the core of Chishti Sabiri practice, the firm foundation upon which all other ritual performances rest. For all Muslims, prayer is an intimate conversation (*munajat*) between the human being and God. Prayer teaches humility and expresses gratitude. Chishti Sabiris make every effort to maintain the schedule of daily devotions, knowing that prayer anchors both faith and practice. In the words of a young Pakistani *murid*, "Prayer is only flexible at certain times, like when you are traveling or if you're not well. He [Wahid Bakhsh] used to say that if you cannot do your prayers at the office then go home and say them. There should not be any excuse. Allah Almighty would be very happy to see someone at the office taking time out to say his prayers. That is real devotion. You must sacrifice other things for your prayers" (November 7, 2000, Lahore).

For the inner core of Chishti Sabiri disciples immersed in *suluk*, the daily diet of devotions is supplemented by two distinct forms of meditative prayer that I explore below: *zikr* and *muraqaba*. Each of these rituals is informed by an underlying theory of psychophysiology that posits a nonmaterial, spiritual body composed of discrete "subtle centers" (*latifa*, plural *lata'if*). The concept of a mystical spiritual body has a long history in Sufi thought and practice.[24] Numerous premodern masters developed sophisticated models of mystical anatomy to explain the psychosomatic states encountered in Sufi experience. One of the most extensive and nuanced systems was formulated by the Kubrawiyya Sufi order in central Asia under the leadership of such luminaries as Najm ad-Din al-Kubra (d. 1220), 'Ala ad-Dawla as-Simnani (d. 1336), and Muhammad Nurbakhsh (d. 1464).[25] Spiritual masters in the Naqshbandi Mujaddidi tradition, including Shah Wali Allah (d. 1762) of Delhi, created equally sophisticated paradigms.[26] This complex of ideas was appropriated into the Chishti Sabiri tradition as well. Hajji Imdad Allah's influential ritual manual *Ziya' al-qulub*, for example, equates seven subtle substances (*lata'if*) with seven distinct levels of the human heart. As Kugle illustrates, *Ziya' al-Qulub* is "not about metaphysics, but rather about metaphysiology: that is, how the human body and especially the heart can be trained to adopt postures and motions that have transcendent ethical effects, so that the body itself can become a mirror for a just cosmic order."[27]

Twentieth-century Chishti Sabiris *shaykhs* inherited this rich premodern tradition. With explicit references to both Shah Wali Allah and Hajji Imdad Allah, their writings theorize a spiritual body that comprises six subtle centers.[28] Each discrete *latifa* is associated with a specific location in the body and a corresponding color. The most succinct summation of Chishti Sabiri mystical physiology is found in Wahid Bakhsh Sial Rabbani's *Islamic Sufism:*

> In Sufism, corresponding to the six physical senses of cognition, sight, hearing, touch, taste, and the hidden sixth sense, there are six spiritual senses of cognition to apprehend higher spiritual realities much beyond the scope of the

physical. These are known as *Lata'if-i sitta*. "*Lata'if*" is the plural of "*latifa*," which means "subtle sense," and "*sitta*" means six. These are:

1) *Latifa-i nafs* (sensual) is located [two fingers] under the navel and the color of its light (*nur*) is yellow.
2) *Latifa-i qalb* (Heart) lies in the left chest and the color of its light is red.
3) *Latifa-i ruh* (Soul) is in the right chest and the color of its light is green.
4) *Latifa-i sirr* (Secret) is in between *latifa-i qalb* and *latifa-i ruh*, and the color of its light is white.
5) *Latifa-i khafi* (Hidden) is located in the middle of the forehead, and the color of its light is blue.
6) *Latifa-i akhfa* (Hidden-most) is located at the top of the head, and the color of its light is black.

These spiritual centers were first reported to exist by the Prophet of Islam in a *hadith* which is as follows: "There is a piece of flesh in the body called *Qalb* (heart), the heart is in the *Soul*, the *Soul* is in the *Sirr*, the *Sirr* is in the *Khafi*, and the *Khafi* is in the *Akhfa* which is in the Divine 'I' (*Ana*)."[29]

These subtle centers within the human body, in turn, are mirrored in the six levels of Divine descent (*tanazzulat-i sitta*). Wahid Bakhsh details this cosmological model as follows:

1) *La Ta'ayyun* (the Infinite Being or Pure Essence)
2) *Ta'ayyun-i Awwal* (the first limitation), also known as *Haqiqat-i Muhammadiyyah* [the reality of Muhammad], which has been given the name of "Logos" in Greek philosophy and "Nous" in Neoplatonism
3) *Ta'ayyun-i Thani* (the second limitation), known as *Haqiqat-al-Insan* (man's reality)
4) *Alam-i-Arwah* (the soul world)
5) *Alam-i-Mithal* (the world of similes) which is a subtle world intervening between the soul world and the phenomenal world
6) The phenomenal or the physical world in which we are living.[30]

In this way, the Chishti Sabiri model expressly links the Sufi's internal spiritual body (microcosm) with both Prophetic realities and the external levels of the cosmos (macrocosm).

During the course of my interviews, I found that most Chishti Sabiri disciples were largely unaware of this nuanced psychophysiology. When asked about the spiritual body, in fact, most *murids* admitted ignorance. This is not entirely surprising, since as a rule Chishti Sabiri *shaykhs* stress practice over theory. Nonetheless, these concepts do play an important, pragmatic function in the *pir-murid* relationship. From the earliest stages of *suluk*, disciples are encouraged to remain especially attentive to the colors they see in dreams and during the practice of *zikr* and *muraqaba*. They relate these visual experiences directly to the *shaykh* who, in turn, interprets their significance. A Pakistani male disciple explains, "That is what the daily *zikr* consists of, trying to illuminate these subtle centers [*lata'if*]. During *zikr*, *muraqaba*, and other practices, some people speak of seeing colors. I recall a number of times when he

[Wahid Bakhsh] questioned me about colors that I had seen, especially in *muraqaba*. Usually he would explain these things in private, not in front of others—just to that particular person, so others were not aware" (August 26, 2001, Lahore). As the Sufi adept progresses along the path, the centers of the spiritual body are gradually activated, one by one. Much like the visions experienced in spontaneous dreams, therefore, the *lata'if* serve as vital heuristic tools for measuring spiritual attainment. Though invisible to the naked eye, the *murid's* spiritual centers are immediately apparent to the spiritual master. The illuminated spiritual body is the definitive mark of spiritual perfection.

Zikr: The Remembrance of God

The backbone of Chishti Sabiri ritual practice is *zikr*: the "remembrance" or "recollection" of God. *Zikr* is a ubiquitous term in the Qur'an. Time and again, human beings are called to remember God and His commandments. By continuously chanting the names of God, either in solitude or in company, Sufis seek nothing less than the interiorization of the Qur'anic message.[31] As a meditative practice, *zikr* aims to replace the insatiable appetites of the concupiscent ego with an abiding awareness of the Divine presence. For the accomplished seeker, a heightened state of consciousness becomes constant and all-consuming. Shahidullah Faridi explains how *zikr* alters perspective:

> If anyone carries out *zikr* constantly, his life no longer remains a meaningless sequence of events, but becomes a series of incidents in his relationship with his Divine Master. If he receives something pleasant he considers it a manifestation of the bounty and mercy of God which He has promised to His servants. If he is overtaken by something unpleasant, he perceives it as the wages of his sins which the Supreme Judge has given him in this world; he realizes that it is a test of his faith and perseverance, and hopes that it will requite for the faults that he has committed. In this way, his whole life becomes a communion with Allah. It could even be described as a conversation with Him, for although to speak directly with the Supreme Being is the privilege of his exceptionally favored servants, through this type of remembrance every believer can converse with his Lord. Allah addresses the believer through the medium of events, and the believer makes his reply by the turning of his heart towards Him in reaction to the event. By means of this *zikr*, the relationship with Allah becomes closer and closer and develops into one of love.[32]

As Shahidullah illustrates, Chishti Sabiris view *zikr* as a conversation with God—an extension and amplification of daily prayer.

Chishti Sabiri teachings posit a symbiotic relationship between the body, mind, and soul. Each must be tamed and trained in succession. In a lecture recorded on March 1, 1978, Shahidullah Faridi details both the form and function of *zikr* practice:

> When we are in *zikr*, we should remember Allah and try to forget ourselves and forget the body. That is why when a person sits in *zikr* he should sit in such a

calm and composed way that he is not bothered by his body . . . That is not
such a difficult thing, but the mind is our great battlefield. To compose and set
the mind at rest is the whole struggle in the spiritual world, but this struggle is
not impossible. Allah has given us the strength to win, but we have to
work . . . In fact you might say that as far as our effort is concerned it is the
most important, because this is what we can do—simply collect our thoughts in
one place, concentrate them, direct them at one point, which is Allah. And then
what Allah does is His will.[33]

This is the very essence of *suluk*. Through one-pointed, focused meditation,
the Sufi adept slowly learns to discipline the body and quiet the mind. And
with the silencing of the self there is the possibility of communion with God.
In practice, however, Chishti Sabiri *zikr* is anything but silent. Concentrating
on the rise and fall of the breath, the practitioner creates a soundscape by
repeating—out loud and with a strong voice—a variety of prescribed litanies.
This distinguishes Chishti Sabiris from their Naqshbandi counterparts who
typically practice a silent, internal form of *zikr*.[34] Although it is not considered "music" per se, there is a definite rhythm and lyricism to Chishti Sabiri
vocal *zikr* (*zikr-i lisani*). As an oral and aural performance, it resembles the
art of Qur'an recitation (*tajwid*).

Chishti Sabiri *murids*—men and women, novices and elders alike—are
encouraged to maintain a strict daily schedule of *zikr*. Disciples regularly perform two foundational *zikr* formulas. The most basic is *zikr-i ism-i dhat*
("the remembrance of the name of the Divine essence"). This involves the
recitation of the name of Allah while simultaneously visualizing a physical
strike (*zarb*) on the heart. Disciples begin by repeating this simple formula-
tion hundreds of times in rapid succession. As their practice deepens, the
number of repetitions increases exponentially. A senior Pakistani *murid*
explains:

> The [daily *zikrs*] are very specific. The typical one is *zikr-i ism-i dhat*. You start
> with five hundred, and then extend it up to as many as ten or twelve thousand.
> It depends on the capacity [of the individual *murid*]. Usually, the minimum is
> reciting one thousand in a sitting. Most people do up to six or seven thousand,
> because that takes about half an hour. You continuously repeat "Allah." The
> strike (*zarb*) of "Allah" is on your heart (*qalb*) [moves his head in motion]. The
> important thing is that it should be done regularly. Unless you do this regularly,
> for a year or so, then you do not increase it. It must be done daily. (March 16,
> 2001, Lahore)[35]

The other standard formula in Chishti Sabiri practice is *zikr-i nafi wa
ithbat* ("the remembrance of negation and affirmation"). In this recitation,
the adept continuously repeats the first half of the testimony of faith
(*shahada*): "there is no god but God" ("*la ilaha 'illa'llah*"). This phrase, of
course, encapsulates the fundamental theological doctrine of Islam: absolute,
uncompromising monotheism (*tawhid*). In Arabic, its alliterative pronunciation rolls easily off the lips, making it an especially powerful mantra for

meditation. Chishti Sabiri disciples recite the second half of the *shahada* as well, affirming the unique status of the Prophet Muhammad as the final messenger (*rasul*) of Divine revelation. In the extended *zikr* practice, the *shahada* is woven together with the names of God and other prescribed formulas to form a single, seamless recitation. The order's ritual manual *Shajara tayyaba* prescribes a daily repertoire that combines these litanies into a standardized format:

> After the evening [*maghrib*] or night ['*isha*] prayers, close the eyes. Two fingers below the left breast is the heart [*qalb*]. From the heart, draw the sound "*la*" ["no"] and pull it towards your right shoulder. From there say "*ilaha*" ["God"] and bring it back to the left and onto the heart with a sharp strike [*zarb*] of "*illa' llah*" ["but Allah"]. After a hundred strikes, say: "Muhammad is the Messenger of God" [*Muhammadu rasul Allah*]. Do this two hundred times. Then strike the heart four hundred times with only "*illa' llah.*" After that recite "*Allahu Allah*" six hundred times. The strike of "*Allahu*" should be two fingers below the right breast, and "*Allah*" should strike onto the heart. Repeat this through the entire rosary [*tasbih*][one thousand two hundred repetitions]. If time is short, then close the eyes and recite "*Allah*" with the voice onto the heart five hundred times. And after the morning prayers, close the eyes and recite in the mind "*Allahu Allah*" with both breaths [i.e., "*Allahu*" while inhaling, "*Allah*" while exhaling] as many times as possible.[36]

By repeating these basic formulas over and over again, the Chishti Sabiri disciple attempts to eradicate all worldly thoughts, tame the ego, and inundate the mind and heart with the memory of God.

In the advanced stages of *suluk*, select Chishti Sabiri adepts engage an alternative form of *zikr* known as *habs-i dam*, or the "keeping of the breath." This rigorous ascetic practice is known as a particular specialty of past Chishti Sabiri spiritual masters. It involves complete submersion in water for prolonged periods of time, a method that is said to cool the "heat" generated by intense *zikr*. This distinct meditation technique—and in particular the concept of spiritual "heat" (*tapas*)—suggests a possible connection with Hindu yogic practices. In *Tarbiyat al-'ushshaq*, Muhammad Zauqi Shah describes the meaning and method of *habs-i dam*:

> Refinement comes to the spirit [*ruh*] through the practice of *habs-i dam*, and through this refinement the spirit gains strength. Whatever is refined [*latif*] possesses immense strength. Electricity is highly refined so it has a greater strength than fire, water or steam which are all dense. When the spirit becomes refined, its ability to comprehend the matters of the higher realm also increases. This helps [the seeker] attain the presence and attention [*tawajjuh*] of Allah.
>
> Generally, *habs-i dam* is performed while submerged in water during the winter. There is rapid progress while sitting in water. In the Holy Qur'an it is said that all things exist from water. Human beings too receive nourishment from water. *Habs-i dam* begins with the recitation of "Allah" twenty one times and then gradually increases. As with all the other spiritual exercises [*mujahadat*], *habs-i dam* should be done consistently.

During the days of my spiritual training, I used to perform this in a river. At first the immersion was difficult, but after some time I did not want to come out of the water. It felt very warm. My *shaykh*, Mawlana Sahab [Shah Sayyyid Waris Hasan], may God be pleased with him, sometimes went into a pond after night prayers and remained under water the entire night. He used to tell the *mu'azzin* [the person who announces the call to prayer], "Tell me when it is time for morning prayers." During the entire night he would take only two or three breaths.[37]

Zauqi Shah's account of his own experiences and the miraculous story of his *shaykh's* spiritual prowess echo common tropes in Sufi hagiographies. Clearly, *habs-i dam* represents the most extreme outer reaches of Chishti Sabiri ritual discipline. Though certainly not a common practice, it illuminates how far some Sufis are prepared to push themselves in the quest for spiritual knowledge.

On a more mundane level, the ultimate goal for most Chishti Sabiri adepts is to make *zikr* constant and continuous. Beyond the fixed hours of private devotion, disciples are encouraged to integrate *zikr* into every moment of their daily lives via a simple technique known colloquially as *pas-i anfas* ("holding the breaths"). This form of silent recitation offers yet another tool for developing the Sufi's powers of concentration. "'*Ya Hayy*' ['Oh, Living'] should be recited with the inward breath and '*Ya Qayyum*' ['Oh, Eternal'] with the outward breath," Shahidullah Faridi explains. "There is another method as well in which 'Allah' is recited with the inward and outward breaths. This is the silent 'remembrance of the heart' [*zikr-i qalbi*]. The goal is to insure that not a single breath is free of the name of God."[38] *Zikr*, Chishti Sabiris say, must be woven into the fabric of the Sufi's heart and mind. In the words of Muhammad Zauqi Shah, "The seeker [*salik*] should always have his heart inclined towards God Most High. Without a doubt, he should continue with his worldly affairs, but even so he must never be neglectful [*ghafil*] of the remembrance of God [*zikr-i Allah*] . . . A *salik* should always remember God, regardless of what he is doing. As the famous saying goes, 'the hand at work, the heart with the Friend' [*dast ba kar, dil ba yaar*]."[39] In short, *zikr* is perfected only when it fully internalized—when the remembrance of God is as constant and effortless as breathing itself.

In keeping with the *adab* of the master-disciple relationship, *zikr* is performed only under the strict supervision of the teaching *shaykh*. During my interviews, disciples often commented that dilettantism and individual experimentation were extremely dangerous and potentially damaging. It is the *shaykh's* sole prerogative to determine a proper course of action for each of his followers. Regardless of the precise program, disciples agree, the efficacy of *zikr* depends on persistence and regularity. Chishti Sabiri masters are especially strict about this. According to a male Pakistani *murid*, "I remember I once told Hazrat Wahid Bakhsh, 'At times when I come home from the office I am very tired and I cannot do all my *zikrs*. Can there be concessions for *zikr*? Could I do less?' Now believe me, he allowed exceptions for everything else—your dress, the way you talk, the way you do things, the way you work. But not these *zikrs*. He said, 'You cannot.' He used to tell me very firmly, 'You have to go out of the way to perform these *zikrs*.' He did not allow a single concession regarding this" (November 7, 2000, Lahore).

Today's Chishti Sabiri disciples typically perform the daily regimen of *zikr* practices in isolation, most often in a quiet, secluded space. Many *murids* have arranged a private meditation chamber in their homes for just this purpose. On Thursday evenings, however, the routine changes and disciples gather together for a weekly communal performance known as the *halqa-i zikr* (the "circle of remembrance"). Given the *silsila's* growing geographic spread, these gatherings are held in multiple locations. In Karachi, Shaykh Siraj 'Ali Muhammad—the order's current teaching *shaykh*—leads a large *zikr* circle in a private home near the tomb complex of Shahidullah Faridi. In Lahore, a senior male *murid* hosts a weekly *halqa-i zikr* in his home. A female disciple of Shaykh Wahid Bakhsh Rabbani does the same, leading a separate session comprised mostly of women. Another female *murid* used to host a similar weekly *halqa* in Islamabad, but this practice has recently been discontinued. In Malaysia, disciples take turns hosting a communal *zikr* in private homes in and around Kuala Lumpur. These sessions are also presided over by a senior disciple of Wahid Bakhsh.

Regardless of location, Chishti Sabiri *halqa-i zikr* is marked by a pervasive attention to the dictates of etiquette and decorum.[40] Disciples learn the rules of *adab* through direct experience and describe them as a vital dimension of the sacrality and efficacy of the ritual. These *zikr* share a common structure as well. On Thursday evenings, *murids* perform ritual ablutions in their own homes and then make their way to the venue. They dress in clean clothes—typically white *shalwar kamiz*. Men wear a white prayer cap (*topi*) and women a thin head covering (*dupatta*). During the ritual performance, disciples sit with legs crossed in ordered rows on the floor. The ritual space is gendered, with women sitting in rows behind the men. The lights are dimmed, and together disciples perform the *maghrib* prayers. When the prayer cycle is completed, the *imam* (prayer leader) turns from the *qibla* (prayer niche) to face the audience, and the *zikr* immediately begins. The leader begins to recite a particular *zikr*, and the audience joins in. This call and response continues through a series of prescribed litanies. *Adab* dictates that *murids* recite in unison with loud voices, energy, and enthusiasm. Physical movements are minimized, though some *murids* sway their heads and move their bodies as they recite.

Tradition places a strong emphasis on the importance of the *zikr's* aesthetics. As Muhammad Zauqi Shah notes in *Tarbiyat al-'ushshaq*, "Exquisite *zikr* [*zikr-i nihayat*] should be done with a beautiful voice, together in unison. If I fall silent [while leading the *zikr*], it is of no consequence. As a rule, you should continue reciting. I will give the indication when it is time to change [the pattern]. Allah is beautiful and He loves beauty. For this reason, *zikr* should always be done in a beautiful manner. You must understand that this is no ordinary matter."[41] While there is no fixed form for *halqa-i zikr*, there is a general pattern that is passed down from generation to generation. The senior male *murid* who leads the weekly session in Lahore explained the logic of the *zikr* format:

> Hazrat Siraj Sahab once mentioned that Hazrat Shahidullah Sahab told him that it is not necessary to plan what you should say in *zikr*. Whatever comes [is suitable]. I remember that Hazrat Captain Wahid Bakhsh told me that *istighfar* [a supplication for forgiveness] in the beginning is important. You must do that, whether it is "*istaghfiru'llah*" ["I ask God's forgiveness"] or "*Rabb igh-fir*" ["Lord, forgive"]. And "*la ilaha illa'llah*" ["There is no god but God"] is important in the middle. Then you should conclude with *salam* [salutations for the Prophet Muhammad]. Either "*salla Allahu 'alaihi wa sallam*" ["God bless him and grant him salvation"] or "*salawat wa salam 'alaikum, ya rasul Allah*" ["blessings and peace be upon you, oh Messenger of God"]. (March 16, 2001, Lahore)

During my fieldwork in Pakistan, I frequently attended the weekly *halqa-i zikr* in Lahore. While the number and arrangement of recitations varied slightly from week to week, the *zikr* performed at a gathering on a Thursday evening in October 2000 is typical:

1. *Rabb ighfir* ("Lord, forgive")
2. *Rabbun Allah* ("Allah is Lord")
3. *tawakkultu Allah* ("surrender to Allah")
4. *Huwa al-Awwal, huwa al-Akhir, huwa al-Zahir, huwa al-Batin* [Qur'an 57:3, "He is the First, the Last, the Outward, the Inward")
5. *Ya khair an-Nasirin* ("Oh, best of helpers!")
6. *Ya khair al-Warithin* ("Oh, best of inheritors!")
7. *Ya khair al-Hafizin* ("Oh, best of preservers!")
8. *la ilaha illa'llah* ("there is no god but God")
9. *illa'llah* ("but God")
10. *Allahu Allah* ("He is God")
11. *salla Allahu 'alaihi wa sallam* ("God bless him [the Prophet Muhammad] and grant him salvation")

This particular repertoire follows the general pattern. The cycle begins by asking for Divine forgiveness (1), continues with a series of incantations of the names of God that emphasize *tawhid* (2–10), and concludes with a blessing for the Prophet Muhammad (11). Despite variations in format, the overall aim of the Chishti Sabiri *halqa-i zikr* remains the same: to expand the Sufi adept's awareness of the presence and power of God.

The atmosphere at these weekly ritual gatherings is serious and somber. Since young children often accompany their parents, however, there is occasionally background noise that threatens to disrupt the *zikr's* focused intensity. In a personal letter to a female Malaysian disciple, Wahid Bakhsh notes that such disturbances actually serve an important role in Sufi training. Within the sacralized space of the *halqa-i zikr*, he asserts, there are no accidents and everything serves a higher purpose. Wahid Bakhsh explains this dynamic in his own inimitable style:

> The virtue of distractions is that the more they break your concentration, the greater becomes your effort to concentrate. One becomes indifferent to what is happening. The principle of opposition is at work in the whole of the universe. Parliaments have opposition parties. The '*ulama* have opposing elements. Even in nature you will find opposition causing good results. The gardener trims the plants which only enhances their growth. The hair that is cut grows longer, while that not cut like eyebrows and eyelashes do not grow. Do not worry about distraction during *zikr*, whether individual or collective. And do not chase your children out of the room. Let them stay and pray with you. The noise they make or the distraction they cause will help your concentration, not spoil it. When a small baby cries during *zikr*, do not worry about it, do not mind it. It has a purpose to serve. It stings you and whips you to be more active and attentive. Allah Almighty has not created Satan in vain! He is there like a trick wrestler, to wrestle with us and make us strong. The more hurdles and obstacles in your way, the greater is your progress.[42]

The entire *halqa-i zikr* typically lasts about half an hour. When the performance concludes, the room falls silent. Disciples quietly rise from their seats and immediately disperse into the night, returning to their homes. Before, during, and after the ritual, talking and socializing are purposefully minimized. I was told that this is absolutely essential if the spiritual blessings (*faiz*) gained during *zikr* are to be retained, internalized, and preserved. According to a senior disciple, "*Halqa-i zikr* is not a social event. Unless it is absolutely necessary, nobody should talk, at least for some time. The best thing is to stay silent, pray your night prayers, and immediately go to bed. Whatever you gain in this weekly *zikr* is so delicate that if you talk, you will lose it. That is why serving any food or even a cup of tea is strictly forbidden, because some people then might come just to socialize" (August 26, 2001, Lahore).

Thus, the *halqa-i zikr* complements and concentrates the daily practices that *murids* carry out in isolation. This weekly ritual is one of the principal forums for the expression and experience of Chishti Sabiri communal identity. "Our *zikr* is particular to our *silsila*," a Pakistani disciple assured me. "It can found in the writings of 'Abd al-Quddus Gangohi [d. 1537] as well as *Ziya' al-qulub* [the ritual manual written by Hajji Imdad Allah (d. 1899)], so it comes to us directly from our Chishti Sabiri *shaykhs*" (March 16, 2001, Lahore).[43] Like all ritual practices, however, *halqa-i zikr* is not static—it changes according to the context of the times. Drawing on his own experiences in the *silsila*, a Pakistani elder recalled that the logistics of the performance were modified over the years. In his words,

> I have attended the *zikr* circles of my *shaykh*, Hazrat Zauqi Shah Sahab, Hazrat Shahidullah Sahab, and now Hazrat Siraj Sahab. I have seen the differences. To start with, the length of *halqa* has shortened. It used to last well over an hour. Traditionally it has always held on Thursdays, except for the month of Ramadan

when it used to be every day. When Hazrat Mawlana Sahab [Shah Sayyid Waris Hasan] visited Bombay or Calcutta, he used to have it every day or on alternate days. Otherwise it was always once a week. Six days of the week the *murid* is supposed to toil by himself, individually. The *shaykhs* also used to hold a stick, Hazrat Mawlana Sahab and Hazrat Zauqi Sahab too. If you were out of line or out of rhythm, then "whap"! [laughter] Try doing that today! You see, human life is an evolutionary process. In that evolutionary process, it is the law of nature that everything adapts to the need of the day. (September 1, 2001, Karachi)

In the eyes of this Chishti Sabiri elder, changes in the form of Sufi ritual practice are natural, unavoidable, and unsurprising. The underlying purpose of *suluk*, however, remains unchanged. This is an important (and widely shared) insight. For today's Chishti Sabiris the *persistence* of ritual practice provides a vital sense of continuity. For disciples of all ages, the daily practice of *zikr* offers an essential outlet for both communication and community. Its performance also cements a powerful link between twenty-first-century *murids* and their spiritual predecessors. Though the Sufi journey toward God is long and arduous, disciples find great comfort in the knowledge that the path is well marked.

Muraqaba: Spiritual Contemplation at Pakistani Sufi Shrines

Another key Chishti Sabiri meditative practice is contemplation (*muraqaba*). Whereas *zikr* is oral and aural, *muraqaba* is primarily a visual experience. As with dreams, disciples view *muraqaba* as a vehicle for states of consciousness beyond the limits of the rational, discursive mind and the descriptive power of language. In the enigmatic words of Muhammad Zauqi Shah, "*Muraqaba* is the guardian of what comes from the heart [*dil*]. It preserves the desire that is imagined [*tasawwur*] in the heart. It turns the slave's own knowledge which disregards the blessings of sacred knowledge in the direction of God Most High."[44]

In Chishti Sabiri *suluk*, contemplation is typically reserved for more advanced disciples. *Murids* are usually introduced to the practice only after they have established a regular, disciplined routine of daily prayer and *zikr*. "*Muraqaba* involves intense concentration and is superior to *zikr*," a senior Pakistani disciple explained. "The unveiling of vision happens in *muraqaba*, but it usually comes only after some time [i.e., later in spiritual training]" (March 16, 2001, Lahore). As Buehler illustrates, the Naqshbandi Mujaddidi tradition developed a complex, formalized routine of twenty-six distinct contemplations.[45] The contemporary Chishti Sabiri system is, by comparison, far less nuanced and systematized. In their writings and oral teachings, Chishti Sabiri *shaykhs* detail three general categories: *muraqaba-i shaykh* ("contemplation of the spiritual guide"), *muraqaba-i rasul* ("contemplation of the messenger," the Prophet Muhammad), and *muraqaba-i dhat* ("contemplation of the Divine essence").

In essence, *muraqaba* is a ritualized form of focused, one-pointed meditation. While following the rise and fall of the breath, the Sufi practitioner imagines herself/himself in the physical presence of the teaching *shaykh*, the Prophet Muhammad, or Allah. Shahidullah Faridi describes the basic practice as follows: "After *'asr* [afternoon prayer] one should try to concentrate one's full heart and soul towards Allah in the form of *muraqaba* (meditation). It means concentrating the mind. Actually, *muraqaba* means watching over the mind so that no foreign thoughts come into it. If they do, then brush them aside. So *muraqaba* from a positive point of view means that one should watch that the mind is at all times directed towards the thought of Allah."[46] Predictably, the specific routine of contemplations is prescribed by the teaching *shaykh* in accordance with the capacities and spiritual status of individual disciples.

As with all Sufi rituals, Chishti Sabiris stress that *muraqaba* must be performed regularly if it is to be effective. At times this presents a formidable challenge, especially when tangible benefits are not readily apparent. "Most people do not feel anything, they just sit there," a Pakistani disciple told me. "Many *murids* often question the *shaykh* about this. They say, 'I do *muraqaba*, but I don't see anything.' The *shaykh* will say, 'That is not your business. You just keep doing it. The rest is our business.' You do not give up the practice because you can't see anything" (March 16, 2001, Lahore). By contrast, other disciples experience immediate results. A male Malaysian *murid*, for example, describes his own experiences in contemplation as a fluid extension of prayer:

> As Muslims we have to pray five times a day. I think that because we pray and do the fast I have found that going into meditation is not that difficult. You are in contact with Allah most of the time, five times a day. So our concentration is there. We always try to refer back to Him. We say "thank God" [*al-hamdu lillah*], even when we sneeze. You are always referring back to Him. The contact is there, in everything we do, even if we're not doing something "religious." So perhaps because of that I find *muraqaba* quite easy. (October 6, 2001, Kuala Lumpur)

An aptitude for intense concentration appears to be largely a matter of personality—a mixture of a disciple's natural abilities and disciplined determination.

For the committed *murid*, the sustained practice of *muraqaba* serves as a gateway to states of ecstasy and insight (*hal*). Chishti Sabiri *adab*, however, dictates that the effects of spiritual intoxication (*sukr*) must always be kept in check. Wahid Bakhsh emphasizes the importance of maintaining sobriety (*sahw*) in a personal letter to a female disciple, describing it as the very essence of Prophetic *sunna:* "We do not make *faqirs* or *majzubs* [a spiritually intoxicated Sufi]. We plan to make full-fledged doctors of spiritual science . . . Sobriety in the middle of storms of intoxication is our system or method which is the same as that of the Holy Prophet, God bless him and grant him salvation. Sobriety in the midst of intoxication is the goal of Islam and this is the real specialty of our *silsila* . . . The kind of *zikrs* and *muraqabas* which we prescribe tend to insure intoxication with sobriety, and not intoxi-cation alone. This is the Holy Prophet's method."[47] Chishti Sabiris insist that the effects of *muraqaba* are especially intense. For this reason, the capacity to maintain focus, discipline, and self-control in the face of spiritual ecstasy is yet another sign of spiritual maturity.

In describing their own experiences, Chishti Sabiri disciples place particu-lar emphasis on the efficacy of *muraqaba-i shaykh*. The importance of the visualization of the spiritual guide once again points to the centrality of the Sufi master-disciple relationship. Reflecting on a similar practice among the Naqshbandiyya, Buehler notes that this visual focus on the teaching *shaykh* "involves both an emotional tie of love and a specific psychological tie of modeling."[48] The same can be said for Chishti Sabiri disciples. Intriguingly, *murids* extend this technique to include the spiritual masters of the entire *silsila*. In addition to their own spiritual guide, for instance, many disciples perform *muraqaba* for Hazrat Khwaja Mu'in ad-Din Chishti Ajmeri, Baba Farid ad-Din, al-Hujwiri, Muhammad Zauqi Shah, and Shah Sayyid Waris Hasan for fifteen to thirty minutes on a daily basis. During meditation, *murids* visualize these spiritual mentors—both living and deceased—in an effort to become more like them. In effect, *muraqaba* is an act of the imagi-nation. Through its practice the genealogical roots and the ethical virtues of the Chishti Sabiri order are remembered and actualized.

"In *muraqaba*," a Malaysian disciple assured me, "you enter a realm of no time and no space" (October 6, 2001, Kuala Lumpur). In practice, however, certain places are more conducive to spiritual reflection than oth-ers. Although Chishti Sabiri disciples typically complete their daily contem-plations in the private sanctity of their own homes, *muraqaba* is also frequently performed at local Sufi shrines. As we have seen, the contempo-rary *silsila* places the tomb of Shaykh Baba Farid ad-Din Mas'ud Ganj-i Shakkar in Pakpattan at the center of Sufi sacred geography in Pakistan. The growing shrine complexes of Shahidullah Faridi in Karachi and Wahid Bakhsh Sial Rabbani in Allahabad are now marked as Chishti Sabiri domain as well. Disciples revere the tombs of saints as places of immense spiritual power. And because they believe that the Friends of God are alive and accessible in their graves, entry into a saint's presence requires careful preparation and an attention to the dictates of etiquette. In *Islamic Sufism*, Wahid Bakhsh Sial Rabbani outlines the requisite decorum for *muraqaba* at Sufi shrines in detail:

> The first and foremost duty of the visitor is to have a bath, change clothes, use perfumes and enter the shrine with love and reverence for the saint, thinking that he is in the presence of the King of whom he has come to pay homage. Next he has to recite the *Fatiha* [the opening chapter of the Qur'an] . . . and sit down facing the grave with closed eyes, thinking that he is sitting in front of the *shaykh* and receiving inspiration from him. To begin with, one must sit, or stand if there is no room to sit, for about half an hour with full attention focused on him. The inspiration automatically comes, of course with varying

degrees for each individual, depending on his level and capacity. Sometimes the recipient remains as if spoon-fed, for he is unable to digest the heavier feasts meant for grown-up and matured spiritualists. When the capacity of the seeker grows, the *shaykh's* inspiration gathers more intensity and vigor and it appears that a full shower of boundless grace has been let loose upon him as compared to the trickling drops he received during the early stages.[49]

Like *zikr*, contemplation is understood as an intimate conversation between the Sufi disciple and the patron saint, alive in his tomb. As a rule, Chishti Sabiri *murids* are discouraged from visiting the tombs of Sufi saints outside the *silsila*. Though they acknowledge that any saint's tomb is potentially a conduit for Divine inspiration, Chishti Sabiri attitudes toward sacred space are remarkably insular. A notable exception is made, however, for the shrine of Sayyid 'Ali ibn 'Uthman al-Hujwiri (d. 1074) in the old city of Lahore. In a personal letter to a female Pakistani disciple, Wahid Bakhsh explains both the rationale for the *silsila's* strict boundaries as well as its concession for al-Hujwiri's shrine:

> Do not go to any *mazar* which is not in our *silsila*. The *shaykhs* of our *silsila* are your real doctors and know what medicine is suitable for you. The *shaykhs* of other *silsilas* just give what [spiritual blessings] they like, and do not discriminate what suits you and what does not suit you. This is very important. There are many *mazars* of unknown *shaykhs* in Lahore. Some of them are *qalandars* [a roaming sect of antinomian Sufis] and can only give their visitors what they have—that is, they make them *qalandars* as well. In our *silsila* we avoid this. Although Hazrat Data Sahab, may God have mercy upon him, is not in the line of our *silsila* directly, he is great enough to know what you need. Moreover, he is very much associated with the *masha'ikh* of our *silsila*. He is very kind to us.[50]

As the saint's moniker, Data Ganj Bakhsh ("The Lavish Giver"), suggests al-Hujwiri's tomb is renowned as a place of intense power—an open and accessible outlet for spiritual grace.

The contemporary Chishti Sabiri appropriation of al-Hujwiri is not surprising since the eleventh-century saint has a long association with the *tariqa*. According to tradition Mu'in ad-Din Chishti Ajmeri (d. 1236), the first Indian Chishti master, was granted the dominion (*wilayat*) of all of South Asia, for himself and his successors, at al-Hujwiri's tomb.[51] This historical linkage runs deep within the Chishti Sabiri *silsila* as well. As we have seen, Shahidullah Faridi and his elder brother Faruq Ahmed converted to Islam after reading al-Hujwiri's classic text *Kashf al-mahjub*. And to this day, Faruq Ahmed lies buried in a small, subterranean room within his patron saint's tomb complex. As a result of these multiple historical trajectories, al-Hujwiri is remembered as an honorary Chishti Sabiri, and his shrine is a focus of local ritual practice. Disciples who live in Lahore regularly visit al-Hujwiri's shrine on Thursday evenings before attending the communal *halqa-i zikr*, and they often repeat the journey on Sundays as well. A senior

Pakistani disciple outlines the routine:

> *Murids* do not go to the *mazar* [of al-Hujwiri] collectively. They go privately
> or as a family, but not as a group. We do not even go for the '*urs* [death anniver-
> sary]. We only go for one-day attendance. We generally keep to our
> *silsila*. Those [shrines] are sufficient for us. But since Data Sahab precedes
> the *silsila* we visit him as a matter of respect. When we go to *shaykhs* other than
> our *silsila*, we recite *Fatiha* twice. You are a stranger there, so you recite one
> *Fatiha* on behalf of your *shaykh* to introduce yourself and then you recite one
> for yourself. But if you go to Data Sahab, you recite it only once because
> you are in his *silsila*. This is done out of respect. (March 16, 2001, Lahore)

Not surprisingly, it was Shaykh Wahid Bakhsh who established this weekly
pilgrimage, instigating a new ritual practice that Chishti Sabiris in Lahore
continue today.

Wherever and whenever it happens, physical proximity to a *wali Allah* pays
spiritual dividends. In the presence of a saint's tomb, disciples assert, there is
a palpable intensity and clarity to the experience of contemplation. After performing the prescribed prayers, *murids* find a quiet place to sit in full view of
the saint's tomb and immediately enter into *muraqaba*. To an outside
observer, the ritual performance appears utterly inconspicuous and unre-
markable. In describing her regular routine at the shrine of al-Hujwiri, however, a female disciple reveals the inner dimensions of contemplation:

> You should say, in your heart, "I am sitting in front of Data Sahab. Data Sahab
> is sitting there, and I am sitting here." Then you just close your eyes, and take
> long, slow, deep breaths. You must become aware of your breathing. With that,
> your thoughts stop. You do not pray and then get up and walk around. You will
> not experience anything that way. This is what Mamu Jan [Wahid Bakhsh]
> taught us when we went for '*umra* [the minor pilgrimage to Mecca]. That is
> how you get your mind blank. Like he used to say, "It takes fifty years [to quiet
> the mind] unless you become aware of your breathing." That is the one way to
> stop your thoughts. This is how you do *muraqaba* for Data Sahab. If you want
> to meditate on Allah, that is even easier. Just close your eyes and say, "Allah is
> with me, inside me, outside me." Of course, you do not picture Allah. When
> you visualize Data Sahab, you see Data Sahab. Many times he will appear to you
> and give you messages. Of course, you do not picture Allah. You just feel Him,
> inside and out. When I go to Data Sahab I sit there for ten to fifteen minutes
> of meditation and receive an answer to all my problems. (October 31, 2000,
> Lahore)

In the meditative silence of contemplation, Chishti Sabiri *murids* try to
establish a direct connection with the saint. In articulating these experiences,
they compare the spiritual energy (*faizan*) that radiates from the saint's tomb
during *muraqaba* to an intense electric current surging through the body. In
the words of another female Pakistani adept, "The main focus at the shrine is
the communication with *Sahab-i Mazar*, because he is your host. The
moments spent at the *mazars* are very valuable. You realize this the moment

you close your eyes [in *muraqaba*]. At that time you wish that you had spent your whole life at the *mazar*. The things which you receive there are invaluable" (June 17, 2001, Lahore).

Marking Chishti Sabiri Space in Malaysia

Intriguingly, the expansion of Chishti Sabiri spiritual domain is not limited to Pakistan. On the opposite side of the Indian Ocean, a Sufi shrine in Malaysia now provides an alternative outlet for pilgrimage and worship. The *mazar* of Sultan al-'Arifin ("The King of Gnostics"), Shaykh Isma'il 'Abd al-Qadir Thani, is located on Pulau Besar ("Big Island"); see figure 5.1. Despite the name, this is a small island (ten square miles) located five miles south of the historical port city of Malacca, three miles off the coastline in the Straits of Malacca. Pulau Besar served as a Japanese military base during the Second World War, and today it is the site of Pandanusa Resort—a small-scale tourist attraction with a restaurant, swimming pool, and a modest eighteen-hole golf course.[52] The island is also rich in history and contains an array of ancient graves. The shrine of Sultan al-'Arifin is located in a prominent position near the beachfront. The grave was covered with an elaborate wooden structure until the 1970s when it was torn down. It has recently been rebuilt as a modest open-air tomb constructed of tiles, covered with a metal roof, and surrounded by a gate. The *mazar* is now funded and administered through a

Figure 5.1   The Shrine of Shaykh Isma'il 'Abd al-Qadir Thani, Pulau Besar, Malaysia
Source: Photograph by Robert Rozehnal

local religious endowment (*waqf*) (interview: October 6, 2001, Kuala Lumpur). Today the local Malay and Indian Muslim communities are the shrine's primary patrons, although groups of Chinese and Hindu devotees visit regularly as well. A senior Malaysian *murid* likened the *mazar* to Ajmer Sharif—the massive tomb complex of the patron Christi saint Mu'in ad-Din Chishti in Rajasthan, north India—describing it a sacred and powerful site that draws devotees from diverse religious backgrounds (interview: October 2, 2001, Pulau Besar).

The story of Sultan al-'Arifin, Shaykh Isma'il 'Abd al-Qadir Thani, is shrouded in mystery. According to several prominent Malaysian disciples, the shrine's caretaker possesses a spiritual genealogy (*shajara*) written in Jawi, the local Malay language in Arabic script. This document names Sultan al-'Arifin as the son of Shaykh 'Abd al-Qadir Jilani Thani (d. 1533), the famous Qadiri saint of Uch Sharif—an ancient city located seventy miles southwest of Multan in Pakistan.[53] With the exception of this text, however, there seems to be no extant archive of the saint, no textual record to document his life and legacy. As a result, Sultan al-'Arifin's memory is now perpetuated through oral histories, some of them conflictive. Local legend suggests that the *shaykh* received instructions to travel to the area for proselytization (*tabligh*) at the tomb of the Prophet during '*umra* (the "lesser pilgrimage" to Mecca). He arrived on a merchant ship and spent most of his life preaching on the mainland before retreating to the island in his later years. The saint is credited with converting large numbers of the local population to Islam. Beyond these standard saintly tropes, little else is known about Sultan al-'Arifin. It is worth noting, however, that the broad stokes of his life closely parallel the biography of Hamzah Fansuri, the famous sixteenth-century Malay scholar, poet, and Qadiri master. According to historian Peter Riddell, "The earliest documented case we have of a Malay scholar traveling to the Arab world to undertake studies of the Islamic sciences is that of Hamzah Fansuri, the great mystic of the late 16th century. He was initiated into the Qadiriyya Sufi Order in Arabia, and in doing so established, or perhaps continued, a tradition which many Malay religious scholars were later to follow."[54]

I visited Pulau Besar in October 2001 in the company of a senior Malaysian disciple from Kuala Lumpur. Though the shrine's caretaker was absent that day, we toured the island with a villager and devotee of the saint who related the local history. According to our interlocutor, Sultan al-'Arifin's own spiritual guide—Sayyid Yusuf Saddiq, a Naqshbandi *shaykh* from Baghdad—is also buried within the confines of the *mazar*. The island is dotted with a host of other unmarked graves as well. These are said to include seven *shaykhs* from Indonesia who were spiritually guided to the island by the nine legendary saints of Java (*wali sanga*), along with two *shaykhs* from Baghdad.[55] All of them are said to be the disciples of Sultan al-'Arifin (interview: October 2, 2001, Pulau Besar). Our guide also led us to two other unmarked graves, both of them women: a local Hindu convert and the wife of the saint who was originally from Palembang (south Sumatra).

A detailed history of this island, its Sufi inhabitants, and their role in the spread of Islam throughout the Indonesian archipelago has yet to be written. What is clear, however, is that historical ambiguity does not deter contemporary religious faith and practice. Today's Malaysian disciples interpret Sultan al-'Arifin's connections to an ancestral South Asian homeland near the birthplace (and now shrine) of their own *shaykh* as an especially auspicious sign. Late in life, Wahid Bakhsh Sial Rabbani made this connection explicit. On a visit to Malaysia in 1991, he accompanied his *murids* to the island for pilgrimage. After performing prayers and *muraqaba*, he publicly sanctioned the place for Chishti Sabiri ritual practice. In the words of a senior Malaysian disciple, "According to my *shaykh*, this *mazar* here at Pulau Besar oversees the care of all Malaysia. He [Sultan al-'Arifin, Shaykh Isma'il 'Abd al-Qadir Thani] is in charge of this territory of Malaysia. He is the real source of spiritualism in this country" (October 2, 2001, Pulau Besar).

The symmetry of this Indian Ocean network is remarkable. The humble tomb of sixteenth-century South Asian Sufi saint buried on a remote island in the heart of Southeast Asia now serves as an alternative center of pilgrimage for the Malaysian disciples of a twentieth-century Pakistani Sufi master. This connection is now sanctified through ritual practice. On the last Sunday of each month, a group of Malaysian *murids* regularly travel to Pulau Besar for pilgrimage. They also make the trip during the annual commemoration of the death anniversary ('*urs*) of major Chishti Sabiri *shaykhs* when they are unable to travel to Pakistan or India. At the shrine, disciples sit in *muraqaba* while facing the tomb. They describe the *faizan* at the shrine as being particular intense. "It's just like electric current, like this wind blowing towards you," states a senior *murid*. "You feel a sensation. It goes right through you. It makes your hair stand up. You feel high" (September 30, 2001, Kuala Lumpur). This experience, Malaysian disciples insist, offers tangible proof of the *silsila's* powerful and enduring connection with Sultan al-'Arifin.

The Malaysian *murids* carry on their ritual practices in an environment that, in many ways, parallels that of their Pakistani counterparts. In contemporary Malaysia too Sufism is a highly contested symbol in a politicized public debate over Islamic authenticity and religion's relationship with state ideology and power. Given this charged atmosphere, *murids* maintain a low profile. In the words of a senior disciple, "We keep quiet because of the government. In Indonesia Sufism is everywhere. In Pakistan, people participate in '*urs* celebrations. But here in Malaysia, there is nothing. In fact, instead of celebrating they destroy the *mazars*. One of the largest ones, in fact, was demolished by the state government" (September 30, 2001, Kuala Lumpur). For the growing ranks of contemporary Chishti Sabiri disciples in Malaysia, Pulau Besar therefore provides a critical space for ritual experience and the expression of Sufi identity. In the twenty-first century, this humble Sufi shrine plays a major role in transplanting the *silsila* into the landscape of Southeast Asia, marking Malaysia as Chishti Sabiri sacred space.

PILGRIMAGE NETWORKS AND MUSICAL
ASSEMBLIES AT SUFI SHRINES

From humble roadside markers to massive institutional complexes, the tombs of Muslim holy men mediate between regional cultural identity and universal Islamic order. As historian Richard Eaton notes,

> In India these shrines displayed, theater-style and in microcosm, the moral order of the Islamic macrocosm. Although such shrines possessed important economic, political and social ties with the masses of villagers who frequented them, their fundamental raison d'etre was religious. For it was through its rituals that a shrine made Islam accessible to nonlettered masses, providing them with vivid and concrete manifestations of the divine order, and integrating them into its ritualized drama both as participants and as sponsors.[56]

Sufi shrines function as heterotopias. As loci of alterity, Sufi tomb complexes provide alternative, liminal spaces that stand in sharp contrast to the realm of everyday experience. They are "something like counter-sites, a kind of effectively enacted utopia in which the real sites, all the other real sites that can be found within the culture, are simultaneously represented, contested, and inverted."[57] As the Pakpattan tragedy of 2001 so clearly illustrated, Sufi shrines are also controversial, contested spaces. At no time is this more evident than during 'urs—the annual death anniversaries of Sufi saints that draw huge crowds of pilgrims and a bright public spotlight.

Contemporary Chishti Sabiri shaykhs are staunch defenders of the efficacy and legitimacy of Sufi shrines in general and the public rituals associated with 'urs in particular. They pointedly reject the critique of Muslim revivalists who denounce shrine worship with accusations of idolatry (shirk) and allegations of outside, Hindu influence. Shahidullah Faridi encapsulates this counter-polemic in a lecture delivered to his disciples during the 'urs at Pakpattan on July 20, 1977:

> Among the signs of Allah, the most significant are those which are associated with his special creatures and prophets. This means that relics of saintly people are signs of God. In the same way, we come here because these relics have an association with a saintly person like Baba Sahib. We come here because they are signs of Allah. The persons who make objections are on the wrong side. They do not realize that signs of God are shown through men. There is no question of shirk. We know that man is not God . . . Whatever we do here, if we respect the mazar, if we kiss it or pay any sort of respect to it, this is because it is one of His signs. Baba Sahab himself is a sign of God. If one understands that, then there is no conflict.[58]

As the "signs of God" (ayat Allah), the Sufi saints are the very embodiment of Islamic orthodoxy. The outpouring of love and respect at Sufi tombs, Shahidullah concludes, is therefore a natural expression of Muslim devotion that violates neither sunna nor shari'a.

For Chishti Sabiris, this theological and legal debate raises another flash-point in the contested legacy of Deoband—the *madrasa* and reformist movement inspired by the nineteenth-century Chishti Sabiri masters, Hajji Imdad Allah al-Faruqi al-Muhajir Makki (1817–1899) and Rashid Ahmad Gangohi (1829–1905). In contemporary Pakistan, Deobandi scholars are known for their sharp critique of the popular practices associated with Sufi shrines. Chishti Sabiris view this as a misreading and ultimately a betrayal of the teachings of their nineteenth-century predecessors. *Malfuzat-i shaykh* records a revealing conversation on this topic. In the text, Shahidullah Faridi is asked by a *murid* to explain the rationale behind the Deobandi *fatwas* (for-mal legal opinions) against worship at Sufi shrines. In response, the *shaykh* draws a distinction between outward (*zahir*) and inward (*batin)* dimensions of knowledge and experience. Sufi masters, he argues, are the true heirs to the Prophet—the custodians of Islamic tradition. "I say that those noble Sufis who have received authority [*ijazat yafta*] in genuine *silsilas* are in real-ity the supreme rulers," Shahidullah tells his audience. "As Hajji Imdad Allah al-Muhajir Makki Sahab, may God have mercy upon him, has said, without inner knowledge [*batini 'ilm*], outer knowledge [*zahiri 'ilm*] is useless. This is absolutely true. A human being does not have the correct perspective with-out inner disclosures [*batini inkishafat*] and inner vision [*batini musha-hada*]."[59] Shahidullah goes on to contextualize the Deobandi polemic against local customs associated with "popular" Sufism. The commoners (*'aam*) who have no appreciation of Sufi doctrine and practice and who lack proper guidance must be protected from improper behavior, he acknowl-edges. But these prohibitions were never meant to apply to elite Sufi adepts (*khass*). In Shahidullah's words,

> A [Deobandi] *mufti* issues a juridical opinion [*fatwa*] for the ignorant com-moners [*jahil 'awam*]. In other words, it is for those who are completely illit-erate. The *fatwa* determines whether something is acceptable for them or not. However, this does not mean that the *fatwa* applies to the people of distinction [*khawas*], those with understanding who are engaged in *suluk*. This is a matter of expedience. Certain saints have declared a general *fatwa* that commoners should not go the shrines. This does not mean that they are denying that one receives spiritual blessing by going to shrines . . . I could give many examples of famous saints who issued this kind of *fatwa*, and yet it is clear from their *mal-fuzat* that they themselves frequented shrines.[60]

Contemporary Chishti Sabiris point to the precedent of the spiritual masters of their own tradition to defend the efficacy and orthodoxy of pil-grimage to Sufi shrines (*ziyarat*). They note that the founders of Deoband were themselves active patrons of shrines. As Ernst and Lawrence illustrate, "The presence of Hindu practices at a Muslim shrine cannot explain centuries of participation of educated Sufi masters in pilgrimage, for they found *ziyarat* pilgrimage to be an authentic expression of Islamic piety, Qur'anic in spirit and firmly based on the model of the Prophet Muhammad."[61] A senior *murid* emphasizes this point by highlighting the example of Hajji Imdad

Allah and Rashid Ahmad Gangohi:

> The Deobandis now quote from [the writings of] Rashid Ahmad Gangohi and say, "Do not go the *mazars*, and do not listen to music [*sama'*]." Our *shaykhs* do not deny this history. In fact, somebody once asked Hazrat Hajji Imdad Allah Muhajir Makki, "Rashid Ahmad Gangohi is your *khalifa*, but he opposes *sama'* whereas you listen to *sama'*. He opposes attendance at the *mazars*, whereas you support it. Why is this?" To which Hazrat Hajji Imdad Allah replied, "He is also right. It is the need of the time." Hazrat Rashid Ahmad Gangohi stopped people from going to *mazars*, although he himself main-tained the *mazar* [of his ancestor] Hazrat 'Abd al-Quddus Gangohi. At the time, the British were trying to exploit Sufism, saying that it was not Islamic. So in the original school of Deoband, they said, "No, do not go to *mazars* because the Hindus also go there." It was never meant that the elite [*khass*] should not go, however! That is the explanation of our *masha'ikh*. (March 16, 2001, Lahore)

In reclaiming what they see as the lost legacy of Deoband's founders, con-temporary Chishti Sabiri disciples champion and defend Sufi tomb complexes such as Pakpattan as doorways to divinity. For them, Sufi shrines serve as fonts of spiritual blessing (*baraka*) and portals to Divine energy (*faizan*), especially during the auspicious occasion of a Sufi saint's death anniversary (*'urs*).

'Urs: The Serial *Khanaqah*

The Chishti Sabiri ritual calendar is highlighted by a pilgrimage network cen-tered on the *'urs* celebrations of the *silsila's* spiritual giants. *'Urs* literally means "marriage." In the context of Sufi practice, it serves as a metaphor for the *wali Allah's* final union with God.[62] According to Shaykh Wahid Bakhsh Sial Rabbani,

> The phenomena of *'urs* has a special significance and importance in the world of Islam. It is not only a festival for social gatherings and exchange of ideas with a recreational flavor, but it is also an occasion for intense spiritual training. People from far and wide come to pay homage to the spiritual benefactor, recite the *Fatiha* for his soul, and flock around the grave for spiritual inspiration (*faizan*). Now because the departed soul himself is the recipient of enhanced favor and blessings characteristic of this occasion, he is in a bountiful mood and bestows more and more favors on his people, giving special preference to the elite engaged in the arduous spiritual journey [*suluk*]. Another advantage of *'urs* is that people get an opportunity to meet their *pir*-brothers, particularly the elder members of the brotherhood and some *Shayukh* [*sic*] as well.[63]

Throughout South Asia, *'urs* celebrations draw massive crowds to the shrines of Sufi saints. These festivals combine religious fervor, public spectacle, and a bustling economic exchange. For Chishti Sabiri disciples, however, the network of annual *'urs* pilgrimages are a platform for ritual practice—the most important venue for the experience and expression of the *silsila's* communal identity.

The Chishti Sabiri order commemorates the *'urs* of four major Chishti saints at key shrines in Pakistan. The schedule for this cycle of communal pilgrimages—measured according to the Muslim lunar calendar—is as follows:

1. Khwaja Mu'in ad-Din Chishti Ajmeri (6 Rajab): at the shrine of Baba Farid Ganj-i Shakkar in Pakpattan;
2. Baba Farid Ganj-i Shakkar (5 Muharram): at the saint's tomb in Pakpattan;
3. Shahidullah Faridi (17 Ramadan): at the saint's tomb in Karachi;
4. Wahid Bakhsh Sial Rabbani (20 Dhu al-Qa'da): at the saint's tomb in Allahabad.

The logic and logistics of this pilgrimage network are significant. It pairs two thirteenth-century Chishti masters—Khwaja Mu'in ad-Din (d. 1246), the first Chishti saint of India, and Baba Farid Ganj-i Shakkar (d. 1265), the patron saint of Pakistan—with a pair of twentieth-century Chishti Sabiri *shaykhs*. Since he died on Hajj and is buried on the plain of 'Arafat, Muhammad Zauqi Shah's *'urs* is not included in this annual cycle, though most disciples do honor his memory in private on the day of his death anniversary.

Chishti Sabiri *'urs* pilgrimages reflect the legacy of Partition. The redrawing of South Asia's geopolitical boundaries in 1947 reconstituted the nation and citizenship, mandating new maps and new passports. With the emergence of an independent (and Islamic) Pakistan, the absence of the Jain, Sikh, and Hindu communities profoundly altered traditional cultural practices and local religious identities. Partition occasioned a parallel shift in Chishti Sabiri ritual practice as well. After 1947, Pakistani disciples could no longer easily travel to the major Sufi shrines in India—including the tomb of Mu'in ad-Din Chishti in Ajmer, central Rajasthan. In response, the *silsila* transferred the *'urs* of Muin ad-Din to the shrine of Baba Farid in Pakpattan. The realignment of Sufi geography is also seen in the emergence of entirely new Chishti Sabiri shrines on Pakistani soil. The growing tomb cults of Shaykh Shahidullah Faridi in Karachi and Shaykh Wahid Bakhsh Sial Rabbani in Allahabad now effectively mark Pakistan as Chishti Sabiri sacred space.

For today's Chishti Sabiris, *'urs* effectively serves as a serial *khanaqah*. Four times a year *murids*—both men and women—travel from all over Pakistan and beyond, gathering together for short but intensive periods of spiritual immersion. *'Urs* offers a rare opportunity for Chishti Sabiri *murids* to live together in the presence of the teaching *shaykh* as a collective, unified community. In the words of a novice disciple, "Sufis used to spend their lives in the *khanaqah*. But these days we experience the *khanaqah* only during *'urs*. We get away from the world there for a short time. It's like going to a monastery and staying there for a week" (September 2, 2001, Karachi). Significantly, disciples mark this break with tradition as a necessary innovation, a pragmatic response to the ground-level realities of the times. As a senior

Pakistani *murid* explains,

> [In the past] there were so many living saints, and travel was difficult, so '*urs* probably did not have as much significance. But now with modern travel, no *khanaqahs*, and fewer living *shaykhs*, this has assumed a greater importance. They [Chishti Sabiri *shaykhs*] encourage people who fly from Canada, or even Jeddah to come and attend the '*urs*. It is that valuable. People are encouraged to part with a lot of money. The Malaysian *murids*, they also come. This is the purification of the lower self [*tazkiya-i nafs*]. Everyone receives a short refresher course, six or seven days. This is what many people do not understand, the traditionalists who think of it ['*urs*] in negative terms. The festive part of '*urs* has existed for a very long time, with people offering ritual gifts [*nazrana*], flowers, and cloths to cover the grave [*chadar*]. But the kind of attendance we have is not for *nazrana*. It is only for the company of the *shakyh* at the *mazar*. (August 26, 2001, Lahore)

As this quote illustrates, Chishti Sabiris view '*urs* as a vital dimension of *suluk*. Many disciples accept significant personal and financial sacrifice in order to participate in these annual events. Given the distance and cost, the logistics of travel to Pakistan are particularly challenging for the Malaysian *murids*. Even so, most of them regularly attend, believing that the spiritual benefits are worth every hardship. In the words of a senior Malaysian disciple, "We go whenever we can. If it is possible, if they have the means, *murids* normally attend. Our *shaykhs* strongly encourage it. We know from experience that '*urs* is a very important training ground, an important part of *suluk*. Once you have tasted it you always want to go" (September 26, 2001, Kuala Lumpur).

The experience of '*urs* provides Chishti Sabiri disciples with ample opportunities for conversation and companionship. The journey to and from the shrine, coupled with the intensive atmosphere at the *mazar*, forges a deep bond between *murids*—a heightened sense of communal identity that anthropologist Victor Turner famously labeled *communitas*.[64] In many ways, the experience of travel and communal living for brief periods of time recalls the practices of the famous South Asian revivalist movement: the Tablighi Jama'at. Founded in 1926 by another Deoband alum named Muhammad Ilyas, Tablighi Jama'at members promote their grassroots agenda via traveling missionary tours designed to teach humility and encourage "a state of permanent vulnerability and uncertainty in which, outside one's normal moorings, one learns to be dependent upon God."[65] Chishti Sabiri *murids* experience a strikingly similar dynamic during '*urs* pilgrimages. The difference, of course, is one of emphasis. While the Tablighi's mission focuses on proselytization (*da'wa*), Chishti Sabiris view pilgrimage as a ritual discipline aimed expressly at the individual *murid's* spiritual development.

Within the liminal space of a Sufi shrine, Chishti Sabiris encounter a sacralized universe in which the normal structures of everyday social practice are temporarily suspended. In Allahabad, Karachi, and Pakpattan, the *silsila* maintains separate living compounds for men and women adjacent to the saint's tomb. During the weeklong 'urs retreats, groups of *murids* share rooms and bathing facilities, gathering together for meals prepared in the on-site kitchens. Each of these temporary *khanaqahs* offers a self-contained, communal environment in close proximity to the shrine complex. The living conditions are austere but comfortable, providing a convenient and accessible oasis for the real work at hand: ritual performance.

In the context of 'urs, disciples view the shrine as an ambivalent space. They approach the *mazar* with a palpable sense of respect and awe, viewing the saint's tomb as a receptacle of immense power and spiritual energy (*faizan*). At the same time, the presence of large, boisterous, and often unruly crowds in the narrow confines of the *dargah* are seen as potentially dangerous and polluting. This is especially true at Pakpattan where thousands of pilgrims are pressed into an extremely cramped area. As a result, *murids* generally avoid lingering in the shrine for extended periods of time. When they do enter the confines of the *dargah*, they navigate through its public spaces with a careful attention to the rules of etiquette. As Wahid Bakhsh notes, "At each 'urs there are special etiquettes of attendance and participation in the traditional rites and rituals peculiar to the place and the occasion, and the attendants are duty-bound to know them for strict observance to facilitate the adequate reception of spiritual benefits."[66]

Chishti Sabiris insist that *adab* protects and preserves the sanctity of the 'urs. Before entering any shrine, *murids* perform ablutions and dress in clean clothes. Both men and women typically wear simple, white *shalwar kamiz*. The men cover their heads with a skull cap or a modest head covering; the women cover their heads with a scarf, or *dupatta*. Decorum also dictates strict rules of bodily comportment and behavior designed to keep the Sufi adepts' attention focused on the saint. This is often difficult amid the carnival-like atmosphere. According to Wahid Bakhsh, however, the jostling crowds at a shrine serve a higher purpose, providing a vital buffer from the overwhelming intensity of the saint's *faizan*:

> While sitting or walking about in the shrine area, the seeker must not take recourse to frivolous activities (laughing, joking, talking loudly, showing off). Quarrelling or outbursts of temper are forbidden. One should remain meek and humble, and subservient to the rules and regulations of the place. The seekers should not hate or talk ill of anybody. The seekers should not meddle with anybody, not even the apparently mad persons whom he sees dancing about or the impertinent mischief-mongers who try to pick a quarrel with him. These things aim at fulfilling a special purpose . . . The greatest purpose which mad men and women and unwanted human beings indulging in antinomian activities serve is this: they are there to counterbalance the enormous torrents of blessings, charms and fascinations which, if left unimpaired by the clowns, would turn people mad by their intensity.[67]

For the duration of 'urs, Chishti Sabiris move in and out of the shrine complex for short periods of intense, focused ritual practice. There is no fixed format for the daily routine, and the logistics vary depending on the exact location. Everywhere and at all times, however, *murids* are meticulous about maintaining their daily prayers throughout the pilgrimage. Prayers take place either in the privacy of the compound or in the public spaces of the shrine. At the Pakpattan '*urs*, for instance, most *murids* offer communal prayers inside the *dargah*. According to a senior Pakistani disciple, "Friday prayers are not obligatory during '*urs*, but we go there to share the company of the *shaykh*. Our attendance [at the shrine] is very short. We arrive just before the call to prayer, pray two obligatory [*farz*] prayers and come back [to the compound]" (April 25, 2001, Lahore). Most disciples perform extra devotions as well, usually in the privacy of their rooms within the *silsila's* compound. As always, prayer—both personal and collective—anchors Chishti Sabiri piety.

Throughout the '*urs* disciples continue their meditative practices. Like prayer, *muraqaba* is a ritual mainstay during any pilgrimage. While the time, frequency, and location are determined by each individual, most devotees try to take full advantage of the auspicious occasion. In the words of a female Pakistani *murid*,

> *Muraqaba* usually takes place in the early morning, after morning prayers [*fajr*]. But it is really up to you, there is no fixed timing for anybody. The two prayers which are performed collectively are *fajr* and *maghrib* [evening prayer]. Beyond that nobody asks you, "Have you done your prayers yet, or not?" It is a personal decision. If you want to pray together or if you do not, it is up to you. *Muraqaba* is typically done before or after *fajr*. And then again after '*asr* [afternoon prayers] or in the evening, after *maghrib*. But in between, I have not seen anybody going down there [to the *mazar*]. (February 26, 2001, Lahore)

At the '*urs*, *muraqaba* is usually performed individually, though on occasion groups of male *murids* accompany the *shaykh* to the shrine for contemplation. This is a regular practice, for example, in Pakpattan where following communal prayers disciples sit together in silent contemplation, facing the saint's tomb. Given the general lack of privacy during '*urs*, however, *zikr* is frequently restricted. Disciples generally avoid *zikr* in Karachi and Pakpattan altogether, though it is performed at the '*urs* in Allahabad. A senior disciple explains,

> *Zikr* does not take place during Hazrat Shahidullah's '*urs* [in Karachi] because it is during Ramadan. At Pakpattan we do not do anything extra because Baba Sahab's influence is so great and so powerful. But in Allahabad, we make a short appearance at the *mazar* and do *zikr*. Hazrat Wahid Bakhsh was a hard taskmaster, and he does not want his *murids* to give up what they are normally doing. So *zikr* is performed individually. Most people look for isolated places, sometimes inside the mosque. The light is shut out, so nobody sees each other. *Murids* try to be as inconspicuous as possible. Those who usually do *zikr* in a loud voice, do it in a low voice. (August 26, 2001, Lahore)

While making necessary allowances for the unique logistics of pilgrimage, Chishti Sabiris aim to deepen and intensify their spiritual devotions during '*urs*.

The Chishti Sabiri living quarters and ritual spaces are segregated by gender during *'urs*. While men and women travel together, once they reach the shrine they separate for the duration of the spiritual retreat. The access for women at the *mazar* varies according to location. During interviews, a number of female disciples expressed a level of frustration with these arrangements. In the words of one female disciple originally from the northwest frontier town of Peshawar,

> I am quite used to the culture of segregation when it comes to the saints and the shrines. In the frontier, we have so many shrines where you can walk into the saint's shrines. Women can go inside, we can touch the graves. At many places there is a separate side for the women. It is not like this at Pakpattan Sharif. I personally feel a bit of, well not resentment, but something else. I just feel that we should also be given a chance. At Hazrat Wahid Bakhsh's *mazar* [in Allahabad] the women can go inside, but when the women are there men don't come, and when the men are there we don't go. Still, at least we can go and touch the grave. At Pakpattan Sharif women cannot even enter [the inner sanctum of the tomb]. The most you can do is touch and kiss the threshold. (October 31, 2000, Lahore)

Although they remain separated at the shrines, male and female disciples follow a similar daily regimen within their own discrete spaces. Amid the chaos of the *'urs* festivities, *murids* move back and forth between the *silsila's* private compound and the public space of the shrine, alternating between communal and private devotions. In between, disciples also have scheduled meetings with their spiritual guide. Today Shaykh Siraj 'Ali is the *silsila's* sole teaching *shaykh*. During the annual cycle of *'urs* commemorations, he is accessible to male and female *murids* alike. The *shaykh* offers collective *dars* in both compounds and also arranges time to meet with disciples individually. Another female *murid* describes a typical day at the *'urs* in Pakpattan Sharif:

> Morning prayer is held at the women's compound or at the shrine. We come back for breakfast around seven thirty or eight o'clock. Some of us take a short rest, others go about preparing to take a bath and changing clothes. At about ten o'clock, Hazrat Siraj Sahab [the current teaching *shaykh*] usually gives us an audience. Apart from anything he may wish to convey to us, we also ask questions. This is for about an hour or so. If he is not present, one of the senior female *murids* answers our questions.
>
> After this we chat and share experiences of a spiritual nature. There is hardly any talk of worldly things, as Hazrat Siraj Sahab discourages that during the *'urs*. We may individually go to the shrine for *muraqaba*, but that is generally between afternoon and evening prayers. We go for communal prayer at the noon prayers, after which we come back for lunch and a little rest. We usually say *'asr* at the compound, and then go to the shrine for *muraqaba* and the communal *maghrib* payers. After that we come back and have our dinner and prepare for the *qawwali*. After *qawwali*, we go back to sleep or talk or mediate individually.[68]

For every Chishti Sabiri *murid*, male and female alike, the fundamental purpose of any *'urs* retreat is to strengthen the connection with both the saint and his living heir: the teaching *shaykh*. *'Urs* offers disciples unparalleled access to the Sufi master and a unique opportunity to encounter the outpouring of spiritual energy (*faizan*) at the saint's tomb. A senior Pakistani disciple illustrates the importance of *'urs* through a story about Shahidullah Faridi:

> Hazrat Shahidullah Faridi was at the shrine of Baba Farid Shakar Ganj [at Pakpattan]. It was the time of the *'urs*, and people were coming out of the Gate of Heaven [*bihishti darwaza*]. Looking towards the crowd that was coming out [from the inner sanctum] he addressed the audience who was sitting there, and said, "The people who waste their life in the colleges and universities for knowledge should come here once. The knowledge they will get can in a fraction of a second cannot be compared to the knowledge they will get in years and years in the universities." And then he said, "These are the real universities, these places. Real knowledge is given to you through the attention of the saint, through inspiration. This knowledge is very precious, and you cannot find it anywhere else." (April 29, 2001, Bahawalpur)

In this narrative, Shahidullah Faridi distinguishes once again between *'ilm* (rational, discursive book knowledge) and the inner realm of *ma'rifa* (the intuitive, esoteric knowledge of the Sufi). For Chishti Sabiris, it is the outpouring of blessings from the Sufi saint that makes *'urs* such an invaluable resource for spiritual insight and transformative experience.

Thus, during the annual *'urs* pilgrimages Chishti Sabiri disciples amplify their daily ritual practices in a concentrated, communal setting. Leaving behind their normal routines and the worries of their everyday lives, they immerse themselves in prayer and rituals of remembrance in close proximity to the tombs of the saints of their *silsila*. Living together in close quarters, disciples share food and stories in between their individual and collective ritual practices. A great deal of learning comes from these personal interchanges. A female Pakistani *murid* attests to the central importance of these horizontal teaching networks during *'urs*:

> The most significant impact of these *'urs* for me and other women I presume is the tremendous sense of sharing and belonging that we experience. Many times you will find us huddled around the elder *murids*, hoping to glean any new piece of information from them. There are groups of women all over the place talking, sharing dreams and experiences—looking for guidance from everything that is said. We talk about anything our *pirs* may have said, or things one of us has read recently. You would be surprised by the amount of reading the *silsila* women do!
>
> There is a tremendous sense of sharing. Even the food we bring along individually is laid out for everyone. Everybody is included, even the children who run and play around the compound. There is of course a certain reverence displayed for the *shaykh's* wife and certain elder *murids*, but otherwise all are treated with the same concern and respect. It is a beautiful experience that I always look forward to.[69]

For twenty-first-century Chishti Sabiris, the intensity of the *'urs* experience serves to strengthen community and cement collective identity.

Mahfil-i Sama': The Musical Assembly

For Chishti Sabiris, the culmination of any *'urs* retreat is the musical assembly (*mahfil-i sama'*). *Sama'*—an Arabic word meaning "listening"—is the ritualized performance of ecstatic Sufi poetry accompanied by music. Cultivated by the Chishti order since the twelfth century, this unique genre of religious expression has inspired poets, spiritual seekers, and popular audiences alike. Along the way, it has also invoked frequent criticism from detractors who question its Islamic credentials. In South Asia, the local variety of *sama'* is known colloquially as *qawwali* ("recited"). From Bollywood film soundtracks to popular music, *qawwali* is ubiquitous, transcending religious and cultural borders. Recently, the growing popularity of "world music" has brought *qawwali* to new international audiences. Accelerated through emerging technologies—from CDs to cyberspace—this growing reach has transformed performers such as the late Nusrat Fateh 'Ali Khan and ensembles such as the Sabri Brothers into mass-marketed, global pop stars. Yet even as *qawwali* expands its boundaries and explores new frontiers, it remains deeply rooted in South Asian Sufi history, piety, and practice. Figure 5.2 is a picture of *qawwali* singers at the 2001 *'urs* festival of Wahid Bakhsh Sial Rabbani in Allahabad, Pakistan.

Figure 5.2 Qawwali Singers at the 2001 *'urs* Festival of Wahid Bakhsh Sial Rabbani, Allahabad, Pakistan

Source: Photograph by Robert Rozehnal

Qawwali is often described as Indo-Muslim "gospel music." Both lyrically and musically, it is emotive, celebratory, inspiring, and potentially transformative. In the context of the Sufi path, however, *sama'* is first and foremost a pedagogical tool—a ritual technology for the molding and shaping of a moral, virtuous self. In response to the often caustic harangues of critics over the centuries, Chishti masters have for centuries marshaled a spirited defense of *sama'*. No less an authority than the famous thirteenth-century luminary Shaykh Nizam ad-Din Awliya' (d. 1325) recognized and defended the use of music as a spiritual catalyst for Sufi adepts willing to engage it with discipline, purpose, and sobriety. In the face of controversy and criticism, the *shaykh* remained unapologetic in his assessment of Sufi musical poetry. "*sama'*," Nizam ad-Din declared, "is a proving ground for men of spiritual prowess." [70]

sama' assumed a central role in Chishti devotional practice by the twelfth century. From the beginning, Chishti *shaykhs* vigorously defended the practice against critics who dismissed musical performance as inappropriate, even blasphemous. In response, Chishti masters championed music as an integral part of Sufi devotion, arguing that it was fully in keeping with the dictates of normative Islamic law (*shari'a*) when performed under the proper conditions. Overt time, Sufi musical traditions gained broad popularity and royal patronage. The use of music for spiritual inspiration, however, remained a hallmark of the Chishti order. As Bruce Lawrence notes,

> In the Indian environment from the period of the Delhi Sultanate through the Mughal era, *sama'* assumed a unique significance as the integrating modus operandi of the Chishti *silsila*. Chishti apologists adopted a distinctive attitude to *sama'*: far from being an embarrassment to them, as the literature sometimes suggests, *sama'* was aggressively defended as an essential component of the spiritual discipline or ascesis incumbent on all Sufis . . . *sama'* became, if not the monopoly of the Chishtiyya, the preeminent symbol crystallizing their position *vis-a-vis* other Indo-Muslim leadership groups. [71]

Postcolonial Chishti Sabiris are as resolute in their defense of this tradition as their premodern counterparts. They too feel the need to marshal evidence and arguments to demonstrate the spiritual efficacy and legality of Sufi music—a defensive posturing that suggests they are aware of (and threatened by) critics of the tradition. The collective writings of twentieth-century Chishti Sabiri *shaykhs* abound with historical and anecdotal references arguing for the orthodoxy of *sama'*. The discourses of Shaykh Muhammad Zauqi Shah, for instance, contain lengthy discussions of the merits of music and the requisite decorum for its apt performance. [72] Shaykh Wahid Bakhsh Sial Rabbani followed in his mentor's footsteps as a passionate advocate of *sama'*. His diverse and eclectic writings offer a broad range of evidence drawn from the Qur'an, the *sunna*, and the lives of myriad Sufi masters to defend music's utility. In *Maqam-i Ganj-i Shakkar* [The Station of "The Treasury of Sugar"] Wahid Bakhsh offers a detailed counterpolemic in a section entitled "Criticism Against the Music of the Sufis" [*sama'-i sufiyya par i'tiraz*]. [73] An equally expansive account is found in the *shaykh's* lengthy introduction to the discourses (*malfuzat*) of the nineteenth-century Chishti master Ghulam Farid (1844–1901) titled *Maqabis al-majalis* [The Lessons of the Spiritual Assemblies].[74] Summarizing his own treatment of the subject, Wahid Bakhsh writes,

> While music is a controversial issue in Islam, its benefits in spiritual develop-ment are of an overwhelming nature. The kind of music and singing which is prohibited in Islam is of the frivolous and corrupt type whose vulgarity is unwholesome in any society. The Islamic society, in particular, stands for all-around purity, chastity and perfection. I have, however, upheld the sanctity of spiritual music with copious references from the Qur'an, Hadith and sayings of the Companions of the Prophet, the leaders of the four schools of *fiqah* [*sic*], *muhaddithin* (the Traditionalists) and the heads of various spiritual orders—Chishtis, Qadiris, Naqshbandis, Suhrawardis and so forth—in the introductions to my books.[75]

Throughout his voluminous writings, Wahid Bakhsh invokes a range of premodern Sufi authorities to bolster his own defense of *sama'*. Here again the famous nineteenth-century Chishti Sabiri master Hajji Imdad Allah al-Muhajir Makki (d. 1899), is especially prominent in Wahid Bakhsh's imag-ination. His reputation for theoretical and intellectual rigor—coupled with deep piety and social activism—mark Hajji Imdad Allah as a prominent moral exemplar and spiritual guide. Yet even as he invokes his Chishti Sabiri predecessor, Wahid Bakhsh adds his own distinct voice to the exposition and defense of *sama'*. As Ernst and Lawrence illustrate, "The approach of Capt. Wahid Bakhsh is at once bolder and more 'rational.' He explicates *sama'* as the culmination of spiritual discipline, which alone can produce the result of annihilation (*fana'*) in God. It is no longer ancillary; it is central. It is, moreover, projected as modern because it recognizes the interior/exterior correspondence of spiritual/physical health that both Europeans and Americans have too narrowly construed as uni-dimensional or physical."[76] Despite the differences of style and emphasis, there is clearly an unbroken trajectory in Chishti discourse. As the living heirs to this legacy, today's Chishti Sabiri disciples continue to view *sama's* credentials as unassailable.

In both theory and practice, the *mahfil-i sama'* is best understood as a for-malized, elaborately structured ritual performance. Chishti Sabiri masters and disciples view the ritual arena of the musical assembly as a sacralized, lim-inal space in which the normal structures and logic of everyday social practice are temporarily suspended.[77] Amid the intensity and intimacy of the *mahfil-i sama'*, music and poetry are transformed into vehicles for heightened spiri-tual insight—opening up the possibility of a deeper union with the Divine. In his Urdu discourses, *Tarbiyat al-'ushshaq*, Shaykh Muhammad Zauqi Shah details the ritual's prerequisites. Echoing a well-known phrase often attrib-uted to the early Sufi theorist, Junayd of Baghdad (d. 910), he asserts that *sama's* efficacy is conditioned by three interdependent factors:

> There are three requirements for *sama'*: place [*makan*], time [*zaman*], and
> companions [*ikhwan*]. *Makan* means the place where *qawwali* is performed. It
> should not be a location where everyone passes by. Rather it should be a
> secluded site. *Zaman* means that there should be a prescribed time for *qawwali*
> when no other duties are at hand. For example, it should not be time for prayer
> or any other obligations that might intervene. *Ikhwan* means that only people
> of taste [*ahl-i zauq*] should be seated in the *qawwali* assembly [*mahfil*], and
> only those in search of God [*talab-i haqq*] ought to listen to the *sama'*. The
> singers [*qawwals*] are also included under the requirement of *ikhwan*.[78]

According to Chishti Sabiris, it is the combination of *makan, zaman,* and
ikhwan that transforms the musical assembly into a sacred space. The careful
attention to atmosphere and audience, they insist, distinguishes the closed,
private performance of the *mahfil-i sama'* from the daily, public displays of
qawwali at Sufi shrines throughout Pakistan. Disciples highlight these elements when comparing *sama'* with the commercialized *qawwali* of the global
recording industry as well. Their criticism of popular *qawwali* reduces mass-
produced music to a form of commercialized entertainment that is often
insensitive to the Sufi tradition. *sama'*, by contrast, constitutes a carefully
choreographed technology for the enrichment of a Sufi adept's inner, spiritual development. Accessible exclusively to an elite cadre of disciples (*murids*)
under the supervision of a teaching *shaykh*, it is always governed by strict rules
of comportment.

The Chishti Sabiri musical assemblies are usually held on the night of a
Sufi saint's death anniversary, most often within an enclosed ritual space adjacent to the tomb. At the annual '*urs* of Shaykh Shahidullah Faridi in Karachi,
for example, the ceremony takes place in an enclosed, open-air courtyard
immediately in front of the tomb. In other locations such as Allahabad and
Pakpattan, the *silsila* maintains a separate indoor room for the occasion in
private compounds near the shrines. Wherever and whenever the *mahfil-i
sama'* takes place, every dimension of the ritual space and the listening audience are tightly controlled by the presiding *shaykh*. With rare exception, only
a select, inner circle of disciples are allowed to participate. During the musical assembly, disciples gather together in the presence of the spiritual master
in view of the patron saint's tomb. There they sit in quiet contemplation as
the singers—professional musicians known as *qawwals* ("reciters")—perform
poetic verses (*kalam*), accompanied by the rhythm of hand clapping, drums
(*tabla*), and the harmonium. Under the proper conditions, *murids* insist,
sama' is transformed into a powerful form of meditative recollection (*zikr*).
Under the watchful and discerning eye of the presiding *shaykh*, participants
are spurred toward mystical insight (*hal*). At times, some experience states of
ecstasy (*wajd*).

The physical space of the *mahfil-i sama'* manifests relationships of power
and authority, both spiritual and temporal. This is clearly reflected in the
seating arrangements of the assembly that mirror the hierarchical social

relations between the leader (*shaykh*), the performers (*qawwals*), and the listening audience (*murids*). At the annual '*urs* in Karachi, for example, the *qawwals* sit at the far end of the compound, directly facing Shaykh Shahidullah Faridi's tomb. As the saint's living heir, the presiding *shaykh* is positioned in the center row to the right of the musicians, facing the direction of the Ka'ba. In both Pakpattan and Allahabad where the musical assembly is held in a room adjacent to the shrine, the *shaykh* sits directly opposite the performers. Disciples, in turn, form a series of rows behind and opposite him. The most senior *murids* position themselves nearest the *shaykh*, while others take seats in the front or back of the rows according to their relative status. While the logistics vary according to the physical landscape of different shrines, the logic remains consistent. This spatial layout places the Sufi master at the very center of the ritual action, even as it confines the singers to the periphery.

Significantly, the *mahfil-i sama'* ritual space is gendered as well. Female disciples typically sit together in rows directly behind the *shaykh*, divided off from the central space by a thin, white sheet. Though recognized as full participants in the ceremony, women remain distanced from the *sama's* ritual action—physically present, but sequestered, silent, and invisible. As we have seen, this is in sharp contrast to the dynamics of everyday experience where many women play integral roles in the Chishti Sabiri order's social and ritual life. Several female *murids*, in fact, are renowned as spiritually advanced mentors with expertise in Sufi ritual practice, including *sama'*. Despite the high standing of women in Chishti Sabiri daily affairs, however, they remain noticeably marginalized within the ritualized confines of the *mahfil-i sama'*.

Aware of the controversy surrounding *sama'*, Chishti Sabiri *murids* are quick to insist that every dimension of the performance is fully in keeping with the dictates of *shari'a*. In their view, the maintenance of ritual etiquette and decorum (*adab*) protect and preserve the *mahfil-i sama's* sanctity. The words of a senior Pakistani disciple are typical:

> In our *mahfil-i sama'* there is nothing that anyone could object to, even Wahhabis. We always keep *shari'a* intact. The women, for example, remain in *pardah*. We are in *wudu* [having performed the ritual ablutions for prayer], neatly dressed, listening to the recitation of *hamd* and *naat* [songs of praise and blessing] to the Prophet, God bless him and grant him salvation. There is nothing at all objectionable in this. Often you feel so moved that you want to shake your body. There is so much pressure that you just want to move. But you are not allowed to do this. Here there is not a single utterance.
>
> We are always careful to protect the *adab* of *sama'*. The proof is the spiritual element in all this. The more you watch and hear it, the more you are attracted to it. It is not like other kinds of music. You can listen to this for years and years and it always moves you, just as it did the first time you heard it. A prayer offered in Mecca is ten thousand times greater than *namaz* done at home. The same is true for *sama'*. The presence of the *shaykh* and the saint make all the difference. (October 7, 2000, Lahore)

For Chishti Sabiris, the requirements of *adab* are as essential to Sufi practice as the ritual prescriptions of formal worship (*'ibadat*). A meticulous attention to the nuances of decorum, in fact, is at the very heart of Chishti Sabiri discipleship. To a large extent, an individual's standing in the community is measured by her/his knowledge of and adherence to these rules of ritual etiquette.

Throughout the *sama'* performance, every effort is made to ensure an atmosphere of piety and propriety. In *Tarbiyat al-'ushshaq*, Zauqi Shah outlines the ritual's parameters in detail. His exposition illustrates how *adab* impacts every dimension of the ceremony, from the listeners' dress to their bodily comportment and physical postures. In Zauqi Shah's words,

> Both the singers and the listeners should arrive clean and well dressed. Everyone who participates in the musical assembly should perform ritual ablutions. As long as they sit in the assembly, they should maintain etiquette [*adab*] and remain seated with crossed legs. During the *qawwali*, everyone should sit and make every effort to focus their attention on God. If they are spurred to inner states of ecstasy, they should focus their attention on the Prophet of God (God bless him and grant him salvation), or on their own *shaykh*, or on any saint of the *silsila* whose virtues are being mentioned [in the *qawwali*]. They should not look around because this only disperses one's thoughts and disrupts the other people of the assembly. Whatever gifts they give [for the *qawwals*] should be presented in front of the master of the assembly [i.e., the *shaykh*]. It is against etiquette to give it directly to the *qawwals* . . . If it is necessary to renew ablutions, one should immediately exit the assembly, perform the ablutions and return. Talking, using prayer beads [*tasbih*] or performing other forms of worship is against the etiquette of the musical assembly. Of course, those who have reached perfection are exempt from these rules.
>
> When overcome with ecstasy [*hal*] a person should remain in control and stay seated. He should continue to refrain from moving that would disturb the people of the assembly. If someone is forced to stand up in ecstasy than everyone should follow his example and stand up as well. As long as the person in ecstasy does not sit down, neither should they. People should never try to seat themselves up front. However, the leader of the assembly [i.e., the presiding *shaykh*] should arrange to have those who have a taste for *sama'* [*arbab-i zauq*] sit in front.
>
> If a novice seeker manages to maintain control when overcome with ecstasy, his status [*maratib*] will improve and the spiritual blessings [*faizan*] will increase as well. If, however, he does not try to stay in control and instead begins to leap and jump about when overcome with ecstasy then all progress stops. When a man becomes intoxicated [*mast*] after drinking only one cup, why would should receive more wine? Of course, it is a different matter with those who have achieved perfection. The character of their ecstasy and rapture [*wajd o hal*] is entirely separate.[79]

*Sama'*s efficacy, Zauqi Shah suggests, presupposes an exacting attention to the details of its performance. As with daily prayer, listening to music demands careful preparation. Ritual purity is maintained through ritual ablutions, the wearing of clean clothes, and the disciplining of the body. With proper intention and the focused concentration of the mind, the *shaykh* notes, disciples open themselves up to spiritual blessings and rarefied states of consciousness that are inaccessible in everyday experience. Yet the mark of spiritual attainment is to maintain sobriety and control, even in the face of spiritual ecstasy. This is only possible, Zauqi Shah insists, if the *murid* maintains an unwavering discipline and adheres to the dictates of decorum. Enshrined in texts and orally communicated among disciples, the rules of *adab* are passed down from generation to generation of Chishti Sabiri disciples. While mediating ritual performance, *adab* also forms a fundamental part of the *silsila's* historical memory, collective wisdom, and corporate identity.

The most important—if controversial—element of *sama'* is the recited lyrics (*kalam*). Sufis long ago discovered poetic images of love and intoxication to be powerful catalysts for enhancing states of spiritual ecstasy. *Fawa'id al-Fu'ad*, for instance, records Shaykh Nizam ad-Din's awe at the transformative power of poetry:

> From his [Nizam ad-Din's] blessed mouth came this pronouncement: "Every eloquent turn of phrase that one hears causes delight, but the same thought expressed in prose when cast into verse causes still great delight." At this point, I [Hasan Sijzi] interjected: "Is there nothing which touches the heart so deeply as listening to devotional music (*sama'*)?" "For those who tread this Path desiring the Divine," replied the master, "the taste which is evoked in them through *sama'* resembles a fire set ablaze. If this were not the case, where would one find eternity (*baqa'*), and how would one evoke the taste for eternity?"[80]

For Sufis past and present, *kalam* is much more than eloquent verse. As the expression of accomplished spiritual masters, Sufi poetry provides a blueprint for spiritual development—a "model of" and a "model for" mystical experience.

Contemporary Chishti Sabiris are equally attuned to the aesthetics and power of *kalam*. As with *zikr, sama'* is characterized by a wide-ranging lyrical repertoire guided by an underlying pattern. In *Tarbiyat al-'ushshaq*, Zauqi Shah links the sequence of *kalam* with the stages of the Sufi path (*suluk*). His commentary offers a nuanced summation of both:

> *Sama'* is a part of *suluk*. Indeed, it is the essence of *suluk*. The singers [*qawwals*] should arrange the *kalam* to match the stages of *suluk* itself. These days the singers are often ignorant of these matters. For this reason, it is the duty of the Sufis to inform them of these nuances.
>
> The essence of *suluk* is this: in the beginning, man is in a state of duality. The mind of the seeker of truth struggles to overcome this. With the blessings of *mujahada*, the signs and secrets of divine unity [*tawhid*] begin to be revealed and the seeker traverses the stages of true love. The result is ultimately union with God. After this, he returns to the state of servitude which is the reward for permanence in God [*baqa' bi Allah*].
>
> This very same path should be followed in *qawwali* as well. According to etiquette, *qawwali* should commence with poems in honor of the Prophet

[*na't sharif*]. This should be followed by songs in praise of the saints of the [Chishti Sabiri] order [*manqabat*]. After that, words of love [should be sung] so that the fire of separation and division warms the hearts of the seekers, and the pleasure of the taste and desire for God is increased . . . Having heard this type of poetry, the seekers immerse themselves in the contemplation of annihilation [*muraqaba-i fana'*]. This kind of *kalam* will help them to achieve effacement in the Divine essence and become overwhelmed with the state of Divine union.

After annihilation, servitude is restored, and this is the final state. For this reason, after the recitation of *kalam* dealing with annihilation and union, the *kalam* associated with servitude—the descent after ascension, separation after union—should be performed . . . The singers should remain attentive to this arrangement. If, having reached one stage they return to a previous stage, the seekers heart will shatter. For this reason, once they have reached the stage of annihilation they must not begin singing about love. Similarly, if the stage of permanence [*baqa'iyat*] is achieved, they should not return to annihilation or *na't* or *manqabat*. If after hearing a particular couplet a *salik* goes into ecstasy [*wajd*], they must continue repeating that same couplet until his state has passed. If this is not kept in mind, he could die under certain circumstances.[81]

As this lengthy quote illustrates, there is nothing arbitrary about the poetic repertoire of the *mahfil-i sama'*. It encapsulates *suluk* itself, serving in effect as a lyrical microcosm of the Sufi's arduous spiritual journey to God. For Chishti Sabiri adepts, poetry and music are merely a medium for a higher goal: the inner concentration on the mystical quest. Under the right conditions, they assert, *sama'* has the power to spur states of heightened consciousness. This power is also potentially dangerous, even destructive. Zauqi Shah's final cautionary note invokes the memory of Shaykh Qutb ad-Din Bakhtiyar Kaki (d. 1235), the famous thirteenth-century Chishti master who died in a state of prolonged spiritual rapture while listening to *sama'*. The musical assembly, Zauqi Shah suggests, is neither a playground nor a venue for worldly entertainment. Instead, it is a ritual training ground open exclusively to devotees who are fully committed to the discipline and rigors of the Sufi path. In the proper context, Chishti Sabiris assert, devotional music becomes a didactic tool that reveals a depth of spiritual insight and knowledge that no text, library, or scholar could ever hope to communicate.

In practice, the Chishti Sabiri *mahfil-i sama'* is led by one or two singers who are supported melodically by a background chorus and several musicians. Though constrained by the ritual's formal structure, *qawwals* are allowed some limited space for creative freedom and spontaneity. As ethnomusicologist Regula Burckhardt Qureshi notes, "The ensemble structure and performing style make possible extended singing, a strongly articulated musical meter, and a flexible structuring process adapted to the changing spiritual needs of the *sama'* listeners."[82] Under the watchful eye of the presiding *shaykh*, the *qawwals* repeat and recombine poetic couplets and individual phrases or words in response to the reactions of the audience. At times the performers choose the lyrics and musical cadence; at other moments, the *shaykh* will call for a specific poem or encourage the *qawwals* to speed up (or slow down) the pace. In this respect, the *mahfil-i sama'* resembles a form of spiritual jazz—fluid, open, and responsive to audience feedback and participation.

The singers' repertoire draws on a diverse range of lyrical poetry communicated in multiple languages. *Qawwals* move fluidly between linguistic registers: from the Persian verses of Jami, Hafiz, and Rumi, to the Punjabi poetry of Mehr 'Ali Shah and Ghulam Farid, and the classical Hindi of Amir Khusrau, among others.[83] Chishti Sabiris have a particular affinity for Persian poetry. In the words of a young *murid*, a disciple of Wahid Bakhsh, "My *shaykh* told me that unless you know Persian you cannot be a Sufi! The poetry in Persian is the essence of *kalam*" (September 2, 2001, Karachi). A senior Pakistani disciple explains the rationale behind this preference: "Most *kalam* for *qawwali* is in Farsi. These poems have been written by the saints [*awliya' Allah*], and because of their spirituality it effects us too when their *kalam* is recited. If I write something, it will not matter. If a *wali Allah* writes something, it will have a different effect. Apart from Farsi, you have *kalam* in Saraiki, Hindi, Sindhi, and Punjabi. Urdu has not been selected by our saints for this purpose. In our *mahfil-i sama'*, the *qawwals* are directed to focus on Farsi" (September 1, 2001, Karachi).

The *qawwals* represent just a single node in a vast web of economic networks and minimarkets that surround the *'urs* pilgrimage and its public rituals. Within the private, sacralized space of the *mahfil-i sama'*, they play a central if at times ambiguous role. As the preservers of poetic and musical tradition, the singers are respected as ritual mediators. As paid service professionals, however, they are simultaneously (and paradoxically) held in low esteem. During the *mahfil-i sama'* the position of the musicians is actually fraught with tension. An accomplished *qawwal* is valued—and financially rewarded—for his musical and poetic talents. Yet a singer's artistic creativity and social authority are constantly kept in check by the Sufi *shaykh* who ultimately controls every dimension of the *sama'* assembly. Qureshi provides a lucid summary of this complex dynamic in her classic study of Sufi musical performance at the shrine of Shaykh Nizam ad-Din Awliya' in Delhi. In her words,

> Issues of spiritual and socio-economic priority, of dominance and submission, of hierarchical order and individual assertion, of conformity and creativity, are being negotiated audibly, in the language of music, through a Qawwali performance. Since the Qawwal is the only one who "speaks" this language, he is in effect charged with being the sole mouthpiece for all this is to be conveyed in the Qawwali. This is why he "speaks" musically not only for himself, but for all his listeners, articulating, in structure and dynamic, the multiplicity of relationships between all participants including himself . . . [Ultimately] the only way to control the Qawwal's musical power over his audience is to give his audience religiously legitimized social and economic power over *him*. Made dependent on his audience in a real way, he can then be controlled in performance through the presence of a strong authority structure and through strict rules of censure for defying it—both of which are realities facing any Qawwali performer.[84]

Within the Chishti Sabiri *mahfil-i sama'*, the presiding *shaykh* is solely responsible for the spiritual welfare of his followers. During the performance, he carefully moderates the actions and reactions of his *murids*, using the *qawwals* to amplify or pacify their responses. The *qawwals*, in turn, are tightly controlled. Loud drumming and theatrical gestures are discouraged. Similarly, pandering to popular tastes by playing "film *qawwali*" is strictly prohibited. Singers who violate these rules are immediately ushered out of the assembly and not invited to return. Not surprisingly, well-known local singers are frequently turned away from the gathering altogether. I was told, for instance, that throughout the 1970s Shaykh Shahidullah Faridi pointedly refused to allow either the Sabri Brothers or Nusrat Fateh 'Ali Khan to perform at the annual *'urs* in Pakpattan (September 30, 2000, Pakpattan).[85] A senior Chishti Sabiri disciple offers a critique of popular *qawwali* that I often heard repeated among *murids*: "*Qawwali* is not *sama'*. With these Nusrat Fateh 'Ali Khan types there is always lots of talk about wine, and the [drum] beats go up [in intensity]. It is a different taste and they [the *qawwals*] play to the gallery. We do not allow them to use loud *tabla*. They must come to us for the blessings of our *shaykhs* and not for the money. They never get much money from us" (December 15, 2000, Karachi). This is a common lament. While disciples may respect popular singers for their musical artistry, they are highly critical of those who commercialize and commodify Sufi music. *sama'*, Chishti Sabiris insist, is not a form of entertainment. It is a powerful spiritual catalyst that should be used only in the presence of an accomplished spiritual master who understands its power. Removing *sama'* from its proper ritual setting, disciples argue, undermines the music's spiritual efficacy and dilutes its transformative power.

In interviews, *murids* often commented on the pervasive decline in standards among today's *qawwals*. Most singers, they claim, are no longer properly trained in the nuances of ritual etiquette and the intricacies of *kalam*. In order to insure that *adab* is maintained, therefore, several senior Chishti Sabiri *murids* assist the *shaykh* in controlling the *mahfil-i sama'*, selecting and guiding the *qawwals'* performance. One of these select disciples explains his role:

We know the *qawwals* and they know us. And having been in the gracious company of our *masha'ikh*, we also have a little more knowledge than the novices about what sort of *kalam* should be recited and the proper order. This is worship ('*ibadat*), it is not a social function. Sometimes the *qawwals* have to be told [what to recite]. There are not many singers left who know that order, and maintain that order. There are various reasons for this. There is a lack of knowledge and there is greed. The *qawwals* only perform for money. They only want to play the songs that people will pay money to hear. That is why the selection of *qawwali* must be done by the Sufi masters (*masha'ikh*) themselves. They alone decide whose name should be called [i.e., what poet should be recited]. (September 1, 2001, Karachi)

By screening the selection of singers and carefully monitoring their performance, Chishti Sabiris effectively maintain a monopoly as the gate-keepers of tradition.

According to disciples, under the proper conditions *sama'* is transformed into a powerful vehicle for states of spiritual insight that no other ritual practice can equal. This is true, they note, even if the recited lyrics are not understood, as is often the case. According to a senior Malaysian disciple, "The *kalam* is central, it brings you to Allah. I do not understand much of the *qawwali*, but there is still such a blessing of the *masha'ikh* who are present there. Even when you do not understand, you keep concentrating on the oneness of Allah. Of course, if you know the meaning of the *qawwali* your heart cries out even more" (October 3, 2001, Kuala Lumpur). At times, Pakistani disciples struggle with the lyrics as well. The rapidly shifting linguistic registers, coupled with the often poor pronunciation of novice *qawwals*, frequently creates translation problems. Nonetheless, disciples assert that the transformative impact of *sama'* ultimately transcends the limits of language. In the words of a senior Pakistani disciple,

> You may hear the same *kalam* elsewhere, but you will not have the same feeling. *Kalam* makes it easier for you to understand the spiritual feelings you receive. You decipher it better. *Kalam* is a vehicle, even when you may not understand it. The *awliya' Allah* frequently explain this by the example of a blind man and a man with vision, sitting together in the sun. The blind man does not see the sun, but he can sense the warmth of the sun, just as a man with eyes. Both will get the same warmth of the sun, without any difference. (September 1, 2001, Karachi)

Remarkably, Chishti Sabiri *murids* claim that even physical distance does not diminish the impact of *sama'*. When they are unable to travel to Pakistan for the annual cycle of *'urs* celebrations, for example, Malaysian disciples frequently commemorate the occasion on the opposite side of the Indian Ocean. During the days of the *'urs*, they gather together in private homes in Kuala Lumpur. There they perform communal prayers and, most intriguingly, listen to taped recordings of *sama'*. Despite the medium, disciples insist that the spiritual blessings (*faizan*) at these gatherings is extremely intense. In the words of a senior female *murid*, "Somebody asked our *shaykh*, 'What is the difference between attending *'urs* at the *mazar* proper and [celebrating] *'urs* here in Kuala Lumpur?' He replied, 'In both places you receive *faizan*, blessings come down. But the blessings you get at the *mazar* itself you do not receive at your house. It is much stronger at the *mazar* because the Shaykh intensifies it.' It is true. We receive a lot of *faizan* when we have our *'urs* here. We play *qawwali* on the tape cassette. It is fantastic!" (September 30, 2001, Kuala Lumpur). Even though taped recordings allow disciples to participate in the ritual performance in absentia, *murids* insist that nothing compares to the direct, unmediated, communal experience of the *mahfil-i sama'*. It is the intimacy and intensity of this experience that cements the annual cycle of '*urs* celebrations as a central fixture of the Chishti Sabiri ritual calendar.

In a letter written to a female disciple, Shaykh Wahid Bakhsh Sial Rabbani recalls his own experience at the Muharram '*urs* of Baba Farid in Pakpattan in 1990:

> I was terribly tired, especially after the exhaustion of a full week of spiritual exercises (*mujahada*) at the shrine (*mazar*) comprising three strenuous hours in the morning from 8 am until 11 am, and three hours in the evening, from 5 to 8 pm. On the night of the '*urs* the *qawwals* sang special Persian and Hindi *ghazals* for our *silsila* people because they know what our taste is. On the arrival of the Diwan Sahib, the *qawwali* reverted to mob entertainment. During mob *qawwali* we fixed our attention on the saint himself who made up for all the deficiency. The three hour evening *sama'* session was filled with ancient Hindi songs of Amir Khusrau and the Persian songs of Hazrat Baba Farid himself. This was very intoxicating and full of ecstasies.[86]

This account captures something of the heightened atmosphere that draws Chishti Sabiri *murids* to the annual '*urs* celebrations, year after year. It also points to the unrivaled intensity and transformative power of *sama'*. For Sufi adepts committed to the rigors of the path, the musical assembly offers a tactile, sensual, and immediate source of knowledge—a passageway to higher states of insight and awareness. At the same time, its structured performance cements a deep sense of social solidarity, shared memory, and communal identity among the select group of listeners. As the paradigmatic ritual practice of the Chishti Sufi order, the *mahfil-i sama'* plays a central role in linking today's disciples to each other and to their spiritual ancestors.

CONCLUSION

Ritual performance is the lifeblood of the Chishti Sabiri order. Contemporary disciples seek spiritual truth in the details of ritual practice. It is through the visceral experience of ritual that the Sufi adept learns to cultivate a bodily habitus in which Muslim virtue is embodied and enacted. Through dreams and dream interpretation, the daily rituals of remembrance, and pilgrimage networks, Chishti Sabiris struggle to remake themselves. They describe this quest as a spiritual *jihad*. For these twenty-first-century Sufis, spiritual wisdom is not found in books. It is possible only through internal combat—a ceaseless striving against one's beastly nature and an aggressive pushing of personal boundaries. Chishti Sabiris view Sufism as a spiritual meritocracy. In this pedagogical system, spiritual knowledge and authority are measured by the intensity of a Sufi's piety, the rigor of a Sufi's practice, and the depth of Sufi's personal experiences. On the Sufi path, *murids* assert, there are no shortcuts. Knowledge must be *earned* through the discipline, sacrifice, and ceaseless striving of ritual work.

Although it is communicated and experienced in community, *suluk* is an intensely personal experience. A senior Pakistani disciple explained this dynamic through a simple technological metaphor:

> "Chishti Sabiri" is our lineage, our family name. It is like an airplane. Passengers buy tickets, check in their luggage, take their seats, and fly. Then they collect their luggage and leave. [On the Sufi path] it is natural that you will develop relationships and even love for your fellow *murids*, but that is not the real purpose. There is no planned group work as such. It is all between the *shaykh* and the *murid*. The most important part of *suluk* is what you do at home, every day and every night. The only objective is the cleaning of the heart in the company of the *shaykh*. (April 25, 2001, Lahore)

This is a revealing statement about Chishti Sabiri identity, both individual and collective. It emphasizes the centrality of personal struggle and the imperative for individual effort in Sufi ritual practice. Above all, it reminds us that Sufi pedagogy remains firmly grounded on the intimate, face-to-face interaction between the novice seeker and the teaching *shaykh*. Yet even when disciples pursue devotions in isolation within the privacy of their own homes, their experiences are authorized and authenticated by the teaching *shaykh* and the horizontal network of *murids*. The individual Sufi self, in other words, is ultimately molded within the moral community of the *silsila*.

Today's Chishti Sabiris negotiate a constant balance between their daily and devotional lives. *Murids* integrate ritual practice into their complex worldly lives through a combination of self-discipline and vigilant time management. They mark these strategies of accommodation as something new, even as they insist that the essential elements of the Sufi path remain unchanged. Like their premodern predecessors, contemporary *murids* are deeply attuned to spiritual genealogy and sacred history. They tell stories about past *shaykhs*, continuously revisiting the words and deeds of the saints and spiritual masters of their shared tradition. Many attend weekly *halqa-i zikr* sessions and regularly visit local shrines in groups for *muraqaba*. Four times a year, disciples travel and live together en masse for short but intensive periods of spiritual immersion, creating a serial *khanaqah* during the annual *'urs* pilgrimages. In every context, the *silsila* maintains strict borders and ritual boundaries. There is, in fact, a pervasive sense of shared experience and a collective identity that unites individual disciples. In twenty-first-century Pakistan and Malaysia, a new generation of Chishti Sabiris perpetuates a nexus of embodied ritual practices and communal networks that links them to a sacred Indo-Muslim past, even as it continues to sacralize the living present.

CONCLUSIONS

The Pakpattan tragedy of April 1, 2001 quickly receded from Pakistan's media spotlight. Over time, the story was eclipsed by a parade of cataclysmic events that consumed public discourse: the aftermath of 9/11, the U.S.-led attack on the Taliban regime in Afghanistan, the invasion of Iraq and the local repercussions of the "war on terror," the devastation of the South Asian earthquake of 2005, and the continued instability of Pakistan's domestic politics. Yet for the families of those who perished amid the confusion and chaos of that night at the shrine of the renowned Chishti Sufi saint, Baba Farid ad-Din Ganj-i Shakkar, April 1, 2001 is a date that will never be forgotten. The same is true for Chishti Sabiri disciples who still mourn the loss of a promising young boy among their ranks—the great-grandson of the twentieth-century Chishti Sabiri master Shaykh Muhammad Zauqi Shah. By interpreting the sudden and violent loss of life as a ritual sacrifice, however, Chishti Sabiris found a deeper sense of meaning amid their pain. This counternarrative consecrated their suffering as a pious act of acquiescence to an inscrutable but transcendent expression of Divine will. In keeping with tradition, Chishti Sabiris continue to make the annual pilgrimage for the Muharram 'urs at Pakpattan, but today the journey carries an added significance. *Murids* now commemorate the "marriage" ('*urs*) of both the saint and the young boy with the God. In both cases, death has been transformed into martyrdom.

The tragedy at Pakpattan frames this book because it illuminates the transformative power of faith for the community of contemporary Chishti Sabiris who live within a sacralized universe. The *silsila's* narrative of redemptive suffering diverges sharply from the rationalist interpretation of the Pakistani state. It is also an interpretation that academic discourse can analyze, dissect, and explain away but never fully comprehend. This study, by contrast, takes the Sufi spiritual quest and the worldview that it engenders seriously. On a more mundane level, my analysis contextualizes the Pakpattan tragedy in the broader contestation over the roots of Islamic authority and the public debates over the authenticity of Sufism in today's Pakistan and Malaysia.

Since Partition and political independence sixty years ago, Pakistan has struggled to define the contours of citizenship and Islamic identity. I argue, however, that the state's control of Sufi tradition—its worldview, its sacred spaces, its spiritual leaders—has never been totalizing or hegemonic. This book illustrates how contemporary Chishti Sabiri Sufi identity is constructed through discourse and constituted through ritual practice, beyond the gaze of the nation and outside the machinery of the state. Today's Chishti Sabiris respond directly to the state's ideology and institutions while adapting their own public image and private practices to accommodate change. In doing so, I argue, they demonstrate that Sufi identity is capacious, broader, and deeper than the parochial constructions of religious nationalism. In the context of late colonial India and postcolonial Pakistan, Chishti Sabiris have articulated an alternative worldview that places Sufi identity and Sufi ritual practices at the very center of Islamic orthodoxy and Pakistani national identity. In my view, today's Chishti Sabiri order embraces an *alternative modernity* that reconfigures the ideology and institutions of the state in multiple ways:

- Expanding the limited boundaries of the geopolitical map, Chishti Sabiris mark an *alternative geography* that delineates an expansive Indo-Muslim sacred landscape centered on a constellation of Sufi shrines.
- Revising the official narrative of Pakistan's sixty-year history, Chishti Sabiris trace an *alternative history* through a spiritual genealogy (*silsila*) that directly links the current generation of disciples with their Sufi predecessors and, ultimately, with the Prophet Muhammad.
- Challenging narrow constructions of Pakistani national identity, Chishti Sabiris perpetuate an *alternative community* rooted in the *silsila's* broad teaching network.
- Reframing Pakistan's identity as an Islamic republic, Chishti Sabiris embrace an *alternative authority* that is rooted in an experiential knowledge acquired through the discipline of Sufi ritual practice.

   In an effort to track these multiple vectors, this book has explored the contemporary Chishti Sabiri order from various perspectives. Combing the philological methods of Islamic Studies with the theory and methodology of Cultural Anthropology, I have examined both texts and contexts. In doing so, my analysis reveals that twenty-first-century Chishti Sabiri identity is complex, fluid, and multifaceted. It is inscribed in texts, mediated through interpersonal networks, transmitted via the intimate master-disciple relationship, and experienced through ritual practice.

   As we have seen, the sacred biographies of Muhammad Zauqi Shah, Shahidullah Faridi, and Wahid Bakhsh Sial Rabbani reflect the traditional paradigm—the hagiographical habitus—of Indo-Muslim sainthood. Despite their diverse backgrounds and life experiences, these twentieth-century Sufi exemplars are each remembered as pious, disciplined, and charismatic teachers. Chishti Sabiri hagiographies characterize Zauqi Shah and Wahid Bakhsh as Sufi masters who were deeply immersed in spiritual life and, at the same time, actively engaged with the social and political issues of their times. As ideologues and social commentators, these Pakistani *shaykhs* articulated a *shari'a*-minded, socially engaged Sufism, firmly grounded in tradition but open to change. Their approach echoes the activist ethos of their nineteenth-century Chishti Sabiri predecessors, Hajji Imdad Allah al-Muhajir Makki and Rashid Ahmad Gangohi—the spiritual founders of Deoband. Shahidullah

Faridi, by contrast, is memorialized in a different manner. As an Englishman and a convert, he stands as a complex figure whose sacred biography marks Sufism as a spiritual meritocracy. Together, the *shaykhs'* legacy sets the standard for a new generation of Chishti Sabiri disciples who combine the rigors of Sufi discipline with a practical, utilitarian approach to the mundane world of everyday experience.

Throughout their voluminous literary corpus, Muhammad Zauqi Shah, Shahidullah Faridi, and Wahid Bakhsh Sial Rabbani responded directly to the momentous social, cultural, and political changes spurred by Partition. The *shaykhs* did not shy away from the realm of politics. Their writings, however, frame politics in terms of religion. As writers and public ideologues, they each defended the orthodoxy of Sufism in Pakistan's contested public sphere. In an eclectic range of essays, articles, and books, they valorized the doctrinal teachings and ritual practices at the core of Chishti Sabiri identity as a bulwark against the tradition's critics and a panacea for the nation's widespread social malaise. In effect, the *shaykhs* made a case for a Pakistani identity that is simultaneously modern, Muslim, and mystic. Adopting the idioms of modernity—the language and logic of science, rationalism, and the market— they used the instruments of mass media to articulate and amplify this message to a broad national and international audience.

Muhammad Zauqi Shah, Shahidullah Faridi, and Wahid Bakhsh Sial Rabbani were also ardent Pakistani nationalists. From their writings it is clear that they envisioned Pakistan as a tabula rasa, a new and welcoming space for South Asian Muslims to resurrect the ideals of the Prophet's Medina. Their imaginings of the nation portray Sufi masters as the true heirs to the Prophet and, by extension, the true spiritual founders of Pakistan. Significantly, their vision of citizenship echoes the logic and structure of the Sufi master-disciple relationship. It equates the nation with a moral community grounded on knowledge and piety and envisions a social order mediated by the Sufi rules of etiquette and decorum (*adab*). This idealized vision of an Islamic state rooted in Sufi tradition made the creation of Pakistan much more palatable to these Chishti Sabiri *shaykhs* than it was for many of their *'ulama* counterparts who resisted Partition. In effect, the *shaykhs'* alternative narrative of the nation frames Pakistan—"The Land of the Pure"—as a utopian promised land for the global Muslim *umma*.

While charting Chishti Sabiri formations of the nation, I have also argued that the *silsila's* public, political dimensions reveal only half the story. Above all, Sufism remains a personal spiritual quest. At its core, the contemporary Chishti Sabiri order is a moral community that aims to reconstitute the Sufi disciple through its networks of knowledge and spiritual pedagogy. Chishti Sabiri ritual practice (*suluk*) begins with a choice. In the pursuit of knowledge, the Sufi adept must willfully submit to the power and authority of a spiritual master. As the embodiment of *sunna*, the *shaykh* serves as the living conduit to Islam's sacred past. In this system, Chishti Sabiri doctrine is interiorized and actualized via a nexus of ritual practices. Drawing on the words of contemporary *murids* in Pakistan and Malaysia, I examined three distinct ritual complexes: dreams and dream interpretation; rituals of remembrance (prayer, *zikr*, and *muraqaba*); and the annual pilgrimage networks and musical assemblies at Sufi shrines ('*urs* and *sama*'). In Sufi ritual, the body serves as a medium for knowledge and a tool for self-transformation. By adhering to a disciplined routine of ritual performance, the Sufi disciple forges a new bodily habitus, transforming the acculturated, socialized self into a sacralized, moral self. While the Chishti Sabiri disciple's progress along the path ultimately rests on individual action and personal responsibility, the Sufi subject is molded within the community of the *silsila*. Through companionship with the spiritual master and the community of fellow disciples, the *murid* learns to navigate the arduous inner journey of the Sufi path.

As a case study of living Sufism in practice, this study demonstrates that Chishti Sabiri *silsila* is both paradigmatic and protean. In both public and private spaces, today's Chishti Sabiris recognize the imperative for reform, the pressing need to respond to changing times and adapt to new environments. The reconfiguration of ritual space by new geopolitical boundaries is only the most obvious example of the altered political and spiritual landscape of postcolonial Pakistan and Malaysia. For individual disciples, the contingencies of modern, urban life have also forced a reassessment of how best to balance the necessities of the practical, lived-in world (*dunya*) with the demands of spiritual discipline. The increased demands of the workplace, the imperative for mobility and travel, and the pervasive ambiguity and anxiety exacerbated by social, political, and economic instability—all these elements have forced a rethinking of the meaning and methods of contemporary Sufi praxis. In response, Chishti Sabiris have altered the frequency and location of their ritual practices in order to accommodate the Sufi path to contemporary ground-level realities.

Despite all these myriad changes, however, there remains a fundamental continuity to Chishti Sabiri identity. The technologies of bodily discipline, the interpretive frameworks of selfhood, and the rules of Sufi decorum remain very much intact. In this sense, I argue, the *silsila* remains true to its historical, genealogical, ontological, epistemic, and heuristic foundations. At the dawn of the twenty-first century, Chishti Sabiri Sufism is imagined and inscribed anew in texts, even as it is embodied and performed in ritual contexts.

Notes

Introduction: Mapping the Chishti Sabiri Sufi Order

1. For an overview of Sufi history and practice, see especially Carl W. Ernst, *The Shambhala Guide to Sufism* (Boston: Shambhala Press, 1997); Annemarie Schimmel, *Mystical Dimensions of Islam* (Chapel Hill: University of North Carolina Press, 1975).

2. For a comprehensive overview of the Chishti order, see Carl W. Ernst and Bruce B. Lawrence, *Sufi Martyrs of Love: The Chishti Order in South Asia and Beyond* (New York: Palgrave Macmillan, 2002). The definitive work on the Chishtiyya is Khaliq Ahmad Nizami's Urdu magnum opus: *Tarikh-i mashayikh-i Chisht* [The History of the Chishti Sufi Masters] (Delhi: Idarah-i Adabiyyat-i Delli, 1980/1985). See also Khaliq Ahmad Nizami, "Chishtiyya," in *Encyclopedia of Islam* (Leiden: E.J. Brill, 1965), 11: 50–56.

3. On the history of Sufism in South Asia, see especially Schimmel, *Mystical Dimensions of Islam*, 370–402, where the author provides a masterful survey of the Sufi contributions to Indo-Muslim culture and the development of regional literary and, in particular, poetic traditions. See also the two-volume work by Saiyid Athar Abbas Rizvi, *A History of Sufism in India* (Delhi: Munshiram Manoharlal Publishers, 1975, 1983/1992).

4. The most comprehensive overview of the history and legacy of the Deoband *madrasa* remains Barbara Daly Metcalf, *Islamic Revival in British India: Deoband, 1860–1900* (Princeton: Princeton University Press, 1982).

5. On the politics and polemics of contemporary Sufism, see Ernst, *The Shambhala Guide to Sufism*, 199–228.

6. Muhammad Qasim Zaman, *The Ulama in Contemporary Islam: Custodians of Change* (Princeton: Princeton University Press, 2002), 3.

7. Dale F. Eickelman and James Piscatori, *Muslim Politics* (Princeton: Princeton University Press, 1996), 37. For a broad discussion of the construction of "tradition" in Muslim discourse, see in particular Chapter Two, "The Invention of Tradition in Muslim Politics," 22–45.

8. Dipesh Chakrabarty, *Habitations of Modernity: Essays in the Wake of Subaltern Studies* (Chicago: University of Chicago Press, 2002), xix.

9. On the connections between modernity and religion, see, e.g., Arjun Appadurai, *Modernity at Large: Cultural Dimensions of Globalization* (Minneapolis: University of Minnesota Press, 1996); Gustavo Benavides, "Modernity," in *Critical Terms for Religious Studies*, ed. Mark C. Taylor (Chicago: University of Chicago Press, 1998), 186–204; Jose Casanova, *Public Religions in the Modern World* (Chicago: University of Chicago Press, 1994). In the specific context of Islam, see also Armando Salvatore, *Islam and the Political Discourse of Modernity* (Reading: Ithaca Press, 1997).

10. Dipesh Chakrabarty, *Provincializing Europe: Postcolonial Thought and Historical Difference* (Princeton: Princeton University Press, 2000), 4.

11. Talal Asad, *Formations of the Secular: Christianity, Islam, Modernity* (Stanford: Stanford University Press, 2003), 13 (emphasis is in the original).

12. Timothy Mitchell, "Introduction," in *Questions of Modernity*, ed. Timothy Mitchell (Minneapolis: University of Minnesota Press, 2000), xxvi.

13. Bruce B. Lawrence, *Defenders of God: The Fundamentalist Revolt against the Modern Age* (San Francisco: Harper and Row, 1989), 17.

14. Jonah Blank, *Mullahs on the Mainframe: Islam and Modernity among the Daudi Bohras* (Chicago: University of Chicago Press, 2001), 286.

15. Katherine P. Ewing, *Arguing Sainthood: Modernity, Psychoanalysis, and Islam* (Durham: Duke University Press, 1997), 4.

16. See, e.g., Linda Alcoff, "The Problem of Speaking for Others," *Cultural Critique*, No. 20 (Winter 1991–1992): 5–32. See also the collection of essays in Russell T. McCutcheon, ed., *The Insider/Outsider Problem in the Study of Religion: A Reader* (New York: Cassell, 1999); James Clifford and George E. Marcus, eds., *Writing Culture: The Poetics and Politics of Ethnography* (Berkeley: University of California Press, 1986).

17. Thomas A. Tweed, "On Moving Across: Translocative Religion and the Interpreter's Position," *Journal of the American Academy of Religion*, Vol. 70, No. 2 (June 2002): 260. Tweed's nuanced theoretical model emerges from his work among Cuban-American Catholic immigrants.

18. Kirin Narayan, *Storytellers, Saints and Scoundrels: Folk Narrative in Hindu Religious Teaching* (Philadelphia: University of Pennsylvania Press, 1989), 62.

19. Tweed, "On Moving Across," 270–271.

20. Carl W. Ernst, "Preface to the Second Edition," in *Eternal Garden: Mysticism, History and Politics at a South Asian Sufi Center* (New Delhi: Oxford University Press, 2004), xi–xviii. On the Orientalist "discovery" of Sufism, see also Ernst, *The Shambhala Guide to Sufism*, 1–18.

21. One of the more ambitious (and influential) historical studies of Sufism comes from J. Spencer Trimingham, a specialist in the history of Islam in Africa. Trimingham's book, *The Sufi Orders in Islam* (London: Oxford University Press, 1971), posits a threefold theory of Sufism's historical devolution. For a trenchant critique of this model, see Ernst and Lawrence, *Sufi Martyrs of Love*, 11–12.

22. Ernst, *The Shambhala Guide to Sufism*, 200.

23. For a concise overview of these two interpretive paradigms, see John R. Bowen, *Muslims through Discourse: Religion and Ritual in Gayo Society* (Princeton: Princeton University Press, 1993), 4–8. See also Vincent J. Cornell, *Realm of the Saint: Power and Authority in Moroccan Sufism* (Austin: University of Texas Press, 1998), xl.

24. See, e.g., the essays in Pnina Werbner and Helene Basu, eds., *Embodying Charisma: Modernity, Locality and the Performance of Emotion in Sufi Cults* (London: Routledge, 1998).

25. The term "discursive tradition" is borrowed from anthropologist Talal Asad. See Talal Asad, "The Idea of an Anthropology of Islam," in *Occasional Paper Series*, by the Center for Contemporary Arab Studies, Georgetown University (Washington, DC: Georgetown University Press, March 1986), 14.

26. Catherine Bell, *Ritual Theory, Ritual Practice* (New York: Oxford University Press, 1992), 140.

27. For a critical review of the literature of South Asian Sufism, see Ernst, "Preface to the Second Edition," xi–xviii. See also David Gilmartin and Bruce B. Lawrence, "Introduction," in *Beyond Turk and Hindu: Rethinking Religious Identities in Islamicate South Asia*, ed. David Gilmartin and Bruce B. Lawrence (Gainesville: University Press of Florida, 2000), 1–20; Marc Gaborieau, "Introduction to the New Edition," in *Muslim Shrines in India: Their Character, History and Significance*, ed. Christian W. Troll (New Delhi: Oxford University Press, 1989), v–xxiv.

28. Pnina Werbner, *Pilgrims of Love: The Anthropology of a Global Sufi Cult* (Bloomington: Indiana University Press, 2003). I offer a detailed review of this book in the *Journal of Asian Studies*, Vol. 63, No. 4 (November 2004): 1187–1189.

29. Arthur F. Buehler, *Sufi Heirs of the Prophet: The Indian Naqshbandiyya and the Rise of the Mediating Sufi Shaykh* (Columbia: University of South Carolina Press, 1998).

30. On the Chishti Sabiri order, see Ernst and Lawrence, *Sufi Martyrs of Love*, 118–127, 130–140.

CHAPTER 1   SUFISM AND THE POLITICS OF ISLAMIC IDENTITY

1. A version of this chapter was published as an article: "*Faqir* or Faker?: The Pakpattan Tragedy and the Politics of Sufism in Pakistan," *Religion* 36 (2006): 29–47.

2. Casanova, *Public Religions in the Modern World*, 6. For a trenchant critique of Casanova's arguments, see Asad, *Formations of the Secular*, Chapter Eight, "Secularism, Nation-State, Religion," 181–201.

3. For perspectives on the public and private spheres in Muslim societies, see the essays in *The Public Sphere in Muslim Societies*, ed. Miriam Hoexter, Shmuel N. Eisenstadt, and Nehemia Levtzion (Albany: State University of New York Press, 2002), 1–8. On contemporary debates of the Islamic public sphere, see also Dale F. Eickelman and Jon W. Anderson, "Redefining Muslim Publics," in *New Media in the Muslim World: The Emerging Public Sphere*, ed. Dale F. Eickelman and Jon W. Anderson (Bloomington: Indiana University Press, 1999), 1–18.

4. Ewing, *Arguing Sainthood*, 67. On the origins and development of the Pakistani state, see also Ayesha Jalal, *The State of Martial Rule: The Origins of Pakistan's Political Economy of Defence* (Cambridge: Cambridge University Press, 1990).

5. For a thorough examination of the Taliban and the rise of the militant Islam within the complex geopolitics of Central Asia, see the recent works by Ahmed Rashid: *Taliban: Islam, Oil and the New Great Game in Central Asia* (London: I.B. Tauris, 2000); *Jihad: The Rise of Militant Islam in Central Asia* (New Haven: Yale University Press, 2002). On the Taliban and its relationship to sectarian Deobandi groups in Pakistan, see Zaman, *The Ulama in Contemporary Islam*, 136–143.

6. The MMA comprises six diverse religious parties—the Jama'at-i Islami; two factions of the Deobandi Jamiat 'Ulama-i Islam; the Barelwi party, the Jamiat 'Ulama-i Pakistan; a small Wahhabi group, the Jamiat Ahl-i Hadith; and a Shi'a group, the Islami Tehrik Pakistan. See Andrew Holden, "Pakistan's Religious Parties: A Threat to Musharraf's Policies?" *Central*

Asia-Caucasus Analyst (Johns Hopkins University, SAIS, November 6, 2002). On the regime of General Musharraf and the landscape of post-9/11 Pakistan, see Ahmed Rashid, "Pakistan on the Edge," *New York Review of Books*, October 10, 2002, 36–40; Isabel Hilton, "The General in His Labyrinth: Where Will Pervez Musharraf Lead His Country?" *New Yorker*, August 12, 2002, 42–55.

7. Seyyed Vali Reza Nasr, *Islamic Leviathan: Islam and the Making of State Power* (New York: Oxford University Press, 2001), 13. On the Islamization of politics in Pakistan, see also Zaman, *The Ulama in Contemporary Islam*, Chapter Four, "Conceptions of the Islamic State," 88–110.

8. For detailed cross-cultural and historical studies on the polemics over Sufism in various Islamic societies, see the essays in Frederick de Jong and Bernd Radtke, eds., *Islamic Mysticism Contested: Thirteen Centuries of Controversies and Polemics* (Leiden: E.J. Brill, 1999). For a more focused study of the debates over Sufism in the context of modernity and colonialism, see Elizabeth Sirriyeh, *Sufis and Anti-Sufis: The Defence, Rethinking and Rejection of Sufism in the Modern World* (Richmond, Surrey: Curzon Press, 1999).

9. Ernst, *The Shambhala Guide to Sufism*, xiii.

10. Ewing, *Arguing Sainthood*, 49. For a more detailed examination of the British policy toward local Sufi institutions and exemplars in the Punjab, see Sarah F. D. Ansari, *Sufi Saints and State Power: The Pirs of Sind, 1843–1947* (Lahore: Vanguard Books, 1992); David Gilmartin, *Empire and Islam: Punjab and the Making of Pakistan* (Berkeley: University of California Press, 1988), 39–72, 205–224.

11. David Gilmartin, "Shrines, Succession, and Sources of Moral Authority," in *Moral Conduct and Authority: The Place of Adab in South Asian Islam*, ed. Barbara Daly Metcalf (Berkeley: University of California Press, 1984), 231.

12. Katherine P. Ewing, "The Politics of Sufism: Redefining the Saints of Pakistan," *Journal of Asian Studies*, Vol. XLII, No. 2 (February 1983): 253. See also Saifur Rahman Sherani, "*Ulema* and *Pir* in the Politics of Pakistan," in *Economy and Culture in Pakistan: Migrants and Cities in a Muslim Society*, ed. Hastings Donnan and Pnina Werbner (New York: St. Martin's Press, 1991), 216–246.

13. Nasr, *Islamic Leviathan*, 62–63.

14. Ewing, *Arguing Sainthood*, 43–44.

15. Ibid., 45.

16. Richard M. Eaton, "Court of Man, Court of God," *Contributions to Asian Studies*, Vol. XII (1982): 58. See also Richard M. Eaton, "The Political and Religious Authority of the Shrine of Baba Farid," in *Moral Conduct and Authority: The Place of Adab in South Asian Islam*, ed. Barbara Daly Metcalf (Berkeley: University of California Press, 1984), 44–61; Gilmartin, "Shrines, Succession, and Sources of Moral Authority," 222.

17. On the life and legacy of Baba Farid, see Khaliq Ahmad Nizami, *The Life and Times of Shaikh Farid-ud Din Ganj-i Shakar* (Delhi: Idarah-i Adabiyat-i Delli, 1973).

18. Lieutenant F. Mackeson, "Journal of Captain C.M. Wade's Voyage from Lodiana to Mithankot by the River Satlaj on His Mission to Lahore and Bahawalpur in 1832–1833," *Journal of the Asiatic Society of Bengal*, Vol. 6 (1837): 192; quoted in Eaton, "Court of Man, Court of God," 56.

19. Tahir Jehangir, "Carnage in Pakpattan," *Friday Times*, April 13–19, 2001, 14–15.

20. The scope and scale of the tragedy of 2001 seem to be unprecedented in Pakpattan's seven-hundred-year history. Given the massive crowds that attend the shrine's annual '*urs* commemoration, however, accidents are not uncommon. As Miles Irving noted in 1911, "Some thirty years ago there was an unfortunate occasion on which several lives were lost by the crush of the Door of Paradise, and before British rule, it is said, this was of yearly occurrence." See Miles Irving, "The Shrine of Baba Farid Shakarganj at Pakpattan," *Journal of the Panjab Historical Society* (Lahore), Vol. 1, No. 1 (1911): 70; reprinted in *Punjab Past and Present*, Vol. 7, No. 2 (October 1973): 412. I am grateful to Professor David Gilmartin for providing me with this historical reference.

21. According to the article, the Diwan had delayed the ceremonies while arguing with the representatives of the Awqaf Department, insisting that the shrine should be paid an annuity of 1,500,000 rupees rather than the 150,000 rupees they were promised. See *Jang*, Monday, April 2, 2001, 1.

22. Quoted in Awais Ibrahim, "Who Locked the Door at Shrine?" *Nation*, Wednesday, April 4, 2001, 9.

23. Werbner and Basu, eds., *Embodying Charisma*, 15.

24. Muhammad Haroon, "Tragedy at the Wedding Anniversary," unpublished article, 2.

25. Ibid., 3.

26. On *faizan* and its connection to Sufi doctrine and ritual practice, see Buehler, *Sufi Heirs of the Prophet*, 117–118.

27. Michael S. Roth and Charles G. Salas, "Introduction," in *Disturbing Remains: Memory, History and Crisis in the Twentieth Century*, ed. Michael S. Roth and Charles G. Salas (Los Angeles: Getty Research Institute, 2001), 3.

28. Excerpt from a personal letter transcribed during an interview: October 6, 2001, Kuala Lumpur, Malaysia.

29. Daniel Brown, *Rethinking Tradition in Modern Islamic Thought* (Cambridge: Cambridge University Press, 1996), 75.

30. For an overview of Sufism in the context of the revivalist movements in the colonial era, see Buehler, *Sufi Heirs of the Prophet*, Chapter Eight, "Mediational Sufism and Revivalist Currents in British Colonial India," 168–189. On the Tablighi Jama'at, see the articles in Muhammad Khalid Masud, ed., *Travellers in Faith: Studies of the Tablighi Jama'at as a Transnational Islamic Movement for Faith Renewal* (Leiden: Brill, 2000). See also Barbara Daly Metcalf, "Nationalism, Modernity, and Muslim Identity in India before 1947," in *Nation and Religion: Perspectives on Europe and Asia*, ed. Peter van der Veer and Hartmut Lehmann (Princeton: Princeton University Press, 1999), 129–143.

31. For a comprehensive overview of the history and legacy of the Deoband *madrasa*, see Metcalf, *Islamic Revival in British India*. On Hajji Imdad Allah, see especially Scott A. Kugle, "The Heart of Ritual Is the Body: Anatomy of an Islamic Devotional Manual of the Nineteenth Century," *Journal of Ritual Studies*, Vol. 17, No. 1 (2003): 42–60.

32. On the Barelwi movement, see Usha Sanyal, *Devotional Islam and Politics in British India: Ahmad Riza Khan Barelwi and His Movement, 1870–1920* (New York: Oxford University Press, 1996).

CHAPTER 2   MUSLIM, MYSTIC, AND MODERN: THREE TWENTIETH-CENTURY SUFI MASTERS

1. Wahid Bakhsh Sial Rabbani, *Muqaddama*, in *Tarbiyat al-'ushshaq*, ed. Wahid Bakhsh Sial Rabbani (Karachi: Mahfil-i Zauqiyya, 1958/1983), 36–37.

2. In transliterating the *shaykhs'* names, I have followed the precedent established by the Chishti Sabiri order's English publications: Zauqi, e.g., with a "z" rather than a "dh"; and "Shahidullah" as opposed to "Shahid Allah."

3. Thomas J. Heffernan, *Sacred Biography: Saints and Their Biographers in the Middle Ages* (New York: Oxford University Press, 1988), 97. Scholarship on medieval Christian sainthood offers important theoretical and methodological insights for a study of Muslim sainthood. See, e.g., Peter Brown, *Authority and the Sacred: Aspects of the Christianisation of the Roman World* (Cambridge: Cambridge University Press, 1995); Peter Brown, *Society and the Holy in Late Antiquity* (Berkeley: University of California Press, 1982); Peter Brown, *The Cult of the Saints: Its Rise and Function in Latin Christianity* (Chicago: University of Chicago Press, 1981); Lynda L. Coon, *Sacred Fictions: Holy Women and Hagiography in Late Antiquity* (Philadelphia: University of Pennsylvania Press, 1997); Pierre Delooz, "Towards a Sociological Study of Canonized Sainthood in the Catholic Church," in *Saints and Their Cults: Studies in Religious Sociology, Folklore and History*, ed. Stephen Wilson (Cambridge: Cambridge University Press, 1983), 189–216; Aviad M. Kleinberg, *Prophets in Their Own Country: Living Saints and the Making of Sainthood in the Later Middle Ages* (Chicago: University of Chicago Press, 1992); Frank E. Reynolds and Donald Capps, eds., *The Biographical Process: Studies in the History and Psychology of Religion* (The Hague: Mouton Press, 1976).

4. The idea of habitus is borrowed from Pierre Bourdieu. See Pierre Bourdieu, *The Logic of Practice*, translated by Richard Nice (Palo Alto: Stanford University Press, 1990), 52. For a trenchant critique of habitus, see also Thomas J. Csordas, "Embodiment as a Paradigm for Anthropology," *Ethos*, Vol. 18, No. 1 (March 1990): 10–12.

5. Cornell, *Realm of the Saint*, xviii.

6. Amir Hasan Sijzi, *Morals for the Heart (Fawa'id al-Fu'ad): Conversations of Shaykh Nizam ad-din Awliya Recorded by Amir Hasan Sijzi*, translated and annotated by Bruce B. Lawrence (New York: Paulist Press, 1992), 95.

7. Michel Chodkiewicz, *Seal of the Saints: Prophethood and Sainthood in the Doctrine of Ibn 'Arabi* (Cambridge: Islamic Texts Society, 1993), 22. For a discussion of *walaya* in Ibn Arabi's *Futuhat al-Makkiyya*, see also the article by Souad Hakim, "The Way of *Walaya* (Sainthood or Friendship of God)," *Journal of the Muhyiddin Ibn 'Arabi Society*, Vol. XVIII (1995): 23–40.

8. Cornell, *Realm of the Saint*, xviii.

9. Ibid., xix.

10. Ibid., 273.

11. Bruce B. Lawrence, "Biography and the 17th Century Qadiriya of North India," in *Islam and Indian Regions*, ed. Anna Libera Dallapiccola and Stephanie Zingel-Ave Lallemant (Stuttgart: Franz Steiner Verlag, 1993), 399.

12. Bruce B. Lawrence, "The Chishtiya of Sultanate India: A Case Study of Biographical Complexities in South Asian Islam," in *Charisma and Sacred Biography*, ed. Michael A. Williams, *Journal of the American Academy of*

Religion Thematic Studies, Vol. XLVIII, Nos. 3 and 4 (1982), 53. See also Bruce B. Lawrence, "An Indo-Persian Perspective on the Significance of the Early Persian Sufi Master," paper delivered at a conference on Early Persian Sufism (George Washington University, Washington, DC, 1992), 2.

13. The definitive work of the Prophet Muhammad's life and legacy remains Annemarie Schimmel's classic study: *And Muhammad Is His Messenger: The Veneration of the Prophet in Islamic Piety* (Chapel Hill: University of North Carolina Press, 1985). See also Earle H. Waugh, "The Popular Muhammad: Models in the Interpretation of an Islamic Paradigm," in *Approaches to Islam in Religious Studies*, ed. Richard C. Martin (Tucson: University of Arizona Press, 1985).

14. Wahid Bakhsh Sial Rabbani, *Malfuzat*, in *Tarbiyat al-'ushshaq*, ed. Wahid Bakhsh Sial Rabbani (Karachi: Mahfil-i Zauqiyya, 1958/1983), 403. On the relationship between sainthood and prophecy, see also Ernst, *The Shambhala Guide to Sufism*, 45–63.

15. On the *mir'aj* as a model for Sufi doctrine and practice, see Earle H. Waugh, "Following the Beloved: Muhammad as Model in the Sufi Tradition," in *The Biographical Process: Studies in the History and Psychology of Religion*, ed. Frank E. Reynolds and Donald Capps (The Hague: Mouton Press, 1976), 64–79. For an examination of early *mir'aj* narratives, see also Frederick Stephen Colby, "Constructing an Islamic Ascension Narrative: The Interplay of Official and Popular Culture in Pseudo-Ibn 'Abbas," unpublished doctoral dissertation (Duke University, 2002).

16. Sijzi, *Morals for the Heart*, 81.

17. Carl W. Ernst, *Eternal Garden: Mysticism, History, and Politics at a South Asian Sufi Center* (New York: State University of New York Press, 1992), 63. For a detailed chronicling of the production, dissemination and impact of *malfuzat* texts in pre-Mughal Indian Sufism, see Bruce B. Lawrence's monograph, *Notes from a Distant Flute: The Extant Literature of Pre-Mughal Indian Sufism* (Tehran: Imperial Iranian Academy of Philosophy, 1978).

18. Khaliq Ahmad Nizami, "Introduction," in Sijzi, *Morals for the Heart*, 5.

19. Lawrence, "The Chishtiya of Sultanate India," 52.

20. Carl Ernst and Bruce Lawrence employ this archetypal model in a brief examination of the life of Muhammad Zauqi Shah in their monograph, *Sufi Martyrs of Love*, 81–83, 123–127. Their analysis, however, focuses largely on a single source: the short biography by Sayyid Sharif al-Hasan, *Sirat-i Zauqi*, in *Tarbiyat al-'ushshaq*, compiled by Wahid Bakhsh Sial Rabbani (Karachi: Mahfil-i Zauqiyya, 1958/1983). Furthermore, their study does not include a detailed survey of either Shahidullah Faridi or Wahid Bakhsh Sial Rabbani.

21. Rabbani, *Muqaddama*, 35–84.

22. al-Hasan, *Sirat-i Zauqi*, 429–504.

23. Shahidullah Faridi, *Malfuzat*, in *Tarbiyat al-'ushshaq*, compiled by Wahid Bakhsh Sial Rabbani (Karachi: Mahfil-i Zauqiyya, 1958/1983), 85–134.

24. Rabbani, *Malfuzat*, 135–426, 507–827. Partial English translations of both *Sirat-i Zauqi* and Shahidullah Faridi's *Malfuzat* were published in a special issue of the order's English language journal dedicated to Zauqi Shah. See Tehzeeb un-Nisa Aziz and Mansoor Ahmad Hashmi, eds., *The Sufi Path* (Book 13) (Islamabad: Association of Spiritual Training, Pakistan, 1995). In this chapter, all translations from the original Urdu texts are my own.

25. Wahid Bakhsh Sial Rabbani, *Hajj-i Zauqi* (Karachi: Mahfil-i Zauqiyya, 1951/1993).

26. al-Hasan, *Sirat-i Zauqi*, 478. Zauqi Shah's complete family genealogy is documented on pages 473–477.

27. Rabbani, *Malfuzat*, 732.

28. al-Hasan, *Sirat-i Zauqi*, 480.

29. Ibid., 480. On Hajji Imdad Allah, see Kugle, "The Heart of Ritual Is the Body," 42–60. See also Ernst and Lawrence, *Sufi Martyrs of Love*, 118–121.

30. al-Hasan, *Siraqt-i Zauqi*.

31. Ernst and Lawrence, *Sufi Martyrs of Love*, 125. For details on the history and curriculum at Aligarh as well as the educational philosophy of its founder, Sir Sayyid Ahmad Khan, see David S. Lelyveld, *Aligarh's First Generation: Muslim Solidarity in British India* (Princeton: Princeton University Press, 1978).

32. Rabbani, *Malfuzat*, 377–378, 598–599, 651.

33. Rabbani, *Muqaddama*, 68–69. See also al-Hasan, *Sirat-i Zauqi*, 463.

34. al-Hasan, *Sirat-i Zauqi*, 453–454. For a partial translation of Zauqi Shah's Sufi lexicon, *Sirr-i dilbaran*, see Marcia K. Hermansen, "Visions as 'Good to Think': A Cognitive Approach to Visionary Experience in Islamic Sufi Thought," *Religion*, Vol. 27 (January 1997): 25–43.

35. Rabbani, *Malfuzat*, 790–791. Another discourse notes that due to excessive bodily strength (*jismani hiddat*) and an inner heat, Zauqi Shah was often forced to drink excess amounts of water, even in winters. This emphasis on inner heat, implicitly caused by ascetic spiritual exercises, recalls the Hindu notion of *tapas*. See al-Hasan, *Sirat-i Zauqi*, 456.

36. Rabbani, *Hajj-i Zauqi*, 43. *Hajj-i Zauqi* has been translated into English by Mrs. Tehzeeb un-Nisa Aziz, though it has yet to be published by the Chishti Sabiri order. Mrs. Aziz graciously provided me with a copy of her translation, and this has proved immensely helpful in guiding my own reading of the Urdu original. The translations that follow, however, are my own.

37. al-Hasan, *Sirat-i Zauqi*, 438–439.

38. Ibid., 439; Rabbani, *Hajj-i Zauqi*, 64–65, 89–90. Uways al-Qarani was a Yemeni contemporary of the Prophet Muhammad. Though they never met, Uways is remembered for his deep devotion to the Prophet. As Ernst and Lawrence note, "The nonphysical binding of two like-minded Sufis is called Uwaysi initiation, and it shows up with particular force in the Sabiri branch of the Chishtiyya" (*Sufi Martyrs of Love*, 22).

39. Rabbani, *Malfuzat*, 799–803.

40. Faridi, *Malfuzat*, 119.

41. Rabbani, *Malfuzat*, 792–793.

42. Ibid., 772–774.

43. Ibid., 757–759.

44. Faridi, *Malfuzat*, 119–120. According to Sayyid Sharif al-Hasan's account, Zauqi Shah also received *bay'at* directly from Rashid Ahmad Gangohi in a dream on October 4, 1934. See al-Hasan, *Sirat-i Zauqi*, 494.

45. Rabbani, *Malfuzat*, 796–799; al-Hasan, *Sirat-i Zauqi*, 487–488.

46. al-Hasan, *Sirat-i Zauqi*, 453.

47. Ernst and Lawrence, *Sufi Martyrs of Love*, 124.

48. On Zauqi Shah's interactions with Christians, see Faridi, *Malfuzat*, 132–143 and Rabbani, *Malfuzat*, 573–574. On the *shaykh's* encounters with Hindus, see Rabbani, *Malfuzat*, 350–351, 379. On his views of other South Asian

religious traditions, see also Rabanni, *Malfuzat*, 689 (on Manu) and 746 (on Guru Nanak and the Sikhs).

49. Rabbani, *Malfuzat*, 271–280, 227–228, 712–715.
50. See Sayyid Muhammad Zauqi Shah, *Letters of a Sufi Saint to Jinnah* [A reprint with additions of the English version of *Muzamin-i Zauqi*], ed. Mansoor Hashmi and Sayyid Tahir Maqsood (Lahore: Talifaat-e Shaheedi, 1949/1998), 138–157.
51. al-Hasan, *Sirat-i Zauqi*, 489.
52. Faridi, *Malfuzat*, 99.
53. Ibid., 124–125.
54. Lawrence, "The Chishtiya of Sultanate India," 49.
55. Sijzi, *Morals for the Heart*, 216.
56. Faridi, *Malfuzat*, 131. In the introduction to *Tarbiyat al-'ushshaq*, Wahid Bakhsh Sial Rabbani summarizes Zauqi Shah's teachings on *hijabat* (veils from God), *kashf* (unveiling), and *karamat* (miracles) in detail. See Rabbani, *Muqaddama*, 74–75.
57. Rabbani, *Hajj-i Zauqi*, 91.
58. al-Hasan, *Sirat-i Zauqi*, 435.
59. Ibid., 437.
60. Ibid., 438.
61. Rabbani, *Hajj-i Zauqi*, 104.
62. Faridi, *Malfuzat*, 125.
63. Ibid., 93.
64. al-Hasan, *Sirat-i Zauqi*, 487.
65. Ibid., 452.
66. Faridi, *Malfuzat*, 89.
67. Rabbani, *Hajj-i Zauqi*, 95–96.
68. al-Hasan, *Sirat-i Zauqi*, 445.
69. Faridi, *Malfuzat*, 94.
70. Ibid., 105.
71. al-Hasan, *Sirat-i Zauqi*, 443. See also 451–452.
72. Ibid., 461.
73. Shahidullah Faridi, *Malfuzat-i shaykh*, compiled by Siraj 'Ali Muhammad (Lahore: Qausin Publishers, 1996). *Malfuzat-i shaykh* has also recently been translated into English by Mrs. Tehzeeb un-Nisa Aziz, though the text has yet to be published. I am grateful to Mrs. Aziz for her willingness to share her fine translation with me. Though I am indebted to her work, in what follows the translations (and any mistakes) are my own.
74. Wahid Bakhsh Sial Rabbani translated *Kashf al-mahjub* from its original Persian into Urdu. See Sayyid 'Ali ibn 'Uthman al-Hujwiri, *Kashf al-mahjub*, Urdu translation from Persian with commentary by Wahid Bakhsh Sial Rabbani (Lahore: al-Faisal Publishers, 1995). The text, with extensive commentary, has also recently been translated into English and published by disciples in Kuala Lumpur, Malaysia. See Sayyid 'Ali ibn 'Uthman al-Hujwiri, *The Kashful Mahjub ("Unveiling the Veiled"): The Earliest Persian Treatise on Sufism*, English translation with commentary by Wahid Bakhsh Sial Rabbani (Kuala Lumpur: A.S. Noordeen, 1997).
75. See Aziz and Hashmi, eds., *The Sufi Path* (Book 14), 9.
76. An excerpt from a lecture given by Shaykh Wahid Bakhsh Rabbani in January 1995 suggests that Faruq Ahmad met Ashraf 'Ali Thanawi on his own.

According to this account, Faruq came to India by himself in 1937, traveling first to Tagore's Ashram in Calcutta and then to Delhi where he spent time at the shrine of Nizam ad-Din Awliya. See Aziz and Hashmi, eds., *The Sufi Path* (Book 14), 53. For broader discussions of Ashraf 'Ali Thanawi and his legacy at Deoband, see Metcalf, *Islamic Revival in British India;* Marcia K. Hermansen, "Rewriting Sufi Identity in the 20th Century: The Biographical Approaches of Maulana Ashraf 'Ali Thanvi (d. 1943) and Khwaja Hasan Nizami (d. 1955)," an unpublished paper presented at the American Academy of Religion Conference, November 1997.

77. Aziz and Hashmi, eds., *The Sufi Path* (Book 14), 10.
78. On Frithjof Schuon and the Sufi Perennialist school in Europe and the United States, see Carl W. Ernst, "Traditionalism, the Perennial Philosophy and Islamic Studies," *Middle East Studies Association,* Bulletin 28 (1994): 176–180.
79. For Shahidullah's lessons on Qur'an interpretation, see Faridi, *Malfuzat-i shaykh,* 58–59, 72–73, 86–89. The text also includes discourses on *hadith* (52) and references to premodern Sufi masters that parallel those of Zauqi Shah, including important allusions to Hajji Imdad Allah's manual, *Zia al-qulub* (20–21, 154–155).
80. Faridi, *Malfuzat-i shaykh,* 77.
81. In one discourse in *Malfuzat-i shaykh,* e.g., Shahidullah Faridi discusses at some length a number of scientific subjects, including evolution (251–253, 256–257); scientific inquiry and invention (254–255); the compatibility of prophecy and science (254); and Islam as a "natural religion" (259–260).
82. Aziz and Hashmi, eds., *The Sufi Path* (Book 14), 10.
83. Rabbani, *Malfuzat,* 664–665. Ernst traces the history and Sufi legacy of Daulatabad and Khuldabad in *Eternal Garden.*
84. Faridi, *Malfuzat-i shaykh,* 116.
85. Rabbani, *Malfuzat,* 400.
86. Ibid., 663. After emigrating to Pakistan, Shahidullah returned to India only once in his life: for pilgrimage in 1962 (Aziz and Hashmi, eds., *The Sufi Path* (Book 14), 39).
87. Shahidullah Faridi's *Wasyat nama* (final will and testament) was published in English in the back of an early Urdu version of *Malfuzat-i shaykh.* In *Tarbiyat al-'ushshaq,* Muhammad Zauqi Shah asserts that neither *khilafat* nor prophecy is possible for women. See Rabbani, *Malfuzat,* 683.
88. Faridi, *Malfuzat-i shaykh,* 236.
89. Ibid., 153. Elsewhere Shahidullah evokes the Prophet Muhammad, Khwaja Mu'in ad-Din Chishti, and Hazrat Maryam (the mother of Jesus) in discussing marital responsibilities. See Faridi, *Malfuzat-i shaykh,* 114–115.
90. Rabbani, *Malfuzat,* 731–732.
91. The will of Shahidullah Faridi, *Wasyat nama,* 1.
92. Faridi, *Malfuzat-i shaykh,* 135–136.
93. Ibid., 135.
94. Aziz and Hashmi, eds., *The Sufi Path* (Book 14), 1.
95. Ibid., 53.
96. Ibid., 9.
97. Ibid., 10.
98. Wahid Bakhsh Sial Rabbani, *Islamic Sufism: The Science of Flight to God, in God, with God, by God and Union and Communion with God, also Showing the*

Tremendous Sufi Influence on Christian and Hindu Mystics and Mysticism (Bahawalpur, Pakistan: Justice Muhammad Akbar Academy, 1995), 417.

99. Aziz and Hashmi, eds., *The Sufi Path* (Book 14), 9.
100. The will Shahidullah Faridi's, in Shahidullah Faridi, *Wasyat nama* [An English translation of Shahidullah Faridi's last will and testament], reprinted in an early addition of *Malfuzat-i shaykh*, no date.
101. Aziz and Hashmi, eds., *The Sufi Path* (Book 14), 17.
102. Rabbani, *Islamic Sufism*, 98.
103. Ewing, *Arguing Sainthood*, 5.
104. Buehler, *Sufi Heirs of the Prophet*, 192.
105. Khwaja Hasan Nizami is mentioned twice in Zauqi Shah's discourses in *Tarbiyat al-'ushshaq* (Rabbani, *Malfuzat*, 336, 380). On Khwaja Hasan Nizami, see Marcia K. Hermansen, "Common Themes, Uncommon Texts: Hazrat Inayat Khan (1882–1927) and Khwaja Hasan Nizami (1878–1955)," in *A Pearl in the Wine: Essays on the Life, Music and Sufism of Hazrat Inayat Khan*, ed., Pirzade Zia Inayat Khan (New Lebanon, NY: Omega Publications, 2001), 323–353. See also Ernst and Lawrence, *Sufi Martyrs of Love*, 113–118.

CHAPTER 3   IMAGINING SUFISM: THE PUBLICATION OF CHISHTI SABIRI IDENTITY

1. Lawrence Grossberg, "Identity and Cultural Studies: Is That All There Is?" in *Questions of Cultural Identity*, ed. Stuart Hall and Paul du Gay (London: Sage Publications, 1997), 89.
2. Sudipta Kaviraj, "The Imaginary Institution of India," in *Subaltern Studies VII: Writings on South Asian History and Society*, ed. Partha Chatterjee and Gyanendra Pandey (Delhi: Oxford University Press, 1992), 33.
3. Benedict Anderson, *Imagined Communities: Reflections on the Origin and Spread of Nationalism* (London: Verso, 1983/1991), 6, 44–45. On the link between ideology and print media, see also Lawrence, *Defenders of God*, 72–73.
4. Salvatore, *Islam and the Political Discourse of Modernity*, 138.
5. On the role of the mass media in the construction of colonial and postcolonial identities in South Asia, see Peter van der Veer, *Religious Nationalism: Hindus and Muslims in India* (Berkeley: University of California Press, 1994); Carol A. Breckenridge, ed., *Consuming Modernity: Public Culture in a South Asian World* (Minneapolis: University of Minnesota Press, 1995); David Ludden, ed., *Contesting the Nation: Religion, Community, and the Politics of Democracy in India* (Philadelphia: University of Pennsylvania Press, 1996).
6. Francis Robinson, "Islam and the Impact of Print in South Asia," in *The Transmission of Knowledge in South Asia: Essays on Education, Religion, History and Politics*, ed. Nigel Crook (Delhi: Oxford University Press, 1996), 63.
7. Ibid., 73–75. See also Metcalf, *Islamic Revival in British India*, 206–210.
8. Eickelman and Anderson, "Redefining Muslim Publics," 2. For comparative analysis, see Richard P. Mitchell's discussion of the Egyptian Muslim Brotherhood, *The Society of the Muslim Brothers* (New York: Oxford University Press, 1969/1993); Brinkley Messick's masterful study of the negotiation of *shari'a* among the *'ulama* of Yemen, *The Calligraphic State: Textual Domination and History in a Muslim Society* (Berkeley: University of

California Press, 1993); Serif Mardin's examination of the legacy of the famous Islamist ideologue and reformist of Turkey, *Religion and Social Change in Modern Turkey: The Case of Bediuzzaman Said Nursi* (Albany: State University of New York Press, 1989).

9. Muhsin Mahdi, "From the Manuscript Age to the Age of Print Books," in *The Book in the Islamic World: The Written Word and Communication in the Middle East*, ed. George N. Atiyeh (Albany: State University of New York Press, 1995), 6–7. For a comparative study of contemporary Egypt, see also Julian Johansen, *Sufism and Islamic Reform in Egypt: The Battle for Islamic Tradition* (Oxford: Clarendon Press, 1996).

10. Carl W. Ernst, "Sufism in Print: The Pakistani Sources," unpublished proposal for the American Institute of Pakistani Studies Research Grant, 1998, 3.

11. Buehler, *Sufi Heirs of the Prophet*, 194–199.

12. Carl W. Ernst, "Between Orientalism and Fundamentalism: Problematizing the Teaching of Sufism," in *Teaching Islam*, ed. Brannon M. Wheeler (New York: Oxford University Press, 2003), 120.

13. On Sayyid Mehr Ali Shah of Golra, see especially Gilmartin, *Empire and Islam*, 58–59. On Khwaja Hasan Nizami, see Ernst and Lawrence, *Sufi Martyrs of Love*, 113–118. On Jama'at 'Ali Shah, see Gilmartin, *Empire and Islam*, 59–61, 103–107; Buehler, *Sufi Heirs of the Prophet*, 190–223.

14. Ernst and Lawrence, *Sufi Martyrs of Love*, 129.

15. Marshall G.S. Hodgson, *The Venture of Islam: Conscience and History in a World Civilization*. Vol. 3, *The Gunpowder Empires and Modern Times* (Chicago: University of Chicago Press, 1974), 176–222.

16. The following taxonomy of Indo-Muslim schools of thought—modernists, traditionalists, Islamists—is based on Marilyn Robinson Waldman, "Tradition as a Modality of Change: Islamic Examples," *History of Religions*, Vol. 25, No. 4 (1986): 318–340.

17. Sami Zubaida, *Islam, the People and the State: Essays on Political Ideas and Movements in the Middle East* (New York: Routledge, 1989), 157.

18. Zaman, *The Ulama in Contemporary Islam*, 86.

19. al-Hasan, *Sirat-i Zauqi*, 483–484. For an abbreviated but insightful discussion of Zauqi Shah's literary legacy, see also Ernst and Lawrence, *Sufi Martyrs of Love*, 81–83, 123–127.

20. Sayyid Muhammad Zauqi Shah, *Sirr-i dilbaran* (Karachi: Mahfil-i Zauqiyya, 1951/1985).

21. al-Hasan, *Sirat-i Zauqi*, 491–492.

22. Ibid., 490.

23. For Zauqi Shah's critique of Wahhabi doctrine, see Rabbani, *Malfuzat*, 667, 726–727, 794. For his views of Mawdudi, see "Tarikh-i Abu al-'Ala," in Sayyid Muhammad Zauqi Shah, *Muzamin-i Zauqi*, compiled by Wahid Bakhsh Sial Rabbani (Karachi: Mahfil-i Zauqia, 1949/1975), 279–302.

24. Sayyid Muhammad Zauqi Shah, "Sufism," originally published in *Islamic Review* in London, 1933; reprinted in *Letters of a Sufi Saint to Jinnah* [A reprint with additions of the English version of *Muzamin-i Zauqi*], ed. Mansoor Hashmi and Sayyid Tahir Maqsood (Lahore: Talifaat-e Shaheedi, 1949/1998), 177.

25. al-Hasan, *Sirat-i Zauqi*, 454. Mawdudi purchased *Tarjuman al-Qur'an* in Hyderabad in September 1932. He remained the journal's sole editor until 1979 and wrote most of the articles himself, though he did solicit articles as

well. See Seyyed Vali Reza Nasr, *Mawdudi and the Making of Islamic Revivalism* (New York: Oxford University Press, 2001), 28.

26. Ernst and Lawrence, *Sufi Martyrs of Love*, 125.

27. The text was completed in Ajmer on April 17, 1943. The Urdu version is available as "Hindi ki Aryon ki asl par tanqid-i jadid," in Zauqi Shah, *Muzamin-i Zauqi*, 313–337. The English version has been reprinted in Zauqi Shah, *Letters of a Sufi Saint to Jinnah*, 93–108.

28. Rabbani, *Malfuzat*, 746.

29. Ernst and Lawrence, *Sufi Martyrs of Love*, 205, footnote 58.

30. Wahid Bakhsh Sial Rabbani, *Reactivization of Islam* (Lahore: Bazm-i Ittehad al-Muslimin, 1988), 97–107. See also Wahid Bakhsh Sial Rabbani, *The Magnificent Power Potential of Pakistan* [An English translation of *Pakistan ki azim ush-shan difai quwwat*], translation and commentary by Brigadier Muhammad Asghar (Lahore: al-Faisal Publishers, 2000), 420–428, 562

31. On Muhammad 'Ali Jinnah and the history of the Pakistan movement, see especially Akbar S. Ahmed, *Jinnah, Pakistan and Islamic Identity: The Search for Saladin* (New York: Routledge, 1997); Ayesha Jalal, *The Sole Spokesman: Jinnah, the Muslim League and the Demand for Pakistan* (Cambridge: Cambridge University Press, 1994).

32. Zauqi Shah, *Letters of a Sufi Saint to Jinnah*, 17.

33. al-Hasan, *Sirat-i Zauqi*, 501.

34. Rabbani, *Muqaddama*, 76–77.

35. Wahid Bakhsh Sial Rabbani, *Maqam-i Ganj-i Shakkar* (Lahore: al-Faisal Publishers, 1994), 26.

36. Shahidullah Faridi, *Inner Aspects of Faith* (Karachi: Mahfil-i Zauqiyya, 1979/1986; reprint edition, Kuala Lumpur: A.S. Noordeen (2nd edition), 1993); Shahidullah Faridi, *Everyday Practice in Islam* (Karachi: Mahfil-i Zauqiyya, 1970/1999); Shahidullah Faridi, *Spirituality in Religion*, compiled by Siraj 'Ali Muhammad (Lahore: Talifaat-e Shaheedi, 1999); Shahidullah Faridi, *The Moral Message of God and His Prophet* (Karachi: Mahfil-i Zauqiyya, 1973/1995).

37. The final will and testament (*Wasyat nama*) of Faridi, *Wasyat nama*, 3–4.

38. Faridi, *Malfuzat-i shaykh*, 120–121, 140–141, 149–150, 212–214.

39. Rabbani, *Maqam-i Ganj-i Shakkar*; 'Abd ar-Rahman Chishti (d. 1683), *Mir'at al-asrar*, Urdu translation from Persian by Wahid Bakhsh Sial Rabbani (Lahore: Ziya al-Qur'an Publications, 1993); al-Hujwiri, *Kashf al-mahjub*.

40. Wahid Bakhsh Sial Rabbani, *Mushahada-i haqq* (Karachi: Mahfil-i Zauqiyya, 1974; reprinted Lahore: al-Faisal Publishers, 1995).

41. Rabbani, *Islamic Sufism*, 4.

42. Ibid., 113.

43. Ibid., 116.

44. Ibid., 117.

45. Ibid., 118.

46. Ibid., 123.

47. Ibid., 126.

48. Ibid.

49. Ibid., 260.

50. On Nadwi, see Muhammad Qasim Zaman, "Arabic, the Arab Middle East, and the Definition of Muslim Identity in Twentieth Century India," *Journal of the Royal Asiatic Society*, Series 3, 8, 1 (1998): 59–81. For Nadwi's critique

of Mawlana Mawdudi, see Nasr, *Mawdudi and the Making of Islamic Revivalism*, 58–59.

51. Rabbani, *Islamic Sufism*, 130. Wahid Bakhsh expounds on this important doctrine in several publications. See especially Wahid Bakhsh Sial Rabbani, *Wahdat al-wujud o wahdat ash-shuhud* (Lahore: Bazm-i Ittehad al-Muslimin, 1988); Rabbani, *Maqam-i Ganj-i Shakkar*, 212–231. Zauqi Shah also wrote an essay by the same title in *Muzamin-i Zauqi*, 107–115.

52. Ibid., 138. On the distinction between these complex metaphysical principles, see Schimmel, *Mystical Dimensions of Islam*, 267–268.

53. Rabbani, *Islamic Sufism*, 132.

54. Ibid., 130.

55. Ibid., 139–140.

56. Ibid., 143. *Islamic Sufism* contains a length essay of Muhammad Zauqi Shah entitled, "The Sufi Path," in which the spiritual path from *fana' fi Allah* (absorption in God) to *baqa' bi Allah* (subsistence in God) is discussed in detail. See pages 73–112.

57. Ibid., 143–144. On ecstatic expressions (*shathiyat*) and the debates over Islamic orthodoxy and heresy, see Carl W. Ernst, *Words of Ecstasy in Sufism* (Albany: State University of New York Press, 1985).

58. Rabbani, *Islamic Sufism*, 145–146.

59. Ibid., 146.

60. Ibid.

61. Ibid., 148.

62. Ibid., 153.

63. Ibid., 154.

64. Ewing, *Arguing Sainthood*, 94. See also pages 66–67, 126.

65. Rabbani, *Islamic Sufism*, 9.

66. Ibid., 6.

67. Ibid., 11.

68. Ibid., 13.

69. Ibid., 4.

70. Ibid., 304.

71. Ibid., 158–159.

72. Ibid., 282.

73. Ibid., 1.

74. Ibid., 9 (emphasis in original text).

75. Ibid., 32–39.

76. Ibid., 39–57. Maurice Bucaille (b. 1920) published his book in 1976 in French under the title *Le Bible, le coran et la science*.

77. On the life and legacy of al-Afghani, see the insightful study by Nikki Keddie, *An Islamic Response to Imperialism: Political and Religious Writings of Sayyid Jamal ad-Din "al-Afghani"* (Berkeley: University of California Press, 1968/1983). On Sayyid Ahmad Khan, see especially Lelyveld, *Aligarh's First Generation*. For the clearest exposition of Muhammad Iqbal's thought, see his classic *The Reconstruction of Religious Thought in Islam* (Lahore: Sh. Muhammad Ashraf, 1934/1982). For a survey of the life and teachings of Said Nursi, see Mardin, *Religion and Social Change in Modern Turkey*.

78. Talal Asad, "Religion, Nation-State, Secularism," in *Nation and Religion: Perspectives on Europe and Asia*, ed. Pater van der Veer and Hartmut Lehmann (Princeton: Princeton University Press, 1999), 191.

79. Wahid Bakhsh Sial Rabbani, *Pakistan ki azim ush-shan difai quwwat* (Lahore: Bazm-i Ittehad al-Muslimin, 1986). The original Urdu text was translated into English at Wahid Bakhsh's request by a senior disciple, Brigadier Muhammad Asghar. In what follows, I quote from Asghar's apt translation. Many of the book's arguments are summarized in another (and much shorter) English text by Rabbani, *Reactivization of Islam*.

80. Nasr offers an overview of the history and enduring legacy of Zia al-Haq in his comparative study *Islamic Leviathan*. For a broader survey of the Afghan war of the 1980s and its long-term implications for Pakistan's domestic politics, see also the works of Ahmed Rashid (*Taliban* and *Jihad*).

81. Rabbani, *The Magnificent Power Potential of Pakistan*, 479–480.

82. Partha Chatterjee, *The Nation and Its Fragments: Colonial and Postcolonial Histories* (Princeton: Princeton University Press, 1993), 49.

83. Zaman, "Arabic, the Arab Middle East, and the Definition of Muslim Identity in Twentieth Century India," 80.

84. Rabbani, *The Magnificent Power Potential of Pakistan*, 475.

85. Ibid., 501.

86. Ibid., 527 (emphasis added).

87. Ibid., 3–4.

88. Ibid., 51.

89. Ibid., 36. *Jihad* is a misunderstood and maligned concept, especially in the wake of the attacks of September 11, 2001. For further insights on this concept, see especially Vincent J. Cornell, "*Jihad*: Islam's Struggle for Truth," *Gnosis Magazine* (Fall 1991): 18–23; Gilles Kepel, *Jihad: The Trail of Political Islam* (Cambridge, MA: Harvard University Press, 2002).

90. Rabbani, *The Magnificent Power Potential of Pakistan*, 15.

91. Ibid., 383.

92. Ibid., 431.

93. Ibid., 382, 449. Clearly, Wahid Bakhsh views the implementation of *shari'a* as the first step to social reform, but he provides no specific details on the codification, interpretation, and institutionalization of Islamic law.

94. Ibid., 441–443, 451, 467.

95. Ibid., 453–466. The debate over *riba* remains a hotly contested issue in Pakistan's domestic politics. Calls for its elimination remain a central item on the political platform of Pakistan's coalition of religious parties.

96. Ibid., 552–562. Wahid Bakhsh's suggestions for military reform are sweeping. He calls for military conscription and civil defense training for every male citizen of Pakistan between the ages of sixteen and sixty; the issuing of licenses for personal weapons; increased support for a national defense industry and military research; and the development of a "Common Defense Council of Islam" to coordinate, finance, and implement a "common foreign policy of the Muslim states."

97. Ibid., 435–441. Wahid Bakhsh provides a broad outline of "Islamic democracy" but few details on its practical implementation.

98. Nasr, *Mawdudi and the Making of Islamic Revivalism*, 87.

99. Rabbani, *The Magnificent Power Potential of Pakistan*, 199.

100. Ibid., 407.

101. Ibid., 428–429, 433–434. For an insightful study of the history and dramatic spread of sectarian politics and violence in contemporary Pakistan, see

Zaman, *The Ulama in Contemporary Islam*, Chapter Five, "Refashioning Identities," 111–143.

102. Ibid., 248–249.
103. Eickelman and Anderson, eds., *New Media in the Muslim World*, 9.
104. The quotation from Shahidullah Faridi is found in a handwritten forward (dated 1393 Hijri/1973) that is reproduced in the introduction to *Tarbiyat al-'ushshaq*, 6.
105. Jon W. Anderson, "The Internet and Islam's New Interpreters," in *New Media in the Muslim World: The Emerging Public Sphere*, ed. Dale F. Eickelman and Jon W. Anderson (Bloomington: Indiana University Press, 1999), 49. For insight on the growing importance of the Internet among contemporary Chishti groups, see also Ernst and Lawrence, *Sufi Martyrs of Love*, 143–145.
106. Dale F. Eickelman, "Communication and Control in the Middle East," in *New Media in the Muslim World: The Emerging Public Sphere*, ed. Dale F. Eickelman and Jon W. Anderson (Bloomington: Indiana University Press, 1999), 38.
107. Blank, *Mullahs on the Mainframe*, 176.
108. Lawrence, *Defenders of God*, 17.
109. Sirriyeh, *Sufis and Anti-Sufis*, 89.
110. Zaman, *The Ulama in Contemporary Islam*, 180.
111. Gayatri Chakravorty Spivak, "Can the Subaltern Speak?" in *Colonial Discourse and Post-Colonial Theory*, ed. Patrick Williams and Laura Chrisman (New York: Columbia University Press, 1994), 76.
112. Kaviraj, "The Imaginary Institution of India," 36.
113. Homi K. Bhabha, *The Location of Culture* (New York: Routledge, 1994), 37.

Chapter 4   Teaching Sufism: Networks of Community and Discipleship

1. Barbara Daly Metcalf, "Introduction," in *Moral Conduct and Authority: The Place of Adab in South Asian Islam*, ed. Barbara Daly Metcalf (Berkeley: University of California Press, 1984), 9–10.
2. Ernst and Lawrence, *Sufi Martyrs of Love*, 25–26. See also Mohammad Ajmal, "A Note on *Adab* in the *Murshid-Murid* Relationship," in *Moral Conduct and Authority: The Place of Adab in South Asian Islam*, ed. Barbara Daly Metcalf (Berkeley: University of California Press, 1984), 241–251; Gerhard Bowering, "The *Adab* Literature of Classical Sufism: Ansari's Code of Conduct," in *Moral Conduct and Authority: The Place of Adab in South Asian Islam*, ed. Barbara Daly Metcalf (Berkeley: University of California Press, 1984), 62–87; Ernst, *The Shambhala Guide to Sufism*, 145–146.
3. For perspectives on the roles of women in Sufi practice, see especially Shemeem Abbas, *The Female Voice in Sufi Ritual: Devotional Practices of Pakistan and India* (Austin: University of Texas Press, 2002); Patricia Jeffery, *Frogs in a Well: Indian Women in Purdah* (London: Zed Press, 1979); Annemarie Schimmel, *My Soul Is a Woman-The Feminine in Islam* (New York: Continuum, 1997). For historical perspective, see also Abu 'Abd ar-Rahman as-Sulami, *Early Sufi Women (Dhikr an-niswa al-muta 'abbidat as-sufiyyat)*, translation and commentary by Rkia E. Cornell (Louisville: Fons Vitae, 1999).

4. Wahid Bakhsh publicly defends the honor and sanctity of the Prophet's family lineage in his book '*Azamat-i Ahl-i Bait-i Rasul* (Lahore: al-Faisal Publishers, 1994). See also Rabbani, *Malfuzat*, 629–630. For a broad discussion of the role of sectarian identities and organizations in the politics of contemporary Pakistan, see Zaman, *The Ulama in Contemporary Islam*, especially 118–131.

5. This personal letter was shared with me during an interview recorded on October 6, 2001 at a private home in Kuala Lumpur. See also the discourse by Shahidullah Faridi, "A Balance between Spiritual and Worldly Obligations," in Faridi, *Spirituality in Religion*, 93–99.

6. On the distinction between "inner" and "outer" knowledge, see the discourses of Shahidullah Faridi in *Spirituality in Religion*, in particular the lectures entitled "Sufis" (41–42) and "Signs" (57–58).

7. Ernst, *The Shambhala Guide to Sufism*, 26.

8. Quoted in Schimmel, *Mystical Dimensions of Islam*, 99.

9. Shahidullah Faridi, "The Spiritual Psychology of Islam," in Faridi, *Inner Aspects of Faith*, 93. For an overview of contemporary Chishti Sabiri doctrine regarding the states and stations of the path, see Zauqi Shah, "*Suluk*," in Zauqi Shah, *Sirr-i dilbaran*, 199–203; Zauqi Shah, "Sufism," 164–182.

10. Rabbani, *Islamic Sufism*, 61. See also Rabbani, *Muqaddama*, 56–57.

11. Ashraf 'Ali Thanawi, quoted in *Perfecting Women: Maulana Ashraf 'Ali Thanawi's Bishishti Zewar*, translated with commentary by Barbara Daly Metcalf (Berkeley: University of California Press, 1990), 200. By contrast, Shah Waliullah (d. 1762), the famous eighteenth-century Naqshbandi Sufi master of Delhi, lists seven criteria of a perfected *shaykh* in his text *Al-qawl al-jamil*, Urdu translation by Khurram 'Ali. 2nd ed. *Shifa' al'alil* (Karachi: Educational Press, 1974). See Buehler, *Sufi Heirs of the Prophet*, 152.

12. Rabbani, *Malfuzat*, 290.

13. Shahidullah Faridi, "Baiat," in Faridi, *Inner Aspects of Faith*, 66. Zauqi Shah also discusses Sufi initiation in his spiritual dictionary *Sirr-i dilbaran*. See the entries under "*Shaykh*" (239–240) and "Sufism" (167–168, 171).

14. Zauqi Shah, "Sufism," 164–182.

15. Faridi, "Baiat," 70. For details on the multiple stages of *fana'* from the Naqshbandi perspective, see Buehler, *Sufi Heirs of the Prophet*, Chapter Six, "Bonding the Heart with the Shaykh," 131–146.

16. Rabbani, *Malfuzat*, 242–243. See also Zauqi Shah, "*Fana' wa baqa'*," in Zauqi Shah, *Sirr-i dilbaran*, 277.

17. Buehler, *Sufi Heirs of the Prophet*, 155. The term in Arabic is *bay'a*, but here I follow the Persian rendering (*bay'at*) favored by contemporary Chishti Sabiri disciples. For details on the history and symbolism of the Sufi initiation ritual, see Buehler, *Sufi Heirs of the Prophet*, 155–163; Ernst, *The Shambhala Guide to Sufism*, 141–146; Ernst and Lawrence, *Sufi Martyrs of Love*, 24–25.

18. Faridi, "Baiat," 72. For an expanded discussion of *bay'at* see especially Zauqi Shah, *Sirr-i dilbaran*, 92–109.

19. Contemporary firsthand accounts of the Sufi master-disciple relationship are rare. Among the more accessible and insightful works are a number of spiritual diaries written by women. See especially Michaela Ozelsel, *Forty Days: The Diary of a Traditional Solitary Sufi Retreat* (Brattleboro, VT: Threshold Books, 1996); Irina Tweedie, *Daughter of Fire: A Diary of Spiritual Training with a Sufi Master* (Nevada City, CA: Blue Dolphin Publishing, 1986). For a more scholarly account that explores *pir-murid* relations through the lens of

sociolinguistics, see Frances Trix, *Spiritual Discourse: Learning with an Islamic Master* (Philadelphia: University of Pennsylvania Press, 1993). For a comparative study of the contemporary Chishti order, see also Desiderio Pinto, *Piri-Muridi Relationship: A Study of the Nizamuddin Dargah* (Delhi: Manohar, 1995). Pinto's analysis is valuable more for its ethnographic material—the book offers lengthy quotes from contemporary Chishti *murids*—than its interpretive analysis.

20. Rabbani, *Malfuzat*, 319.
21. Zauqi Shah, "Sufism," 171. See also Faridi, "Baiat," 69–70.
22. Carl W. Ernst, "Mystical Language and the Teaching Context in Early Lexicons of Sufism," in *Mysticism and Language*, ed. Steven T. Katz (New York: Oxford University Press, 1992), 191. Frances Trix provides a detailed ethnography of the importance and nuances of language in Sufi pedagogy in her book *Spiritual Discourse*. Trix's monograph focuses on a contemporary Albanian Bektashi community in Michigan.
23. Buehler, *Sufi Heirs of the Prophet*, 138.
24. Trix, *Spiritual Discourse*, 150.
25. Faridi, "Baiat," 70. See also Schimmel, *Mystical Dimensions of Islam*, 103; Buehler, *Sufi Heirs of the Prophet*, 133.
26. Zauqi Shah, "Sufism," 168. See also Rabbani, *Malfuzat*, 790.
27. This is an extract from a personal letter communicated during a personal interview in Kuala Lumpur, Malaysia on October 6, 2001.
28. Rabbani, *Malfuzat*, 205.
29. Ashraf 'Ali Thanawi, quoted in *Perfecting Women*, 200. Thanawi's expanded list of thirteen rules for Sufi adepts appears on pages 200–202. See also Ajmal, "A Note on *Adab* in the *Murshid-Murid* Relationship," 243–244.
30. Rabbani, *Malfuzat*, 663.
31. Sijzi, *Morals for the Heart*, 143. See also Ernst and Lawrence, *Sufi Martyrs of Love*, 19.
32. Katherine P. Ewing, "Dreams from a Saint: Anthropological Atheism and the Temptation to Believe," *American Anthropologist*, Vol. 96 (1994): 578. For an insightful ethnographic analysis of contemporary *pir-murid* relationships, see also Katherine P. Ewing, "The Modern Businessman and the Pakistani Saint: The Interpenetration of Worlds," in *Manifestations of Sainthood in Islam*, ed. Grace Martin Smith (Istanbul: Isis Press, 1993), 69–84.
33. Rabbani, *Malfuzat*, 613.
34. Narayan, *Storytellers, Saints and Scoundrels*, 247.
35. On the importance of silence in Sufi training, see Trix, *Spiritual Discourse*, 122.
36. Buehler, *Sufi Heirs of the Prophet*, 148–149.
37. Rabbani, *Malfuzat*, 172.
38. Faridi, "*Baiat*," 69.
39. Zauqi Shah echoes this belief in *Tarbiyat al-'ushshaq*: "The friends of God continue to progress even after death. There is no limit to the divine essence [*dhat*], so there is no limit to progress" (Rabbani, *Malfuzat*, 305).
40. Faridi, *Malfuzat*, 108.
41. Rabbani, *Malfuzat*, 244.
42. On the life and legacy of Khwaja Hasan Nizami, see Ernst and Lawrence, *Sufi Martyrs of Love*, 113–188. See also Hermansen, "Common Themes, Uncommon Contexts," 323–353.
43. The final will and testament of Faridi, *Wasyat nama*, 3–4.

44. Rabbani, *Malfuzat*, 642.
45. The final will and testament of Faridi, *Wasyat nama*, 2.
46. Bell, *Ritual Theory, Ritual Practice*, 183.
47. Ewing, *Arguing Sainthood*, 163.
48. The final will and testament of Faridi, *Wasyat nama*, 2–3.
49. Chakrabarty, *Provincializing Europe*, 243.
50. Ibid., 113.
51. Zauqi Shah, "Sufism," 171.

CHAPTER 5 EXPERIENCING SUFISM: THE DISCIPLINE OF RITUAL PRACTICE

1. This is a selection from a personal letter narrated during an interview on October 6, 2001 in Kuala Lumpur. Wahid Bakhsh provides a detailed overview of the theory and practice of *suluk* in *Mushahada-i haqq*. See in particular the chapter entitled "*Suluk illa Allah ya'ni tariq-i husul-i maqsad-i hayat*" ("The Spiritual Journey to God, or the Path to Attaining the Purpose of Life"), 82–134.

2. Michel Foucault, "Technologies of the Self," in *Technologies of the Self: A Seminar with Michel Foucault*, ed. Luther H. Martin, Huck Gutman, and Patrick H. Hutton (Amherst: University of Massachusetts Press, 1988), 18. See also Michel Foucault, "About the Beginning of the Hermeneutics of the Self," in *Religion and Culture*, ed. Jeremy R. Carrette (New York: Routledge, 1999), 158–181. For a critique, see Ladelle McWhorter, "Culture or Nature?: The Function of the Term 'Body' in the Work of Michel Foucault," *Journal of Philosophy*, Vol. 86, No. 11 (November 1989): 608–614.

3. Michael Jackson, "Knowledge of the Body," *Man*, Vol. 18, No. 12 (June 1983): 337. Scholars in various academic disciplines have studied the role of the body in ritual practice. For an overview, see especially Catherine Bell, "The Ritual Body," in Bell, *Ritual Theory, Ritual Practice*, 94–117; Thomas J. Csordas, ed., *Embodiment and Experience: The Existential Ground of Culture and Self* (Cambridge: Cambridge University Press, 1994); Csordas, "Embodiment as a Paradigm for Anthropology," 5–47; Margaret Lock, "Cultivating the Body: Anthropology and Epistemologies of Bodily Practice and Knowledge," *Annual Review of Anthropology*, Vol. 22 (1993): 133–155.

4. An extract from a personal letter dated March 2, 1932, republished in Zauqi Shah, *Letters of a Sufi Saint to Jinnah*, 160–161.

5. Kugle, "The Heart of Ritual Is the Body," 42. On the application of ritual studies to Sufi practice, see also Qamar-ul Huda, *Striving for Divine Union: Spiritual Exercises for Suhrawardi Sufis* (London: Routledge Curzon, 2003), 83–89.

6. Ibn Khaldun, *The Muqaddimah: An Introduction to History*, translated by Franz Rosenthal (Princeton: Princeton University Press, 1967), 81. For a detailed examination of Ibn Khaldun's description of dreams, see also Gordon E. Pruett, "Through a Glass Darkly: Knowledge of the Self in Dreams in Ibn Khaldun's *Muqaddimah*, " *Muslim World*, Vol. LXXV (January 1985): 29–44.

7. On the importance of dreams in classical Islam and the historical development of the science of *ta'bir*, see especially John C. Lamoreaux, *The Early Muslim Tradition of Dream Interpretation* (Albany: State University of New York Press, 2002). See also Taufiq Fahd, "*Ru'ya*: The Meaning of Dreams," in

Encyclopedia of Islam, Vol. VIII, ed. C.E. Bosworth et al. (Leiden: E.J. Brill, 1995), 645–647; Taufiq Fahd, "The Dream in Medieval Islamic Society," in *The Dream and Human Societies*, ed. G.E. von Grunebaum and Roger Caillois (Berkeley: University of California Press, 1966), 351–363; Leah Kindberg, "Literal Dreams and Prophetic Hadiths in Classical Islam: A Comparison of Two Ways of Legitimation," *Der Islam*, Vol. LXX (1993), 279–300; Miklos Maroth, "The Science of Dreams in Islamic Culture," *Jerusalem Studies in Arabic and Islam*, Vol. 20 (1996): 229–238.

8. Bernd Radtke and John O'Kane, trans. and eds., *The Concept of Sainthood in Early Islamic Mysticism: Two Works by al-Hakim al-Tirmidhi* (Richmond, Surrey: Curzon Press, 1996), 9. For an overview of the importance of dreams in Sufi theory and practice, see also Hermansen, "Visions as 'Good to Think,' " 25–43.

9. Ruzbihan Baqli, *The Unveiling of Secrets: Diary of a Sufi Master*, translation and commentary by Carl W. Ernst (Chapel Hill: Parvardigar Press, 1997). For a detailed account of Ruzbihan's life and legacy, see Carl W. Ernst, *Ruzbihan Baqli: Mysticism and the Rhetoric of Sainthood in Persian Sufism* (Richmond, Surrey: Curzon Press, 1996).

10. This is an extract from the personal letter of a female Pakistani disciple dated February 9, 1988.

11. This taxonomy is found in Katherine P. Ewing, "The *Pir* or Sufi Saint in Pakistani Islam," unpublished doctoral dissertation, University of Chicago, 1980, 90–139.

12. Valerie J. Hoffman, "The Role of Visions in Contemporary Egyptian Religious Life," *Religion*, Vol. 27 (January 1997): 48–49.

13. Faridi, "Baiat," 71.

14. Ewing, "The Modern Businessman and the Pakistani Saint," 76–81. For comparative ethnographic material on dreams, see Pinto, *Piri-Muridi Relationship*, 262–263. For similar accounts among both Muslims and Coptic Christians in contemporary Egypt, see also Hoffman, "The Role of Visions," 48, 52.

15. Katherine P. Ewing, "The Dream of Spiritual Initiation and the Organization of Self Representations among Pakistani Sufis," *American Ethnologist*, Vol. 17 (1990): 60.

16. Rabbani, *Malfuzat*, 894.

17. Hoffman, "The Role of Visions," 49.

18. Thanawi, *Perfecting Women*, 201.

19. This is an excerpt from a personal letter dated April 10, 1988.

20. Quoted in Jonathan G. Katz, *Dreams, Sufism and Sainthood: The Visionary Career of Muhammad al-Zawawi* (Leiden: E.J. Brill, 1996), 205.

21. Taufiq Fahd, "*Istikhara*," in *Encyclopedia of Islam*, Vol. IV, ed. Evan Daniel et al. (Leiden: E.J. Brill, 1978), 259–260. See also Hermansen, "Visions as 'Good to Think,'" 27. Ibn Khaldun describes his own experiments with *istikhara* in his book *The Muqaddimah*, 84.

22. Faridi, *Malfuzat-i Shaykh*, 116.

23. Ewing, "The *Pir* or Sufi Saint in Pakistani Islam," 110.

24. For an overview of *lata'if* in the context of Sufi meditation practices, see Ernst, *The Shambhala Guide to Sufism*, 106–111; Buehler, *Sufi Heirs of the Prophet*, 106–109.

25. On the Kubrawi tradition, see especially Jamal J. Elias, *The Throne Carrier of God: The Life and Thought of 'Ala ad-dawla as-Simnani* (Albany: State University of New York Press, 1995). See in particular Chapter Five, "The Spiritual Body and the Mirror of God," 79–99. See also Shazad Bashir, *Messianic Hopes and Mystical Visions: The Nurbakhshiya between Medieval and Modern Islam* (Columbia: University of South Carolina Press, 2003).

26. On the Naqshbandi theory of *lata'if*, see especially Marcia K. Hermansen, "Shah Wali Allah's Theory of the Subtle Spiritual Centers (*Lata'if*): A Sufi Model of Personhood and Self-Transformation," *Journal of Near Eastern Studies*, Vol. 47, No. 1 (January 1988): 1–25; Buehler, *Sufi Heirs of the Prophet*, 103–113; Schimmel, *Mystical Dimensions of Islam*, 174. Muhammad Zauqi Shah summarizes the Naqshbandi Mujaddadi system in *Sirr-i dilbaran*, 299. He also provides a comprehensive summary of Shaykh Ahmad Sirhindi's three-tiered cosmological model in a detailed foldout chart (200–201). Hermansen reproduces and translates Zauqi Shah's chart in her article "Shah Wali Allah's Theory of the Subtle Spiritual Centers," 8–9.

27. Kugle, "The Heart of Ritual Is the Body," 48. See also Ernst and Lawrence, *Sufi Martyrs of Love*, 130–134.

28. Wahid Bakhsh Sial Rabbani refers to both of his Chishti Sabiri predecessors in *Mushahada-i haqq*, 102–103. Shahidullah Faridi references *Ziya' al-qulub* in *Malfuzat-i Shaykh*, 20–21.

29. Rabbani, *Islamic Sufism*, 71–72. Wahid Bakhsh provides no reference for this *hadith*, though it is also found in Hajji Imdad Allah's book *Ziya' al-qulub, in Kulliyat-i Imdadiyya* (Deoband: Kutub Khana Hadi, no date) (see Ernst and Lawrence, *Sufi Martyrs of Love*, 131). The same typology is repeated in Wahid Bakhsh Sial Rabbani's *Mushahada-i haqq* (100) and Zauqi Shah's *Tarbiyat al-'ushshaq* (Rabbani, *Muqaddama*, 58; Rabbani, *Malfuzat*, 357, 704). Zauqi Shah details the *lata'if* in *Sirr-i dilbaran* as well (298–300). On the whole, however, the writings of contemporary Chishti Sabiri *shaykhs* regarding the *lata'if* provide far less nuance and detail than those of their premodern predecessors.

30. Rabbani, *Islamic Sufism*, 306. On Chishti Sabiri cosmology, see also pages 62–67, 307. For comparison with the Naqshbandi Mujjadadi model, see Buehler, *Sufi Heirs of the Prophet*, 105–107.

31. Ernst and Lawrence, *Sufi Martyrs of Love*, 27. For a broad analysis of *zikr* in the Qur'an and Sufi practice see especially Ernst, *The Shambhala Guide to Sufism*, 92–98; Schimmel, *Mystical Dimensions of Islam*, 167–178.

32. Faridi, *Inner Aspects of Faith*, 110–111. Shahidullah's words echo those of his nineteenth-century Chishti Sabiri predecessor Hajji Imdad Allah. See Kugle, "The Heart of Ritual Is the Body," 57, footnote 28.

33. Faridi, *Spirituality in Religion*, 68. Wahid Bakhsh Sial Rabbani provides an overview of Chishti Sabiri *zikr* in *Maqam-i Ganj-i Shakkar*, 420–425.

34. For a comparative analysis of the Naqshbandi practice of silent *zikr* (*zikr-i qalbi* or "remembrance of the heart"), see Buehler, *Sufi Heirs of the Prophet*, 127–130. The Suhrawardi order also practices vocal *zikr*. See Huda, *Striving for Divine Union*, 101–107, 157–164.

35. On *zikr-i ism-i dhat*, see Rabbani, *Mushahada-i haqq*, 101–102; Rabbani, *Islamic Sufism*, 307–308.

36. *Shajara tayyaba ma'a awrad aur waza'if* [The Exalted Spiritual Genealogy with Devotional Exercises and Daily Prayers], the unpublished, official handbook of the contemporary Chishti Sabiri order, compiled by Shaykh Muhammad Zauqi Shah, 38.

37. Rabbani, *Malfuzat*, 403–404. On the links of early Chishti Sabiri masters with Hindu ascetics, see Simon Digby, "'Abd al-Quddus Gangohi (1456–1537 A.D.): The Personality and Attitudes of a Medieval Indian Sufi," *Medieval India—A Miscellany*, Vol. 3 (1975): 1–66; Ernst and Lawrence, *Sufi Martyrs of Love*, 106.

38. Shahidullah Faridi, *Malfuzat-i Shaykh*, 20–21. Wahid Bakhsh Rabbani labels these forms of silent *zikr* as "*zikr-i khafi*" ("hidden *zikr*") and describes them as *mashaghil* ("duties"). See Rabbani, *Mushahada-i haqq*, 102; Rabbani, *Islamic Sufism*, 305–306.

39. Rabbani, *Malfuzat*, 149.

40. *Malfuzat-i Shaykh* contains a lengthy lecture by Shaykh Shahidullah Faridi on the proper *adab* for *halqa-i zikr*. See pages 185–190.

41. Rabbani, *Malfuzat*, 154.

42. This extract from a personal letter was read during an interview on October 6, 2001 in Kuala Lumpur.

43. On Hajji Imdad Allah and 'Abd al-Quddus Gangohi, see Ernst and Lawrence, *Sufi Martyrs of Love*, 130–133; Digby, "'Abd al-Quddus Gangohi," 1–66. On *zikr-i nafi ithbat*, see also Rabbani, *Mushahada-i haqq*, 101; Rabbani, *Islamic Sufism*, 308.

44. Zauqi Shah, *Sirr-i dilbaran*, 304. See also Rabbani, *Mushahada-i haqq*, 102–103; Rabbani, *Maqam-i Ganj-i Shakkar*, 426–434.

45. For a detailed description of the Naqshbandi system, see Buehler, Appendix Two, "Mujaddidi Contemplations," in *Sufi Heirs of the Prophet*, 241–248.

46. Faridi, *Spirituality in Religion*, 23. See also Faridi, *Malfuzat-i Shaykh*, 56.

47. This is an extract from a personal letter dated October 31, 1989.

48. Buehler, *Sufi Heirs of the Prophet*, 140.

49. Rabbani, *Islamic Sufism*, 282. Regarding the proper *adab* at shrines of saints, see also Faridi, *Malfuzat-i Shaykh*, 60.

50. This is an extract from a personal letter written to a female Pakistani *murid* dated October 31, 1989. See also Rabbani, *Islamic Sufism*, 275. Zauqi Shah issues a similar warning in *Tarbiyat al-'ushshaq*, advising his followers to avoid the *mazars* of spiritually intoxicated saints (*majzub*). See Rabbani, *Malfuzat*, 201.

51. Ernst and Lawrence, *Sufi Martyrs of Love*, 96.

52. See the Web site http://www.abcmalaysia.com/tour_malaysia/mlka_pbsr.htm.

53. Shaykh 'Abd al-Qadir Jilani Thani was the eldest son of Shaykh Muhammad al-Husseini al-Jilani, the founder of the first Qadiriyya *khanaqah* at Uch. A native of Turkey, Shaykh Muhammad traveled to Khurasan and then Multan before settling with his family in Uch. In tracing the history of this family, Rizvi quotes extensively from the famous hagiographic dictionary *Akhbar al-akhyar* [Tales of the Great Ones], compiled by Shaykh 'Abd al-Haqq Muhaddith Dihlwawi, the Qadiri loyalist of the Mughal era. See Rizvi, *A History of Sufism in India*, II: 58. On the rich history of Uch, see also Mas'ud Hasan Shahab, *Khitta-i pak Uch* (Bahawalpur: Urdu Academy, 1967/1993), 257–261.

54. Peter Riddell, *Islam and the Malay-Indonesian World* (Honolulu: University of Hawai'i Press, 2001), 104. On Hamzah Fansuri, see also Mark R. Woodward, *Islam in Java: Normative Piety and Mysticism in the Sultanate of Yogyakarta* (Tucson: University of Arizona Press, 1989), 125–128; G.W.J. Drewes and L.F Brakel, *The Poems of Hamzah Fansuri* (Dordrecth: Foris Publications, 1986). For an overview of the history of Sufism in Southeast Asia, see also Bruce B. Lawrence, "The Eastward Journey of Muslim Kingship: Islam in South and Southeast Asia," in *The Oxford History of Islam*, ed. John L. Esposito (New York: Oxford University Press, 1999), 395–431; M.C. Ricklefs, *A History of Modern Indonesia since 1300* (Stanford: Stanford University Press, 1981/1993). None of these sources, however, documents the history of Pulau Besar or the life of Shaykh Isma'il 'Abd al-Qadir Thani.

55. On the *wali sanga* and their role in the establishment of Islam in the Indonesian archipelago during the fifteenth and sixteenth centuries, see Woodward, *Islam in Java*, 96–101.

56. Eaton, "The Political and Religious Authority of the Shrine of Baba Farid," 334.

57. Michel Foucault, "Of Other Spaces, Heterotopias," *Diacritics*, Vol. 16, No. 1 (1986): 24.

58. Faridi, *Spirituality in Religion*, 59. See also the lecture entitled "Attendance at the *Mazars*" (115–130) where Shahidullah Faridi invokes the Qur'an, al-Ghazali, Rumi, and Ibn 'Arabi to articulate a comprehensive defense of the tradition of *ziyarat* and defend the orthodoxy of intercession. Wahid Bakhsh offers a detailed defense of both *ziyarat* and *'urs* in *Maqam-i Ganj-i Shakkar*, 340–364.

59. Faridi, *Malfuzat-i Shaykh*, 77.

60. Ibid., 75–76. For a broad analysis of the Chishti response to the controversies over pilgrimage to Sufi shrines, see Ernst and Lawrence, *Sufi Martyrs of Love*, 90–98.

61. Ernst and Lawrence, *Sufi Martyrs of Love*, 90–91.

62. Wahid Bakhsh notes that Hajji Imdad Allah traced the term *'urs* to a *hadith* directed at the saints as they prepare for death: "Sleep with the sleep of a bridegroom (*'arus*)." See Rabbani, *Maqam-i Ganj-i Shakkar*, 38; quoted in Ernst and Lawrence, *Sufi Martyrs of Love*, 91. For an overview of *'urs* festivals, see Ernst, *The Shambhala Guide to Sufism*, 77–78; Syed Liyaqat Hussain Moini, "Rituals and Customary Practices at the Dargah of Ajmer," in *Muslim Shrines in India: Their Character, History and Significance*, ed. Christian W. Troll (Delhi: Oxford University Press, 1989), 60–75.

63. Rabbani, *Islamic Sufism*, 281. See also Wahid Bakhsh's introduction to Khwaja Ghulam Farid (compiled 1893–1901), *Maqabis al-majalis*, Urdu translation from Persian by Wahid Bakhsh Sial Rabbani (Lahore: al-Faisal, 1979/1993), 239–242. Zauqi Shah details the spiritual blessings of *'urs* in numerous lectures in *Tarbiyat al-'ushshaq*. See, e.g., Faridi, *Malfuzat*, 122; Rabbani, *Malfuzat*, 545.

64. Victor Turner, "The Center Out There: The Pilgrim's Goal," *History of Religions*, Vol. 12, No. 1, 195.

65. Barbara Daly Metcalf, "Tablighi Jama'at and Women," in *Travellers in Faith: Studies of the Tablighi Jama'at as a Transnational Islamic Movement for Faith Renewal*, ed. Muhammad Khalid Masud (Leiden: Brill, 2000), 48. See also Barbara Daly Metcalf, "Living Hadith in the Tablighi Jama'at," *Journal of Asian Studies*, Vol. 52, No. 3 (August 1993): 584–608; Metcalf,

"Nationalism, Modernity, and Muslim Identity in India before 1947," 129–143.

66. Rabbani, *Islamic Sufism*, 282. See also Rabbani, *Malfuzat*, 146, 152, 238, 280.
67. Rabbani, *Islamic Sufism*, 283–284.
68. This is an extract from a personal e-mail dated February 19, 2002, 1.
69. Ibid., 2.
70. Sijzi, *Morals for the Heart*, 132.
71. Bruce B. Lawrence, "The Early Chishti Approach to *Sama*'," in *Islamic Society and Culture: Essays in Honor of Professor Aziz Ahmad*, ed. Milton Israel and N.K. Wagle (Delhi: Manohar Publications, 1983), 73–74. For an analysis of the defense of *sama*' by Chishti theorists, see Ernst and Lawrence, *Sufi Martyrs of Love*, 34–46. For an overview of Sufi music, see Ernst, *The Shambhala Guide to Sufism*, 179–198; Schimmel, *Mystical Dimensions of Islam*, 179–186.
72. Muhammad Zauqi Shah, e.g., offers a lengthy exposition and defense of *sama*' in both *Sirr-i dilbaran* (203–226) and *Tarbiyat al-'ushshaq* (Rabbani, *Malfuzat*, 248–250, 254–257, 390, 772–776, 806–816).
73. Rabbani, *Maqam-i Ganj-i Shakkar*, 365–416.
74. Faridi, *Maqabis al-majalis*, 131–212. The title of this lengthy chapter is "The Taste of *Sama*'" (*Zauq-i sama*').
75. Rabbani, *Islamic Sufism*, 285.
76. Ernst and Lawrence, *Sufi Martyrs of Love*, 134–135.
77. On liminality and the transformative power of ritual, see Victor Turner, *The Ritual Process: Structure and Anti-Structure* (Ithaca: Cornell University Press, 1977), 95–96.
78. Rabbani, *Malfuzat*, 810. A similar typography is found in the appendix to *Naghmat-i sama* [*The Melodies of Listening to Music*], a sourcebook for *qawwali* performers published in Pakistan in 1972. For a partial translation of this Urdu manual, see Carl W. Ernst, *Teachings of Sufism* (Boston: Shambhala Press, 1999), 105–117.
79. Rabbani, *Malfuzat*, 811–812. On the spiritual effects of listening to music, see also 248–250, 749–750, 772–776.
80. Sijzi, *Morals for the Heart*, 154.
81. Rabbani, *Malfuzat*, 812–815.
82. Regula Burckhardt Qureshi, "Sufi Music and the Historicity of Oral Tradition," in *Ethnomusicology and Modern Music History*, ed. Stephen Blum, Philip V. Bohlman, and Daniel M. Neuman (Urbana: University of Illinois Press, 1991), 106–107. See also Regula Burckhardt Qureshi, "The *Mahfil-e Sama*: Sufi Practice in the Indian Context," *Islam and the Modern Age*, Vol. 17, No. 3 (August 1986): 133–165.
83. In a detailed discussion of *kalam*, Muhammad Zauqi Shah recites a range of his favorite poetic couplets. These include the Persian verses of Shams-i Tabriz, Amir Khusrau, Hafiz, Khaqani, Maghribi, Rumi, Niyaz Ahmad Barelwi, Shah Bahlul, 'Abd al-Quddus Gangohi, and Qutb ad-Din Bakhtiar Kaki. Zauqi Shah also includes two couplets in Urdu: one from the popular singer 'Aziz Miyan and one that he composed himself. See Rabbani, *Malfuzat*, 812–814. On the *qawwali* lyrical repertoire, see also Regula Burckhardt Qureshi, *Sufi Music of India and Pakistan: Sound, Context and Meaning in Qawwali* (Cambridge: Cambridge University Press, 1986), 19–45.
84. Qureshi, *Sufi Music of India and Pakistan*, 231.

85. On the spread of South Asian *qawwali* to an international audience in the twentieth century through the global recording industry see Regula Burckhardt Qureshi, "Muslim Devotional: Popular Religious Music and Muslim Identity under British, Indian and Pakistani Hegemony," *Asian Music*, Vol. 24 (1992–1993): 111–121; Ernst, *The Shambhala Guide to Sufism*, 189–191.

86. This is an extract from a personal letter written to a female disciple dated August 8, 1990.

BIBLIOGRAPHY

PRIMARY SOURCES

al-Hasan, Sayyid Sharif. *Sirat-i Zauqi*. In *Tarbiyat al-'ushshaq*. Compiled by Wahid Bakhsh Sial Rabbani, 429–504. Karachi: Mahfil-i Zauqiyya, 1958/1983.

al-Hujwiri, Sayyid 'Ali ibn 'Uthman (d. 1074). *Kashf al-mahjub*. Urdu translation from Persian with commentary by Wahid Bakhsh Sial Rabbani. Lahore: al-Faisal Publishers, 1995.

———. *The Kashful Mahjub ("Unveiling the Veiled"): The Earliest Persian Treatise on Sufism*. English translation with commentary by Wahid Bakhsh Sial Rabbani. Kuala Lumpur: A.S. Noordeen, 1997.

Aziz, Tehzeeb un-Nisa, and Mansoor Hashmi, eds. *The Sufi Path*. Books 13/14. Islamabad: Association of Spiritual Training Pakistan, 1995/1996.

The Bible, the Qur'an and Science. Translated by Alistair D. Pannell. Crescent Publishing Company, 1978.

Chishti, 'Abd ar-Rahman (d. 1683). *Mir'at al-asrar*. Urdu translation from Persian by Wahid Bakhsh Sial Rabbani. Lahore: Ziya al-Qur'an Publications, 1993.

Farid, Khwaja Ghulam (d. 1901). *Maqabis al-majalis* (compiled 1893–1901). Urdu translation from Persian by Wahid Bakhsh Sial Rabbani. Lahore: al-Faisal, 1979/1993.

Faridi, Shahidullah. *'Awarif al-ma'arif ke chand dars*. Lahore: Talifaat-e Shaheedi, 1996.

———. "Baiat." In *Inner Aspects of Faith*, 65–74. Karachi: Mahfil-i Zauqiyya, 1979/1986. Reprinted Kuala Lumpur: A.S. Noordeen (2nd edition), 1993.

———. *Everyday Practice in Islam*. Karachi: Mahfil-i Zauqiyya, 1970/1999.

———. *Gul-i sad barg*. Karachi: Mahfil-i Zauqiyya, 1962/1985.

———. *Inner Aspects of Faith*. Karachi: Mahfil-i Zauqiyya, 1979/1986. Reprinted Kuala Lumpur: A.S. Noordeen (2nd edition), 1993.

———. *Malfuzat*. In *Tarbiyat al-'ushshaq*. Compiled by Wahid Bakhsh Sial Rabbani, 85–134. Karachi: Mahfil-i Zauqiyya, 1958/1983.

———. *Malfuzat-i Shahidi*. Compiled by Hajji Ahmad Allah. Karachi: Ta'rif Printers, 1995.

———. *Malfuzat-i Shahidi*. Compiled by Muhammad Yamin. Karachi: Matba' 'Imdadi Press, 1993.

———. *Malfuzat-i shaykh*. Compiled by Siraj 'Ali Muhammad. Lahore: Qausin Publishers, 1996.

———. *The Moral Message of God and His Prophet*. Karachi: Mahfil-i Zauqiyya, 1973/1995.

———. "The Spiritual Psychology of Islam." In *Inner Aspects of Faith*, 79–98. Karachi: Mahfil-i Zauqiyya, 1979/1986. Reprinted Kuala Lumpur: A.S. Noordeen (2nd edition), 1993.

Faridi, Shahidullah. *Spirituality in Religion*. Compiled by Siraj 'Ali Muhammad. Lahore: Talifaat-e Shaheedi, 1999.

———. *Wasyat nama* [An English translation of Shahidullah Faridi's last will and testament]. Reprinted in an earlier edition of *Malfuzat-i shaykh*, no date.

Gangohi, 'Abd al-Quddus (d. 1537). *Maktubat-i Quddusiyya*. Urdu translation from Persian by Wahid Bakhsh Sial Rabbani. Lahore: Bazm-i Ittehad al-Muslimin, 1988.

Haroon, Muhammad. "Tragedy at the Wedding Anniversary." Unpublished article. 2001.

Hasan, Shah Sayyid Waris (d. 1936). *A Guide for Spiritual Aspirants* [A partial English translation of *Shamamat al-'ambar*]. Translated by Wahid Bakhsh Sial Rabbani. Kuala Lumpur: A.S. Noordeen Publishers, 1990.

———. *Shamamat al-'ambar*. Compiled by Muhammad Zauqi Shah. Karachi: Mahfil-i Zauqiyya, 1931/1990.

Jami, Nur ad-Din 'Abd al-Rahman (d. 1492). *Sharh-i lawa'ih-i Jami*. Urdu translation and commentary by Wahid Bakhsh Sial Rabbani. Bazm-i Ittehad al-Muslimin, 1988.

The Kashf al-Mahjub: The Oldest Persian Treatise on Sufism. Translated by Reynold A. Nicholson. Leiden: E. J. Brill, 1911.

Nizami, Khwaja Hasan (d. 1955). *A Diary of a Disciple of Nizamudin Aulia* [An English translation of *Nizami Bansari*]. Translated by H. Sajun. Lahore: Talifaat-e-Shaheedi, 2001.

———. *Nizami Bansari*. Lahore: Qausin Publishers, 1996.

Qudusi, Muhammad Akram. *Iqtibas al-anwar* (completed 1729). Urdu translation from Persian by Wahid Bakhsh Sial Rabbani. Lahore: Ziya al-Qur'an Publications, 1993.

Rabbani, Wahid Bakhsh Sial. *'Azamat-i Ahl-i Bait-i Rasul*. Lahore: al-Faisal Publishers, 1994.

———. *Hajj-i Zauqi*. Karachi: Mahfil-i Zauqiyya, 1951/1993.

———. *Islamic Sufism: The Science of Flight to God, in God, with God, by God and Union and Communion with God, also Showing the Tremendous Sufi Influence on Christian and Hindu Mystics and Mysticism*. Lahore: Sufi Foundation, 1984. Reprinted editions, Kuala Lumpur: A.S. Noordeen (4th edition), 1992; Bahawalpur: Justice Muhammad Akbar Academy, 1995.

———. *The Magnificent Power Potential of Pakistan* [An English translation of *Pakistan ki azim ush-shan difai quwwat*]. Translation and commentary by Muhammad Asghar. Lahore: al-Faisal Publishers, 2000.

———. *Malfuzat*. In *Tarbiyat al-'ushshaq*. Compiled by Wahid Bakhsh Rabbani, 135–426, 507–827. Karachi: Mahfil-i Zauqiyya, 1958/1983.

———. *Maqam-i Ganj-i Shakkar*. Lahore: al-Faisal Publishers, 1994.

———. *Muqaddama*. In *Tarbiyat al-'ushshaq*, ed. Wahid Bakhsh Sial Rabbani, 35–84. Karachi: Mahfil-i Zauqiyya, 1958/1983.

———. *Mushahada-i haqq*. Karachi: Mahfil-i Zauqiyya, 1974. Reprinted Lahore: al-Faisal Publishers, 1995.

———. *Pakistan ki azim ush-shan difai quwwat*. Lahore: Bazm-i Ittehad al-Muslimin, 1986.

———. *Panj pir* [Selections from the Urdu translation of *Mir'at al-asrar* by 'Abd ar-Rahman Chishti]. Lahore: al-Faisal Publishers, 1993.

———. *Reactivization of Islam*. Lahore: Bazm-i Ittehad al-Muslimin, 1988.

———. *Ruhaniyat-i Islam*. Lahore: al-Faisal Publishers, 1995.

——. *Wahdat al-wujud o wahdat ash-shuhud*. Lahore: Bazm-i Ittehad al-Muslimin, 1988

Zauqi Shah, Sayyid Muhammad. *Bada u saghir*. Karachi: Mahfil-i Zauqiyya, 1955.

——. *Barzakh*. Karachi: Mahfil-i Zauqiyya, 1976/1987.

——. *Haqiqat-i tasawwuf*. Lahore: al-Kitab, 1978.

——. *Islam, Pakistan aur jamhuriyat*. Mahfil-i Zauqiyya, 1950.

——. *Islamic Spiritualism*. Lahore: Sufi Foundation, 1933/1984.

——. *Letters of a Sufi Saint to Jinnah* [A reprint with additions of the English version of *Mudamin-i Zauqi*], ed. Mansoor Hashmi and Sayyid Tahir Maqsood. Lahore: Talifaat-e Shaheedi, 1949/1998.

——. *Muzamin-i Zauqi*. Compiled by Wahid Bakhsh Sial Rabbani. Karachi: Mahfil-i Zauqia, 1949/1975.

——. *New Searchlight on the Vedic Aryans*. Lahore: Sufi Foundation, 1943. Reprinted in *Letters of a Sufi Saint to Jinnah* [A reprint with additions of the English version of *Muzamin-i Zauqi*], ed. Mansoor Hashmi and Sayyid Tahir Maqsood, 93–108. Lahore: Talifaat-e Shaheedi, 1949/1998.

——. *Shajara tayyaba ma'a awrad aur waza'if* [The Exalted Spiritual Genealogy with Devotional Exercises and Daily Prayers]. The unpublished, official handbook of the contemporary Chishti Sabiri order. Compiled by Shaykh Muhammad Zauqi Shah.

——. *Sirr-i dilbaran*. Karachi: Mahfil-i Zauqiyya, 1951/1985.

——. "Sufism." Originally published in *Islamic Review*, London, 1933. Reprinted in *Letters of a Sufi Saint to Jinnah* [A reprint with additions of the English version of *Muzamin-i Zauqi*], ed. Mansoor Hashmi and Sayyid Tahir Maqsood, 164–182. Lahore: Talifaat-e Shaheedi, 1949/1998.

——. *Tarbiyat al-'ushshaq*. Compiled by Wahid Bakhsh Sial Rabbani. Karachi: Mahfil-i Zauqiyya, 1958/1983.

SECONDARY SOURCES

Abbas, Shemeem. *The Female Voice in Sufi Ritual: Devotional Practices of Pakistan and India*. Austin: University of Texas Press, 2002.

Ahmed, Akbar S. *Jinnah, Pakistan and Islamic Identity: The Search for Saladin*. New York: Routledge, 1997.

Ajmal, Mohammad. "A Note on *Adab* in the *Murshid-Murid* Relationship." In *Moral Conduct and Authority: The Place of Adab in South Asian Islam*, ed. Barbara Daly Metcalf, 241–251. Berkeley: University of California Press, 1984.

Alcoff, Linda. "The Problem of Speaking for Others." *Cultural Critique*, No. 20 (Winter 1991–1992): 5–32.

Anderson, Benedict. *Imagined Communities: Reflections on the Origin and Spread of Nationalism*. London: Verso, 1983/1991.

Anderson, Jon W. "The Internet and Islam's New Interpreters." In *New Media in the Muslim World: The Emerging Public Sphere*, ed. Dale F. Eickelman and Jon W. Anderson, 40–56. Bloomington: Indiana University Press, 1999.

Ansari, Sarah F.D. *Sufi Saints and State Power: The Pirs of Sind, 1843–1947*. Lahore: Vanguard Books, 1992.

Appadurai, Arjun. *Modernity at Large: Cultural Dimensions of Globalization*. Minneapolis: University of Minnesota Press, 1996.

as-Sulami, Abu 'Abd ar-Rahman. *Early Sufi Women (Dhikr an-niswa al-muta 'abbidat as-sufiyyat)*. Translation and commentary by Rkia E. Cornell. Lousiville: Fons Vitae, 1999.

Asad, Talal. *Formations of the Secular: Christianity, Islam, Modernity.* Stanford: Stanford University Press, 2003.

———. *Genealogies of Religion: Discipline and Reasons of Power in Christianity and Islam.* Baltimore: Johns Hopkins University Press, 1993.

———. "The Idea of an Anthropology of Islam." In *Occasional Paper Series,* by the Center for Contemporary Arab Studies, Georgetown University, 1–23. Washington, DC: Georgetown University Press, March 1986.

———. "Religion, Nation-State, Secularism." In *Nation and Religion: Perspectives on Europe and Asia,* ed. Peter van der Veer and Hartmut Lehmann, 178–196. Princeton: Princeton University Press, 1999.

Baqli, Ruzbihan. *The Unveiling of Secrets: Diary of a Sufi Master.* Translation and commentary by Carl W. Ernst. Chapel Hill: Parvardigar Press, 1997.

Bashir, Shahzad. *Messianic Hopes and Mystical Visions: The Nurbakhshiya between Medieval and Modern Islam.* Columbia: University of South Carolina Press, 2003.

Bell, Catherine. *Ritual Theory, Ritual Practice.* New York: Oxford University Press, 1992.

Benavides, Gustavo. "Modernity." In *Critical Terms for Religious Studies,* ed. Mark C. Taylor, 186–204. Chicago: University of Chicago Press, 1998.

Bhabha, Homi K. *The Location of Culture.* New York: Routledge, 1994.

Blank, Jonah. *Mullahs on the Mainframe: Islam and Modernity among the Daudi Bohras.* Chicago: University of Chicago Press, 2001.

Bourdieu, Pierre. *The Logic of Practice.* Translated by Richard Nice. Palo Alto: Stanford University Press, 1990.

Bowen, John R. *Muslims through Discourse: Religion and Ritual in Gayo Society.* Princeton: Princeton University Press, 1993.

Bowering, Gerhard. "The *Adab* Literature of Classical Sufism: Ansari's Code of Conduct." In *Moral Conduct and Authority: The Place of Adab in South Asian Islam,* ed. Barbara Daly Metcalf, 62–87. Berkeley: University of California Press, 1984.

Breckenridge, Carol A., ed. *Consuming Modernity: Public Culture in a South Asian World.* Minneapolis: University of Minnesota Press, 1995.

Brown, Daniel. *Rethinking Tradition in Modern Islamic Thought.* Cambridge: Cambridge University Press, 1996.

Brown, Peter. *Authority and the Sacred: Aspects of the Christianisation of the Roman World.* Cambridge: Cambridge University Press, 1995.

———. *The Cult of the Saints: Its Rise and Function in Latin Christianity.* Chicago: University of Chicago Press, 1981.

———. "The Saint as Exemplar in Late Antiquity." In *Saints and Virtues,* ed. John Stratton Hawley, 3–14. Berkeley: University of California Press, 1987.

———. *Society and the Holy in Late Antiquity.* Berkeley: University of California Press, 1982.

Buehler, Arthur F. *Sufi Heirs of the Prophet: The Indian Naqshbandiyya and the Rise of the Mediating Sufi Shaykh.* Columbia: University of South Carolina Press, 1998.

Butler, Judith. "Foucault and the Paradox of Bodily Inscriptions." *Journal of Philosophy,* Vol. 86, No. 11 (November 1989): 601–607.

Casanova, Jose. *Public Religions in the Modern World.* Chicago: University of Chicago Press, 1994.

Chakrabarty, Dipesh. *Habitations of Modernity: Essays in the Wake of Subaltern Studies.* Chicago: University of Chicago Press, 2002.

———. *Provincializing Europe: Postcolonial Thought and Historical Difference.* Princeton: Princeton University Press, 2000.

Chand, Tara. *The Influence of Islam on Indian Culture.* Allahabad: Indian Press, 1963.

Chatterjee, Partha. *The Nation and Its Fragments: Colonial and Postcolonial Histories.* Princeton: Princeton University Press, 1993.

Chodkiewicz, Michel. *Seal of the Saints: Prophethood and Sainthood in the Doctrine of Ibn 'Arabi.* Cambridge: Islamic Texts Society, 1993.

Clifford, James, and George E. Marcus, eds. *Writing Culture: The Poetics and Politics of Ethnography.* Berkeley: University of California Press, 1986.

Colby, Frederick Stephen. "Constructing an Islamic Ascension Narrative: The Interplay of Official and Popular Culture in Pseudo-Ibn 'Abbas." Doctoral dissertation, Duke University, 2002.

Coon, Lynda L. *Sacred Fictions: Holy Women and Hagiography in Late Antiquity.* Philadelphia: University of Pennsylvania Press, 1997.

Cornell, Vincent J. "*Jihad*: Islam's Struggle for Truth." *Gnosis Magazine* (Fall 1991): 18–23.

———. *Realm of the Saint: Power and Authority in Moroccan Sufism.* Austin: University of Texas Press, 1998.

Csordas, Thomas J., ed. *Embodiment and Experience: The Existential Ground of Culture and Self.* Cambridge: Cambridge University Press, 1994.

———. "Embodiment as a Paradigm for Anthropology." *Ethos*, Vol. 18, No. 1 (March 1990): 5–47.

Currie, P.M. *The Shrine and Cult of Mu'in al-Din Chishti of Ajmer.* Delhi: Oxford University Press, 1989.

De Jong, Frederick, and Bernd Radtke, eds. *Islamic Mysticism Contested: Thirteen Centuries of Controversies and Polemics.* Leiden: E. J. Brill, 1999.

Delooz, Pierre. "Towards a Sociological Study of Canonized Sainthood in the Catholic Church." In *Saints and Their Cults: Studies in Religious Sociology, Folklore and History,* ed. Stephen Wilson, 189–216. Cambridge: Cambridge University Press, 1983.

Digby, Simon. "'Abd al-Quddus Gangohi (1456–1537 A.D.): The Personality and Attitudes of a Medieval Indian Sufi." *Medieval India—A Miscellany*, Vol. 3 (1975): 1–66.

Drewes, G.W.J., and L.F. Brakel. *The Poems of Hamzah Fansuri.* Dordrecth: Foris Publications, 1986.

Eaton, Richard M. "Court of Man, Court of God." *Contributions to Asian Studies,* Vol. XVII (1982): 44–61.

———. "The Political and Religious Authority of the Shrine of Baba Farid." In *Moral Conduct and Authority: The Place of Adab in South Asian Islam,* ed. Barbara Daly Metcalf, 333–356. Berkeley: University of California Press, 1984.

Eickelman, Dale F. "Communication and Control in the Middle East: Publication and Its Discontents." In *New Media in the Muslim World: The Emerging Public Sphere,* ed. Dale F. Eickelman and Jon W. Anderson, 29–40. Bloomington: Indiana University Press, 1999.

———. "The Religious Public Sphere in Early Muslim Societies." In *The Public Sphere in Muslim Societies,* ed. Miriam Hoexter, Shmuel N. Eisenstadt, and Nehemia Levtzion, 1–8. Albany: State University of New York Press, 2002.

Eickelman, Dale F., and James Piscatori. *Muslim Politics.* Princeton: Princeton University Press, 1996.

Eickelman, Dale F., and Jon W. Anderson, eds. *New Media in the Muslim World: The Emerging Public Sphere.* Bloomington: Indiana University Press, 1999.

Elias, Jamal J. *The Throne Carrier of God: The Life and Thought of 'Ala ad-dawla as-Simnani.* Albany: State University of New York Press, 1995.

Ernst, Carl W. "Between Orientalism and Fundamentalism: Problematizing the Teaching of Sufism." In *Teaching Islam*, ed. Brannon M. Wheeler, 108–123. New York: Oxford University Press, 2003.

———. "Chishti Meditation Practices of the Later Mughal Period." In *The Heritage of Sufism: Late Classical Persianate Sufism (1501–1750)*, ed. Leonard Lewisohn and David Morgan, 344–357. Boston: Oneworld Publications, 1999.

———. *Eternal Garden: Mysticism, History, and Politics at a South Asian Sufi Center*. New York: State University of New York Press, 1992.

———. "Mystical Language and the Teaching Context in Early Lexicons of Sufism." In *Mysticism and Language*, ed. Steven T. Katz, 181–201. New York: Oxford University Press, 1992.

———. "Preface to the Second Edition." In *Eternal Garden: Mysticism, History and Politics at a South Asian Sufi Center*, xi–xviii. New Delhi: Oxford University Press, 2004.

———. *Ruzbihan Baqli: Mysticism and the Rhetoric of Sainthood in Persian Sufism*. Richmond, Surrey: Curzon Press, 1996.

———. *The Shambhala Guide to Sufism*. Boston: Shambhala Press, 1997.

———. "Sufism in Print: The Pakistani Sources." Unpublished proposal for the American Institute of Pakistani Studies Research Grant, 1998.

———. *Teachings of Sufism*. Boston: Shambhala Press, 1999.

———. "Traditionalism, the Perennial Philosophy and Islamic Studies." *Middle East Studies Association*, Bulletin 28 (1994): 176–180.

———. *Words of Ecstasy in Sufism*. Albany: State University of New York Press, 1985.

Ernst, Carl W., and Bruce B. Lawrence. *Sufi Martyrs of Love: The Chishti Order in South Asia and Beyond*. New York: Palgrave Macmillan, 2002.

Ewing, Katherine P. *Arguing Sainthood: Modernity, Psychoanalysis, and Islam*. Durham: Duke University Press, 1997.

———. "The Dream of Spiritual Initiation and the Organization of Self Representations among Pakistani Sufis." *American Ethnologist*, Vol. 17 (1990): 56–74.

———. "Dreams from a Saint: Anthropological Atheism and the Temptation to Believe." *American Anthropologist*, Vol. 96 (1994): 571–583.

———. "The Modern Businessman and the Pakistani Saint: The Interpenetration of Worlds." In *Manifestations of Sainthood in Islam*, ed. Grace Martin Smith, 69–84. Istanbul: Isis Press, 1993.

———. "The *Pir* or Sufi Saint in Pakistani Islam." Unpublished doctoral dissertation, University of Chicago, 1980.

———. "The Politics of Sufism: Redefining the Saints of Pakistan." *Journal of Asian Studies*, Vol. XLII, No. 2 (February 1983): 251–267.

Fahd, Taufiq. "The Dream in Medieval Islamic Society." In *The Dream and Human Societies*, ed. G.E. von Grunebaum and Roger Caillois, 351–63. Berkeley: University of California Press, 1966.

———. "*Istikhara*." In *Encyclopedia of Islam*, Vol. IV, ed. Evan Daniel et al., 259–260. Leiden: E.J. Brill, 1978.

———. "*Ru'ya*: The Meaning of Dreams." In *Encyclopedia of Islam*, Vol. VIII, ed. C.E. Bosworth et al., 645–647. Leiden: E.J. Brill, 1995.

Foucault, Michel. "About the Beginning of the Hermeneutics of the Self." In *Religion and Culture: Michel Foucault*, ed. Jeremy R. Carrette, 158–181. New York: Routledge, 1999.

———. "Of Other Spaces, Heterotopias." *Diacritics*, Vol. 16, No. 1 (1986): 22–27.

————. "Technologies of the Self." In *Technologies of the Self: A Seminar with Michel Foucault*, ed. Luther H. Martin, Huck Gutman, and Patrick H. Hutton, 16–49. Amherst: University of Massachusetts Press, 1988.

Gaborieau, Marc. "Introduction to the New Edition." In *Muslim Shrines in India: Their Character, History and Significance*, ed. Christian W. Troll, v–xxiv. New Delhi: Oxford University Press, 1989.

Gilmartin, David. *Empire and Islam: Punjab and the Making of Pakistan*. Berkeley: University of California Press, 1988.

————. "Shrines, Succession, and Sources of Moral Authority." In *Moral Conduct and Authority: The Place of Adab in South Asian Islam*, ed. Barbara Daly Metcalf, 221–240. Berkeley: University of California Press, 1984.

Gilmartin, David, and Bruce B. Lawrence, eds. *Beyond Turk and Hindu: Rethinking Religious Identities in Islamicate South Asia*. Gainesville: University Press of Florida, 2000.

Grossberg, Lawrence. "Identity and Cultural Studies: Is That All There Is?" In *Questions of Cultural Identity*, ed. Stuart Hall and Paul du Gay, 87–107. London: Sage Publications, 1997.

Hakim, Souad. "The Way of *Walaya* (Sainthood or Friendship of God)." *Journal of the Muhyiddin Ibn 'Arabi Society*, Vol. XVIII (1995): 23–40.

Heffernan, Thomas J. *Sacred Biography: Saints and Their Biographers in the Middle Ages*. New York: Oxford University Press, 1988.

Hermansen, Marcia K. "Common Themes, Uncommon Contexts: Hazrat Inayat Khan (1882–1927) and Khwaja Hasan Nizami (1878–1955)." In *A Pearl in the Wine: Essays on the Life, Music and Sufism of Hazrat Inayat Khan*, ed. Pirzade Zia Inayat Khan, 323–353. New Lebanon, NY: Omega Publications, 2001.

————. "Interdisciplinary Approaches to Islamic Biographical Materials." *Religion*, Vol. 18 (April 1988): 163–182.

————. "Rewriting Sufi Identity in the 20th Century: The Biographical Approaches of Maulana Ashraf 'Ali Thanvi (d. 1943) and Khwaja Hasan Nizami (d. 1955)." An unpublished paper presented at the American Academy of Religion Conference, November 1997.

————. "Shah Wali Allah's Theory of the Subtle Spiritual Centers (*Lata'if*): A Sufi Model of Personhood and Self-Transformation." *Journal of Near Eastern Studies*, Vol. 47, No. 1 (January 1988): 1–25.

————. "Visions as 'Good to Think': A Cognitive Approach to Visionary Experience in Islamic Sufi Thought." *Religion*, 27 (January 1997): 25–43.

Hilton, Isabel. "The General in His Labyrinth: Where Will Pervez Musharraf Lead His Country?" *New Yorker*, August 12, 2002, 42–55.

Hodgson, Marshall G.S. *The Venture of Islam: Conscience and History in a World Civilization*. Vol. 3, *The Gunpowder Empires and Modern Times*. Chicago: University of Chicago Press, 1974.

Hoexter, Miriam, Shmuel N. Eisenstadt, and Nehemia Levtzion, eds. *The Public Sphere in Muslim Societies*. Albany: State University of New York Press, 2002.

Hoffman, Valerie J. "The Role of Visions in Contemporary Egyptian Religious Life." *Religion*, Vol. 27 (January 1997): 45–64.

————. *Sufism, Mystics, and Saints in Modern Egypt*. Columbia: University of South Carolina Press, 1995.

Holden, Andrew. "Pakistan's Religious Parties: A Threat to Musharraf's Policies?" *Central Asia-Caucasus Analyst* (Johns Hopkins University, SAIS, November 6, 2002).

Huda, Qamar-ul. *Striving for Divine Union: Spiritual Exercises for Suhrawardi Sufis.* London: Routledge Curzon, 2003.

Ibrahim, Awais. "Who Locked the Door at Shrine?" *Nation,* Wednesday, April 4, 2001, 1, 9.

Iqbal, Muhammad. *The Reconstruction of Religious Thought in Islam.* Lahore: Sh. Muhammad Ashraf, 1934/1982.

Irving, Miles. "The Shrine of Baba Farid Shakarganj at Pakpattan." *Journal of the Panjab Historical Society* (Lahore), Vol. 1, No. 1 (1911): 70–76. Reprinted in *The Punjab Past and Present,* Vol. 7, No. 2 (October 1973): 405–414.

Jackson, Michael. "Knowledge of the Body." *Man,* Vol. 18, No. 12 (June 1983): 327–345.

Jalal, Ayesha. *Self and Sovereignty: Individual and Community in South Asian Islam since 1850.* London: Routledge, 1998.

———. *The Sole Spokesman: Jinnah, the Muslim League and the Demand for Pakistan.* Cambridge: Cambridge University Press, 1994.

———. *The State of Martial Rule: The Origins of Pakistan's Political Economy of Defence.* Cambridge: Cambridge University Press, 1990.

Jeffery, Patricia. *Frogs in a Well: Indian Women in Purdah.* London: Zed Press, 1979.

Jehangir, Tahir. "Carnage in Pakpattan." *Friday Times,* April 13–19, 2001, 14–15.

Johansen, Julian. *Sufism and Islamic Reform in Egypt: The Battle for Islamic Tradition.* Oxford: Clarendon Press, 1996.

Katz, Jonathan G. *Dreams, Sufism and Sainthood: The Visionary Career of Muhammad al-Zawawi.* Leiden: E.J. Brill, 1996.

Kaviraj, Sudipta. "The Imaginary Institution of India." In *Subaltern Studies VII: Writings on South Asian History and Society,* ed. Partha Chatterjee and Gyanendra Pandey, 1–39. Delhi: Oxford University Press, 1992.

Keddie, Nikki. *An Islamic Response to Imperialism: Political and Religious Writings of Sayyid Jamal ad-Din "al-Afghani."* Berkeley: University of California Press, 1968/1983.

Kepel, Gilles. *Jihad: The Trail of Political Islam.* Cambridge, MA: Harvard University Press, 2002.

Khaldun, Ibn. *The Muqaddimah: An Introduction to History.* Translated by Franz Rosenthal. Princeton: Princeton University Press, 1967.

Kindberg, Leah. "Literal Dreams and Prophetic Hadiths in Classical Islam: A Comparison of Two Ways of Legitimation." *Der Islam,* Vol. LXX (1993): 279–300.

Kleinberg, Aviad M. *Prophets in Their Own Country: Living Saints and the Making of Sainthood in the Later Middle Ages.* Chicago: University of Chicago Press, 1992.

Kugle, Scott A. "The Heart of Ritual Is the Body: Anatomy of an Islamic Devotional Manual of the Nineteenth Century." *Journal of Ritual Studies,* Vol. 17, No. 1 (2003): 42–60.

Lamoreaux, John C. *The Early Muslim Tradition of Dream Interpretation.* Albany: State University of New York Press, 2002.

Lawrence, Bruce B. "An Indo-Persian Perspective on the Significance of the Early Persian Sufi Masters." Paper delivered at a conference on Early Persian Sufism, George Washington University, Washington, DC, 1992.

———. "Biography and the 17th Century Qadiriya of North India." In *Islam and Indian Regions,* ed. Anna Libera Dallapiccola and Stephanie Zingel-Ave Lallemant, 399–415. Stuttgart: Franz Steiner Verlag, 1993.

————. "The Chishtiya of Sultanate India: A Case Study of Biographical Complexities in South Asian Islam." In *Charisma and Sacred Biography*, ed. Michael A.Williams. *Journal of the American Academy of Religion Thematic Studies*, Vol. XLVII, Nos. 3 and 4 (1982): 47–67.

————. *Defenders of God: The Fundamentalist Revolt against the Modern Age*. San Francisco: Harper and Row, 1989.

————. "The Early Chishti Approach to *Sama'*." In *Islamic Society and Culture: Essays in Honor of Professor Aziz Ahmad*, ed. Milton Israel and N.K. Wagle, 69–93. Delhi: Manohar Publications, 1983.

————. "The Eastward Journey of Muslim Kingship: Islam in South and Southeast Asia." In *The Oxford History of Islam*, ed. John L. Esposito, 395–431. New York: Oxford University Press, 1999.

————. *Notes from a Distant Flute: The Extant Literature of pre-Mughal Indian Sufism*. Tehran: Imperial Iranian Academy of Philosophy, 1978.

Lelyveld, David S. *Aligarh's First Generation: Muslim Solidarity in British India*. Princeton: Princeton University Press, 1978.

Liebeskind, Claudia. *Piety on Its Knees: Three Sufi Traditions in South Asia in Modern Times*. Delhi: Oxford University Press, 1998.

Lock, Margaret. "Cultivating the Body: Anthropology and Epistemologies of Bodily Practice and Knowledge." *Annual Review of Anthropology*, Vol. 22 (1993): 133–155.

Ludden, David, ed. *Contesting the Nation: Religion, Community, and the Politics of Democracy in India*. Philadelphia: University of Pennsylvania Press, 1996.

Mahdi, Muhsin. "From the Manuscript Age to the Age of Print Books." In *The Book in the Islamic World: The Written Word and Communication in the Middle East*, ed. George N. Atiyeh. Albany: State University of New York Press, 1995.

Malik, Jamal. *Colonization of Islam: Dissolution of Traditional Institutions in Pakistan*. New Delhi: Munshiram Manoharlal Publishers, 1996.

Mardin, Serif. *Religion and Social Change in Modern Turkey: The Case of Bediuzzaman Said Nursi*. Albany: State University of New York Press, 1989.

Maroth, Miklos. "The Science of Dreams in Islamic Culture." *Jerusalem Studies in Arabic and Islam*, Vol. 20 (1996): 229–238.

Martin, Luther H., Huck Gutman, and Patrick H. Hutton, eds. *Technologies of the Self: A Seminar with Michel Foucault*. Amherst: University of Massachusetts Press, 1988.

Masud, Muhammad Khalid, ed. *Travellers in Faith: Studies of the Tablighi Jama'at as a Transnational Islamic Movement for Faith Renewal*. Leiden: Brill, 2000.

McCutcheon, Russell T., ed. *The Insider/Outsider Problem in the Study of Religion: A Reader*. New York: Cassell, 1999.

McWhorter, Ladelle. "Culture or Nature?: The Function of the Term 'Body' in the Work of Michel Foucault." *Journal of Philosophy*, Vol. 86, No. 11 (November 1989): 608–614.

Messick, Binkley. *The Calligraphic State: Textual Domination and History in a Muslim Society*. Berkeley: University of California Press, 1993.

Metcalf, Barbara Daly. *Islamic Revival in British India: Deoband, 1860–1900*. Princeton: Princeton University Press, 1982.

————. "Living Hadith in the Tablighi Jama'at." *Journal of Asian Studies*, Vol. 52, No. 3 (August 1993): 584–608.

————, ed. *Moral Conduct and Authority: The Place of Adab in South Asian Islam*. Berkeley: University of California Press, 1984.

Metcalf, Barbara Daly. "Nationalism, Modernity, and Muslim Identity in India before 1947." In *Nation and Religion: Perspectives on Europe and Asia*, ed. Peter van der Veer and Hartmut Lehmann, 129–143. Princeton: Princeton University Press, 1999.

———. "Tablighi Jama'at and Women." In *Travellers in Faith: Studies of the Tablighi Jama'at as a Transnational Islamic Movement for Faith Renewal*, ed. Muhammad Khalid Masud, 44–58. Leiden: Brill, 2000.

Mitchell, Richard P. *The Society of the Muslim Brothers*. New York: Oxford University Press, 1969/1993.

Mitchell, Timothy, ed. *Questions of Modernity*. Minneapolis: University of Minnesota Press, 2000.

Moini, Syed Liyaqat Hussain. "Rituals and Customary Practices at the Dargah of Ajmer." In *Muslim Shrines in India: Their Character, History and Significance*, ed. Christian W. Troll, 60–75. Delhi: Oxford University Press, 1989.

Narayan, Kirin. *Storytellers, Saints and Scoundrels: Folk Narrative in Hindu Religious Teaching*. Philadelphia: University of Pennsylvania Press, 1989.

Nasr, Seyyed Vali Reza. *Islamic Leviathan: Islam and the Making of State Power*. New York: Oxford University Press, 2001.

———. *Mawdudi and the Making of Islamic Revivalism*. New York: Oxford University Press, 2001.

———. *The Vanguard of the Islamic Revolution: The Jama'at-i Islami of Pakistan*. Berkeley: University of California Press, 1994.

Nizami, Khaliq Ahmad. "Chistiyya." In *Encyclopedia of Islam*, Vol. 11, 50–56. Leiden: E.J. Brill, 1965.

———. *The Life and Times of Shaikh Farid-ud Din Ganj-i Shakar*. Delhi: Idarah-i Adabiyat-i Delli, 1973.

———. *The Life and Times of Shaikh Nizam-u'd-din Auliya*. Delhi: Idarah-i Adabiyat-i Delli, 1991.

———. *Tarikh-i mashayikh-i Chisht*. Delhi: Idarah-i Adabiyyat-i Delli, 1980/1985.

Ozelsel, Michaela. *Forty Days: The Diary of a Traditional Solitary Sufi Retreat*. Brattleboro, VT: Threshold Books, 1996.

Pinto, Desiderio. *Piri-Muridi Relationship: A Study of the Nizamuddin Dargah*. Delhi: Manohar, 1995.

Pruett, Gordon E. "Through a Glass Darkly: Knowledge of the Self in Dreams in Ibn Khaldun's *Muqaddimah*." *Muslim World*, Vol. LXXV (January 1985): 29–44.

Qureshi, Regula Burckhardt. "The *Mahfil-e Sama*: Sufi Practice in the Indian Context." *Islam and the Modern Age*, Vol. 17, No. 3 (August 1986): 133–165.

———. "Muslim Devotional: Popular Religious Music and Muslim Identity under British, Indian and Pakistani Hegemony." *Asian Music*, Vol. 24 (1992–1993): 111–121.

———. "Sufi Music and the Historicity of Oral Tradition." In *Ethnomusicology and Modern Music History*, ed. Stephen Blum, Philip V. Bohlman, and Daniel M. Neuman, 102–120. Urbana: University of Illinois Press, 1991.

———. *Sufi Music of India and Pakistan: Sound, Context and Meaning in Qawwali*. Cambridge: Cambridge University Press, 1986.

Radtke, Bernd, and John O'Kane, trans. and eds. *The Concept of Sainthood in Early Islamic Mysticism: Two Works by al-Hakim al-Tirmidhi*. Richmond, Surrey: Curzon Press, 1996.

Rashid, Ahmed. *Jihad: The Rise of Militant Islam in Central Asia*. New Haven: Yale University Press, 2002.

———. "Pakistan on the Edge." *New York Review of Books*, October 10, 2002: 36–40.

———. *Taliban: Islam, Oil and the New Great Game in Central Asia*. London: I.B. Tauris, 2000.

Reynolds, Frank E., and Donald Capps, eds. *The Biographical Process: Studies in the History and Psychology of Religion*. The Hague: Mouton Press, 1976.

Ricklefs, M.C. *A History of Modern Indonesia since 1300*. Stanford: Stanford University Press, 1981/1993.

Riddell, Peter. *Islam and the Malay-Indonesian World*. Honolulu: University of Hawai'i Press, 2001.

Rizvi, Saiyid Athar Abbas. *A History of Sufism in India*. Vol. I, *Early Sufism and Its History in India to 1600 A.D.* Delhi: Munshiram Manoharlal Publishers, 1975.

———. *A History of Sufism in India*. Vol. II, *From the Sixteenth Century to the Modern Century*. Delhi: Munshiram Manoharlal Publishers, 1983/1992.

Robinson, Francis. "Islam and the Impact of Print in South Asia." In *The Transmission of Knowledge in South Asia: Essays on Education, Religion, History and Politics*, ed. Nigel Crook. Delhi: Oxford University Press, 1996.

Roth, Michael S., and Charles G. Salas, eds. *Disturbing Remains: Memory, History and Crisis in the Twentieth Century*. Los Angeles: Getty Research Institute, 2001.

Salvatore, Armando. *Islam and the Political Discourse of Modernity*. Reading: Ithaca Press, 1997.

Sanyal, Usha. *Devotional Islam and Politics in British India: Ahmad Riza Khan Barelwi and His Movement, 1870–1920*. New York: Oxford University Press, 1996.

Schimmel, Annemarie. *And Muhammad Is His Messenger: The Veneration of the Prophet in Islamic Piety*. Chapel Hill: University of North Carolina Press, 1985.

———. *My Soul Is a Woman: The Feminine in Islam*. New York: Continuum, 1997.

———. *Mystical Dimensions of Islam*. Chapel Hill: University of North Carolina Press, 1975.

Shahab, Mas'ud Hasan. *Khitta-i pak Uch*. Bahawalpur: Urdu Academy, 1967/1993.

Sherani, Saifur Rahman, "*Ulema* and *Pir* in the Politics of Pakistan." In *Economy and Culture in Pakistan: Migrants and Cities in a Muslim Society*, ed. Hastings Donnan and Pnina Werbner, 216–246. New York: St. Martin's Press, 1991.

Sijzi, Amir Hasan. *Morals for the Heart (Fawa'id al-Fu'ad): Conversations of Shaykh Nizam ad-din Awliya Recorded by Amir Hasan Sijzi*. Translated and annotated by Bruce B. Lawrence. New York: Paulist Press, 1992.

Sirriyeh, Elizabeth. *Sufis and Anti-Sufis: The Defence, Rethinking and Rejection of Sufism in the Modern World*. Richmond, Surrey: Curzon Press, 1999.

Spivak, Gayatri Chakravorty. "Can the Subaltern Speak?" In *Colonial Discourse and Post-Colonial Theory*, ed. Patrick Williams and Laura Chrisman, 66–111. New York: Columbia University Press, 1994.

Talbot, Michael. *Mysticism and the New Physics*. New York: Bantam Books, 1981.

Thanawi, Ashraf 'Ali. *Perfecting Women: Maulana Ashraf 'Ali Thanawi's Bishishti Zewar*. Translated with commentary by Barbara Daly Metcalf. Berkeley: University of California Press, 1990.

Trimingham, Spencer J. *The Sufi Orders in Islam*. London: Oxford University Press, 1971.

Trix, Frances. *Spiritual Discourse: Learning with an Islamic Master*. Philadelphia: University of Pennsylvania Press, 1993.

Troll, Christian W. *Muslim Shrines in India: Their Character, History and Significance*. Delhi: Oxford University Press, 1989.

Turner, Victor W. "The Center Out There: The Pilgrim's Goal." *History of Religions*, Vol. 12 (1973): 191–230.

———. *The Ritual Process: Structure and Anti-Structure*. Ithaca: Cornell University Press, 1969.

Tweed, Thomas A. "On Moving Across: Translocative Religion and the Interpreter's Position." *Journal of the American Academy of Religion*, Vol. 70, No. 2 (June 2002): 253–277.

Tweedie, Irina. *Daughter of Fire: A Diary of Spiritual Training with a Sufi Master*. Nevada City, CA: Blue Dolphin Publishing, 1986.

van der Veer, Peter. *Religious Nationalism: Hindus and Muslims in India*. Berkeley: University of California Press, 1994.

van der Veer, Peter, and Hartmut Lehmann, eds. *Nation and Religion: Perspectives on Europe and Asia*. Princeton: Princeton University Press, 1999.

von Grunebaum, and Roger Caillois, eds. *The Dream and Human Societies*. Berkeley: University of California Press, 1966.

Waldman, Marilyn Robinson. "Tradition as a Modality of Change: Islamic Examples." *History of Religions* Vol. 25, No. 4 (1986): 318–340.

Waugh, Earle H. "Following the Beloved: Muhammad as Model in the Sufi Tradition." In *The Biographical Process: Studies in the History and Psychology of Religion*, ed. Frank E. Reynolds and Donald Capps, 63–85. The Hague: Mouton Press, 1976.

———. "The Popular Muhammad: Models in the Interpretation of an Islamic Paradigm." In *Approaches to Islam in Religious Studies*, ed. Richard C. Martin, 41–58. Tucson: University of Arizona Press, 1985.

Weinstein, Donald, and Rudolph M. Bell. *Saints and Society: The Two Worlds of Western Christendom, 1000–1700*. Chicago: University of Chicago Press, 1982.

Werbner, Pnina. *Pilgrims of Love: The Anthropology of a Global Sufi Cult*. Bloomington: Indiana University Press, 2003.

Werbner, Pnina, and Helene Basu, eds. *Embodying Charisma: Modernity, Locality and the Performance of Emotion in Sufi Cults*. London: Routledge, 1998.

Woodward, Mark R. *Islam in Java: Normative Piety and Mysticism in the Sultanate of Yogyakarta*. Tucson: University of Arizona Press, 1989.

Zaman, Muhammad Qasim. "Arabic, the Arab Middle East, and the Definition of Muslim Identity in Twentieth Century India." *Journal of the Royal Asiatic Society*, Series 3, 8, 1 (1998): 59–81.

———. *The Ulama in Contemporary Islam: Custodians of Change*. Princeton: Princeton University Press, 2002.

Zubaida, Sami. *Islam, the People and the State: Essays on Political Ideas and Movements in the Middle East*. New York: Routledge, 1989.

INDEX

'Abd ar-Rahman Chishti (d. 1683)
102
adab (etiquette and decorum)
of pilgrimage 27, 31, 55, 110
of ritual practice 180, 192, 193,
197–8, 209
of sama' 217–19, 222–3,
of Sufi discipleship 16, 44, 69, 79,
106, 131, 138, 143, 150, 154–5,
158–9, 163, 167, 168, 170, 186
Afghanistan 3, 22, 113, 227
see also Taliban
Ahl-i Hadith 36, 48, 87, 92
Ahmad Khan, Sayyid (1817–1898) 49,
92, 111
see also Aligarh Muslim University
Ajmer Sharif 26, 48, 51, 52, 58, 64,
68, 79, 99, 198, 199, 202, 207
Aligarh Muslim University 39, 40, 49
Arya Samaj 87, 92
Ashraf 'Ali Thanawi (1864–1943) 63,
140–1, 154, 180
awliya' Allah (Friends of God; Sufi
saints) 35, 37, 39, 42–4, 45, 56,
59, 65, 84, 86, 147, 153, 163,
200, 206, 221, 223
see also saints/sainthood

baqa' (permanence in God) 106, 109,
140, 165, 219, 220
baraka (blessing; spiritual energy) 3,
26, 33, 146, 150, 182, 206
see also faizan
Barelwi 36, 92, 119
batin (inward knowledge and
experience) 42, 63, 89, 101, 131,
139, 194, 205
bay'at (initiation ceremony) 16, 49,
63, 67, 70, 80, 144, 145–50,
178–9, 182, 184, 186

bihishti darwaza (Gate of Heaven) 26,
27, 28, 29, 30, 212
see also Pakpattan Sharif
body
and ritual practice 50–1, 66, 130–1,
139, 161, 172, 173–5, 189–90,
200, 218–19, 230
spiritual body 109, 186–9
see also lata'if
British colonialism 3, 7, 21, 23, 36,
41, 48, 59–60, 64, 77–8, 92, 94,
97, 108, 113, 119, 127, 206
see also Orientalism; postcolonialism

chilla (spiritual retreat) 53
Chishti Nizamis 3, 14, 87, 94, 164
Chishti Sabiris
and Islamic orthodoxy 30–38
disciples 7–9, 129–38
history 3–5, 17, 227–30
master-disciple relationship 139–62
publication campaign 120–7
ritual practices 175–225
texts and teaching networks 162–72
see also Malaysian disciples
Christianity 21, 53, 60, 73
colonialism, see British colonialism
communalism 53, 108, 118

dargahs (Sufi shrines) 3, 209–10
see also mazar; shrines
Daudi Bohras 8–9, 125
Deoband madrasa 3, 36, 48, 63, 87,
89, 92, 119, 140, 205–6, 208
din (religion) 8–9, 31, 36, 46, 135–8,
185–6
see also dunya
dreams 33, 63, 69, 71, 176–84
dream theory 176–81, 183
of Jesus 177–8

dreams—*continued*
   of Sufi saints   48, 51–2, 66–7, 68,
      79–80, 83, 85, 130, 179, 182
   of the Prophet Muhammad   44,
      181–2
   see also istikhara; ta'bir
dunya (the mundane world)   8–9, 31,
   73, 135–8, 185–6, 230

ecstasy   2, 33–4, 45, 56–7, 72, 84–5,
   197–8, 216, 218–20
   see also hal; wajd
ethnographic fieldwork   10–15, 80–1,
   82, 132–3, 169, 194

faizan (overflowing; spiritual energy)
   33–4, 154, 200, 203, 206, 209,
   218, 223
   see also baraka
fana' (annihilation in God)   40,
   139–40, 142, 165, 181, 215, 220
faqir (impoverished one; a Sufi master)
   19, 24, 73, 110, 197
Farid ad-Din Ganj-i Shakkar (d. 1295)
   4, 15, 19, 25–6, 32, 66–7, 69–70,
   71, 83, 114, 149, 166–7, 198, 227
   see also Pakpattan Sharif
Faruq Ahmad (d. 1945)   62–6, 78–9,
   199
Frithjof Schuon (1907–1998)   63
fundamentalists   13, 23, 93, 125
   see also Islamists

God   32, 38, 42–4, 53, 55, 56–7, 58,
   103, 106–7, 108, 136, 139–40,
   142, 160, 173–4, 177, 184,
   189–96, 204, 219–20
Golden Age   6, 13, 112, 114, 117, 120
Great Western Transmutation   94–5

habs-i dam (holding the breath)   191–2
   see also zikr
hadith (traditions of the Prophet
   Muhammad)   35, 43, 45, 49, 63,
   64, 69, 77, 92, 96, 104, 106, 110,
   118, 137–8, 171, 173–4, 181
   see also Muhammad the Prophet; *sunna*
hagiography   41, 43, 51, 62, 71–2
   see also sacred biography;
      saints/sainthood

hagiographical habitus   41, 45, 68, 74,
   75, 80, 86, 228
Hajj (pilgrimage to Mecca)   31, 46,
   47, 48, 51, 55, 57–8, 173
hal (states on the Sufi path)   33, 109,
   139, 150, 197, 216, 218
   see also ecstasy
halqa-i zikr (circle of remembrance)
   193–5, 199, 225
   see also zikr
Hasan Nizami, Khwaja (1878–1955)
   87, 94, 164
Hindus/Hinduism   8, 25–6, 53–4, 55,
   73, 92, 97–9, 105–6, 110, 136,
   158, 164, 191, 202, 205, 207
horizontal pedagogy   167–70
Hujwiri, 'Ali (d. 1074)   62, 65–6,
   102, 114, 163, 165, 198,
   199–201

'ibadat (worship; normative Islamic
   ritual practices)   37, 136, 137,
   174, 184, 185, 218, 222
identity   1, 4, 6–9, 14, 17–24, 90–6,
   112, 119–20, 125–7, 130–1,
   169–70, 179, 224–5, 227–30
ijtihad (independent reasoning)   56,
   94, 176
ikhlas (sincerity)   37, 139, 184
'ilm (outward, discursive knowledge)
   63, 95, 122, 137, 140, 205, 212
Imdad Allah al-Muhajir Makki, Hajji
   (1817–1899)   3, 5, 36, 48, 52,
   58, 63, 89, 97, 146, 187, 195,
   205–6, 215, 228
   see also Deoband *madrasa*
Internet   9, 90, 91, 125, 147, 158
   see also mass media
'ishq (love)   109, 140, 160
Islamic Sufism   102–12
Islamists (Muslim "fundamentalists")
   2, 6, 13, 19, 22–3, 35–7, 92–3,
   95–6, 97, 98, 103, 107–8, 110,
   118–19, 125, 217
   see also fundamentalists; Wahhabism
istikhara (induced dreams)   182–3
   see also dreams

Jama'at 'Ali Shah (d. 1951)   87, 93, 94
   see also Naqshbandi Sufi order

Jama'at-i Islami 36, 92, 97, 98
 see also Islamists; Mawdudi
Jesus 54, 83, 178
jihad (struggle, striving) 8, 101, 116,
 140, 174, 186, 224
Jinnah, Muhammad 'Ali (1876–1948)
 50, 59, 83, 99–100

Kalyar Sharif 2, 26, 52, 53
 see also Sabir, 'Ala ad-Din 'Ali Ahmad
karamat (saintly miracles) 45, 55–6,
 71–2
 see also miracles
Karbala 32
khalifa (spiritual successor) 40, 52, 64,
 66–7, 75, 79–80, 132, 163
khanaqah (Sufi lodge) 3, 45, 47, 53,
 68, 80, 175, 185
Khizr 51, 83
knowledge 40, 49–50, 51, 63–4, 77,
 86–7, 89, 94–6, 103, 106–8,
 110–11, 114, 122, 130–1, 137–42,
 150–3, 158, 162–3, 166–9, 171–6,
 205, 212
 see also 'ilm; ma'rifa

lata'if (subtle centers) 109, 187–9
 see also spiritual body
letter writing 35, 50, 54, 76, 82–3,
 99–100, 136, 148, 153, 165–6,
 173, 177, 179, 180–1, 194–5,
 197–8, 199, 224

madrasa (Islamic religious school) 3,
 21, 22, 34, 36, 48, 49, 64, 77,
 86–7, 95, 97, 137–8, 149, 155, 205
 see also Deoband madrasa; 'ulama
Magnificent Power Potential of Pakistan
 112–20
mahfil-i sama' (musical assembly)
 213–24
 see also qawwali; sama'
malfuzat (discourses of a Sufi master)
 15, 40, 44–5, 46–7, 53, 75–6, 94,
 102, 121, 123, 163, 165, 205, 215
Malaysia 7, 17, 41, 80, 82, 103, 123,
 124, 130, 164, 171, 201–3, 227, 230
Malaysian disciples
 background 5, 8–9, 132, 134–6,
 138, 169, 193, 197–8, 225

interactions with Sufi masters 35,
 68, 78, 80, 82, 83, 130, 134–6,
 148, 149–50, 153, 155, 161,
 165–6, 170, 173, 177–9, 182,
 194–5
pilgrimage 27–8, 33–4, 201–3, 208,
 223
publications and mass media 49,
 103, 120–1, 123–5, 127, 163–4
 see also Pulau Besar; Sultan al-'Arifin
maqam (stations of the Sufi path) 109,
 139, 150, 156, 180
Maqsuda Begam ('Amma Jan', d. 1997)
 11, 83–4, 85
ma'rifa (esoteric, intuitive knowledge)
 40, 51, 60, 95, 107, 109, 122,
 137, 212
 see also 'ilm; knowledge
mass media 9, 90–102, 120–7, 147,
 158
master-disciple relationship 14, 16, 24,
 80, 95, 122, 129, 132, 139–62,
 171, 192, 198, 228, 229
 see also Chishti Sabiris; pir-murid
Maudud Mas'ud Chishti, Diwan 26–7,
 29, 31
 see also Pakpattan Sharif
Mawdudi, Abu al-'Ala' (1903–1979)
 96, 97, 98, 107, 111, 113, 118
 see also Jama'at-i Islami
mazars (Sufi tombs) 36, 52, 53, 65–6,
 67, 70, 110, 199–201, 202–4, 206,
 209, 210–11, 223–4
 see also dargahs; shrines
Mecca 23, 31, 44, 47, 48, 58, 86,
 117, 200, 202
Medina 23, 62, 71, 115, 117, 120,
 124, 142, 229
miracles 40, 43, 45, 55–6, 71–2,
 84–5, 97, 144
 see also karamat
mi'raj (Prophet Muhammad's
 ascension) 44
modernity 5–9, 19–24, 30, 86–7, 90,
 94–5, 111–12, 120, 125–7, 133,
 169, 227–30
Muhammad al-Ghazali (d. 1111) 104,
 113, 126, 163
Muhammad the Prophet (570–632) 1,
 4, 8, 32, 34–6, 43–4, 47, 51, 55,

Muhammad the Prophet—*continued*
  62, 65, 72, 77, 86, 101–2, 107,
  114, 117, 133, 136, 139, 142–3,
  145–6, 160, 170–1, 173–4, 181–2,
  188, 192, 197–8, 229
  see also sunna
Mu'in ad-Din Chishti (d. 1236)   48,
  51, 52, 68, 78
mujahada (spiritual striving)   50–1, 54,
  70, 173–5, 184–6, 191–2, 219–20,
  224
muraqaba (contemplation)   27, 50–1,
  64, 81, 142–3, 186, 188–9,
  196–201, 203, 210, 211
murids (Sufi disciples)
  and modern life   6–9, 135–8, 185–6,
    230
  background of   9, 132–8
  master-disciple relationship   139–62
  texts and teaching networks
    129–32, 162–72
  women   27, 32, 33–5, 67, 69–71,
    72, 77–8, 83–4, 86, 101–2, 132,
    133, 136, 137, 143, 147, 148–9,
    162, 165, 166, 169, 170, 180,
    181–2, 193, 200–1, 210,
    211–12, 217, 223
  see also adab; Chishti Sabiris;
    Malaysian disciples
Musharraf, Pervez   22
music   2, 39, 45, 52, 56–8, 72, 110,
  149, 190, 206, 213–24
  see also mahfil-i sama'; *qawwali; sama'*
Muttahida Majlis-i Amal (MMA)   22

Nadwi, Sayyid Abu'l Hasan 'Ali
  (1914–1999)   105, 113
nafs (lower self, ego)   34, 50–1, 58,
  106, 139–40, 168, 173–5, 179,
  181, 183, 188, 208
  see also psychology; self
Naqshbandi Sufi order   14, 39, 87, 93,
  94, 146, 151, 187, 190, 196, 198,
  202, 215
Nizam ad-Din Awliya' (d. 1325)   42,
  44–5, 52, 53, 54, 55, 163–4, 214,
  219, 221
Nizami Bansari   163–4
Nusrat Fateh 'Ali Khan   213, 222
  see also qawwali

Orientalism   13, 93, 95, 97, 103–8,
  113, 126
  see also British colonialism
orthodoxy   5, 12–3, 19–24, 30–8, 90,
  92, 94–6, 97, 102, 105, 107–10,
  114–15, 125–7, 204–6, 214,
  227–9

Pakistan
  and Chishti Sabiri identity   25–38,
    40–1, 96, 112–20, 206–8,
    227–30
  and Islamic identity   19–24, 34,
    74–5
  and Sufism   15, 19–26, 75
Pakpattan Sharif   19, 66–7, 70, 112,
  121, 149–50, 166, 198, 204, 207,
  209, 210–12, 216, 217, 222, 224,
  227
  see also Farid ad-Din Ganj-i Shakkar
Pakpattan tragedy   25–38, 227
Partition (of South Asia in 1947)
  21–6, 35, 40–1, 53, 62, 73, 75, 77,
  79, 96, 101–2, 112–20, 134, 207,
  227–30
  see also British colonialism; Pakistan;
    postcolonialism
pilgrimage networks   204–13
  see also 'urs; ziyarat
pir (a Sufi master), *see* master-disciple
  relationship; *shaykh*
pir bhai (brother of the master; Sufi
  disciples)   28, 167, 184
pir-murid (master-disciple)   24, 80,
  129, 130, 132, 135, 139–62, 170,
  172, 188
  see also master-disciple relationship
postcolonialism   6–7, 9, 13, 22–4, 30,
  41, 47, 75, 78, 86–7, 91, 92, 94–6,
  126–7, 169, 171, 228, 230
  see also British colonialism; Pakistan;
    Partition
poverty   19, 24, 58, 73, 136
  see also faqir
prayer   15, 27, 50, 51, 56, 65, 77, 79,
  81, 109, 136, 152, 160, 183,
  186–9, 197, 210–11
psychology   109, 139–40, 151, 154–5,
  172–5, 187–90
  see also self

Pulau Besar (Big Island) 201–3
  see also Sultan al-'Arifin; Malaysia;
    Malaysian disciples

qalb (heart) 109, 139, 140, 141, 188,
    190, 191, 192
qawwali (South Asian Sufi music)
    33–4, 57–8, 211, 213–24
  see also mahfil-i sama'; music; sama'
qawwals (singers) 2, 110, 216–17,
    218, 219, 220–3, 224
Qur'an 1, 6, 35, 42–3, 45, 49, 50, 58,
    63, 64, 69, 77, 91, 92, 94, 98,
    104, 106, 107, 109, 110, 111,
    114, 116, 123, 139, 142, 145,
    149, 153, 155, 157, 162, 163,
    171, 173, 174, 177, 186, 189,
    190, 191, 194, 205, 214, 215
qutb (axis; head of the Sufi saints) 70

Rashid Ahmad Gangohi (1829–1905)
    3, 5, 36, 52, 89, 97, 205–6, 228
  see also Deoband madrasa
Rashida Khatun ('Ammi Jan', d. 1990)
    54, 69–71, 74
ritual practice 14, 64, 173–225
  see also suluk
ruh (soul; breath of God) 57, 106,
    109, 139, 140, 179, 188, 191

Sabir, 'Ala ad-Din 'Ali Ahmad (d. 1291)
    2, 3, 4, 52, 71
  see also Kalyar Sharif
sabr (patience) 32, 139
Sabri Brothers 213, 222
  see also qawwali
sacred biography 41, 43, 44, 60, 72,
    75, 86, 229
  see also hagiography
saints/sainthood 2, 13–14, 19, 24,
    32, 35, 37, 41–6, 47, 49, 55–6, 59,
    65, 66, 72, 75, 76, 80, 84–5, 86–7,
    100, 105, 110, 114, 137, 160,
    161, 163, 166, 198–9, 200, 202,
    204–5, 207, 209, 211–12, 216,
    221, 228
  see also awliya' Allah; hagiography
sajjada nishin (hereditary shrine
    custodian) 23, 26, 37, 51
Sakhi Hassan cemetery 68, 71

sama' (listening to music) 33, 45, 52,
    57–8, 72, 110, 119, 149, 206,
    213–24
  see also mahfil-i sama'; music; qawwali
sayyid (descendant of the Prophet
    Muhammad) 32, 47, 69
science 8, 39, 40, 49, 56, 64, 82, 104,
    110–12, 114, 115, 118, 197, 229
sectarianism 21, 29, 74, 95, 101,
    118–19, 133
secularism 6, 7, 8, 21, 24, 47, 95,
    100, 101, 108, 112, 114, 120,
    137, 172
self 5, 17, 24, 34, 51, 58, 106–7, 109,
    116, 129, 131, 139–40, 154, 170,
    172–5, 179, 187–90, 214, 225,
    230
  see also nafs; psychology
September 11, 2001 15, 21, 35, 38
shahadat (martyrdom) 30–1, 38
Shahidullah Faridi (1915–1978)
  biography 5, 16, 40–1, 54, 59–64,
    68–75, 78–9, 86–7, 100, 101,
    121, 137, 199, 207
  interaction with non-Muslims 68,
    102, 138, 155
  qualities as a Sufi master 66–8,
    100–1, 132, 137, 143, 144, 148,
    178–9, 182, 228–9
  spiritual training and teachings 37,
    64–6, 71–2, 80, 89–90, 140–1,
    142, 145–6, 152, 160, 168, 170,
    177, 183, 189–90, 192, 197,
    204, 205, 212, 222
  writings of 47, 93–4, 96, 100–2,
    109, 112, 123–4, 126–7, 140,
    164–5, 183, 205, 229
shajara (tree, Sufi genealogy) 4, 143,
    186–7, 191, 202
shari'a (Islamic law) 1, 6, 12, 34, 35,
    37, 50, 53, 69, 72, 76, 84, 95,
    107, 109, 118, 126, 139, 141,
    144, 160, 161, 171, 172, 177,
    182, 204, 214, 217, 228
shaykh (Sufi master) 3, 43–6, 139–45,
    150–3
  see also master-disciple relationship
Shi'a 8–9, 92, 101, 118–19, 125,
    133
  see also Daudi Bohras; sectarianism

shrines 2, 3, 13, 23–4, 25–6, 29, 34,
    36, 37–8, 43, 53, 64–6, 68, 110,
    133, 158, 168, 196–213, 216, 228
  see also dargah; mazar; 'urs
silsila (chain, Sufi genealogy) 1, 4, 17,
    43, 130
Siraj 'Ali Muhammad 5, 27–8, 30, 33,
    121, 132–3, 134, 137, 143, 149,
    157, 158, 161, 193, 194, 195, 211
sobriety 56–7, 72, 84–5, 106–7,
    197–8, 214, 219
spiritual body 187–9
  see also lata'if
storytelling 60–1, 72, 74, 83, 90, 130,
    137, 144, 158, 160, 167–8, 172,
    176, 212
Sufism (tasawwuf)
  and mass media 9, 90–102, 120–7,
    147, 158
  and modern life 6–9, 135–8, 185–6,
    230
  definitions of 1–5, 12–14, 103–8
  in Malaysia 7, 8–9, 17, 33–4, 49,
    103, 120–1, 123–5, 127, 130,
    134–6, 148, 163–4, 166, 169,
    171, 193, 201–3, 225, 230
  in Pakistan 15, 19–38, 40–1, 74–5,
    96, 112–20, 206–8, 227–30
  master-disciple relationship 14, 16,
    24, 80, 95, 122, 129, 132,
    139–62, 171, 192, 198, 228, 229
  ritual practices 173–225
  teaching networks 1, 13, 16, 17, 96,
    129–32, 145, 158, 162–72, 212,
    228
suhbat (companionship) 76, 83, 158–9
Suhrawardi Sufi order 10, 39, 47, 146,
    215
Sultan al-'Arifin (King of the Gnostics,
    Shaykh Isma'il 'Abd al-Qadir
    Thani) 201–3
  see also Malaysia; Pulau Besar
suluk (journey, path; Sufi practice) 5,
    32, 54, 64, 65, 71, 79, 131, 136,
    140, 152, 154, 157, 167, 173,
    177, 183, 184–6, 187, 188–9, 190,
    191, 196, 206, 208, 219–20,
    224–5
sunna (the Prophetic model) 1, 6, 8,
    12–13, 34–6, 43–4, 72, 76, 84,

    94–5, 114, 123, 160, 170, 171,
        182, 197–8, 204, 214, 229
  see also hadith; Muhammad the Prophet

ta'bir (classical Islamic science of dream
    interpretation) 176
  see also dreams
Tablighi Jama'at 36, 208
Taliban 22, 36, 227
  see also Afghanistan
Tarbiyat al-'ushshaq (Training of the
    Lovers) 40, 46–7, 50–1, 64–6, 69,
    97, 98, 100, 141, 150, 153, 154,
    156, 161–2, 163, 178, 179–80,
    191–2, 193, 215–16, 218–20
tariqa (path; a Sufi order) 1, 37, 43,
    107, 109, 129, 139, 146, 154,
    160, 172, 184, 199
tasawwuf, see Sufism
tawwakul (surrender to God) 32, 58
teaching networks 1, 13, 16, 17, 96,
    129–32, 145, 158, 162–72, 212,
    228
tradition 5–6

Uch Sharif 10, 47, 202
'ulama (Muslim religious scholars) 6,
    19, 21, 23–4, 30–1, 34, 37, 39, 49,
    86–7, 92, 94–6, 105, 106, 126,
    142, 195, 229
  see also madrasa
'urs (marriage; death anniversary of a
    Sufi saint) 10, 26, 29, 31, 32,
    33–4, 57, 64, 66, 79, 133, 149,
    161, 168–9, 203, 204–13, 216,
    221, 223–4, 227
  see also pilgrimage networks; ziyarat
Uwaysi initiation 51, 68, 178

vertical pedagogy 150–3
visions 33, 40, 44, 47, 48, 51, 52, 65,
    66–7, 83, 130, 176–7, 179–80,
    181–2, 183, 196, 205
  see also dreams

wahdat al-wujud (unity of being)
    105–6, 109
Wahhabism 31, 35–6, 58, 95, 97, 118,
    217
  see also Islamists

Wahid Bakhsh Sial Rabbani
    (1910–1995)
  biography   5, 16, 40–1, 75–8, 83–4,
    85–6, 86–7, 100, 121, 134, 137,
    207
  interaction with Malaysians   123,
    124, 134–5, 148, 149–50, 173,
    178–9, 182, 194–5, 203
  interaction with non-Muslims   81–2,
    123, 136, 144, 155
  letter writing   35, 76, 153, 165–6,
    173, 180, 194–5, 197–88
  photograph of   10–11
  qualities as a Sufi master   76, 80–3,
    132, 135, 148–9, 153, 161, 182,
    210, 228–9
  spiritual training and teachings   35,
    50, 56, 62, 66, 68, 78–80, 84–5,
    89–90, 100–1, 133, 136, 137,
    140, 144, 147–8, 160, 166–7,
    173–4, 177, 180–1, 187–8, 192,
    194–5, 197–8, 198–9, 200, 203,
    206, 209, 214–15, 221, 224
  writings of   46–7, 49, 75, 93–4, 96,
    99, 102–20, 121, 124, 126–7,
    164–5, 187–8, 198–9, 214–15,
    229
wajd (spiritual ecstasy)   57
walaya (closeness)   42–3, 44
  see also awliya' Allah;
    saints/sainthood
wali Allah (Friend of God; a Sufi saint),
  see awliya' Allah; saints/sainthood
Waris Hasan, Shah Sayyid (d. 1936)
    40, 48–9, 50, 51, 52, 63, 70, 83,
    123, 137, 192, 196, 198
wasyat nama (final will and testament)
    67, 70, 170
wilaya (guardian; intercessor)   26,
    42–3, 80, 199
  see also awliya' Allah;
    saints/sainthood
women disciples   27, 32, 33–5, 67,
    69–71, 72, 77–8, 83–4, 86, 101–2,
    132, 133, 136, 137, 143, 147,
    148–9, 162, 165, 166, 169, 170,
    180, 181–2, 193, 200–1, 210,
    211–12, 217, 223

zahir (outward knowledge and
    experience)   42, 63, 89, 101, 131,
    139, 194, 205
Zauqi Shah, Muhammad (1877–1951)
  biography   5, 16, 28, 39–41,
    46–50, 54–5, 58–9, 66, 69–70,
    79, 80, 86–7, 100, 134, 137,
    161, 207
  interactions with non-Muslims
    50–2, 53–4, 55, 97–9
  qualities as a Sufi master   39–40,
    52–8, 63, 65, 67, 132, 137, 153,
    195–6, 228–9
  spiritual training and teachings
    50–2, 55–8, 64–5, 66–7, 69,
    78, 89–90, 141, 142, 150,
    152–3, 154, 156, 160, 161–2,
    163, 166, 172, 174–5, 179–80,
    191–2, 193, 196, 214, 215–16,
    218–20
  writings and discourses of   40, 46–7,
    49–51, 64–6, 69, 93–4, 96–100,
    102, 109, 112, 121, 123, 124,
    126–7, 141, 150, 153, 154, 156,
    161–2, 163, 164–5, 178,
    179–80, 186, 191–2, 193,
    215–16, 218–20, 229
Zia al-Haq, Muhammad (President of
    Pakistan 1979–1989)   24, 101,
    113
zikr (remembrance of God)   50, 53,
    64, 66, 68, 79, 80, 82, 110, 133,
    134, 136, 149, 157, 174, 180,
    184–5, 186, 189–96, 198, 199,
    210, 216, 225, 229–30
  see also habs-i dam; halqa-i zikr
ziyarat (pilgrimage to Sufi shrines)   15,
    79, 110, 205
  see also pilgrimage networks; 'urs

Lightning Source UK Ltd.
Milton Keynes UK
UKOW01f1201280916

284000UK00002B/12/P